DISCARD

The Economics of Technical Change and International Trade

The Economics of Technical Change and International Trade

Giovanni Dosi
Università degli Studi di Roma, La Sapienza, Rome

Keith Pavitt
Science Policy Research Unit, University of Sussex, Brighton

Luc Soete
Maastricht Economic Research Institute on Innovation and Technology, University of Limburg, Maastricht

 NEW YORK UNIVERSITY PRESS
Washington Square, New York

First published in the U.S.A. by
NEW YORK UNIVERSITY PRESS
Washington Square
New York, NY 10003

Typeset in 10/12 pt Times
by MCS Ltd, Salisbury

Printed and bound in Great Britain by
BPCC Wheatons Ltd, Exeter

Library of Congress Cataloging-in-Publication Data

Dosi, Giovanni 1953–
    The economics of technical change and international trade /
Giovanni Dosi, Keith Pavitt, Luc Soete.
        p.   cm.
    ISBN 0-8147-1834-5
    1. International trade.   2. Technological innovations—Economic
aspects.   I. Pavitt, Keith.   II. Soete, Luc.   III. Title.
HF1379.D67   1990
382—dc20   90-13302
                                                                CIP

Contents

Preface and acknowledgements

This book is the result of a convergence of research interests that began when Giovanni Dosi, Keith Pavitt and Luc Soete were together in the early 1980s in the Science Policy Research Unit at the University of Sussex. Giovanni Dosi's broad interests in redesigning the contours of economic theory based on new insights into the nature and process of technological change seemed, at least at first sight, to fit well with the more specific and eclectic interest and expertise of Keith Pavitt on the determinants, causes and impacts of sectoral patterns of innovation and technological progress, and the more empirically focussed trade and technology research interests of Luc Soete.

The original idea was to go for a relatively quick publication building on some of the work already published by each one of us and leaving each author responsible for his chapter. However, it quickly appeared that such an approach would suffer from the overlap in theoretical visions, empirical tests and policy conclusions which each one of us wanted to draw in his chapters. A richer, more demanding approach was chosen, aiming at a fully integrated book, redesigning, so to speak, the theoretical foundations of the economics of technological change and international trade, while drawing on each other's previous research expertise. This approach required, however, as quickly became apparent, a far more comprehensive undertaking than any one of us would have predicted five years ago, not in the least because from the 'symbiotic' SPRU atmosphere couched in the Sussex South Downs, we got dispersed across Europe before a final draft could be written.

Giovanni Dosi was appointed Professor in Rome, Keith Pavitt was appointed Professor and Deputy Director of SPRU in Sussex and Luc Soete was appointed Professor and Director of MERIT in Maastricht.

Geographical distance appeared a major disruptive factor in progressing along what became known as the 'trade book'.

For the reader, fond of original acknowledgements, the following extract from a letter, dated 1 March 1988, of one of the authors to his fellow co-authors gives a fairly impressionistic picture of some of the problems involved in getting the 'trade book' into its final format.

> It was with a great sense of intellectual excitement and 'remembrance of things past' that I returned to the preparation of our above-named masterpiece. Thus, I have found correspondence with Wheatsheaf in 1983 making romantic and idealistic promises of prompt delivery. And in a recent visit, Edward Elgar (with whom the deal was negotiated at Wheatsheaf, and who now has his own publishing business) re-affirmed his admiration for the book, and confirmed advanced bookings worthy of the latest offerings of Andrew Lloyd Webber (or La Cicciolina) on Broadway. ... In addition, Linda and Lesley have spent weeks printing out large volumes of text from a disc found with Vanessa. For a moment, I wondered whether it might be an undiscovered masterpiece by Proust (or Joyce). But with some regret I remembered that the prevailing artistic ethos surrounding the preparation of our book was closer to that of Marx (Harpo) and Monty Python.

But with the spread of information technologies, the benefits of communication technologies finally did filter through. The organisational support of MERIT, in the form of Wilma Coenegrachts taking things under control, paid off, and rather than 2015 – which we have seen somewhere the 'trade book' being referred to – it has become 1990, half a decade after a first draft was put on paper.

Over the last five years, as will be clear from the extensive reference list, many things have happened in international trade and growth theory. With time passing by, many of the sometimes radical critiques of traditional trade theory which we had put forward in the eighties and restate here more extensively, can now also be found in many so-called 'new' trade and growth contributions and are even beginning to become 'reviewed' in some of the new trade textbooks (Krugman and Obstfeld, 1988; Markusen and Melvin, 1988). However, there remain substantial differences between this new rich body of trade and growth contributions and *our* analysis based as it is on a different conceptual framework, starting from the economics of technical change. We certainly benefited from the new trade and growth theoretical insights; we did, however, also benefit from the progresses made in the less traditional approaches to the economics of technological change, such as those published in Dosi *et al.* (1988).

We have, in other words and maybe paradoxically, profited from the slow process of getting this book to its final draft. None of the issues raised have lost their importance. On the contrary, we would even argue that with the increasing trend in the internationalisation of technology, issues of trade and innovation policy will be even higher on the agenda of the 1990s.

The time it took to produce this book also implies a long list of names of persons and institutions to thank. We have benefited greatly from the support of – and debate with – numerous colleagues at SPRU, in particular Tibor Barna, Chris Freeman, Christopher Saunders and Nick von Tunzelmann; at the University of Venice and Rome in Italy, in particular Mario Cimoli and Luigi Orsenigo; and at MERIT, University of Limburg, the Netherlands we thank in particular Gerald Silverberg, Bart Verspagen and Rohini Acharya. Financial support came from the Designated Research Center on Science, Technology and Energy Policy of the ESRC (Economic and Social Research Council); from the Leverhulme Trust; from the Italian National Research Council (CNR); and from MERIT. We are also greatly indebted to Lesley Elliot, Linda Gardiner, Heather Page, Rob Maessen, Corien Gijsbers, Mieke Donders and Wilma Coenegrachts, for their patience, dedication and a firm hand in extracting this final text from the three of us.

Tables and figures

1

Introduction

Once upon a time, so international trade theorists like to tell each other, [1] there was paradise, where everybody lived efficiently, producing and trading whatever was demanded in the most efficient combination. Then an angel came and stamped a different colour on each one's forehead, you could say a national flag, allowing him or her to produce and trade only with capital and land having the same colour. The diaspora which followed led to large differences in efficiency across the world, with a huge world welfare loss. Since that unhappy moment, trade theorists — by definition economists with a world rather than national welfare vision — have been trying to show how to return to this paradisiac situation.

The first main direction of analysis, returning to classical economics, attempted to show how despite a country's poor efficiency, there could nevertheless be gains in welfare by specialising in those products/industries in which the country was, relatively, most efficient. Such gains were by and large based on the principles of division of labour applied to an international world. The *neo*-classical extension of this line of analysis introduced 'factor endowments' to explain a country's comparative advantage and establish a number of crucial links with factor-price equalisation, income distribution and growth. In terms of our parable, it could be said that trade theory illustrated how paradise could be re-established through free trade all over the world, despite national differences in 'factor endowments'.

Whatever one's views on the success of the 'traditional trade theory' explanations of trade flows and gains from trade, it is difficult not to be surprised by the large amount of trade flows which do not fit such trade explanations, and by the relatively limited nature of the estimated gains

1

from opening up to free trade (such as in the case of the European Common Market or the Canada–United States free trade agreement) compared to the significant structural trade gains obvious to anyone.

A second 'new' line of analysis, developed over the last ten years, started from a fundamentally different assumption, namely that most economic activities are characterised by increasing, rather than decreasing, returns. In other words, gains from trade are, in the first instance, the result of the scale economies that each national economy can achieve through free trade, whether applied to a small country such as Luxembourg or to a large one such as the United States. These gains are far more significant than traditional trade theory would lead one to believe. Many empirical studies within the 'new' trade theory tradition have pointed towards the significance of such gains (Smith and Venables, 1988; Harris, 1984; Cox and Harris, 1986). Just as in large nations, where particular activities have been concentrated in particular locations – Krugman's favourite example being mushroom production in Pennsylvania – paradise for the world as a whole can be achieved by bringing resources together, whether it be motor car manufacturing in Japan or ceramic tiles in Italy. The advantages accruing to the region or country from the 'agglomeration' of a particular set of activities, are of little importance as compared to the advantages accruing to *every* world consumer of the efficient exploitation of world economies of scale.

In this book, we concentrate on a different, i.e. third, stream of analysis. Compared to the 'new' trade theories discussed above, we place greater emphasis on the dynamics of increasing returns, particularly those associated with production technology and innovation. In terms of our parable, to the extent that technological development and growth are irreversible processes, there is no possible return to paradise: like virginity, once lost it is lost for ever. As emphasised in many locational theories, the main reasons concern the way in which industrialisation locations are 'selected' early on and how, by appropriating the available agglomeration economies, they exercise some 'competitive exclusion' – to use Arthur's (1988, 1989) term – on other locations. In other words, from a dynamic technology perspective it does matter whether a region or country is specialised in mushroom production or in silicon chips. By focussing on these dynamic 'learning' features, our analysis falls within the 'evolutionary' framework (as broadly set out in Freeman *et al.* (1982) and in an earlier book edited by Dosi, 1988), which also takes as one of its starting points the substantial evidence and insights brought together within a relatively large body of literature on the nature and process of technological change and innovation.

Is there no 'normative' world paradise to be attained in our vision of the world? To some extent the answer to that question is 'no'. The normative counterpart of our analysis brings to the forefront the crucial role of history, of 'man-made' interventions, of institutions, of particular international investment decisions, of 'multinational' corporations, etc., of the whole spectrum of individual and collective decisions made in a complex system such as the international economic environment.

The analysis presented in this book, which is reflected in the title, thus *starts* from differences of technological capabilities and innovativeness between countries and then focuses on the effects of such differences on international patterns of trade and growth. By technological capabilities we mean the skills and knowledge necessary to develop, produce and sell products; by innovativeness we mean the actual realisation of that capacity to generate and commercialise new and better products and production processes. Innovations are produced by innovative activities, in which technology is both an input and an output.

Both historians and practitioners in industry and government are well aware of the significant influence of technology and innovative activities on international competitiveness, and on the relative efficiency and income of firms, regions and countries. From the most recent OECD, EC or UN document to the various individual countries' international think-tank recommendations, the importance of technical change as a 'chronic disturber of existing patterns of comparative advantage' (Johnson, 1975), as well as an essential factor in the achievement of the necessary adjustment to structural change resulting from technical change itself, is well recognised.[2] In a similar way, the most recent Economic Report of the President recognises the increased 'international scope of science and technology' over the 1980s and subscribes to the view already expressed ten years earlier in the Report on US Competitiveness, directly linking the erosion of the international competitiveness of the United States over the 1960s and 1970s to deficient investment in innovative activity in the United States as compared to its major industrial competitors.[3]

Despite what one may think on reading many traditional trade contributions, many economists over the past thirty years *have* become increasingly aware of the importance of technology and innovation, often partly as a result of empirical studies on the determinants of economic growth and trade performance. While some significant progress has been made in empirical studies in this area over recent years, analysis has remained constrained by two major difficulties: inadequate data measuring innovative activities, and problems with the broad theoretical framework representing the characteristics of such activities and their impact on the economy.

With regard to the latter, as Vernon noted in his introduction to the influential readings on *The Technology Factor in International Trade*: 'Researchers have an extraordinary capacity to screen out the evidence that does not fit well with their preconceptions; to relegate uncomfortable observations to the dustbins of the unconscious; or, better still, to reshape the observations so that they may be perceived in a way that eliminates the discomfiture.'[4] Twenty years after Vernon's remarks, a good deal of analysis on technology, growth and international trade has a 'reductionist' flavour, attempting more often than not to squeeze genuine dynamic problems of innovation, learning, uncertainty and change into the more familiar cloth of endowments, relative scarcities and optimisation under budget constraints.

Notwithstanding the impression of naïvety conveyed in our opening parable, there is in our mind no doubt that one of the great achievements of economic analysis has been the formulation of rigorous and coherent theories of international trade and investment. In essence, these are theories of general market equilibrium extended to explain trade in goods and exchanges of productive agents between countries. The critical insight they contain is that the direction of trade in different commodities, or the movement of productive agents, is to be explained by the existence of differences in autarky price structures, differences which free trade eliminates. In turn, different autarky price structures are to be explained by appropriate combinations of intercountry differences in consumer preferences (including the willingness to save), in process technology, and in stocks of productive agents, labour, capital goods, etc.

Certainly, the two sets of traditional trade theory (classical and neoclassical) differ in their emphasis as to the origin of price differences. The Ricardian theory stresses international differences in technology in conjunction with international differences in real wage levels, while the Heckscher–Ohlin theory assumes the international identity of tastes and technology, tracing the origins of trade to given differences in endowments of productive agencies. Non-trivial propositions may be derived concerning the determinants of the terms of trade, the distribution of the gains from trade, and the costs and benefits of policies to restrict trade. Moreover, the effect of hypothetical changes in tastes, technology and resources on these dimensions of a trading world is readily deduced. However, a critical deficiency of these theories is their treatment of technological data as exogenous to the economic system and, consequently, their failure to offer any understanding of the fact that changes in technology are properly to be viewed in terms of an economic process.

New trade theory (Krugman, 1986; Helpman and Krugman, 1985, 1989) has added an important qualification to these, by now well-established, theories, namely, that for the most simple of theorems to hold, some of the basic assumptions of perfect competition and decreasing returns were essential. The many cases of imperfect competition and increasing returns analysed under the umbrella of 'new' trade theory have led to a plethora of 'new', sometimes reversed, sometimes similar, results with respect to gains from trade, income distribution, etc. One of the most damaging normative results for traditional trade theory has undoubtedly been the illustration by Brander and Spencer, 1983, 1985) that free trade might no longer be the only world maximum welfare gain policy, but that a 'strategic' trade policy might in some cases be justified and actually needed. As Dixit pointed out in his contribution to Krugman's book on strategic trade policy:

> Recent research contains support for almost all the vocal and popular views on trade policy that only a few years ago struggled against the economists' conventional wisdom of free trade. Now the mercantilist arguments for restricting imports and promoting exports are being justified on grounds of 'profit sharing'. The fears that other governments could capture permanent advantage in industry after industry by giving each a small initial impetus down the learning curve now emerges as results of impeccable formal models. The claim that one's own government should be aggressive in the pursuit of such policies because other governments do the same is no longer dismissed as a non sequitur. (Dixit, 1986a)

Such strategic trade theories have undoubtedly brought to the forefront many features which appear, at least at first sight, to be of particular relevance to analyses of technical change and international trade. The importance of monopoly rents, of profit sharing and strategic trade manipulation indeed seem of particular relevance to many high-technology industries. Furthermore, the actual emergence of these new theories on the US academic scene occurred at a time of increasing fear in the United States of the Japanese challenge in trade and technology (Mowery and Rosenberg, 1989).

As we illustrated in the opening parable of this book, there is undoubtedly more affinity between a more realistic trade theory, such as 'new' trade theory, and the view presented here. At the same time, it is difficult not to remain rather critical about the way the technology factor has been introduced in such theories (see a.o. Aghion and Howitt (1989), Helpman, 1990a and b). The interpretation given to technology in the new trade vision remains in our view relatively far from the complexity of the process of technological change and innovation as described in Chapter 4. The simplicity of the way technological change is reduced either to 'learning curves' or to the generation of new intermediate inputs under monopolistic competition in 'new' trade theory is to some extent reflected in the simplicity of some of the policy recommendations.

For us, technology plays a major role in two fundamental topics pertaining to economic analysis: (i) the problem of coordination and interdependence between agents and, by implication, between countries; and (ii) the patterns of change and transformation of each economy. Classical economists saw both questions as essential ones. One of their major analytical tasks was to explain the determinants of, and the possible regularities in, the dynamics of modern economies and, using the same theoretical framework, also to explain the pattern of allocation and the related coordination of economic activities that would produce relatively ordered and efficient outcomes from a multiplicity of decisions of individual agents. They were clearly only partly successful in making the link between such explanations of dynamic patterns and the analysis of (static) allocative mechanisms. None of them really produced a rigorous model of interaction between agents which yielded those macroeconomic 'laws of change and transformation' in which they were so interested. Moreover, their investigation was essentially developed in terms of a closed-economy model.

The main classical economist to undertake explicitly the task of analysing the open-economy case in a rigorous manner was Ricardo. His main concern was, however, the short-term mechanism and efficiency properties of the international allocation of productive activities, whenever one would allow foreign trade to take place. In his famous example of England and Portugal trading cloth and wine, he illustrated that even when a country is characterised by absolute advantages (i.e. higher production efficiency) in both commodities, the mechanism of comparative advantages would yield patterns of trade beneficial to both partners. Clearly, major international technological differences appeared in the background of the analysis, in the form of country-specific advantages/disadvantages in their input coefficients. However, neither Ricardo nor, for that matter, the other classical contributors tried to answer the more fundamental *dynamic* questions such as: Where do absolute advantages come from? What are the effects of these absolute advantages/disadvantages upon the levels and rates of growth of income? What is the relationship between the allocation of resources stemming from a given pattern of absolute advantages and the long-term evolution of the latter?

Within neo-classical theory, on the other hand, the analytical attention focussed upon the issue of coordination/interdependence between the agents, elegantly formalised under highly simplified hypotheses on the nature of the technology and the behaviour of the agents. The theory of international trade became one of the sub-headings of the general model – General Equilibrium Analysis – confined to the original

Ricardian question, namely: what is the pattern of comparative advantage in the allocation of productive activities between countries and what are its efficiency properties? Not only that: the standard neo-classical answer to the question ruled out *ex-hypothesi* the existence of international technological differences. Trade patterns were simply explained by the relationship between factor endowments and factor intensities. In the standard model, 'technology' appears only as the exogenously given form of the production function. Moreover, even when technological differences between countries were allowed into the model, one hypothesis had to be retained, namely the existence by assumption of a generalised market-clearing process, necessary to the explanation of equilibrium prices and quantities in terms of relative scarcities.

Within such a framework it is hardly possible to accommodate dynamic, evolutionary questions related to change and transformation, other than by means of a reduction to exercises of comparative statics between different equilibrium positions. As mentioned above, in its essence the Heckscher–Ohlin model of international trade is nothing but a particular illustration of an open-economy general equilibrium, with all its usual assumptions, restrictions and beliefs. As Lerner (1953) put it:

> The constructions ... apply to any kind of trade, between individuals, towns, regions, countries and continents as well as between social classes or between people at different points in time; and ... it is only historical accident of the development of the Economics Theory that all these problems are called 'International Trade'.[5]

Prevailing contemporary economic theory, facing the two 'classical problems', concerning (i) the mechanisms of coordination and interdependence between the agents, and (ii) the pattern of transformation of the economy, addresses mainly the former and tackles it with elegance and rigour, formulating its underlying assumptions without any reference to technological and behavioural evidence.[6] This applies even more so in relation to the international context. There are probably few pieces of prevailing economic thought that are in more direct contrast with available empirical evidence than the hypothesis of identical production functions across countries.

One can also easily see the intrinsic difficulty of accommodating a reasonable account of technological progress into prevailing economic theory: How can we maintain a notion of 'scarcity' when technical progress concerns, precisely, a continuous improvement in the productive efficiency of the inputs? Does the model make any sense in explaining trade between countries that are often characterised by excess supply of labour or labour and capital? How can one account for the fact that differences in innovativeness are often much more important than primary endowments as determinants of trade flows?

But it is at the empirical level in particular that the difficulties of the traditional trade view appear, as already indicated above, most serious. After Leontief's well-known findings that the total capital intensity (direct plus indirect capital content, via input/output flows) of US exports was lower than US imports,[7] a good deal of research effort went into the attempt to explain away what was curiously termed a 'paradox' instead of the, probably more accurate, description of a 'falsifying test' of the endowment theory.[8] In a sense, 'neo-factor proportion' theories, which added some technology-related variables to the list of primary endowments, became the conventional analytical answer to 'facts' which did not conform to the 'endowment theory' in its original and cleanest form.

Until the late 1970s, nearly all empirical tests of 'neo-factor' and 'neo-technology' trade theories for industrially advanced countries were based on country-specific, cross-sectoral trade data, together with measures of technology intensity derived from sectoral patterns of research and development (R&D) expenditures in the United States. This form of analysis was dictated largely by the inadequacy of R&D statistics, and of other measures of innovative activities, across country, sector and time. Unfortunately, it meant that theories that explained sector-specific differences between countries were tested with data that measured country-specific differences between sectors. It also meant that the sectoral patterns of R&D intensity in the United States were generally assumed to hold in all countries, and to reflect technology intensity in all sectors accurately.

Since the late 1970s, systematic data on innovative activities have improved considerably, as a result of three interrelated factors: first, the painstaking activities of the OECD in developing internationally comparable time-series on R&D activities; second, the 'science indicators' movement, which was instigated in the United States through the National Science Board, with the purpose of exploring and improving a wide range of statistical indicators of scientific and technological activities; and third, the pioneering activities of academic and commercial organisations in developing systematic counts of scientific papers, citations, innovations, etc.

As a result of this progress, the inadequacies of previous data and analysis not only became clearer; the opportunities for more complete, satisfactory and novel analysis also became greater. In particular, it became possible to test the sensitivity of the results of empirical analyses to the use of different measures of technological activity, and to undertake more ambitious statistical analyses based on the rich and detailed data on other science and technology indicators.

In this book we make detailed use of this evidence within the framework of a theoretical analysis of innovation, trade and growth, which differs in some important respects from most traditional analyses.

First, we share Nelson's (1981a) concern, in particular that the widely accepted representation of 'technical progress' as a shift in the production function resulting from disembodied or embodied technical change inadequately represents the more complex and interesting reality that emerges from a variety of industry and firm-based studies, as well as from the more systematic international evidence now available. It is, as we have already indicated above, a popular economic assumption to represent technology as exogenously generated and applicable either as information or embodied in producers' goods. In most sectors, however, technology is generated endogenously; it is often firm-specific, differentiated and tacit in nature; and is practically, by definition, cumulative in development.

Second, we reject the assumption that the generation of technology is independent of investment and production. In most sectors, it is strongly dependent on them.

Third, the assumption that firms' technical choices are exogenously determined and optimal is rejected in favour of the proposition that such choices are generally discretionary and non-optimal, given the impossibility of foreseeing the nature and likelihood of all possible future technological and market developments.

The implications of these and other discrepancies between traditional 'economic theory' assumptions and what we view as the 'stylised' empirical reality have already been the subject of the book *Technical Change and Economic Theory* (Dosi *et al.*, 1988) in which two of us participated. Building on some of the contributions in this book, and on Nelson and Winter's celebrated evolutionary theory of firm behaviour and economic change (Nelson and Winter, 1982),[9] as well as on some of our own earlier work (Dosi, 1982; Pavitt, 1984; Soete, 1981a; Dosi and Soete, 1983, 1988; Pavitt and Soete, 1982),[10] we attempt in this book to develop a model of trade, the fundamental features of which are international technology gaps, reflecting superior and inferior techniques and what we will call cost-based adjustment mechanisms. International differences in innovative capabilities, in the sources and uses of innovations, in corporate strategies and institutional conditions contribute to determine these gaps. In turn, the latter are, we will argue, of fundamental importance in explaining the participation of each country in international trade flows, and international differences in income levels.

From a microeconomic perspective, we believe, a satisfactory theory will need to be based on assumptions, on behaviours and on the characteristics of technology, innovation and competitive processes that can account for the prevailing observed behaviour at the level of the firm, and the observed characteristics of the pattern of international trade. In our view, the key features of such a theory must be as follows:

- Technological decisions in firms are not generally about adjustment along a given and widely accessible production function, but, rather, about movements to techniques that are superior under almost any income distribution and relative prices, and to products characterised by superior performances.
- Movements by firms to these superior techniques are not automatic, given that techniques are generally firm-specific in nature, and are both cumulative and uncertain in their development.
- Patterns of strategic interactions on international markets are generally influenced by an *asymmetric* distribution between firms and between countries of technological, organisational and financial capabilities.
- Static and dynamic efficiency are not necessarily simultaneously compatible with certain behavioural patterns and economic signals.

In many ways, the emphasis of our analysis is opposite to the conventional one. As argued in greater detail in the next chapter, the century of economic discussion which has focussed primarily on allocative optimality *for given techniques* has obscured the importance of differences in techniques and product characteristics between countries, and has neglected the analysis of their origin. It is quite evident, for example, that the wide international differences in per capita income stem primarily from the joint effect of differences in the degrees of capital accumulation and differences in technology rather than from differences in relative prices only (or 'distortions' in the price mechanism).

However, the investigation of these phenomena developed separately from trade theory, which until recently did not take technology gaps as one of the fundamental facts from which to begin theorising. This, as we indicated above, applies in different ways to both 'classical' and neoclassical theories. For the validity of the most general theorems such as international factor-price equalisation to hold, the latter excludes from the core of the model the implications of straightforward inferiority/superiority of techniques between countries. The former allows the existence of such international technological differences, but − as in the 'neo-Ricardian' reformulations[11] − takes a rather general and agnostic view, describing the equilibrium specialisations, irrespective of the nature of the techniques available in each country.

In this book we will discuss some hypotheses on the determinants of trade flows in those cases, which evidence suggests are rather widespread, where techniques and product-technologies can be univocally ranked, irrespective of domestic income distribution and relative prices.

Technology gaps, we will argue, are of paramount importance in determining the participation of each country in international trade flows and, through that, the maximum levels of income that each country can attain, compatible with the foreign balance constraint. Our empirical results, admittedly based on highly imperfect data, point to the dominance of a set of absolute advantages over the factors pushing towards comparative advantages and specialisation. In other words, the international composition of trade by countries within each sector appears to be essentially explained by technology gaps, while comparative advantage mechanisms appear to be of lesser importance.

In so far as technology gaps and their changes are a fundamental force in shaping international competitiveness, their impact on domestic income, by inducing and/or allowing relatively high rates of growth via the foreign trade multiplier, will be significant. However, the 'virtuous circle' between technological levels, foreign competitiveness and domestic growth is not entirely automatic and endogenous to the process of economic development. As we will argue at length, country-specific and sector-specific innovative or imitative capabilities can be isolated as one of the single most important factors which originate these 'virtuous circles' and contribute to explaining the patterns of international convergence or divergence in terms of trade performance, per capita incomes and rates of growth.

From such a perspective, it is the relationship between technology, trade and growth which is at the centre of the analysis, rather than the question about the short-term gains from trade stemming from the open-economy allocation of resources, so crucial in the conventional view. The latter are indeed once-and-for-all gains, by their very nature: their dynamic relevance, if any, concerns the link between the 'static' pattern of allocation and the long-term performance of the economy.

Here again, a close link between the analysis presented in the following chapters and 'new' trade theory can be envisaged. Indeed, the characteristics of technology and innovation that we describe below, generally imply forms of industrial organisation that differ from perfect competition and, hence, also 'strategic' behaviours by individual agents. However, contrary to 'new' trade theories, which often assume 'equilibrium' interactions amongst symmetric agents, our argument will be consistent with more 'evolutionary' microfoundations, whereby firms with different technologies and organisational traits interact under conditions of persistent disequilibrium.

The empirical findings presented in Chapter 3 are broadly consistent with the theoretical model. The most important conclusions can be summarised as follows:

1. A variety of science and technology measures – R&D, patenting and innovation counts – gives a consistent picture of the aggregate international distribution of innovative activities among countries. Innovative activities are concentrated in relatively few countries. Although there have been significant changes since the beginning of this century in the relative importance of these countries, there has been only one major newcomer to the group – Japan.

2. International differences in innovative activities are reflected in differences in shares of world exports in most sectors, and in manufacturing as a whole.

3. Export performance is positively associated with differences in per capita innovative activities and differences in labour productivity.

4. Changes in trade performance are more strongly associated with changes in innovative activities than changes in relative labour costs.

5. Since the beginning of the century, international differences in per capita income have been closely related to international differences in per capita innovative activity. International differences in the rate of growth of per capita income have been associated with similar differences in the rate of investment and in the rate of growth of innovative activities.

We are only too well aware of the imperfections and gaps in our analysis. Both the theoretical model and its empirical test can be extended and improved. More attention needs to be devoted to the characteristics and mechanisms of the international diffusion and adaptation of innovation, and to identifying the determinants of international differences in technology and, in particular, in the level and pattern of innovative activities. On a theoretical level, a major effort is still required to develop a complete theory of the relationship between the international pattern of economic change, and its microeconomic, 'microtechnological' and institutional foundations.

After half a century of unchallenged rule of neo-classical trade theory, the 1980s has led to a revolution in thinking about the determinants of international trade flows and the gains from trade in a world dominated by imperfect competition and increasing returns. This revolution is far from over. It has led to the laying out of an alternative, more realistic, but still primarily static framework, within which international trade flows should be studied. The first dynamic models in this area are now being developed (see, e.g. Grossman and Helpman, 1990a and b; Markusen, 1990). Coming from a completely different analytical perspective, the economics of technological change, we hope to provide here some first building blocks for a more complete dynamic picture of the interactions between technology, trade and growth.

For our part we hope that the 1990s might see a further change in ways of thinking of the dynamics of international competitiveness, technology and growth. The issue of the internationalisation of technology has to some extent only come to maturity in the 1980s. It is now high on any policy agenda, [12] with frequently challenging questions put to both the economic theoretician and the empirical researcher. By concentrating on some of the empirical measurement issues and on the, in our view, essential consistency of theoretical assumptions with empirical observation, we also hope to provide some first responses to these new policy challenges.

Notes

1. The parable is from Paul Krugman, who quotes Paul Samuelson.
2. In the OECD Report's words:

   Both the need for adjustment and the possibilities of achieving it are strongly influenced by the underlying pace and directions of technological change, by its rates of diffusion within different national economies, and by the ease with which the technology is transferred from one country to another... . The countries of the OECD have become partners in a world system of dynamic interdependence based upon continued innovation and the unimpeded flow of technology within and across frontiers. In such a system, successful adjustment will depend on the ability of governments to mobilise the inventive, entrepreneurial talents of their people by creating an appropriate climate for technological innovation. (OECD, 1979, p. 44)

3. According to the Report of the President on US Competitiveness:

   Many indicators of U.S. trade competitiveness such as export market shares suggest that there has been an erosion of U.S. competitiveness in world markets. The increased international competition facing U.S. producers is mainly the result of changing world resource supplies and technological capabilities. Because of higher rates of growth in investment and expanded research activity in other countries, the United States has experienced a relative decline in its trade performance over the past two decades even though the level of U.S. exports has increased substantially in recent years. (US Department of Labour, Report of the President on US Competitiveness, 1980, pp. 1.1, 1.2)

4. Vernon (1970), p. 2.
5. Lerner (1953), also quoted in De Marchi (1976).
6. An important exception is the so-called 'new' growth theory; see also Romer, 1986, 1987, 1990 and Lucas, 1988.
7. See Leontief (1956).
8. As argued, among others, by Leamer (1984) and Deardorff (1984), it is true that Leontief's analysis is incomplete as a rigorous test of the Heckscher–Ohlin–Samuelson model. However, it is equally certain that 'The Leontief

14   *Introduction*

test, though not perfectly controlled, is probably about as clear an example of a "crucial experiment" as one is likely to encounter in economics' (De Marchi, 1976, p. 113).

9. Nelson and Winter (1982)
10. Dosi (1984), Soete (1981a).
11. cf. Steedman (1979) and (1980).
12. See for example Ostry (1990) and Mowery and Rosenberg (1989).

2
Technology and trade: An overview of the literature

2.1 Introduction

In contrast to many other fields of economic theory, international trade theory has traditionally retained the importance of technical change in explaining international trade flows or the international 'competitiveness' of a country or an industry at the centre of much economic debate. This can be explained to a large extent by the almost unique influence of 'classical' thinking in the area of international trade, with many contemporary trade theorists still expressing doubts (particularly with regard to the technology assumption) as to the actual contribution of 'neo-classical' thinking.

The fact that 'pure' neo-classical trade theory is still so prominent in international trade textbooks and is held in such esteem by policy-makers, at least until the 1970s, has little to do with the way 'factor endowments' (pure Heckscher–Ohlin–Samuelson) trade theory explains international trade flows. Its value as a *descriptive* theory, i.e. national differences in endowments of productive factors form the basis for trade, is reputedly very limited.

Like so many other fields of economic analysis, the old 'strength' of the pure orthodox theoretical framework lies primarily in the relatively straightforward normative implications – in terms of the gains from trade for both trading partners, as well as free trade prescriptions – which can be built around the model. The fact that in order to do so it has to rely on a set of extreme 'heroic' assumptions is then generally justified in terms of cost–benefit analysis: the insights gained by such a simple but complete trade/welfare picture by far outstrip the disadvantages of more realistic but more complex and less clear analyses.

Such a view, however, requires first that a 'reasonably accurate' explanation is offered for these main causal interdependencies identified by the theory, and second that the distortions and imperfections of the real world lead only to minor or 'shortlived' aberrations with relatively little consequence for the normative or policy conclusions of the theory. In the case of 'orthodox' trade theory and, rather uniquely, in nearly all fields of economic inquiry there has been growing recognition from all sides that both conditions do not hold.

Nowhere is this more clearly illustrated than in the seminal review Hufbauer (1970) presented twenty years ago, on the emerging and growing evidence and support in favour of the so-called 'neo-technology' accounts of international trade flows. In interpreting his neo-technology results, Hufbauer, himself the author of one of the most detailed 'technology gap' trade studies on synthetic materials (1966), remained, if anything, rather schizophrenic. His 'neo-technology' results, while powerful in explaining the actual trade flow and admittedly closer to the real world, represented an approach which, in Hufbauer's words, was 'not geared to answering the traditional questions of economic inquiry'. And Hufbauer added with some irony: 'It can as yet offer little to compare with Samuelson's magnificent (if misleading) factor–price equalisation theorem.'[1]

While Hufbauer's contribution was exceptional in its frankness, it was in no way exceptional in bringing out the dilemma between relevance and consistency with a general and established theoretical framework which has characterised the analysis of technical change in economic theory.

Some authors privilege the first criterion (relevance) and find in the evidence on technological change a powerful challenge pushing towards the search for a radically different theory. As Rosenberg puts it:

> in a world where rapid technological change is taking place we may need an analytical apparatus which focusses in a central way upon the process of technological change itself, rather than treating it simply as an exogenous force which leads to disturbances from equilibrium situations and thereby sets in motion an adjustment process leading to a new equilibrium. (Rosenberg, 1970, pp. 69–70)

Conversely, other economists stress, as a necessary condition for the theoretical consideration of the phenomena related to technological change, precisely their tractability within the traditional model, or simply consider the absence of any alternative as a sufficient condition for their neglect. In Bhagwati's words, writing some twenty years ago:

> the realistic phenomena ... such as the development of new technologies in consumption and production involve essentially phenomena of

imperfect competition for which, despite Chamberlain and Joan
Robinson, we still do not have today any serious theories of general
equilibrium... . Unless therefore we have a new powerful theoretic
system... we cannot really hope to make a dent in the traditional frame
of analysis. (Bhagwati, 1970, p. 23)

It is only fair to say that, particularly in the area of imperfect competition, major new insights have been developed over the last twenty years, providing a major 'dent' in traditional trade theory.[2]

However, in keeping with the broad spirit of this book, as discussed in the preceding chapter, we will, in the following review, try to circumscribe 'new' trade theory contributions to the class of what we will call here 'revisionist' contributions, in the most positive meaning of the term, pursuing a gradual and progressive incorporation of an increasing number of more realistic phenomena into modified forms of general equilibrium analysis. These contributions will be opposed to the 'heretic' tradition, searching for alternative models no longer based on 'generally accepted', neo-classical assumptions. Our attempt to use such theoretical benchmarks to review a highly selected literature is of course less and less successful, in keeping with the high variance in 'degree of orthodoxy', scope and realism of the assumptions, which are being introduced, particularly on the 'new' trade theory side.

In this short review we shall start from what could be called an 'incrementalist' analysis of technology-related phenomena, broadly along the lines of the neo-classical approach.[3]

2.2   The 'pure' trade theory: neo-classical extensions and the 'revisionists'

Consider first the neo-classical 'pure' theory of trade in its simplest textbook form. There are generally four fundamental assumptions:

1. *On technology*. Differences in techniques can be adequately represented by production functions. The latter are assumed to represent the essential features of production activities of the real world, are well-behaved, continuous, differentiable, exhibit non-increasing returns to scale, etc. Moreover, they are assumed identical across countries.
2. *On behaviour*. Perfect competition prevails throughout. Agents are maximisers under budget constraints.
3. *On demand*. Identical tastes across countries and well-behaved utility functions.
4. *On adjustment mechanism*. Adjustments are such as to guarantee *ex hypothesi* the clearing of all commodity and factor markets.

This leads to the following subsidiary assumption:

> Hypotheses (1)–(4) offer a reasonably accurate description of the prevailing 'state of the world' and the main interdependencies in the international arena, so that any possible distortions or imperfections of the real world lead only to minor or 'shortlived' aberrations with relatively little consequence for the interpretative and normative conclusions of the theory.

In its simplest form, the 'pure' theory of international trade then goes on to prove some of the most 'classic' theorems of economic theory: on relative specialisation determined by relative factor endowments (Heckscher–Ohlin–Samuelson), on factor–price equalisation and the theorems of comparative statics, on the effects of changing prices on factors' returns (Stolper–Samuelson–Rybczynski theorem) and of changing endowments upon commodity outputs.

Here we will not consider the developments and refinements of all four hypotheses listed above, but will limit our review to some of those contributions which do not entirely subscribe to the derived hypothesis that distortions are short-lived and have tried to modify some of the assumptions (1)–(4). Typically, the scientific strategy is to hold the rest as true and work out the implications of the additional (more 'realistic') hypotheses. Assumption (4) remains, however, *the* core proposition which is generally left untouched, since the entire model, irrespective of how it is precisely defined, needs a link of some kind between relative scarcities and relative prices.

One way of relaxing the simplest technological assumptions has been to allow production functions to differ between countries. Jones (1970) analyses some of the implications: factor-price equalisation no longer occurs, 'differential rates of technical differences between countries come to dominate the determination of comparative advantages',[4] but the Heckscher–Ohlin theorem on specialisation still applies in a modified form. Berglas and Jones (1977) embody in their model a mechanism of learning-by-doing, characterised by 'local learning',[5] on the techniques effectively in use. Findlay (1978) develops a steady-state dynamic model including technology transfers between an 'advanced' country and a 'backward' one. Chipman (1970) considers the case of moving production functions whereby technical progress is itself endogenous, along Kennedy–von Weizsäcker–Samuelson lines.[6] Purvis (1972) presents a model with international technological differences and capital mobility, illustrating that in this case, contrary to the standard model, factor mobility and trade may be complementary. The issue of capital mobility is also considered by Ferguson (1978) and Jones (1980):

interestingly, the patterns of trade turn out to be essentially determined by technology gaps and relative labour costs.

Another way of relaxing the standard assumption with regard to the production function is by introducing economies of scale. Since the analysis of the latter must be generally associated with assumptions that differ from the pure competitive model,[7] one may consider these two variations on the standard model together.[8] First, as Drèze (1960 and 1961) and Ohlin (1933) himself pointed out over fifty years ago, taken on their own, economies of scale can be an explanatory variable of trade patterns. Second, from a more normative point of view, they may well influence the welfare effects of trade so that a country may even lose from trade, as suggested originally by Graham (1923).

Over the last ten years many interesting theoretical developments have of course been produced in this area, giving rise to a rapidly expanding literature which can only be reported upon in part here, and which is generally referred to as the 'new' trade theory.[9]

Ethier (1979) and (1982a) has explored the conditions under which Graham's arguments hold: they depend on the nature of the increasing returns (which are either 'national' or 'international') and the pattern of change in relative prices due to the transition from autarky to trade. Imperfect competition due to increasing returns *may* imply gains from trade for both trading partners (cf. Melvin, 1969; Krugman, 1979a), but may also imply losses (cf. Kemp, 1969). In the case of 'imperfect competition' a large number of conclusions emerge which may be diametrically in conflict with the standard Heckscher–Ohlin–Samuelson model:[10] for example, factor prices will not be equalised, but, on the contrary, the price of the factor used intensively in the production of the export good may actually be high in each country (cf. Markusen and Melvin, 1984). Similarly, factor mobility, instead of substituting for trade (trade in factors as opposed to trade in commodities) as in the standard model, will be complementary to trade, with each country achieving an equilibrium where it is well endowed with the factor used intensively in the production of its export good. As Markusen and Melvin (1984) note: 'In the Heckscher–Ohlin model this is, of course, the basis for trade whereas in the present model it is the result of trade'.

In general, as shown by Markusen and Melvin (1984), sufficient conditions for the gains-from-trade theorems to hold are (i) marginal pricing on the behavioural side; and (ii) the convexity of the production possibility sets on the technological side. More recently, many of such 'new' trade contributions have focussed on estimating some of the gains from trade that are directly related to economies of scale, particularly within the framework of the further harmonisation of the internal EC market (Smith and Venables, 1988) and the Canada–US free trade agreement.[11] In the specific Canadian case, for example, Harris (1984) shows, using a general equilibrium model but introducing scale economies and imperfect competition, that the gains from trade liberalisation are four times as great as under conditions of perfect competition.[12] Within the small country context, Dixit (1986b) has illustrated that for small countries there may be gains from strategic trade policy which are sometimes greater than for large countries.

On the other hand, analysis of differentiated products has led to attempts at synthesis between theories of monopolistic competition, intra- and interindustry trade. Differentiation is supposed to come from a demand for a variety of product characteristics (cf. Barker, 1977; Dixit and Stiglitz, 1977; Krugman, 1979a, 1980, 1981; Helpman and Krugman, 1985; Markusen, 1986, 1989) or from different combinations of some fundamental attributes (cf. Lancaster, 1979, 1980) embodied in each product. Thus whereas intraindustry trade is explained on the grounds of monopolistic competition,[13] the explanation for the inter-industry trade flows will be left to the traditional Heckscher–Ohlin model. These models predict that intraindustry trade will be highest between similar countries (in terms of per capita income and patterns of demand; see Linder, 1961), whereas interindustry trade flows will be more important the greater the difference between countries in terms of 'endowments'.[14] An alternative (Ricardian) model of intraindustry trade is provided by Petri (1980), where intraindustrial specialisation for any given pattern of demand is determined by relative labour productivities and cost conditions within sector-specific and country-specific structures of production.

More generally speaking, it can be said that 'new' trade theory places the microfoundations of intraindustry trade in the strategic behaviours of firms operating in conditions of 'monopolistic competition', with product differentiation and, sometimes, increasing returns (Markusen and Melvin, 1984, Grossman and Helpman, 1989, and Markusen, 1989). Other 'new' trade theory versions consider oligopolistic interactions whereby countries are equated to single firms and the ensuing game-theoretic equilibria are then analysed. In these circumstances, it is shown that bilateral trade of identical products will or can take place. The formal introduction of market structures that differ from pure competition pioneered by authors who attempted to link instruments and concepts of industrial organisation (multinational corporation, oligopolistic competition, strategic behaviours) with a general equilibrium trade model,[15] has led to two separate directions. The first one, whereby results can be formally presented in terms of the traditional model with specific factors,[16] has drawn attention to the significance of the link between industrial structures and trade flows, whatever the 'endowments'; the second one has focussed attention on a different adjustment mechanism: international capital mobility in the form of multinational investment rather than intranational intersectoral mobility. This latter direction allows, at least in principle, the consideration of *country-specific* variables of both an institutional and economic nature which as such also represent an incentive/obstacle to the location of international capital. [17]

Under the broad heading of 'industrial organisation and international trade', one must thus also mention parts of the vast literature on the origins and effects of multinational corporations. Some of the studies deviate in both spirit and constructions from the neo-classical assumptions we listed above (e.g. Hymer, 1976): technological differences between companies and countries, country-specific absolute advantages and high degrees of 'imperfection' of the markets in general and the market for technology in particular are implicit from the start. These features of the world are indeed the necessary structural conditions for the existence of multinationals. Other interpretative models also try to incorporate some neo-classical elements. This appears to be the case in Dunning's 'eclectic theory', [18] whereby Heckscher–Ohlin mechanisms of adjustment in prices, quantities and relative specialisations are considered to be *one of* the processes at work, whose relative importance depends on the sectors, the degrees of development of the countries and the nature of the technology. Finally, other interpretations – such as Rugman (1980) – attempt to reconcile the existence of multinationals, intrafirm trade, etc., with traditional analysis. Rugman recognises the widespread existence of 'imperfections' (and thus the limited validity of assumptions 1 and 2 above). However, he assumes that companies face and overcome these imperfections by *internalising* the relevant transactions. Therefore, multinationals become some sort of 'second best approximation' to the working of the standard model.

An increasing number of the theories discussed above are now becoming formalised. In particular, a number of contributions by Horstmann and Markusen (1986, 1987a,b, 1989) have illustrated in a number of cases how conclusions are reached that are at variance with the canonic model: factor prices are not generally equalised; there are oligopolistic rents; trade patterns do not depend only on countries' endowments; and the degrees and forms of market 'imperfections' become a determinant on their own of productive locations and trade.

A different group of models adopts 'Ricardian' hypotheses on technology – with coefficients of production fixed and different between countries – while generally retaining general equilibrium assumptions on prices, determined through a market-clearing process. Dornbush, Fisher and Samuelson (1977) present a two-country Ricardian model with a 'continuum' of commodities and the patterns of specialisation determined by relative wages and relative productivities.[19] Wilson (1980) extends the model to many countries and non-homotetic demand schedules. Jones (1979) considers the conditions under which technical progress may produce 'immiserizing growth' for either of the trade partners.

A simple but illuminating picture of the technology–trade relationship emerges from Krugman's North–South trade model (1979) and (1982). Starting with an innovative North and a non-innovative South, where the North's innovations only take the form of new products produced immediately in the North, but only after a lag in the South. Krugman (1979) shows how new industries must constantly emerge in the North in order to maintain its living standards, since the new industries decline and disappear sooner or later in the face of low-wage competition from the South. In Krugman's model, this is because the North's wages reflect the rent on the North's monopoly of new technology: 'This monopoly is continually eroded by technological borrowing and must be maintained by constant innovation of new products. Like Alice and the Red Queen, the developed region must keep running to stay in the same place' (Krugman, 1979, p. 262). In other words, while the North will be able to achieve some 'moving equilibrium' through a sufficiently large rate of innovation in order to maintain its living standards, any slowing of innovation or acceleration of technology transfer will narrow the wage differentials between North and South and might even lead to an absolute decline in living standards in the North. The most interesting aspect of Krugman's model is, perhaps paradoxically, the set of simplistic and, from a traditional trade point of view, totally 'unrealistic' assumptions behind the model: there are no differences in factor endowments because there is only one factor of production (labour); and all goods, old and new, are produced with the same function, leaving no room for differences in labour productivity; neither neo-classical nor Ricardian trade explanations are relevant; there is no fixed pattern of trade, but trade is determined by a continuing process of innovation in the North and technology transfer to the South. Yet despite these simplifications, some of the conclusions which emerge from the model are very appealing, not in the least because, as Krugman observes: 'The picture of trade seems in some ways more like that of businessmen or economic historians than that of trade theorists' (Krugman, 1979, p. 265).

Within a different analytical framework, Krugman (1982) considers the patterns of trade stemming from technological gaps and different 'technological intensities' of the various commodities in a Ricardian model, with a continuum of commodities, which shows some similarities with the model and the conclusions that we will present in Chapter 6: for example, technological differences turn out to be a fundamental force which shape comparative advantages.

More generally, a recent stream of analysis (Krugman, 1987; Grossman and Helpman, 1989, 1990a and 1990b; Markusen, 1989) has attempted to formalise equilibrium trade patterns with endogenous technical change and monopolistic competition in the 'innovative' intermediate inputs. These models somewhat link trade theory with increasing-returns growth theories (Romer, 1986, 1989, 1990; Lucas, 1988; Aghion and Howitt, 1989): an equilibrium rate of technical change is endogenously determined and, with that, the steady-state properties of trade flows (an exception being Markusen (1989), which considers a set of equilibria which might not be steady-state ones).

It is obviously very difficult to provide a synthetic assessment of these quite heterogeneous streams of literature, characterised as they are by very different directions and degrees of 'revisionism'. However, three general conclusions may be drawn.

First, there is probably little disagreement about the inadequacy of the 'canonic' factor proportions theory to explain international trade flows *by itself*. As Krugman (1979b) puts it: '...causal observation seems to militate against a simple factor proportions theory. The emphasis on factor proportions in international trade is... not the result of an empirical judgement' (p. 14).

Second, most of the studies we reviewed implicitly highlight the lack of robustness of the major Heckscher–Ohlin results in terms of both predictions and welfare implications. Relaxation of the least realistic assumptions (i.e. perfect competition, constant returns to scale, factor immobility, immediate and free diffusion of technology, existence of well-behaved production functions) leads, generally speaking, to indeterminate prediction in relation to the direction and volume of trade. Moreover, the factor–price equalisation theorem does not generally follow. In terms of welfare implications, depending on which assumption is relaxed, conclusions about the 'gains from trade' are sometimes in accordance and sometimes at variance with the orthodox model.

Third and, from our own perspective, of more direct relevance, quite interesting results sometimes emerge, *despite* the continuing presence of highly restrictive assumptions. This set of conclusions, which will be discussed later, will prove to be even more important when placed in an alternative theoretical framework: for example, the role of technology gaps, country-specific absolute advantages and different forms of industrial organisations; the importance of economies of scale and various types of learning; the absence of any general tendency toward factor–price equalisation.

It has already been mentioned that a core assumption shared by most of the models reviewed so far is a *scarcity* link between factors, commodities and prices, irrespective of the particular hypotheses on technology, forms of competition, etc. In this sense, the contributions reviewed above share all the points of strength and weakness of general equilibrium analysis. The strength, in our view, relates to the capacity to handle, using a simple and general theoretical device, the question of *interdependence* among national and international markets. Not surprisingly, the main question addressed by the standard Heckscher–Ohlin theory and by most of its 'revisionist' developments concerns the *patterns of specialisation* of each country in relation to some country-specific characteristics.

The other side of the coin is that such analyses, undertaken in terms of equilibrium positions, take as given that (i) there are adjustment mechanisms which generally lead to such equilibria; and (ii) these mechanisms based on price/quantity adjustments – as assumed in the standard Walrasian model – lead to the clearing of all markets. Both points are difficult to accept on either theoretical or empirical grounds. The difficulties in accounting for the adjustment processes in the standard general equilibrium framework when neither the fantastic 'auctioneer' nor a complete set of contingency markets exist[20] are well-known and need not be discussed here.[21] There is no reason to believe that such adjustment processes are any easier in the open-economy case.

On more empirical grounds, it is difficult to believe that relative prices are explained by relative scarcities in a world characterised not only by various forms of static and dynamic economies of scale, but also by continuous technical progress and by national economies which are themselves often characterised by some degree of unutilised labour or labour *and* capital.

The very formulation of the standard model in its 'timeless' form becomes even harder to accept whenever one of the factors of endowment – capital – is a set of reproducible (and heterogeneous) commodities. The question has been discussed in a 'capital controversy',[22] with many points in common with the famous 'Cambridge debate' on capital theory, focussing on the problems arising from the heterogeneity of capital goods[23] to the measurement of the 'aggregate capital' which must appear among the 'endowments'.[24]

Another feature common to practically all the models reviewed so far is the behavioural assumption concerning maximising agents. This is equally true for the models of 'pure' competition as it is for those based on imperfect competition or oligopolistic strategic interaction. With regard to technical change in particular, this assumption becomes rather questionable. As argued at greater length elsewhere[25] and following Nelson and Winter (1982), it is difficult to maintain that maximisation

procedures are an adequate representation of the general behaviour of
the agents whenever one accounts properly for the fundamental features
of technical change (including uncertainty about choices and outcomes,
patterns of search generally embodying tacit heuristics, various kinds of
irreversibilities, etc.). It is not only, or even primarily, a matter of
realism of assumptions. The fundamental point is that behaviours are
also directly relevant in terms of the equilibrium positions towards
which the system might tend to converge. In other words, even the
sequences of 'attractors' for the microeconomic adjustments of the
system may well be *path-* and *behaviour-dependent.* [26]

2.3   The less pure theory: the 'heretics'

The discussion so far has focussed upon that stream of economic
analysis concerned primarily with one theoretical question, namely *the
determinants of specialisation*, and one functional mechanism, namely
the adjustment processes induced in the latter by the *interdependencies
between markets*, both within each country and between countries. It is
a line of enquiry which – despite the great differences in the assumptions
on technology, demand and nature of the markets – links Ricardo, the
neo-classical school and all those new, 'revisionist' contributions based
on a general equilibrium framework. One of the fundamental premises
of such a stream of thought is that trade (or the notional transition from
autarky to trade) affects the intersectoral (and, sometimes, international)
allocation of inputs, quantities, and prices, but *does not* affect the rate
of utilisation of the stocks of inputs themselves (and, thus, the rates of
macroeconomic activity). [27] This is straightforward in modern general
equilibrium analysis, where, as already discussed, full employment of all
factors is assumed by hypothesis. It is equally true for that part of
Ricardo's *Principles* that is concerned with international trade, based,
as it was, on the assumption that

> no extension of foreign trade will immediately increase the amount of
> value in a country, although it will very powerfully contribute to increase
> the mass of commodities, and therefore the sum of enjoyments. As the
> value of all foreign goods is measured by the quantity of the produce of
> our land and labour, which is given in exchange for them, we should
> have no greater value if, by the discovery of new markets, we obtained
> double the quantity of foreign goods in exchange of a given quantity of
> our's. (Ricardo, 1951, p. 128)

Since in Ricardo's model production techniques are given, the assumption concerning an unchanged 'amount of value of a country' is

precisely equivalent to an assumption of constancy of the rates of macroeconomic activity throughout the notional transition from autarky to trade. In the history of economic thought, however, one can also identify another group of contributions that are highly heterogeneous in scope and nature, seldom thoroughly formalised, heretic in spirit and often produced by outsiders of the dominant economic tradition. In this composite group one may include early economists from the eighteenth and nineteenth centuries, such as the Reverend Tucker, Count Serra of Naples, Ferrier, List and Hamilton, as well as parts of the analysis of Adam Smith. In more recent times one finds an equally heterogeneous set of writers ranging from some technology-gap and product-cycle authors (Posner, Freeman, Vernon, Hirsch, Kaldor, Cornwall and Thirlwall) broadly in the post-Keynesian tradition; 'structuralist' writers in development economics, especially within the Latin American tradition; economic historians, such as Gerschenkron, Kuznets and Balogh; some modern French writers such as Bye, de Bernis, Lafay and Mistral. Obviously, these contributions are highly different in nature and scope. However, one may state that they have in common, explicitly or implicitly, one or several of the following assumptions:

1. International differences in technological levels and innovative capabilities are a fundamental factor in explaining the differences in both levels and trends in the exports, imports and income of each country.
2. General equilibrium mechanisms of international and intersectoral adjustment are relatively weak, so that trade has important effects upon the rates of macroeconomic activity of each economy. Putting it in another way, the growth of each economy is often balance-of-payment constrained and this constraint becomes tighter or looser according to the levels and composition of the participation of each country to world trade flows. The weakness of price/quantity adjustments between sectors and between countries has to do partly with the nature of technology (fixed coefficients, irreversibilities, etc.) and partly with the nature of demand (sticky baskets of consumption, etc.). As a result, what adjust in the international arena are world market shares within each sector and, through that, the levels of macroeconomic activity generated by foreign demand.
3. That same weakness of general equilibrium mechanisms is such that the intrasectoral distribution of trade shares between countries and their evolution through time can be explained by a set of country-specific absolute advantages/disadvantages and without explicit reference, at least in a first approximation, to price/quantity adjustments between sectors and between factors' returns.

4. Technology is not a free good.
5. The allocative patterns induced by international trade have dynamic implications which may either yield 'virtuous' or 'perverse' feedback in the long term.

These assumptions have generally been stated in a rather confused way by the early writers, who did not share the rigour and depth of Ricardo or Samuelson, and were often motivated simply by policy issues such as protection versus free trade. None the less, they had precious, if confused, insights into complex problems of economic dynamics which were later neglected in the cleaner but more restrictive formalisations of modern trade theory. For example, Tucker (1774) (quoted also by Hufbauer, 1970) assumes that there is a macroeconomic link between technological advantages, international competitiveness and incomes, and discusses whether the product-cycle effects induced by the lower wages of the 'poor country' will eventually reverse the competitive position of the 'rich' vis-à-vis the 'poor'. His answer is reassuring for the United Kingdom: continuous technical progress, higher capabilities of accumulation and institutional factors will ensure an absolute advantage there, despite the lower wages of the more backward countries. Ferrier (1805) deals with the relationship between trade and rates of macroeconomic activity in the light of the historical experience of the Continental Blockade, arguing that there is a direct negative link between import penetration and employment levels in the relatively backward country due to a generalised technological disadvantage and to the long-term effect that despecialisation in the most advanced products (in this case, manufactures) exerts upon the capability of progress and accumulation: 'I compare a nation which with its money buys abroad commodities it can make itself, although of a poorer quality, with a gardener who, dissatisfied with the fruits he gathers, would buy juicier fruits from his neighbours, giving them his gardening tools in exchange.'[28]

Interestingly, Adam Smith was equally aware of the dynamic implications of trade,[29] and his position appears to be almost symmetrical to that of Ferrier, from the 'advanced country' point of view. First, he argues, trade has a beneficial effect upon the rates of macroeconomic activity and employment because, in contemporary words, exports increase aggregate demand. This is close to what Myint (1958) later defined as a 'rent-for-surplus' model of trade. Second, the enlargement of the market due to international trade feeds back upon the domestic division of labour and thus on the trends in productive efficiency.

The argument of German and nationalist List (1904) was directly opposed to those of Ricardo and Say. The practical matter at stake, as was well known, was the political advocacy of protectionism and industrialisation. In List's view, there is nothing in the adjustment mechanisms on the international market (in List's terminology, the adjustments 'based on the theory of exchange values') which guarantees dynamic convergence between nations in terms of productive capabilities and incomes (the 'growth of productive forces of a Nation'). In several respects, this view involves much more than an 'infant industry argument', the idea being that the long-term position of each country depends jointly on its degrees of capital accumulation, its global, technical and learning capabilities,[30] and a set of institutional factors (social consensus, factory discipline, political conditions). According to List, the adjustment processes set in motion by international trade, might well be detrimental to the development of these aspects of the 'national productive forces'. Putting it in modern terms, static and dynamic economies of scale and differing income elasticities of the various commodities, under free-trade conditions will lead to divergence rather than factor–price equalisation, and growth polarisation, with concentration of production in one country rather than welfare gains for both partners.

In a similar perspective, these points have been emphasised in much of the early development/trade/dependency literature,[31] and in the historical analysis of the early industrialisation/opening of trade process in the United Kingdom.

More recently and along the lines suggested by Kaldor (1970, 1975 and 1980), Thirlwall and Vines (1983) have formalised such views in a multisector North–South model and have studied the 'consistency conditions' between the two countries and the various sectors. The Kaldor–Thirlwall–Vines approach, while incorporating some ideas similar to earlier 'two-gap' models of development – whereby the growth of industrialising countries is shown to be constrained by either saving/investment capacity or foreign exchange requirements[32] – embodies a general hypothesis on world growth as being determined by 'asymmetrical' patterns of change in technical coefficients and demand composition. In this view, processes of interfactorial and intercommodity substitution in response to relative prices and excess factor supplies are of minor importance. What adjusts is the level of sectoral and macroeconomic activity.

An ambitious multisector model along similar lines is that of Pasinetti (1981), whose open-economy version determines the relative rates of growth between economies in terms of evolution of relative productivities and income elasticities of the commodities that each country produces. Such a model also generates 'comparative advantages' as the endogenous result of sector-specific dynamics and country-specific dynamics of technological change.

In all these models the difference in the income elasticity of the various commodities plays a fundamental role and is assumed to dominate over price/quantity adjustments in consumption baskets. Thus, as Thirlwall (1980) shows, the income elasticities enter into the determination of the foreign-trade multiplier of each economy (via import propensities and export elasticities to world income). The other fundamental factor is obviously technology. 'Polarisation' in innovativeness is shown to imply 'polarisation' in growth.

Interestingly, while both the Ricardian and neo-classical perspectives focus upon the determinants of the *patterns of specialisation*, the set of contributions reviewed above focusses on the relationship between trade, levels of activity and growth. In terms of adjustment mechanisms, both Ricardo and the neo-classical school hold the rates of activity constant and study trade-induced changes in relative prices and relative quantities; conversely, the 'heretic' stream often assumes away price/quantity adjustments and studies the link between trade and rates of activity in both the short and long terms.

In order to highlight these differences, one may represent the early heretic model as follows. Imagine, two countries, Portugal and England, producing two commodities, wine and cloth, with labour only. Suppose that, at the beginning, the two countries are absolutely identical: the same technical coefficients, same relative prices, same patterns of consumption, same absolute prices as expressed in their respective currencies whose exchange rate is equal to one. Suppose also the existence of a non-reproducible asset, say gold or, alternatively, tradeable shares representing titles of ownership over the productive activities. Finally, suppose that each economy has some surplus labour which can be mobilised without any extra cost whenever this is required. Clearly, the two countries, even if opened to international markets, will not trade. Assume now an across-the-board improvement in the Portuguese technical coefficients which leaves *unchanged relative productivities* and *relative prices*. In the perspective of both Ricardo and the neo-classicists, still no trade will occur. As Findlay puts it, '...greater technological efficiency cannot be the cause of trade if the relative difference is the same in both goods'.[33]

On the contrary, in what we could call a Smith–Ferrier–List model of trade a *one-way* trade occurs, with Portugal progressively gaining market shares on the English market in *both* wine and cloth. Correspondingly, gold or ownership titles will move from England to Portugal. The rates of macroeconomic activity will grow in Portugal and fall in England. The adjustment process to the Portuguese technological advance will not stop until the exchange rate has entirely adjusted to the new purchasing power parity determined by the new levels of productivities in Portugal as compared to English ones. It is easy to define the dynamic counterpart of the model. Imagine a *continuous* flow of technical improvements in Portugal. One will observe a continuously increasing market penetration of Portugal on the English markets. Essentially, the adjustment process takes three forms.

First, the English currency continues to devaluate. Second, gold or ownership titles continue to flow out of England. Third, rates of activity in Portugal continue to grow and the English ones continue to fall. Notably, the increasing technological gap is reflected in the changing world-market share of *each* commodity, even if no international specialisation occurs. One could broaden the model, for example by introducing a third commodity, whisky, which only England can produce due to some natural advantage. Then, under the above assumptions, England will slowly converge toward an absolute specialisation in whisky while its short-term rate of activity and its long-term growth will depend upon the levels and changes in the Portuguese propensity to drink whisky as compared with the English propensity to drink wine and wear clothes.

Needless to say, such a model embodies gross oversimplification. However, it illustrates the evidence of the free-trade adjustment processes following major technological polarisations better than the Ricardian alternative. This is precisely what continental writers from the early nineteenth century had in mind: given the European backwardness vis-à-vis England, *laissez-faire* regimes would not have yielded mutual gains from trade, but, rather, would have reduced Europe to a condition more similar to that in India.

A major factor counteracting this link between polarisation in technology and in income levels is of course the international diffusion of technology. Indeed, most modern technology-gap models focus on the crucial time element between innovation and imitation abroad, as trade and income-polarising 'reversal' factor.

The basic assumption of most modern technology-gap trade accounts is that technology is not a freely, instantaneously and universally available good, but that there are substantial advantages in being first. Thus, in Posner's seminal model it is suggested that while technical changes and developments may influence some industries and not others, it is the technical change originating in one country and not in others which will induce trade 'during the lapse of time taken for the rest of the world to imitate one country's innovation' (Posner, 1961, p. 323).

A similar point is made in Freeman's case study of the plastics industry: 'Technical progress results in leadership in production in this industry, because patents and commercial secrecy together can give the innovator a head start of as much as 10–15 years' (Freeman, 1963, p. 22). Once imitation has taken place, more traditional factors of adjustment and specialisation would again take over and determine

trade flows. In Hufbauer's words: 'Technology gap trade is...the impermanent commerce which initially arises from the exporting nation's
industrial breakthrough and which is prolonged by static and dynamic
scale economies flowing from the breakthrough' (Hufbauer, 1966,
p. 23). There is of course nothing necessarily 'impermanent' about these
static and dynamic scale economies. Coupled with new or improved
product innovations they might well lead to a more or less continuous
trade flow.

Product cycle theories (Hirsch, 1965; Vernon, 1966) provide an
articulated trade picture along similar lines. They also integrate foreign
direct investment and view technology as part of a wider set of market
structure factors, including entry, product differentiation/standardisa-
tion and nature of demand. Vernon's original model is primarily
demand-determined: high levels of income and sophisticated demand
patterns induce innovative responses from domestic firms. More
recently, the introduction of supply factors has dealt with some of the
weaknesses of the original model (for a critical assessment see Walker,
1979). Further developments within this perspective are based on explicit
theories of technological innovation and are likely to involve extensions
of post-Schumpeterian 'evolutionary' models[34] to the international
field, where the emphasis is on the dynamic nature of international
competition.[35]

Another recent direction of investigation relates to the importance
given to the import and export of technology in shaping a country's
future trade pattern. It opens the way for a future integration of foreign
investment theories,[36] technology transfer and catching-up models,[37]
and dynamic diffusion models[38] within a theoretical trade framework.
In particular, explicit dynamic analyses of the interactions between
company-specific and country-specific advantages (Cantwell, 1989), and
their bearing on the explanation of both trade flows and international
investments, seems a highly promising direction of inquiry which is
indeed highly complementary to the interpretation presented in this
book.

2.4   The empirical evidence

The picture which emerges from the numerous empirical trade studies is,
as one might expect, far from uniform. Moreover, the correspondence
between theoretical models and empirical tests is generally poor. As
Deardorff notes in his thorough review of trade studies:

> Empirical tests of the theories are often faulted on the grounds that they
> test propositions that do not derive rigorously from the theories. The

reason is not usually that empirical models are sloppy. Rather, the problem seems to lie in the theories themselves, which are seldom stated in forms that are compatible with the real world complexities that empirical research cannot escape. (Deardorff, 1984, p. 468)

We will organise our review of an even more selected literature with reference to the same themes and approaches discussed above.

Not surprisingly, a major stream of research has been concerned with the explanation of the so-called 'Leontief paradox' within a mainly orthodox factor-proportions framework. As is well known, Leontief (1953) found that the composition of trade in the United States, clearly a capital-abundant country, was biased in favour of labour-intensive exports and capital-intensive imports. While the typical research strategy in the theoretical field was simply to neglect the potentially disruptive implication of such a falsification of the theory, the empirical strategy focussed upon additional variables which could explain away the 'paradox'. This has been one of the analytical procedures which has drawn attention toward technology-related variables, typically labour skills and what has become known as 'human capital'. Many empirical studies, primarily concerned with the US case, found these latter variables to be significantly correlated with the American composition of trade.[39]

Moreover, Leamer (1980) has recently argued that a proper test of the Heckscher–Ohlin model must not be based on the factor content of trade but on the relative factor intensity of production as compared to consumption. Using this criterion, Stern and Markus (1981) found that the Leontief 'paradox' did hold for 1958 but not for 1947 and 1972. These empirical findings and refinements seem, at first sight, comforting to the prevailing theory in its generalised version, including a 'technology-production' factor and extending the concept of capital not only to human capital, but also to 'intellectual capital', defined as the 'capitalised value of productive knowledge created by research and development'.[40] However, one must have severe reservations about these 'revisionist' attempts to accommodate the evidence with a traditional factor-proportion view of trade flows.

First, as regards the conclusions based on Leamer's methodological suggestions the results are far from 'non-paradoxical' and depend crucially on the chosen years. They therefore appear to be not particularly robust.

Second, as argued by Deardorff, the 'acknowledgement of additional factors of production cannot in theory explain Leontief's paradoxical results regarding capital and labour'.[41]

Third, the higher the distance of the underlying model from the original labour/land framework, the lower appears to be the plausibility of the basic assumptions. As already discussed in Section 2.3, one can hardly consider 'capital' as an endowment when it is actually produced under conditions of non-decreasing returns. It is even harder to define R&D as an endowment, for its 'size' depends on highly discretionary decisions of firms and public institutions.

Fourth, proper 'tests' of the Heckscher–Ohlin model must be based on direct *plus* indirect factor contents. As discussed at length by Momigliano and Siniscalco (1984) this correct procedure has been followed by only a few studies.[42] The majority of studies simply consider direct product characteristics. This methodological difference matters. Thus, for example, Italy's trade performance is *negatively* correlated with the direct R&D content of each commodity but is *positively* correlated with the total content (direct plus indirect, via input/output flows).[43]

Finally, there is the question as to whether empirical analyses of trade flows can be usefully carried out at the level of intracountry intersectoral studies only. This methodological issue has been raised at a general level by Leamer (1974) and Leamer and Bowen (1981). The problem stems from different technology-specific characteristics which are likely to influence trade flows and can be accounted for only in intercountry intrasectoral analysis.

Given all these methodological problems and caveats, it is fair to conclude that most of the empirical studies based on cross-sectoral analyses relating trade flows (either measures of comparative advantages or net exports) to a menu of product characteristics, while useful in presenting the possible *regularities* in the structural features of domestic supply and their statistical correlation with the patterns of competitiveness, are far from useful in highlighting any causal mechanism *explaining* international competitiveness and specialisation.[44]

The empirical validity of the endowment-based theory of trade remains, therefore, very much subject to debate.[45] As Hufbauer puts it: 'Leontief's findings dealt an apparently telling blow to the simplistic two-factor version. Various authorities have sought to repair the damage; their work in some respects resembles the tortured efforts of pre-Copernican astronomers.'[46]

A different line of empirical enquiry has been concerned with the patterns of relative intersectoral specialisations based on a simple Ricardian framework. MacDougall (1951–2) showed that the sectoral ratio of US to UK exports was well correlated with relative American and British labour productivities. These results, confirmed by Stern (1962) and Balassa (1963) do not, of course, explain the *sources* of intersectoral differences in productivity and – as has been argued – could also be consistent with a Heckscher–Ohlin model of trade. On the other hand, they could also highlight the mechanisms leading to comparative advantages on the grounds of sector-specific gaps or leads in technology.

Empirical studies using the technology-gap trade framework or product-life-cycle theory, on the other hand, emphasise in the first instance the intercountry differences in innovativeness as the basis of international trade flows. Rather than interindustry variations in the technological 'endowment' of a specific country, it is the variation in innovativeness within each sector across countries which seems crucial.[47] Most sectoral studies (e.g. on chemicals, plastics, process plants, electronics products, semiconductors) highlight the dynamic relationship between early innovative leads,[48] economies of scale, learning by doing, oligopolistic exploitation of these advantages, and international competitiveness. As referred to in the introduction, one of the most ambitious attempts of intercountry and intersectoral comparison of technology-based and product-cycle-based models as compared to the other explanations of trade flows was carried out by Hufbauer (1970).

Hufbauer found that the commodity characteristics, by country, were related to a set of country characteristics, including variables related to technology, economies of scale, product differentiation and patterns of domestic demand. Whereas some of the proxies used implied high levels of 'heroism', they pointed to the widespread existence of country-specific advantages/disadvantages related to technological innovation, national 'context' conditions and forms of corporate behaviour that differed from 'pure competition'.

Similarly, the findings by Gruber and Vernon (1970), while broadly in line with the Leontief 'paradox', highlighted the homogeneity in the structure of exports (and production) among the major industrial countries and their general correlation with per capita GDP. Walker (1979) critically analysed the sectoral evidence on product-cycle patterns of production and exports, finding that there are groups of products which do conform with the prediction of a 'flow' from advanced to intermediate and backward low-wage countries, while other groups appear more in line with straightforward technology-gap theories, whereby the advantage remains over long periods in the most innovative country(ies).

Irrespective of whether the analysis deals with intracountry, intersectoral comparisons or international, intersectoral ones, an important methodological issue concerns the proxies used for the technology variable.[49] With the exception of Davidson (1979), Pavitt and Soete (1980) and Soete (1980 and 1981a), most empirical studies use technology *input* proxies, such as R&D expenditure or R&D employment. Yet, the exact relationship between technology input and technology output remains unclear. However, by emphasising the crucial role of new products and process innovations, most technology-gap models make explicit the need to use a technology output proxy instead of an input proxy in explaining international trade flows.

2.5   Conclusions

There are many gaps in our understanding of the role of innovation in international trade. Despite much progress, particularly over the last decade, we are only beginning to analyse (i) the determinants of different national capabilities to innovate, imitate and generally exploit innovation efforts competitively; (ii) the nature and relative importance of the various adjustment mechanisms within and between countries following such innovative processes; (iii) the relationship between sector-specific patterns of competitiveness and 'general equilibrium' factors, in the broader sense linked to relative prices, intersectoral capital and labour mobility, etc; (iv) the implications of economies of scale, dynamic increasing returns, oligopolistic forms of marked organisation, international investment and all the factors which are generally gathered under the headings 'imperfect competition' and 'new' trade theory; (v) the relationship between innovation, trade and growth. All these issues, of course, present an empirical counterpart which is also in need of more detailed study.

The ability to carry out such studies is obviously very much subject to data availability. Nevertheless, over recent years many new data sources have come into existence. The data are never perfect and rarely conform to what is ideally needed. However, perhaps the major bottleneck can be found in the lack of *joint* development of empirical analysis and strictly consistent theoretical models. In this respect, highly 'eclectic' methodologies trying to reconcile the orthodox framework with the evidence by means of an increasingly cumbersome apparatus are likely to yield rapidly decreasing returns.

In Kindleberger's words,

> neo-factor proportion theories assume that there is a standard world technology and that factor endowments determine the direction of trade. Neo-technological theories assume that technology is continuously changing unevenly, and that these changes alter the trade pattern. Innovations lead to exports; the spread of technology to the world establishes a pattern based on factor proportions, which may or may not differ from that included by the initial gap. To the extent that the pattern based on factors differs from that based on innovation, the neo-factor and neo-technological explanations differ rather than harmonize. (Kindleberger, 1970, p. 281)

Recognising this divide which, no doubt, an increasing number of 'new' trade theories are trying to bridge,[50] one cannot avoid choosing which 'vision' one deems is nearest to the evidence. We hope it is clear from this chapter which vision we believe conforms best to reality and is theoretically consistent. Our general theoretical propositions are as follows. *First*, the 'microfoundations' of international trade analyses, easily consistent with the available evidence, should be found in the extension of an 'evolutionary' interpretation to the international arena. *Second*, in such evolutionary dynamics, what appears to be, *ex-post*, a 'comparative advantage' is in no proper sense the result of any 'endowment' but rather the outcome of processes of learning – innovation, imitation, organisational change – which have both sector and country specificities. *Third*, the innovative process, by allowing various sorts of (static and dynamic) increasing returns, generally also entails forms of market interactions that differ from perfect competition. *Fourth*, these same properties of technical change imply the possibility of those *irreversible processes* discussed, for example, by Arthur (1989) and thus also, from a normative point of view, the possibility of 'virtuous' or 'vicious' circles in innovativeness, competitiveness and growth. *Fifth*, the *micro*economic and sectoral levels and changes in international competitiveness, so determined under conditions of continuous technological learning and limited short-term substitution in both production and consumption, also represent the microfoundations of those *macro*economic analyses, with some 'Keynesian' ascendancy whereby (western) economic systems seldom hit any powerful scarcity constraint, but, on the contrary, are often limited in their growth by aggregate demand and foreign balance requirements.

Admittedly, most of the theoretical analysis of these propositions and processes is still to be done. In the following chapters, we turn to a more detailed discussion of these propositions and the insight they contain in interpreting the links between trade patterns and processes of innovation, industrial evolution and patterns of growth. First, however, we turn to a brief 'empirical' review of some 'stylised' and 'less stylised' facts on technology, growth and trade.

Notes

1. Hufbauer (1970), p. 197.
2. The position taken 20 years later by Bhagwati is also interesting to note, Bhagwati (1989).
3. Extensive reviews of the trade literature can be found in Bhagwati (1964), Chipman (1965–6), Stern (1975) and Jones and Kenen (1984); more specifically on the issues related to technology and international trade, in

Hufbauer (1966) and (1970), Chesnais and Michon-Savarit (1980), Aho and Rosen (1980), Soete (1985) and Lyons (1986).

4. Jones (1970), p. 84.
5. Cf. Atkinson and Stiglitz (1969).
6. Cf. Kennedy (1964), von Weizsäcker (1965), Samuelson (1965).
7. Of course this is necessarily so if the economies of scale are internal to each firm.
8. For a thorough review, see Helpman (1984). An interesting collection of some of the 'state-of-the-art' contributions in the field can be found in Kierzkowski (1984).
9. See, among others, Dixit and Norman (1980), Chapter 9, Krugman (1979a), (1980), (1986), Helpman and Krugman (1985), (1989), Brander (1987), Markusen and Venables (1988), Markusen and Melvin (1988).
10. For 'imperfect competition' models, among others, Markusen (1981), Lancaster (1980), Helpman (1981), Helpman and Razin (1980), Melvin and Warne (1973). The implications of economies of scale in a neo-classical open-economy growth model are analysed in Krugman (1984a), Grossman and Helpman (1989, 1990a and b).
11. There exists not surprisingly an extensive literature on this subject. With respect to Europe see Jacquemin and Sapir (1988), Smith and Venables (1988) and Onida (1990); with respect to the United States and Canada, see Harris (1984), Cox and Harris (1986) and Stern, Tresize and Whalley (1987).
12. See also Markusen and Wigle (1989).
13. Grubel and Lloyd (1975).
14. See Helpman (1984a). This line of enquiry is in many ways an attempt at a synthesis between the Heckscher–Ohlin–Samuelson model and Linder's model (cf. Linder, 1961). For a model accounting also for multinational investment, see Helpman (1984). A general discussion of intraindustry trade and its interpretations can be found in Greenaway and Milner (1986). Results of empirical applications of the intraindustry literature to the Nordic countries can be found in Andersson (1987).
15. Cf. the special issue of *The Journal of Industrial Economics* edited by Caves (1980) and since then Brander (1981), Jacquemin (1982), Brander and Krugman (1983), Harris (1984), etc.
16. That is a general equilibrium model with sector-specific and intersectoral immobile factors (see Jones and Neary, 1984).
17. See also Jones (1980).
18. See Dunning (1977), (1981) and (1981a), Buckley and Casson (1976).
19. Krugman (1979, p. 262).
20. See Hahn (1984), Leijonhufrud (1981).
21. We refer the interested reader to the book edited by Dosi *et al.* (1988).
22. On this issue, for a 'Cambridge view', see Steedman (1979) and (1980), Metcalfe and Steedman (1981), and the replies by Ethier (1981) and Dixit (1981).
23. Interestingly, the standard neo-classical way out of the difficulties with regard to capital measurement has been, in the closed-economy case, through general equilibrium models of Walrasian ascendancy. This possibility is generally precluded in the field of international trade, since the specification of a long vector of 'endowments' implies nearly tautological conclusions. It is of little interest as Corden puts it crudely to have a 'theory' which says, 'that Switzerland has a comparative advantage in

watches because she is watchmaker-intensive or that the United States exports 747s because she is intensive in firms or engineers capable of making 747s' (Corden, 1979, p. 9). In trade-related capital theory the standard procedure is simply to assume that the measurement problem does not exist *ex hypothesi*: 'Suppose that ... the common technology has no factor-intensity reversal ...' (Ethier, 1981, p. 274).

24. This is not the place to discuss these issues. Suffice to make one remark. With time and reproducibility of capital (in the form of machines, etc.) the 'dynamic' equivalent of the timeless Heckscher–Ohlin model becomes one where the 'scarcity constraints' are the rate of growth of the labour supply and the savings rate. This strictly pre-Keynesian view of the growth process raises many questions: How does one account for those periods and those many countries in modern history characterised by structural unemployment of one kind or another? Do 'scarcity constraints' functionally define the system, even in the presence of continuous technical progress and widespread economies of scale? Where is there proof that it is the rate of saving which determines the rate of investment and not vice versa, such as in the Keynesian–Kaleckian view? Where is the evidence that countries characterised by higher saving propensities also present higher capital 'endowments' and relatively capital-intensive exports?

25. Dosi (1984) and Dosi *et al.* (1988).
26. On this point, cf. Nelson and Winter (1982) and Dosi and Orsenigo (1988).
27. Obviously, this assumption is necessary to base the analysis on unit functions, indifference curves, isoquants, etc.
28. Ferrier (1805), p. 288.
29. Adam Smith (1937), volume I.
30. For a reappraisal of List's view on the importance of the national techno-scientific systems, cf. Freeman (1982a).
31. Cf. Prebisch (1950).
32. See Chenery and Bruno (1962), Chenery and Strout (1966), Findlay (1973). For a thorough critical analysis of the debate on North–South differences, terms of trade, development, see Bacha (1978). A review of the trade/development literature, cf. Findlay (1984).
33. Findlay (1973), p. 57.
34. See Nelson and Winter (1982), Dosi (1984) and Silverberg, Dosi and Orsenigo (1988).
35. See B. Klein (1977) and (1979). Klein's work focusses on individual firm behaviours in relation to industrial innovation. For an overview of this line of enquiry, see E. Graham (1979).
36. Cf. Buckley and Casson (1976 and 1981), Dunning (1981).
37. Cf. Cornwall (1977), Gomulka (1971), Koizumi and Kopecky (1980).
38. See Nelson (1968), Nelson, Winter and Schuette (1976), Nelson and Winter (1982), Metcalfe and Soete (1984) and Metcalfe (1988).
39. See, among others, Keesing (1965) and (1967), Baldwin (1971), Harkness and Kyle (1975), Branson and Monoyios (1977), Stern and Maskus (1981).
40. Johnson (1970), p. 14.
41. Deardorff (1984), p. 481.
42. Cf. Horn (1976), Stern (1976), Bodenhofer (1976), Wolter (1977).
43. Cf. Katrak (1973), Horn (1976), Owen, White and Smith (1978).
44. Cf. Hulsman-Vejsova and Koekkoek (1980).
45. Cf. Horn (1976).

46. Cf. Helg and Onida (1985). Some scattered and less convincing evidence also exists for Sweden (Bergstrom-Balkestahl, 1979) and Canada (Hanel, 1976). Thorough reviews can be found in Deardorff (1984) and Onida (1984).
47. See Momigliano and Siniscalco (1984).
48. See, among others, Freeman (1963) and (1965), Hirsch (1965), Hufbauer (1966), Tilton (1971), Dosi (1984).
49. For a more detailed argument along these lines, see Chapters 3 and 4.
50. See, e.g. Markusen and MacDonald (1985) or Markusen (1989).

3

The empirical evidence: 'Stylised', and 'less stylised' facts on technology, growth and trade

Contrary to a tradition in economic theory that commences its analysis by choosing a set of assumptions on the grounds of formal tractability and/or consistency with the established doctrine, and more in line with the spirit of the preceding chapter, we begin our analysis by presenting a list of what we shall refer to as 'stylised facts' – that is, broad empirical regularities – which are in need of theoretical explanation. These 'stylised', and some 'less stylised', facts are based on a long stream of empirical investigations and theoretical explorations undertaken by a number of authors in the area of technical change who have retained an empirical interest in the patterns of structural change in modern economies.

Many of the pioneering investigations on the complex dynamics linking technical change, growth and transformation, undertaken by such major contributors to economics as Schumpeter, Kuznets, Gerschenkron and Svenilsson have often been neglected in the broad reductionist vein that was characteristic of the economic approach prevailing after the Second World War, particularly in Anglo-Saxon countries. Our central interest in innovative phenomena brings us quite naturally closer to these often neglected 'classics'. It leads us to present the empirical evidence on technological activities within a framework which focusses on change, through time and differences between countries, instead of on timeless equilibria and uniformity between countries. The 'stylised facts' that follow thus aim to provide the reader with an account of some of the regularities, differences and similarities through time and across countries in innovation, efficiency in inputs use, particularly in labour productivities, and composition of trade flows.

3.1 The international and intersectoral patterns of innovation

The international location of innovation: some preliminary evidence

We begin with two measures of long-term trends in the location of innovative activities among countries. One method is simply to identify significant innovations and their locations and to trace any change over time. This is (not surprisingly) a difficult undertaking involving difficult methodological problems about definition of concepts (significant innovations), consistency over time, comparability between countries, etc. Some authors have attempted to carry out such inventory listings. Feinman and Fuentevilla (1976), Davidson (1976) and Townsend *et al.* (1981) have tried to do this, but none of them have yet completed a sample of innovations that is comprehensive, representative and international. In Table 3.1, we present some country-share data based on a list of 1,012 major inventions, discoveries and innovations since 1750, based on Streit, as reported in Pavitt and Soete (1982). This is one of the rare lists which identifies the country of origin. We limited the sample to primarily technical inventions and innovations, excluding major 'social innovations' for which the definitional problems appeared too severe.

Compiled shortly after the Second World War, Table 3.1 is probably biased towards the United States. Nevertheless, the picture which

Table 3.1 Major inventions, discoveries and innovations by country, 1750–1950 (as a percentage of total)

Period	Total	Inventions, discoveries and innovations (Percentage of total)				
		Britain	France	Germany	United States	Others
1750–75	30	46.7	16.7	3.3	10.0	23.3
1776–1800	68	42.6	32.4	5.9	13.2	5.9
1801–25	95	44.2	22.1	10.5	12.6	10.5
1826–50	129	28.7	22.5	17.8	22.5	8.5
1851–75	163	17.8	20.9	23.9	25.2	12.3
1876–1900	204	14.2	17.2	19.1	37.7	11.8
1901–25	139	13.7	9.4	15.1	52.5	9.4
1926–50	113	11.5	0.9	12.4	61.9	13.3

Source: Calculated from Streit, 1949.

emerges is consistent with what we know from economic historians: the very strong position of the United Kingdom as the major innovating country in the period 1750–1825, which very rapidly saw its position challenged by both the United States and Germany by the middle of the late nineteenth century; the overall decline of France from the middle of the nineteenth century until 1950; and the emergence in the twentieth century, of the United States as the major technological power, leading to a huge technological gap between the United States and Europe. As for the other countries, their innovative activity in terms of major innovations, inventions or discoveries has remained relatively limited, with the partial exception of Sweden and Switzerland.

Using an alternative technology indicator, we present in Table 3.2 the share of each of a number of OECD countries in the total number of foreign patents granted in the United States over the period 1883–1986. With the exception of Canada, whose proximity to the United States overstates its importance, Table 3.2 shows a similar pattern to Table 3.1: the long-term decline of the United Kingdom only temporarily halted by the First and Second World Wars; and the steadily growing importance of Germany as a technological power which, after the Second World War, returned to its pre-War patenting level in less than nine years. It also shows the emergence of Italy, the Netherlands, Sweden and Switzerland with larger shares in the twentieth century, and a somewhat increased share for France since the Second World War.

But the most striking change in patent share relates to Japan. Its level of innovative activity, as measured by the number of US patents granted, remained until the 1920s among the lowest of all OECD countries; and it was only in the late 1950s and 1960s that, after having returned by 1957 to its pre-War patenting level, its share of foreign US patents started to grow very rapidly. In 1986, the latest year for which data were available, Japan was the major foreign country patenting in the United States, accounting for more than 40 per cent of total US patents of foreign origin.

Apart from Japan, there have been no newcomers to the very select group of world innovators. The share of Eastern Europe and the USSR has remained small throughout the twentieth century. What are now called the newly industrialising countries (NICs) have increased their share slightly, but it remains very small.

In terms of R&D expenditures, a similar picture emerges. Figure 3.1 shows industrial R&D shares for a number of OECD countries for 1967 and 1987, the latest year for which international comparable R&D data were available. As in Table 3.2, the increase in the Japanese share is worth noting. But it is the decline in the US share which is probably the most striking feature of Figure 3.1. In 1967, the United States was

Table 3.2 Patents granted in the United States by country of origin, 1883–1986 (as a percentage of all foreign patenting)

Country	1883	1890	1900	1913	1929	1938	1950	1958	1965	1973	1979	1986
Australia	1.11	1.20	2.33	1.97	1.96	1.18	1.54	0.60	0.94	0.92	1.12	1.14
Austria	2.62	3.37	3.36	3.99	2.47	2.91	0.48	1.12	1.16	1.02	1.19	1.09
Belgium	1.59	0.86	1.35	1.28	1.30	1.23	1.07	1.14	1.50	1.23	0.98	0.74
Canada	19.94	17.63	10.54	13.22	10.25	6.35	11.16	7.99	7.00	6.20	4.56	4.01
Denmark	0.56	0.38	0.46	0.67	0.71	0.71	1.36	0.74	0.74	0.70	0.56	0.56
France	14.22	8.46	9.79	8.07	9.76	9.23	15.54	10.36	10.90	9.38	8.46	7.22
Germany	18.67	21.47	30.72	34.02	32.36	38.18	0.57	25.60	26.40	24.25	23.87	20.80
Italy	0.24	0.29	0.92	1.31	1.91	1.43	0.86	3.02	3.38	3.39	3.14	3.05
Japan	0.16	0.10	0.03	0.45	1.40	1.51	0.03	1.93	7.43	22.10	27.69	40.35
Netherlands	0.24	0.29	0.75	0.47	1.57	3.38	8.10	5.71	4.15	3.03	2.80	2.20
Norway	0.32	0.14	0.49	0.74	0.71	0.54	0.95	0.61	0.42	0.42	0.43	0.25
Sweden	0.95	1.52	1.32	2.07	3.19	3.13	6.67	4.64	4.50	3.40	3.02	2.70
Switzerland	1.75	2.66	2.27	3.11	4.46	3.72	9.73	8.80	6.97	5.79	5.40	3.70
United Kingdom	34.55	36.15	30.52	23.29	22.23	22.70	36.00	23.45	20.62	12.56	10.07	7.37
Eastern Europe including USSR	0.40	0.67	1.49	1.19	1.62	1.61	1.23	0.55	0.89	2.53	2.76	1.13
NICs	0.40	1.19	1.12	1.21	1.03	0.90	1.41	1.31	1.71	1.36	1.45	1.50
Others	3.28	3.62	2.54	2.94	3.07	1.29	3.28	2.43	1.29	1.72	2.50	2.19

Source: Calculated from US Department of Commerce (OTAF, 1977, 1980).

still responsible for more than two-thirds of total OECD R&D expenditures, which is consistent with the 1950 figure obtained for our sample
of major inventions and innovations in Table 3.1. By 1987, this figure
had dropped to just under 53 per cent. Nevertheless, as in the case of
major innovations and international patenting, R&D expenditure is and
has remained highly concentrated, with the five major OECD countries
responsible for more than 94 per cent of the total in 1987.

In contrast to the patent data, the R&D expenditures data also illus-
trate the very rapid growth of such activities in the NICs. In terms of
R&D/GDP ratios, some of these countries, such as South Korea or
Taiwan, now have ratios above those of many OECD countries.

In the next section we go somewhat deeper into differences and
complementarities between both indicators.

R&D and patenting: what do these indicators tell us?

A meaningful use of technological indicators depends of course on an
understanding of the relationship between them, and of their economic
significance. Our basic hypothesis is that both R&D and patent statistics
show different aspects of the same process of industrial *innovation*. This
is somewhat different from the assumption that, since patents by
definition involve novelty, and since invention is defined as novelty,
patents capture and measure the earlier stages of a process that leads
from novelty/invention, through development, testing and engineering,
to full-scale innovation.

Such a view neglects the fact that, as Schumpeter pointed out, the
essential process for the industrial firm is innovation, not invention.
Patents can thus be viewed as one of the means by which entrepreneurs
protect their innovations. Or, to put it another way, patents are means
by which entrepreneurs try to augment the monopoly profits from
innovation by making it more difficult for potential competitors to copy
or imitate. Other methods of discouraging imitation involve secrecy,
further technological advance based on firm-specific R&D and skill,
influence over suppliers or marketing outlets and manipulation of
standards. Patenting activity may extend over the whole of the product
lifecycle: from the patents protecting the basic invention, through those
related to product and process engineering, to a myriad of improvement
and blocking patents. What concern us here are the relationships
between industrial R&D activity, patenting and innovation. In
interpreting the data, we shall have two working hypotheses in mind.

First, in spite of the many perversities (real and imagined) of imperfect and oligopolistic competition, it is implausible that a firm would

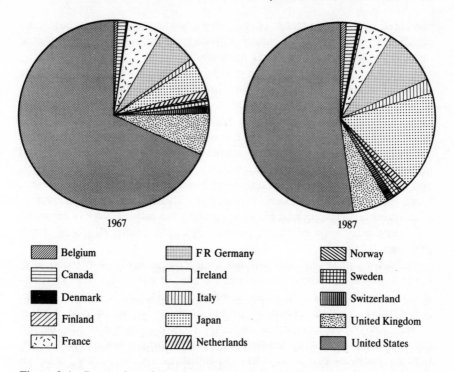

Figure 3.1 Research and development expenditures in the business enterprise sector as a percentage of the OECD-total (1967 and 1987)

commit resources to R&D and to patenting activities in order not to innovate. It might not wish to be the first to innovate; it might even wish to control or to delay the innovation process. But eventually it knows that it will have to innovate. In other words, we argue that R&D activities and patenting activities are positively related to innovative activities.

Second, we suggest that R&D and patenting activities are also positively related to each other; in other words, that they are complementary activities in the sense that higher or lower R&D activities are reflected in higher or lower patenting activities. However, we recognise that R&D and patent activities are not always perfect reflections of each other. The results of R&D activity may not be patented because secrecy is felt to be a better protection than patenting or because its results are in the form of unpatentable know-how (especially in relation to production and to systems design); in this case R&D will be a more reliable indicator of innovative activity than patenting. On the other hand, innovative activities undertaken outside formal R&D institutions may not be measured in the R&D statistics, but may none the less result in patenting activity. In this case, patenting will be a more reliable indicator of innovative activities than R&D activities.

Both R&D and patenting vary widely in productivity and economic significance, and both can miss such important aspects of the innovative activity as software. International comparisons of R&D activities are made difficult when conventional exchange rates do not equalise R&D input costs in different countries. Longitudinal comparisons of patenting can be misleading when the propensity to patent inventions and innovations changes over time. Further discussions of the advantages and drawbacks of each measure have been pursued elsewhere[1] (Soete, 1980; Pavitt, 1985a; Patel and Pavitt, 1987). Suffice to say that in sectors as different as whaling and plastics, strong correlations have been found between the location of R&D, patents and innovations (Basberg, 1982; Freeman, 1963).

However, problems of international comparability of technology input and output indicators remain. Patents in particular are extremely sensitive to differences in national patent legislation. It is well known, for instance, that the ratio of patent applications to patents granted varies widely from country to country. The difference between the two patent measures can be illustrated, using a simple statistical test, by relating both measures to R&D expenditures. Alternatively, using as dependent variables the number of domestic patent applications and the number of domestic patents granted, we regressed these variables, with intramural R&D expenditure in the business sector as the independent variable, for a number of years.[2]

The following results were obtained:[3]

$$PA_i = 7129.05 + 3.11 \ R\&D_i \qquad \bar{R}_2 = 0.29$$
$$(1.10) \qquad\qquad F(1,16) = 8.07 \qquad \textbf{(3.1)}$$

$$PG_i = 1525.29 + 1.75 \ R\&D_i \qquad \bar{R}_2 = 0.81$$
$$(0.20)^* \qquad\qquad F(1,16) = 75.20^* \qquad \textbf{(3.2)}$$

where PA_i is the number of patent applications in country i, PG_i is the number of patents granted in country i and $R\&D_i$ the amount spent on R&D in the business enterprise sector in country i. The results suggest that, not surprisingly, the patents-granted measure is a better technology output indicator. For example, in terms of patent applications, Japan would be by far the most technologically advanced country, twice as advanced as the United States and four times as advanced as Germany, as compared to an estimated R&D expenditure figure of only a fourth of the US figure. In terms of patents granted, though, Japan's patent figure falls back to just below the US figure.

One should, however, remain cautious about such simple regression exercises. Both the number of patents and R&D expenditure measures are partly a function of the size of the countries considered. To eliminate this influence, we repeated the analysis, dividing both the patent and R&D figures by population. The following results were obtained:

$$PAC_i = 0.099 + 3.66 \; R\&DC_i \qquad \bar{R}_2 = 0.32$$
$$(1.23) \qquad\qquad\qquad F(1,16) = 8.87 \qquad (3.3)$$

$$PGC_i = 0.001 + 2.25 \; R\&DC_i \qquad \bar{R}_2 = 0.72$$
$$(0.34)^* \qquad\qquad\qquad F(1,16) = 43.83^* \qquad (3.4)$$

where PAC_i is the patent-applications intensity in country i, PGC_i the patents-granted intensity in country i and $R\&DC_i$ the R&D intensity in country i. These results give further support to what was said above about the superiority of the patents-granted measure.

By looking at patenting in a particular country, one can overcome some of the international variations in patent evaluation mentioned above, to the extent that all patents have now undergone a similar screening treatment. One obviously loses the information on the country in which foreign patenting is taking place. In the light of the regression results obtained above, one can ask how 'foreign' patent data would relate to national R&D expenditure data. To answer this, regressions identical to the ones above were carried out using foreign patents granted and foreign patents granted per capita as dependent variables and the same R&D expenditure data as independent variables.

Data limitations forced us to sacrifice two countries (Iceland and Portugal); however we now also had patent data for Italy. The sample thus consisted of the seventeen major OECD countries, each time, however, excluding the country in which foreign patenting was taking place. Patenting of foreign origin in the United States, Japan, France, Germany and the United Kingdom was analysed.

The following results were obtained:

In the United States:

$$FP_i = -18.51 + 0.965 \; R\&D_i \qquad \bar{R}_2 = 0.97$$
$$(0.46)^* \qquad\qquad\qquad F(1,14) = 444.59^* \qquad (3.5)$$

$$FPC_i = -0.01 + 1.143 \; R\&DC_i \qquad \bar{R}_2 = 0.94$$
$$(0.076)^* \qquad\qquad\qquad F(1,14) = 228.79^* \qquad (3.6)$$

In Japan:

$$FP_i = 28.15 + 0.151 \; R\&D_i \qquad \bar{R}_2 = 0.99$$
$$(0.004)^* \qquad\qquad\qquad F(1,14) = 1291.22^* \qquad (3.7)$$

$$FPC_i = -0.004 + 0.245 \; R\&DC_i \qquad \bar{R}_2 = 0.86$$
$$(0.025)^* \qquad\qquad\qquad F(1,14) = 92.63^* \qquad (3.8)$$

In France:

$$FP_i = 499.61 + 0.240 \ R\&D_i \qquad \bar{R}_2 = 0.73$$
$$(0.038)^* \qquad \qquad F(1,14) = 41.07^* \qquad \textbf{(3.9)}$$

$$FPC_i = -0.019 + 0.977 \ R\&DC_i \qquad \bar{R}_2 = 0.71$$
$$(0.159)^* \qquad \qquad F(1,14) = 37.71^* \qquad \textbf{(3.10)}$$

In Germany:

$$FP_i = 227.97 + 0.127 \ R\&D_i \qquad \bar{R} = 0.84$$
$$(0.014)^* \qquad \qquad F(1,14) = 80.63^* \qquad \textbf{(3.11)}$$

$$FPC_i = -0.012 + 0.585 \ R\&DC_i \qquad \bar{R}_2 = 0.74$$
$$(0.094)^* \qquad \qquad F(1,14) = 38.79^* \qquad \textbf{(3.12)}$$

In the United Kingdom:

$$FP_i = 978.97 + 0.073 \ R\&D_i \qquad \bar{R} = 0.01$$
$$(0.068) \qquad \qquad F(1,14) = 1.4 \qquad \textbf{(3.13)}$$

$$FPC_i = -0.013 + 0.991 \ R\&DC_i \qquad \bar{R}_2 = 0.68$$
$$(0.174)^* \qquad \qquad F(1,14) = 32.43^* \qquad \textbf{(3.14)}$$

where FP_i is the number of foreign patents granted to each country i, and FPC_i the foreign-patent intensity of each country in the United States, Japan, France, Germany and the United Kingdom respectively. With the exception of the United Kingdom, these results suggest that foreign patenting is a more 'reliable' technology output proxy than domestic patenting.

Particularly in the case of the United States, good results between foreign patenting and domestic R&D expenditures were obtained, both in absolute as well as in per capita terms.

The good results obtained here using US foreign patenting as a technology output indicator supports the use of this innovation proxy in a number of earlier studies,[4] where foreign patenting in the United States was used as a direct measure of international innovative performance. The United States as a major technology 'market' indeed appears to be a good mirror of the OECD or world technology market.

The analysis presented has been based on patent data collected and published by the World Intellectual Property Organisation (WIPO) and OECD R&D data. It might be useful to verify whether the results obtained above in relation to foreign patenting in the United States also hold for US patent data.

Results are given in equations (3.15)–(3.18):

$$FP_i = 4.97 + 0.735 \ R\&D_i \qquad \bar{R}_2 = 0.97$$
$$(0.034)^* \qquad \qquad F(1,13) = 476.40^* \qquad \textbf{(3.15)}$$

$$FPC_i = -0.005 + 0.825 \ R\&DC_i \qquad \bar{R}_2 = 0.93$$
$$(0.061)^* \qquad F(1,13) = 187.44^* \quad \textbf{(3.16)}$$

$$\ln FP_i = -1.06 + 0.966 \ \ln R\&D_i \qquad \bar{R}_2 = 0.98$$
$$(0.040)^* \qquad F(1,13) = 591.89^* \quad \textbf{(3.17)}$$

$$\ln FPC_i = -0.62 + 0.902 \ \ln R\&DC_i \ \ \bar{R}_2 = 0.90$$
$$(0.079)^* \qquad F(1,13) = 120.14^* \quad \textbf{(3.18)}$$

The graphical representation of the results obtained in equations (3.17) and (3.18), shown in Figures 3.2 and 3.3, illustrates the 'neatness' of the fit well.

The United Kingdom's, Spain's and Portugal's 'number-of-patents-

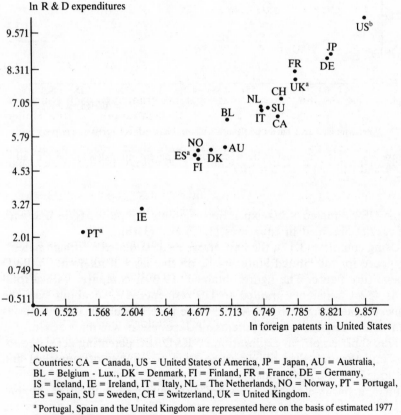

Notes:

Countries: CA = Canada, US = United States of America, JP = Japan, AU = Australia, BL = Belgium - Lux., DK = Denmark, FI = Finland, FR = France, DE = Germany, IS = Iceland, IE = Ireland, IT = Italy, NL = The Netherlands, NO = Norway, PT = Portugal, ES = Spain, SU = Sweden, CH = Switzerland, UK = United Kingdom.

[a] Portugal, Spain and the United Kingdom are represented here on the basis of estimated 1977 R & D expenditure.

[b] The US figure is estimated on the basis of regression equation (3.17).

Figure 3.2 The relationship between foreign patenting in the United States and national R&D expenditure

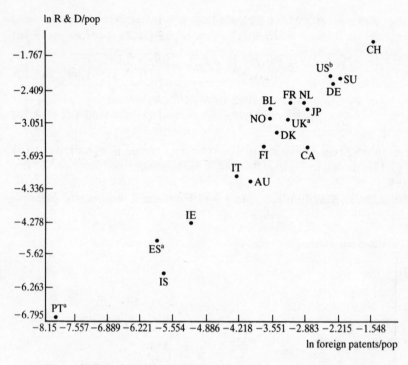

Note: as for Figure 3.2, but the US figure is estimated on the basis of regression equation (3.18).

Figure 3.3 The relationship between foreign patent-intensity in the United States and national R&D intensity

in-the-US-estimated-R&D-expenditure' points lay perfectly in line with the results obtained in equations (3.17) and (3.18).

Using equation (3.17), the best fit, we also estimated a foreign patenting figure for the United States itself, on the basis of its domestic R&D expenditure figure. The figure obtained, 19,095, compares with a total of 41,452 US patents granted to US residents, i.e. to about half the domestic patenting activity. At the same time it is about three times as high as the number of US patents of Japanese or German origin.

This short empirical exploration of R&D and patenting across countries and through time allows us to draw a number of empirical and methodological conclusions.

First, it shows a highly diversified distribution of innovative capabilities, however measured, between countries. The number of participants to the 'club of innovators' is rather small and relatively stable through time. Following a predominant British position from the time of the industrial revolution, the United Kingdom was joined in the second part of the nineteenth century by a small group of Western countries (Germany, the United States, France, etc.), while the only major newcomer in the post-War period has been Japan. In most recent times, one or two NICs – in particular South Korea – might also have joined this still very select club. For our purpose, this differentiated pattern of innovative capabilities corresponds to an equally differentiated distribution of country-specific advantages/disadvantages which demand a theoretical explanation: What determines them? How are they being reproduced? What explains different trends in different countries?

Second, on more methodological grounds, despite many of the shortcomings of the patent concept, the above analysis supports the robustness of the variable 'patenting in the United States' as proxy for the relative innovative capability of a country in empirical analyses of technological change and innovation. Consequently, we shall use it extensively in the empirical testing of the theoretical frameworks set out in the following chapters.

3.2   International and intersectoral differences in productivity

Gross domestic product per head

Innovation in products and processes continuously modifies production structures, input efficiencies, consumption baskets, levels and distribution of income, etc. Whatever may be the precise causal mechanisms linking innovative processes and productive efficiency – which we analyse in greater detail in Chapter 4 – an important 'stylised fact' of modern economies is the (by historical standards) exceptionally high growth of output per head since the industrial revolution. In Rosenberg's words:

> the industrial revolution, beginning in Great Britain in the last third
> of the eighteenth century, had at its center a rapidly expanding
> armamentarium of new technologies involving new power sources, new
> techniques of metallurgy and machine-making and new modes of
> transportation. These new technologies, when successfully organised and
> administered, brought in their wake immense improvements in
> productivity which eventually transformed the lives of all participants.
> (Rosenberg, 1984, p. 9)

This process of industrialisation, analysed by classical economists such as Smith and Marx and by modern economic historians including, among others, Rosenberg himself and Landes,[5] spread unevenly across a relatively small group of countries in Europe, the United States and, later, Japan. The national specificities in the timing, intensity and success in industrialisation and development correspond to distinguishable levels and patterns of evolution of productivities and incomes. The persistent difference in the levels and rates of growth of output per head and per man hour is a fundamental feature of industrialised economies and, *a fortiori*, of the whole set of developed and developing countries.

The measurement problems involved in any comparison over time and across countries of 'the amount of product per unit of labour input' are of course formidable. Any estimating procedure is bound to involve high degrees of 'informed guesswork'. None the less, one may still obtain useful information on the orders of magnitude and approximate pace of change. Tables 3.3 and 3.4, taken from Maddison (1987), show the patterns over a century in GDP per man hour for sixteen countries. It is difficult to rely on the precise values of the estimates. However, it is striking that these productivity gaps, even within the group of OECD countries, have remained persistently high. Moreover, the only period of evident convergence appears to have been after the Second World War. The century from 1870 to 1970 also witnessed a changing world leadership among the major countries, from the United Kingdom to the United States, which took the lead around the turn of the century.

Table 3.3 Comparative levels of productivity, 1870–1985 (US GDP per man hour = 100)

	1870	1890	1913	1938	1950	1973	1979
Australia	186	153	102	89	72	73	78
Austria	61	58	54	(47)	29	62	71
Belgium	106	96	75	70	50	75	88
Canada	87	81	87	67	78	87	85
Denmark	63	58	60	60	43	63	64
Finland	41	35	43	44	35	63	64
France	60	55	54	64	44	76	86
Germany	61	58	57	56	33	71	84
Italy	63	44	43	49	32	66	70
Japan	24	(23)	22	33	14	46	53
Netherlands	106	(92)	74	68	53	81	90
Norway	57	53	49	62	48	69	80
Sweden	44	42	50	59	55	79	81
Switzerland	79	70	60	70	52	62	62
United Kingdom	114	100	81	70	56	64	66
United States	100	100	100	100	100	100	100
Arithmetic average of 15 countries (excluding the United States)	77	68	61	61	46	69	75

Source: Maddison (1982), p. 98.

Table 3.4 Productivity growth (GDP per man hour), 1870–1979

| | Annual average compound growth rate | | | | |
	1870–1913	1913–50	1950–73	1973–9	1870–1979
Australia	0.6	1.6	2.6	2.6	1.5
Austria	1.7	0.9	5.9	3.8	2.4
Belgium	1.2	1.4	4.4	4.2	2.1
Canada	2.0	2.3	3.0	1.0	2.3
Denmark	1.9	1.6	4.3	1.6	2.3
Finland	2.1	2.0	5.2	1.7	2.7
France	1.8	2.0	5.1	3.5	2.6
Germany	1.9	1.1	6.0	4.2	2.6
Italy	1.2	1.8	5.8	2.5	2.4
Japan	1.8	1.3	8.0	3.9	3.0
Netherlands	1.2	1.7	4.4	3.3	2.1
Norway	1.7	2.5	4.2	3.9	2.6
Sweden	2.3	2.8	4.2	1.9	2.9
Switzerland	1.4	2.1	3.4	1.3	2.1
United Kingdom	1.2	1.6	3.1	2.1	1.8
United States	2.0	2.6	2.6	1.4	2.3
Arithmetic average	1.6	1.8	4.5	2.7	2.4

Source: Maddison (1982), p. 96.

The pace of change in the aggregate productivity gap between countries seems to have accelerated in the post-War period, with every country reducing the gap between itself and the United States, as compared to the 1950 values. Among the countries catching up, Japan shows the most striking performance.

In earlier work (Pavitt and Soete, 1982), we showed that increases in the 1960s and 1970s in countries' productivity levels relative to the world frontier, were associated with increases in innovative activities, measured in terms of R&D expenditure and foreign patenting. More recently, Fagerberg (1987, 1988b) has shown strong correlations between countries' levels of GDP per capita, and their levels of innovative activities. He has also explained international differences in growth rates between 1960 and 1983 in terms of each country's scope for catching up with world best-practice productivity, its investment share, and its rate of increase of technological activities.

Manufacturing

Figures on aggregate output are necessarily impressionistic. A somewhat more accurate picture can be gathered by looking at manufacturing. First, its degree of international openness guarantees smaller international price differences than for the economy as a whole. Second, a separate treatment of manufacturing and, even more so, of a set of manufacturing subsectors, reduces the problems of biases stemming from a simple 'composition effect'. Third, and more importantly, manufacturing is both the major source and the primary field for economic application of technical change.

The construction of internationally comparable labour productivity estimates, even those that are limited to manufacturing, remains heroic by any standard. In particular, the problem of comparability remains severe. It is related to possible international differences in price levels (expressed in current exchange rates), different prices of intermediate inputs, different product mixes, different degrees of vertical integration (and thus different ratios of value added to output), etc. Ideally, one would have liked some kind of 'physical' measure of output with precise weights for the commodity mix. These problems can be partially dealt with in the case of time series by means of the 'double deflation' procedure which yields the value-added deflator.[6] In terms of international comparisons, however, equivalents of double deflators are not generally available.[7]

Straightforward utilisation of the detailed analysis undertaken by Kravis *et al.*[8] on purchasing power parities is not possible either, since the latter produces estimates which may not bear any simple relationship with producer prices and costs. On the other hand, the instability of exchange rates over the most recent period is likely to lead to significant biases in international comparisons of value added per employee.[9]

One must also be aware of the fact that labour productivity indices in multiproduct sectors are a synthetic indicator both of labour productivities in each product and of the mix between high-value-added and low-value-added products.[10] Such indicators, even for our purposes, are nevertheless still useful in two senses. First, from a behavioural point of view, changing product mixes towards higher value-added products and improving labour productivity on existing lines of products are sometimes alternative strategies, both of which represent 'technological upgrading' by microeconomic units. Second, and as a consequence, the resulting proxy for labour productivity at each level of disaggregation is a 'mixed' indicator of output in terms of value added, irrespective of whether it is obtained through high 'physical' productivity, or through the manufacturing of products that yield a higher value added (e.g. through a higher 'use value' compared to competing products).[11]

With these caveats in mind, let us consider the patterns of manufacturing value added per employee in a sample of developed and developing countries. These are shown in Figure 3.4, calculated at current exchange rates and based on 1977–80 averages. Figure 3.4 also indicates comparable proxies for capital/labour and capital/output ratios.[12] Below, we present a number of regression equations, correlating the intercountry variation in level of development, manufacturing labour productivity, capital intensity, capital/output ratios, wages and profit margins.

$$\pi = 40.15 - 113.62 \ (K/Y)$$
$$(-2.678)$$

$\bar{R}_2 = 0.37$
$F = 7.17$ **(3.20)**
$n = 14$

$$\ln K/Y = -1.955 - 0.237 \ln (K/N)$$
$$(-0.859)$$

$\bar{R}_2 = 0.04$
$F = 0.72$ **(3.21)**
$n = 19$

$$K/Y = 0.159 - 0.004 \ (GDP/N)$$
$$(-1.10)$$

$\bar{R}_2 = 0.07$
$F = 1.20$ **(3.22)**
$n = 19$

$$\ln \pi = -0.876 + 0.870 \ln (GDP/N)$$
$$(9.186)^*$$

$\bar{R}_2 = 0.86$
$F = 84.3$ **(3.23)**
$n = 14$

$$\ln K/N = -0.04 + 0.297 \ln (GDP/N)$$
$$(3.704)$$

$\bar{R}_2 = 0.45$
$F = 13.7$ **(3.24)**
$n = 19$

$$\ln \pi = 2.384 + 1.36 \ln (K/N)$$
$$(4.774)^*$$

$\bar{R}_2 = 0.66$
$F = 22.7$ **(3.25)**
$n = 14$

where

π = value added per employee (1977–80 averages at current prices and exchange rates);

GDP/N = per capita income (1970–80 average at current prices and exchange rates);

K/N = gross fixed capital investment per employee (1968–80 averages divided by one plus the average rate of growth of manufacturing output at constant prices over the period);

K/Y = gross fixed capital investment per output (1968–80 averages divided by one plus the average rate of growth of manufacturing output at constant prices over the period);

$$K/Y = 0.152 - 0.0029w$$
$$(-0.86)$$

$\bar{R}_2 = 0.04$
$F = 0.72$ **(3.26)**
$n = 16$

$$m = 0.482 + 0.214 \ (K/Y) \qquad \bar{R}_2 = 0.005$$
$$(0.29) \qquad\qquad F = 0.08 \qquad (3.27)$$
$$n = 18$$

$$w = 0.358 + 1.094 \ (GDP/N) \qquad \bar{R}_2 = 0.79$$
$$(7.43)^{*} \qquad\qquad F = 55.2 \qquad (3.28)$$
$$n = 16$$

$$m = 0.652 - 0.24 \ (GDP/N) \qquad \bar{R}_2 = 0.25$$
$$(2.33) \qquad\qquad F = 5.42 \qquad (3.29)$$
$$n = 18$$

where

w = wages and supplementary benefits per employee (1968–80 averages); and

m = one minus the ratio of wages and benefits to value added (1968–80 averages)

Analysis of the trends in these various proxies and their correlation with levels of per capita income point to the following broad relations.

First, and not surprisingly, there is a strong correlation between inter-country differences in levels of manufacturing labour productivity and levels of per capita income (equation (3.23)).

Second, the differences between countries in productivity in manu-facturing are bigger than for the economy as a whole (compare the right-hand top quadrant of Figure 3.4 with the last two rows of Table 3.5 for those countries included in both samples). In other words, the activity of the economy – manufacturing – where a large part of innovations are generated and used, is also the one where the international diffusion of technology does not easily keep pace with the generation of innovations, thus leading to relatively wide productivity gaps between countries.

Third, both per capita incomes and manufacturing productivities are strongly correlated with the levels of capital accumulation, and 'mechanisation' as approximated by investment/labour ratios (equations (3.24) and (3.25)). These positive relations show 'increasing returns' of accumulation in terms of productivity. In our interpretation, this would tend to suggest that increasing levels of development are associated with a set of dynamic and static economies of scale, positive externalities, and increasing innovative capabilities, as argued more recently in the so-called 'new' growth tradition by Romer (1987, 1990) and Lucas (1988). This feature makes the differential efficiency of the advanced countries more than proportional to the differential degrees of capital accumulation.

The same property holds in relation to the capital/output ratios

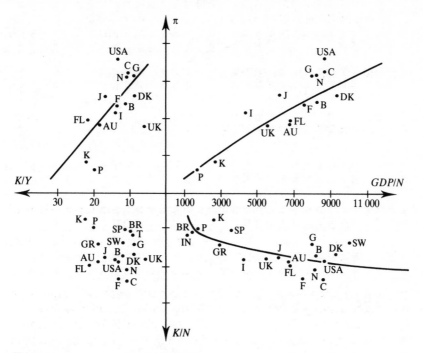

Notes:

π = value added per employee (1977–80 averages at current prices and exchange rates).

GDP/N = per capita income (1970–80 average at current prices and exchange rates).

K/N = gross fixed capital investment per employee (1968–80 averages divided by one plus the average rate of growth of manufacturing output at constant prices over the period).

K/Y = gross fixed capital investment per output (1968–80 averages divided by one plus the average rate of growth of manufacturing output at constant prices over the period).

Countries: USA = United States of America, N = The Netherlands, G = West Germany, DK = Denmark, B = Belgium, F = France, J = Japan, SW = Sweden, FL = Finland AU = Austria, UK = United Kingdom, I = Italy, SP = Spain, GR = Greece, K = South Korea, BR = Brazil, T = Turkey, P = Portugal, IN = India.

Source: elaboration on UN, *Yearbook of Industrial Statistics*, various years, and national sources.

Figure 3.4 Labour productivity, capital/labour and capital/output ratios (manufacturing, 1968–80)

(equation (3.20)). Higher levels of manufacturing productivity are associated with lower capital/output ratios, or higher capital productivity rather than lower capital productivity – as one would expect from a traditional production-function model. Higher degrees of development are, in other words, associated with both higher labour productivity and higher capital productivity. This is consistent with the finding that higher-growth countries in the post-War period are generally

Table 3.5 Labour productivity by country and by sector, 1977–8 (unweighted mean = 100)

ISIC	Austria	Belgium	West Germany	Japan	Norway	Netherlands	Portugal	Sweden	United Kingdom	United States	France	Switzerland	Italy	Mean	Standard deviation
330	95.93	120.29	166.08	80.95	–	134.67	19.74	115.21	53.51	134.14	110.17	107.88	61.42	100.0	38.74
3312	72.79	185.67	131.64	51.80	–	130.05	21.24	129.71	51.93	146.97	112.54	–	65.65	100.0	47.91
32	78.52	95.80	136.60	51.40	106.56	149.58	27.96	138.52	59.69	127.84	98.72	149.12	79.67	100.0	37.81
321	79.19	102.26	141.19	58.46	103.18	151.45	27.10	144.23	61.85	134.18	102.69	122.01	72.19	100.0	36.87
322	76.93	91.35	129.69	43.17	113.02	132.28	25.82	119.85	52.15	126.84	89.80	210.94	88.16	100.0	45.90
323	78.76	–	140.81	–	99.72	115.83	37.96	128.88	64.89	134.92	103.29	–	94.35	100.0	30.90
324	80.95	134.71	126.92	76.78	104.94	141.36	24.31	136.23	69.88	114.57	116.17	–	73.17	100.0	33.80
33	80.63	126.63	157.40	121.80	120.83	100.88	20.31	140.05	65.40	106.08	75.92	117.02	67.03	100.0	35.55
34	82.92	94.80	132.12	78.03	93.10	(161.41)	32.48	140.80	65.21	156.12	90.31	93.50	79.18	100.0	35.95
341	85.53	102.84	139.52	91.93	83.46	131.45	42.45	126.40	61.64	165.49	102.70	91.78	74.81	100.0	32.33
342	79.50	93.91	122.56	70.04	100.47	161.15	24.48	158.04	67.34	145.57	–	94.88	82.05	100.0	38.91
35	63.68	85.42	160.03	121.94	82.60	22.19	–	118.20	62.15	163.53	119.12	141.95	59.18	100.0	42.39
351	56.09	–	143.19	72.19	62.99	167.60	22.39	105.15	–	172.13	107.41	141.44	49.42	100.0	48.70
3511	–	–	143.04	59.07	74.27	141.28	23.50	109.76	65.59	183.49	–	–	–	100.0	49.99
3512	–	–	–	71.86	78.44	127.59	18.03	128.99	–	175.11	–	–	–	100.0	50.36
3513	71.58	–	102.13	139.33	–	–	29.99	120.29	59.28	177.39	–	–	–	100.0	46.78
352	70.71	–	150.70	119.97	89.60	131.25	26.21	120.04	65.23	189.72	68.29	–	68.26	100.0	44.75
3521	–	–	–	–	86.40	146.95	41.27	125.18	60.79	161.96	–	–	77.45	100.0	42.02
3522	64.21	–	146.08	136.26	86.14	123.14	20.39	119.21	71.64	172.85	–	–	60.06	100.0	44.57
3523	–	–	146.54	63.68	79.48	123.02	25.47	110.50	58.58	231.91	–	–	60.81	100.0	58.45
3529	–	–	–	93.10	117.52	131.91	26.45	129.62	62.24	154.31	–	–	84.86	100.0	39.15
355	84.91	106.67	136.41	111.98	87.70	129.05	33.37	113.45	61.06	165.57	91.75	–	78.08	100.0	33.82
356	74.55	–	119.24	105.86	98.11	162.58	34.13	126.83	61.76	142.70	99.58	–	74.65	100.0	35.62
36	83.95	89.88	132.47	78.29	121.64	146.08	26.59	122.99	61.81	144.14	107.13	122.18	62.84	100.0	34.78
361	94.35	–	123.73	69.81	113.48	150.86	31.96	114.73	61.60	139.48	–	–	–	100.0	36.75
362	68.88	–	115.46	121.39	96.38	161.14	22.64	107.25	66.35	137.63	102.87	–	–	100.0	37.43
369	81.67	–	136.42	72.84	122.83	–	26.68	122.75	60.74	136.29	139.78	–	–	100.0	38.38
37	66.49	83.59	125.82	148.21	–	163.01	36.16	97.06	54.78	159.73	116.85	73.64	74.67	100.0	40.49
371	62.23	–	121.44	174.17	–	–	38.02	91.18	49.86	152.12	110.98	–	–	100.0	45.63
372	84.17	–	134.18	74.25	107.65	–	25.27	113.26	67.50	171.47	127.24	–	–	100.0	40.49
38	81.79	111.55	144.76	96.28	100.77	–	27.50	130.32	61.13	166.20	–	109.77	69.92	100.0	37.60
381	82.02	–	131.90	58.64	108.31	133.91	29.19	126.42	62.60	148.27	147.00	–	71.73	100.0	38.99

3813	—	—	151.49	—	98.83	112.54	20.31	114.53	71.97	130.33	—	—	—	100.0	39.78
382	79.80	—	139.89	126.58	97.47	125.99	15.95	118.07	61.80	158.44	98.84	—	77.16	100.0	38.35
3822	—	—	112.07	52.15	—	125.64	27.57	—	87.18	195.39	—	—	—	100.0	54.16
3823	—	—	127.76	74.73	99.42	137.08	23.41	118.07	61.60	157.92	—	—	—	100.0	41.54
3824	—	—	130.55	63.25	—	118.06	25.48	130.99	65.37	166.30	—	—	—	100.0	45.85
3825	—	—	190.83	—	—	—	15.55	70.81	51.60	123.97	—	—	—	100.0	59.70
3829	—	—	141.42	—	97.43	122.32	22.58	114.87	57.36	144.02	—	—	—	100.0	41.73
383	81.33	—	138.90	83.73	120.60	153.33	32.43	122.18	56.96	147.42	91.22	—	71.90	100.0	37.44
3831	—	—	130.98	—	117.26	118.85	29.42	98.86	61.98	142.64	—	—	—	100.0	37.53
3832	72.14	—	159.89	—	114.27	—	28.34	126.03	55.11	144.23	—	—	—	100.0	45.28
3833	—	—	129.74	93.65	93.56	—	34.40	136.52	46.74	165.40	—	—	—	100.0	44.27
3839	—	—	120.33	—	115.95	—	37.20	105.40	—	121.12	—	—	—	100.0	31.89
384	75.67	—	144.43	116.15	—	108.60	28.90	131.21	54.27	173.53	99.74	—	67.49	100.0	41.81
3841	63.60	—	130.69	78.60	—	133.91	35.69	165.75	57.46	134.29	—	—	—	100.0	43.76
3843	69.73	—	135.45	108.08	—	107.10	27.04	133.07	51.58	167.94	—	—	—	100.0	44.25
3844	—	—	141.27	—	103.93	114.68	30.85	114.92	56.19	136.08	—	—	—	100.0	39.48
3845	—	—	100.36	106.18	—	111.41	—	97.81	43.87	147.84	—	—	—	100.0	30.27
3849	—	—	97.04	—	—	—	—	98.13	—	93.42	—	—	—	100.0	6.81
385	64.00	—	125.42	79.50	138.45	—	27.49	135.64	62.57	193.96	87.25	—	85.70	100.0	45.79
3851	—	—	132.25	64.26	—	—	22.84	129.55	—	151.10	—	—	—	100.0	48.49
3852	—	—	85.37	66.61	—	—	27.44	96.08	—	224.50	—	—	—	100.0	66.50
390	88.35	—	156.21	25.36	115.91	—	30.23	138.46	72.11	150.25	105.15	139.21	78.76	100.0	43.47
3	78.25	106.60	145.45	86.26	88.88	146.44	24.08	126.01	59.56	149.31	106.84	112.91	68.39	100.0	32.02
(at constant prices and exchange rates)[a]	(86.91)	(99.65)	(142.42)	(77.64)	(90.80)	(135.82)	(28.97)	(127.62)	(63.37)	(157.76)	(112.92)	(103.19)	(72.92)	(100.0)	(34.23)
Normalised standard deviation by country[b]	13.4	28.3	14.3	39.0	16.4	13.4	22.3	14.8	13.5	18.5	17.6	28.3	14.8		
Mean of the standard deviations by sector															42.8

Notes:

(a) Manufacturing at 1975 prices and exchange rates.

(b) Standard deviation of the values across each column at the maximum available disaggregation, normalised by the unweighted mean of the corresponding sectors.

N.B. – The standard deviations have been calculated on a marginally greater set of data including a few more disaggregated sectors not shown here.
– The value of the manufacturing aggregate for the Netherlands has been estimated by the authors on the grounds of a set of sub-sectors falling short of the total.

Source: UN Yearbook of Industrial Statistics (various issues), see also the Appendix to Chapter 6.

characterised by lower marginal capital/output ratios, as compared to slow-growing ones (see Maddison, 1964).

Fourth, and as shown in Figure 3.5, wide international gaps in per capita income are associated with equally wide differences in wage rates (equation (3.28)). Conversely, if one considers the percentage part of non-wage value added as a proxy for gross profits, there is no evident trend in the relationship profitability/development/accumulation. One can see from the left-hand side of Figure 3.5 that no significant correlation exists between profit margins, capital intensity and wage rates.[13] Certainly, measurement of profit rates involves considerable statistical difficulties, related to the measurement of both capital stock and net profits.[14] However, what we can argue on the basis of the available data is that: (i) international differences in profit rates are not big enough to determine a clear pattern in gross margins as a percentage of value added;[15] (ii) these differences, even when they exist, do not show any evident correlation with the technological level of the manufacturing process and in particular with the proxies for capital/output ratios; (iii) international differences in profitability are orders of magnitude smaller than differences in wage rates.[16]

Sectoral patterns in labour productivity

Additional insights can be obtained from a more disaggregated analysis of some of the sub-sectors within manufacturing. Table 3.5 shows the indices of labour productivity for each sector, compared to the unweighted mean for the sample of countries within that same sector. Data availability restricted the investigation to the group of OECD countries and to 1977–8 averages.

A typical feature of modern industrial economies is the persistence of wide productivity gaps, even among the group of industrialised countries within the OECD area. These differences do not depend only (or primarily) on a composition effect between different industrial sectors; a wide variance across countries remains at all levels of available disaggregation. By the mid-1970s, a few countries appeared to have almost caught up with (and in some sectors even overtaken) the productivity levels of the United States. This group of 'productivity leaders' included (in addition to the United States) Germany, the Netherlands, Sweden, Switzerland, France and, somewhat behind, Belgium and Japan. A second group of industrialised countries still presented productivity levels significantly 'below the frontier': this group included Austria, Norway, Italy and the United Kingdom. Within this group the United

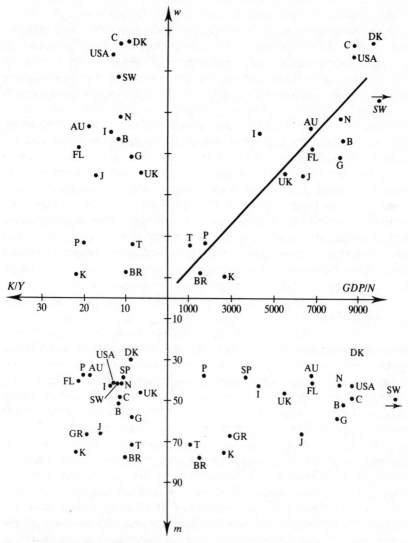

Notes: as for Figure 3.4, and
w = wages and supplementary benefits per employee (1968–80 averages).
m = one minus the ratio of wages and benefits to value added (1968–80 averages).

Figure 3.5 Wages, profit margins and capital/output ratios (manufacturing, 1968–80)

Kingdom was at the lower productivity end. Finally, Portugal can be taken as representative of an entire group of NICs, still characterised by a wide productivity gap vis-à-vis industrialised countries.

These productivity gaps – whereby Japan has moved up further in the 1980s and probably overtaken the 'productivity-leading' countries in most manufacturing sectors – characterise all sectors. They are somewhat lower only in those activities where one would *a priori* expect a relatively easier international diffusion of best-practice technologies such as textiles.[17]

A closer examination of the international and intersectoral differences in labour productivity highlights two general factors which account for the observed patterns. The first relates to the sectoral specificities which hold across countries. The second refers to country specificities which hold across sectors. As regards the former, statistical analysis of the intracountry deviations of sectoral productivities around the manufacturing mean shows that the 'sectors' – at the maximum available levels of disaggregation – are a significant variable explaining around two-thirds of the intersectoral intranational variance in the absolute levels of productivity:[18] perhaps not surprisingly, a sector such as clothing always has levels of productivity below the manufacturing average in all countries, whereas a sector such as chemicals always has one above the manufacturing average.

More interestingly, there are also country-specific regularities which significantly account for the productivity gaps vis-à-vis the OECD average in all sectors within that same country. In other words, there is a broad country-specificity of productivity gaps so that one country's average gap for manufacturing as a whole is not generally strikingly different from the sectoral ones. This can also be seen from a direct examination of Table 3.5. The patterns of variation of relative productivity differences across countries, holding the sector constant, is wider than the variation of productivity gaps/leads across sectors, holding each country constant.[19]

Again, these considerations would, *a fortiori*, apply to a larger sample of countries including NICs and developing ones, which are likely to show levels of labour productivity well below those of the United States, Japan or Germany. The broad intersectoral, intranational homogeneity in productivity gaps is common to all the countries considered here (again, see the last row of Table 3.5), although less strong in the case of two small countries (Belgium and Switzerland)[20] and, interestingly, in Japan. This latter case probably shows the outcome of a fast process of technological catching-up characterised by more sectoral selectivity. This general country-specificity of productivity gaps/leads is also confirmed by formal statistical analysis: the country-variable accounts for around three-quarters of the variance in relative sectoral productivity levels.[21]

International and intersectoral diversity in productive efficiency

The analysis so far points to a few, in our view fundamental, 'stylised facts' which require a proper theoretical account, namely:

1. There are wide international gaps in labour productivity.
2. There are equally broad wage gaps.
3. While there is a rather strict correlation between productivity levels, wage levels and per capita income levels, there seems to be no evident correlation between the former indicators and the capital intensity of production.
4. There seems to be no striking international difference in the rates of profit, as far as this can be indirectly inferred from gross margins and the proxy for the capital/output ratios.
5. A more detailed analysis of manufacturing sub-sectors shows that property holds irrespective of the levels of disaggregation.
6. Each country shows a relatively ordered pattern of productivity gaps/leads so that the intersectoral intranational variance in productivity levels, relative to the corresponding OECD averages, is rather low; moreover such a pattern does not show any evident correlation with sectoral 'factor intensities'.[22]

A more traditional way of summarising these observations is by saying that the dominant difference between countries rests in the 'different production functions' that they have, and *not* in different 'factor combinations' along the same production function. Moreover, the patterns between countries are such that they show generalised absolute advantages/disadvantages characterising, to a higher or lower extent, all manufacturing sub-sectors. These features raise some important questions, which need to be discussed in the following chapters. A number come immediately to the forefront. For example: what explains international differences in labour productivity if these do not appear to be the result of interfactoral substitution along an identical production function? How do these productivity gaps relate to the innovative differences analysed in Section 3.1? What accounts for the country-specificity of these productivity advantages/disadvantages?

3.3   International competitiveness, specialisations and trade

Trade flows and market shares

A third set of 'stylised facts', which will serve as a basis for our analysis of the relationship between technical change, trade and growth, relates to the volume, commodity composition and intercountry distribution of trade flows. From a secular point of view, one observes a great acceleration in the rate of growth of international exchanges of commodities around the time of the industrial revolution and a persistently high growth of trade flows throughout the nineteenth century, with a deceleration between the two world wars and, again, an accelerated growth after the Second World War. According to Kuznets, per capita trade in 1913 was twenty-five times higher than in 1800 and the proportion of foreign trade to world productivity increased over eleven times in the same period. [23] This high elasticity of world trade to world growth fell below one in the inter-War period and rose again to a value of around one-and-a-half in the post-War period. However, in 1963, the proportion of world trade to world production was still below its 1913 value. [24]

This secular growth of trade is associated with a long-term shift in the commodity composition from agricultural and primary products to manufactures. Moreover, within the trade of manufactures, one observes a secular relative growth of producer goods, transport equipment and chemicals and a marked relative decline of textile and clothing products. These divergent commodity trends are even more impressive if measured at constant prices, since the most dynamic commodities are generally characterised by falling relative prices. For example, the share of chemicals in the exports of the industrial countries rose only from 8.3 per cent in 1899 to 11.5 per cent in 1971, when measured at current values. However, that corresponded to a threefold increase in volume terms.

As regards the market shares of the various countries within trade of manufactures, Table 3.6 shows their evolution for a group of OECD countries from 1899 to 1980, while Figures 3.6 ((a), (b) and (c)) present the trends in some manufacturing sub-sectors for the United States, United Kingdom, Germany, France, Japan and Italy. Three features are worth noticing.

First, one may observe pronounced country-specific trends which characterise the international distribution of manufacturing exports. In particular, there is a marked decline in UK shares throughout this century. The US share rises until the 1950s and then starts declining rather rapidly. France, after a disappointing first half of the century, improves

Table 3.6 Export shares of manufactures, by country, 1899–1980

	1899(a)	1913(a)	1929	1937	1950	1957	1971	1980
United States	11.7	13.0	20.4	19.2	26.6	25.3	17.0	17.8
United Kingdom	33.2	30.2	22.4	20.9	24.6	17.7	10.9	10.6
Germany	22.4	26.6	20.5	21.8	7.0	19.9	20.1	20.4
Japan	1.5	2.3	3.9	6.9	3.4	5.8	13.0	15.4
France	14.4	12.1	10.9	5.8	9.6	7.9	8.8	10.4
Italy	3.6	3.3	3.7	3.5	3.6	3.7	7.2	8.4
Netherlands	na	na	2.5	3.0	2.9	3.5	4.7	4.7
Belgium–Luxembourg	5.5	5.0	5.4	6.6	6.2	5.9	5.9	5.9
Canada	0.4	0.6	3.5	4.8	6.1	5.4	5.9	4.3
Switzerland	4.0	3.1	2.8	2.8	4.1	3.3	3.0	3.4
Sweden	0.9	1.4	1.7	2.6	2.8	2.8	3.3	3.0
Total industrialised countries	100	100	100	100	100	100	100	100

Notes:
(a) 'World' totals exclude the Netherlands.

Sources: Maizels (1963), Batchelor, Mayor and Morgan (1980) and our elaborations on OECD data. Total figures include the United States, the United Kingdom, Germany (West Germany since 1950), Italy, France, Switzerland, Netherlands, Austria, Sweden, Belgium, Canada, Japan.

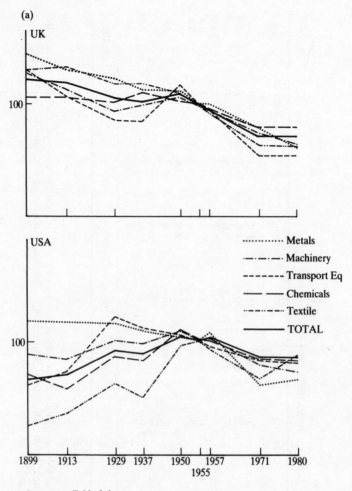

Source: as Table 3.6

Figure 3.6 Export shares, manufacturing and some manufacturing sub-sectors; United Kingdom, United States, France, Japan, Germany and Italy; 1899–1980; indices, 1955 = 100

its export performance, especially since the late 1950s. Japan presents a spectacular performance with a steady and rapid growth of its share, interrupted only by the period around the Second World War. The German share, which achieved its maximum just before the First World War, tends to reach the pre-War levels at the end of the 1930s. Again, after the Second World War rapid West German export growth leads to

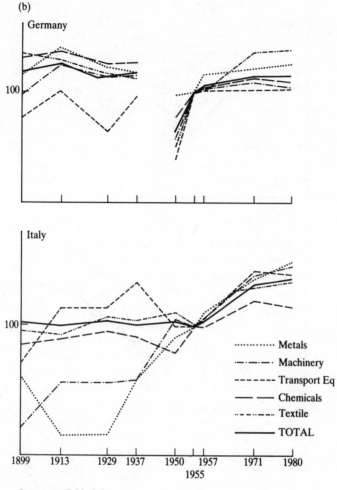

(b)

Source: as Table 3.6

Figure 3.6 *continued*

levels not far from those of pre-War Germany. The relative stagnation of Italian export shares ends in the 1950s with a steeply rising trend matched only by Japan.

Second, one can see that these differing national trends in manufacturing export shares correspond to similar trends for each of the major groups of commodities shown in Figure 3.6. In other words, there seem to be sector-independent patterns of evolution of national competitiveness which go beyond the changes in sectoral comparative advantages.

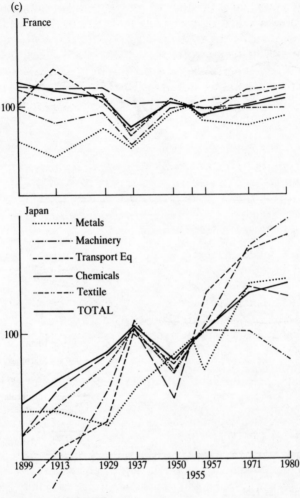

Source: as Table 3.6

Figure 3.6 *continued*

Certainly, there are changes in the latter, as represented in Figure 3.6 by the different slopes of the sectoral shares compared to the total manufacturing shares. However, in most cases these varying 'comparative advantages' appear to be the result of somewhat different sectoral rates of change along an underlying trend common to all sectors in any particular country.

Third, this national homogeneity between sectoral and average trends appears to be more pronounced after the Second World War (for all countries, except Japan). In other words, the forces leading to sectoral specialisation seem relatively weaker as compared to those leading to an across-the-board increase or decrease in foreign competitiveness. This 'absolute' notion of 'competitiveness', it may be noticed, bears some similarity to that familiar among businessmen (or to the view of the 'heretic' trade writers mentioned in Chapter 2). Conversely, it can hardly be expressed by means of the 'relative' (intercommodity) notion familiar among trade economists.

Diversity in the patterns of national competitiveness and specialisation

A more detailed analysis of the patterns of specialisation over the more recent period suggests the following:[25]

1. Even at a much higher level of commodity disaggregation, the standard deviation in revealed 'comparative advantages' is relatively low for most of the OECD countries.
2. The degree of similarity in the commodity composition of exports among this same group of countries is quite high.[26]
3. That degree of similarity in trade patterns has, if anything, increased (for all major countries except Italy) through the last two decades so that − on average − there could be talk of a tendency to 'despecialise' in the sectors of 'comparative advantage' and vice versa.[27]

In general terms, the change over time in the export of any one country in any one sector can be attributed to the interplay between four major factors, namely: (i) the general change in the degree of world interdependence in production and consumption; (ii) the change in the commodity composition of world trade; (iii) the change in the 'absolute' degree of competitiveness of the country; (iv) the change in the comparative advantage of that country in that sector relative to other sectors of that same country.

This can be written as the following simple identity:

$$\dot{x} \equiv \dot{Y} + (X/Y) + (y/Y) + C\dot{A}$$

where x represents the exports of country j in sector i, X are total world exports in sector i, Y are total world exports, y are total exports of country j, CA is the comparative advantage[28] of j in i, and the dots stand for rates of change.

The broad tendencies mentioned above highlight some fundamental questions. For example: what determines the general trend in national

Table 3.7 The evolution of comparative advantages in some industrial sectors, 1899–1980(a)

	1899	1913	1929	1937	1950	1955	1971	1980
Metals								
United Kingdom	1.07	0.85	0.96	0.83	0.67	0.65	0.75	0.51
United States	2.26	2.00	1.22	1.10	0.71	0.72	0.44	0.46
Japan	1.13	0.71	0.15	0.36	1.41	1.25	1.55	1.43
France	0.51	0.45	0.90	1.09	1.30	1.59	1.14	1.14
Germany (b)	0.72	1.05	0.91	0.78	1.54	0.74	0.90	0.96
Italy	0.17	0.06	0.05	0.18	0.35	0.48	0.58	0.68
Machinery/other electrical equipment								
United Kingdom	1.19	0.93	0.80	0.93	0.96	1.03	1.06	0.87
United States	2.32	1.85	1.72	1.65	1.57	1.41	1.25	1.05
Japan	0	0.04	0.15	0.34	0.26	0.31	0.81	1.14
France	0.39	0.34	0.46	0.43	0.56	0.62	0.89	0.80
Germany (b)	0.86	1.28	1.31	1.29	1.14	1.29	1.18	1.05
Italy	0.11	0.27	0.24	0.29	0.86	0.82	1.03	1.05
Transport equipment								
United Kingdom	1.68	1.19	0.92	0.96	1.59	1.39	0.92	0.94
United States	1.17	1.37	2.07	2.20	1.33	1.31	1.31	1.21
Japan	0	0.13	0.13	0.39	0.44	0.47	1.11	1.25
France	0.47	1.25	0.68	0.72	0.75	0.76	0.94	0.93
Germany (b)	0.49	0.70	0.40	0.75	0.64	1.18	0.93	0.93
Italy	0.22	0.70	0.62	1.12	0.43	0.48	0.65	0.53
Chemical								
United Kingdom	0.60	0.66	0.78	0.76	0.72	0.86	0.99	1.03
United States	1.24	0.87	0.83	0.88	1.30	1.17	1.13	1.11
Japan	0.27	0.42	0.46	0.43	0.24	0.47	0.56	0.38
France	0.97	1.10	1.24	1.71	1.05	1.02	1.11	1.12
Germany (b)	1.58	1.50	1.50	1.45	1.49	1.14	1.12	1.04
Italy	0.64	0.76	0.78	0.76	0.51	0.97	0.72	0.57
Textile/clothing								
United Kingdom	1.27	1.42	1.48	1.56	1.09	1.07	0.88	0.91
United States	0.21	0.23	0.27	0.21	0.44	0.51	0.35	0.52
Japan	1.67	1.79	2.45	2.70	2.44	2.96	1.40	0.69
France	1.05	1.25	1.38	1.14	1.35	1.29	1.28	1.10
Germany (b)	0.74	0.55	0.58	0.49	0.34	0.50	0.83	0.87
Italy	1.75	1.76	2.30	2.24	2.43	2.09	1.97	1.99

Notes:
(a) Comparative advantages are, as usual, the ratio of the sectoral share in 'world' export for any one particular country to that country's share in total 'world' manufacturing exports. That is:

$$\frac{x_{ij} / \Sigma_j x_{ij}}{\Sigma_i x_{ij} / \Sigma_{ij} x_{ij}}$$

with $i = 1 \dots n$, the sectors, $j = 1 \dots m$, the countries.
(b) West Germany only since 1950.

competitiveness – as expressed by the changing trends in export shares in, for example, Table 3.7? What is the relationship between sectoral trends and overall national trends? How do the determinants of sectoral comparative advantages relate to the determinants of these general changes in the competitive position of each country?

Answers to these questions require an analysis of the relationship between commodity/sector characteristics and national characteristics, and of the way different national characteristics affect competitive inter-actions on world markets. At this preliminary stage of exploration of the main 'stylised facts', it is useful to observe in greater detail the commodity composition of trade by country as revealed by the changing patterns of comparative advantages shown in Table 3.7.

Here one can identify important national specificities which could add to the phenomena to be explained. For example: the relatively stable German strength in chemicals and machinery; the Japanese comparative advantage – after the Second World War – in metals and electro-mechanical machinery and equipment;[29] the continuing Italian advan-tage in textile and clothing, and its rising advantage in machinery; the worsening British performance in transport equipment and machinery, and its emerging comparative advantage in chemicals.[30] Another set of important questions relates to what accounts for those country-specific regularities in relative specialisations? What reproduces or changes them through time?

At this level of aggregation it is obviously difficult to match sectors with precise commodity/country characteristics. However, casual empiricism hints at an apparent inadequacy of traditional endowment-based explanations. For example, if one accepts the conventional view that metal production is a relatively capital-intensive activity, it is difficult to believe that Japan and France are the most 'capital endowed' OECD countries or that in 1899 Japan was among the 'capital abun-dant' countries. Conversely, France has in addition to metals, an advan-tage in textile/clothing, traditionally considered a labour-intensive activity. The 'paradoxes' are numerous. In general, the patterns shown in Table 3.7 do not show any intuitive correspondence with the 'informed guesses' about the commodity/country correlations that one could make on the grounds of traditional trade theory.

3.4   Conclusions

In this chapter we have tried to explore some 'stylised' and 'less stylised' regularities in the international distribution of innovative capabilities (Section 3.1), international differences in input coefficients (Section 3.2) and the trends and characteristics of trade patterns (Section 3.3). More precisely, we identified a rather asymmetric distribution of innovative activities between countries, matched by an equally asymmetric pattern of efficiency in the use of production inputs (and, first of all, labour inputs). These two broad 'stylised facts' represent two fundamental sources of country-specific absolute advantages, which are important in terms of international competitiveness and trade.

In the following chapter we shall investigate their origins, the causes of their changes through time and the links they show with each other. Moreover, we shall analyse their sectoral specificities and study how different features of the various technologies affect the ways in which innovative advances are appropriated and/or diffused among firms, sectors and countries. In the following chapters we will then focus on the relationship between these sector-specific and country-specific technological leads/lags and the corresponding trade patterns.

Notes

1. See, among others, some of our own contributions to this measurement issue (Patel and Soete, 1987; Soete, Verspagen, Pavitt and Patel, 1989).
2. The patent data were based on IPO's Industrial Property Statistics, obliging us to sacrifice one observation; i.e. Italy, for which no domestic patent data were available. The R&D data were based on the 1975 and 1977 OECD data. No R&D data were available for New Zealand, Austria, Greece and Turkey.
3. Standard errors between brackets;

    $\bar{R} = R^2$ adjusted for the degrees of freedom
    *: significant at 1 per cent.

4. Cf. Pavitt, 1979; Pavitt and Soete, 1980; Patel and Pavitt, 1987, 1988.
5. Cf. Rosenberg (1976) and Landes (1969).
6. Even in a single-economy context serious problems remain and among them the question of the (fixed or moving) weights attributed to changing product mixes.
7. For an attempt, unfortunately limited to the United Kingdom and the United States, cf. Paige and Bombach (1959).
8. Cf. Kravis *et al.* (1975), (1982). Adjusted figures also based on Kravis' data can be found in Jones (1976), Smith *et al.* (1982) and Roy (1982).
9. Note, however, that the relative intercountry ratios of aggregate manufacturing productivities obtained on the ground of current prices and exchange rates are rather similar to those obtained through constant prices and exchange rates (see Table 3.4).
10. By high-value-added products, we mean products with higher value per 'physical unit', which ideally should be the numerator of the productivity ratio.
11. More detail on the statistical data base can be found in the appendix to

Chapter 6. The reader must be warned about the difference between the results presented here and similar attempts elsewhere. In particular, a significant difference emerges between the productivity ratio Germany/USA from Smith *et al.* (1982) and our estimates, even at current prices. This is due to different statistical sources, whose merits and faults are difficult to assess. Here we consistently use the Industrial Statistics of each country, which are easily comparable throughout the sample of chosen countries, despite some intercountry differences in the sampling coverage. National Accounts data, on the other hand, yield in some cases (as the one mentioned) relatively different figures. *A priori*, one should prefer the latter data which are meant to be adjusted to the universe of industrial activities. However, the sectoral breakdown in the National Accounts is sometimes smaller. Moreover, the adjustment criteria from the sample to the universe are often quite different between countries. For these reasons we chose the former option for the analysis of all manufacturing subsectors (cf. Table 3.5). The comparison of aggregate manufacturing productivity for the sample of developed and developing countries shown in Figures 3.5 and 3.6 is based on the United Nations, *Yearbook of Industrial Statistics*, various years, and on national sources.

12. These proxies are calculated through the yearly averages of investment/labour and investment/value-added ratios over the period 1968–80, divided by one plus the average rate of growth of output and constant prices. This adjustment through the growth rate is necessary in order to approximately 'discount' that part of investment aimed at the expansion of productive capacity, especially if one considers averages over relatively long periods. Calling v the marginal (= average) capital/output ratios; I, the gross investment; Y, output; g, the rate of growth of output; λ, the rate of scrapping; K, the capital stock, then

$$I = v \cdot \Delta Y + \lambda K$$
$$I/Y = v \cdot g + \lambda \cdot v$$
$$v = (I/Y)(g + \lambda)$$

The actual rate of scrapping is not generally available. However, if these rates do not differ too much between countries, then the ranking of the various $(I/Y)/(1 + g)$ for each country should not be very different from the actual $(I/Y)/(g + \lambda)$. Identical considerations apply to the capital/labour ratios.

13. Here and throughout the text, by 'capital intensity' we properly mean the ratio of capital inputs to output at current prices.

14. For an attempt at estimation, see Hill (1979).

15. On the cross-country stability in distributive share, see also Loftus (1969).

16. Some elaborations of ours on the same set of data as those given in Table 3.5 show that (a) the international standard deviation in wage rates, even within our sample of OECD countries, is around three times higher than the standard deviation in gross margins (which can be taken as a rough proxy for the profit rates); (b) international variations in gross margins do not show any strong correlation, with either sign, with GDP per head, where the latter can be taken as a proxy for 'capital abundance'.

17. See, for example, the standard deviation in textiles and clothing, ISIC 32, and compare this with the cross-sectoral average in the standard deviations (last column of Table 3.5).

18. In order to overcome, in a rather simple manner, the problems stemming from a variable number of observations for each country and sector, due to data availability, we regressed the vector of sectoral productivities, normalised by the manufacturing weighted mean of the corresponding countries (X_{ij}) against a number of dummy variables representing the sectors (D_i with $i = 1, ..., 23$, the sectors at the maximum level of available disaggregation), which assume as required the values 0 and 1. The estimate

$$X_{ij} = \alpha + \beta_1 D_1 + ... + \beta_{23} D_{23} + \mu$$

yielded

$$\bar{R}^2 = 0.62 \text{ and } F = 15.8$$

19. Compare again the mean of the standard deviations in productivities across countries for each sector (yielding a value of 42.8, last column of Table 3.5) with the normalised standard deviation within each country (see the last row of Table 3.5).

20. However, the reliability of the data related to these countries may be biased by a small number of strictly comparable sectoral observations.

21. I.e. the variance across the rows of Table 3.5. We used the same procedure as outlined in note 18, above. In this case the vector of observations of the dependent variable (Y_{ij}) is the set of sectoral productivities normalised with the unweighted OECD mean for the corresponding sector, which is regressed against a number of dummy variables (C_j with $j = 1, ..., 13$, for each country), taking the values 0 or 1 as appropriate. The estimate

$$Y_{ij} = \alpha + \beta_1 C_1 + ... + \beta_{13} C_{13} + \mu$$

yielded

$$\bar{R}^2 = 0.77, \quad F = 95.9$$

with all the β's significantly different from 0 at 1 per cent level of significance.

22. We tested the correlation between relative productivity gaps, as shown by each column in Table 3.5, and a proxy for capital/output ratios (averages of investment/output ratios) for the corresponding sector and country. The results have uncertain signs and are statistically insignificant.

23. Kuznets (1967), p. 7.

24. *Ibid.*, p. 9.

25. Kuznets (1967), p. 9.

26. *Ibid.*, pp. 36–8. The index of rank correlation between each of the major six countries and the OECD average is always above 0.70 (Italy being the lowest), and for each pair of countries always above 0.55 (with the exceptions of the pairs Italy-USA and Italy-Japan).

27. *Ibid.*, pp. 38–41.

28. I.e.

$$\frac{x/X}{y/Y}$$

29. Note that 'machinery – other electrical equipment' includes here electronics and electrical consumer durables.

30. For a detailed analysis of the evolution of the patterns of specialisation among OECD countries in the post-War period, see CEPII (1983).

4

The innovative process: International and intersectoral differences and determinants

The empirical evidence discussed in the preceding chapter illustrates the crucial importance of a better understanding of the international dimension of the nature, sources and determinants of technology and technological innovation (including the knowledge of design, production, sale of products, processes, systems, and services). In spite of this, little attention has generally been paid to the nature and determinants of what we shall refer to as 'firm-', 'sector-' and 'country-specific' technological advantage, or, put in another way, to the description, measurement and explanation of processes of technological *accumulation*.

In this chapter we begin to remedy this deficiency. In the first two sections, we define some properties of the innovative activities that emerge both from empirical studies and recent theoretical explorations. In the third section, we analyse and explain the intersectoral differences in patterns of innovation. In the fourth and final section, we consider the causes of the international differences in innovative capabilities, and provide a brief analysis of their relationship with other sources of country-specific and sector-specific advantages.

4.1 Entrepreneurship, demand and relative prices

By way of introduction we shall consider three contributions to the analysis of the innovative process, each of which, from a very different perspective, has attempted to explain international differences in the pace and direction of technical change. They can be summarised as follows: the discussion among economic historians on the relationship between relative factor prices and the comparative rates of technological innovation in nineteenth-century England and the United States; Asa Lindbeck's suggestions on the role of entrepreneurship in explaining international patterns of innovation; and Raymond Vernon's hypothesis on the link between patterns of demand and patterns of innovation.

The debate on the forces that account for different rates of technical progress and, in particular, different rates of mechanisation between the United States and England, following Habakkuk's work,[1] focusses on whether different relative prices of labour to capital (higher in the United States) can explain different rates of *induced* technical progress. It is impossible here to provide a full account of this debate. Suffice to mention two general implications that are relevant to our discussion.

First, there is evidence that levels and changes in the relative price of labour to machinery has been *one* of the important stimuli to the mechanisation of the US economy (cf. David, 1975). Second, there is no rigorous way in which this empirical regularity can be directly deduced from a traditional, neo-classical theory of production. To put it another way, there is no general theorem on the *biases* in the direction of technological change that can be derived from any exercise of comparative statics, if one maintains all neo-classical assumptions of rationality of the agents, instant adjustments and pure competition.[2] In this respect, David's analysis is illuminating. He starts by assuming some notional production function (which he calls 'Fundamental Production Function'), but only a finite group of techniques readily available to the economic agents. The following step involves considering a change in relative price, and an explicit adjustment process involving *local learning* and *technology-constrained* directions of change. Thus, the link between changes in relative prices and patterns of technological advances is accounted for by the introduction of (non-neo-classical) hypotheses regarding disequilibrium adjustment processes, irreversibility in the patterns of change and technological boundaries to the likely direction of progress.

Lindbeck and Vernon are both economists who have stressed the importance of the technology factor in international competition, and both have discussed the determinants of firm- and country-specific technological advantages. However, they come to different conclusions. For Lindbeck (1981), such advantages emerge from essentially unpredictable and immeasurable entrepreneurial activities, while for Vernon (1966), they emerge strictly as a result of perceived market opportunities. According to Lindbeck:

> ... the comparative advantages of the various highly developed countries are rather similar when looking at broad aggregates of products; ... when studying the 'fine' structure of production, the comparative advantages are too complex to be explained or predicted either by central planners or

by academic economists with the help of available methods of analysis ...
this largely results from the fact that some energetic and creative persons
happened to take initiatives in just that sector and product class ...
success stories in a specific country can occur in practically any branch of
manufacturing, services and marketing ... the possibility of predicting
where such success stories will occur is actually small. (pp. 394–5)

In other words, firm- and country-specific technological advantages
emerge, according to Lindbeck, from the random search processes of
Schumpeterian entrepreneurs.

For Vernon (1966), on the other hand, demand factors are all
important:

We begin with the assumption that the enterprises in any one of the
advanced countries of the world are not distinguishably different from
those in any other advanced country, in terms of their access to scientific
knowledge and their capacity to comprehend scientific principles ... . It is
a mistake to assume, however, that equal access to scientific principles in
all the advanced countries means equal probability of the application of
those principles in the generation of new products ... producers in any
market are more likely to be aware of the possibility of introducing new
products in that market than producers located elsewhere would be.
(p. 191)

In other words, for Vernon all firms in advanced countries have equal
access to the technological knowledge for innovation, but international
differences in market demand lead to different national inducements for,
and rates of, innovation. He argued in 1966 that, given scarce labour,
the US demand for labour-saving innovations had been higher than in
other parts of the world, and hence the pioneering development there of
such innovations as the sewing machine, the typewriter and the tractor.
Along similar lines Davidson (1976, 1979) and Franko (1976) argued
that natural resource scarcities had induced different directions of
innovative activities in such countries as Germany and Japan. Vernon
has been said to have rejected his original hypotheses in later papers
(1979, 1982). In fact, he simply observed that, by the late 1970s, the
greater similarities among the industrially advanced countries in their
relative factor prices would lead to greater similarities in their patterns
of innovative activities.

A related explanation has been put forward in Denmark. Building on
the earlier analysis of Burenstam Linder (1961), Andersen *et al.* (1981)
have argued that sophisticated national buyers of capital goods can have
a strong influence on national patterns of innovation, given the important role of users in developing, testing and modifying capital goods,
and their close relations with local suppliers through preferential purchasing, and through flows of information and skills. They argue that

Danish comparative advantage in exports of agricultural equipment derives from the downstream linkages with a well-endowed and technically sophisticated agricultural sector.

Vernon also argued that the links between the geographical location of innovative activities and production tend to diminish over the so-called product cycle. In the early stages of this cycle, high rates of product innovation, of market uncertainty, of volatility in industrial structure and of price inelasticity in demand, will all induce the innovating firm to locate its production activities close to its research and development (R&D) activities, to the sources of specialised inputs, and to its markets. As the product matures and its market grows, a slower rate of innovation and a shift from product towards process innovation will progressively cause firms to seek production locations on the basis of factor and transport costs.

The very different conclusions of Lindbeck and Vernon about the determinants of national patterns of innovative activity reflect different assumptions about their nature. For Lindbeck, the entrepreneurial function is fulfilled by talented individuals; for Vernon it is part of the deliberate search process of industrial firms. And for Vernon, the technology necessary for innovation consists of widely accessible knowledge of scientific principles, while for Lindbeck it consists of very specific knowledge of particular products, processes and markets.

At first sight, 'demand'-based explanatory models appear persuasive. They build on Schmookler's earlier conclusions (1966) that invention and innovation are essentially economic activities, responding to movements in market demand. US innovations abound in mechanisation, mass production and durable consumer goods. Scarce natural resources were clearly a strong stimulus for the development of the German chemical industry and the synthetic rubber industry during the Second World War. Relatively scarce space and energy are reflected in the small, energy-economic automobiles of Western Europe and Japan, and in Japanese innovations in small television sets. Similarly, sophisticated national buyers of capital goods have been a strong stimulus to national innovative activities, most notably in the purchase of weapons in the United States, the United Kingdom and France, but also in equipment for public utilities in a number of countries, including newly industrialising ones (Lall, 1980).

However, the models are sometimes inconsistent with one another, and there are certain national patterns of innovative activity that they cannot explain. In particular, strong patterns of innovative activity can be stimulated by an abundance, as well as a scarcity, of natural resources. Rosenberg (1976) has described how the United States rose to pre-eminence in woodworking technology in the nineteenth century on the basis of abundant natural resources. More recently, local natural resources have been the basis of innovative activity in the United States in petrochemicals, and in Sweden in a range of activities beginning with wood and iron ore, and moving through paper and steel, to high-grade furniture, metal products and machinery. Very often, the exploitation of abundant natural resources creates local demands for sophisticated capital goods in just the manner postulated by Andersen *et al.* (1981).

Several examples of these differentiated inducement mechanisms can be found in analyses of modern technology history, by, among others, Landes (1969), Freeman (1982), David (1975) and Rosenberg (1976). More recently, Altshuler *et al.* (1984) have shown that different energy prices and physical space constraints between the United States, on the one hand, and Western Europe and Japan, on the other, have generated different mixes of demand for large and small automobiles and that these are also reflected in the accumulated skills in the local firms supplying automobiles.

However, the peculiarities of national demand cannot explain all significant areas of national innovative activity. In what is, relatively speaking, the most innovative country in the world, namely Switzerland, we doubt whether the strong concentration of innovative capabilities in pharmaceuticals can be explained by any national inclination of the Swiss population to disease or hypochondria, any more than the Swiss highly developed innovative capabilities in marine engines can be explained by the activities of the Swiss Navy or merchant fleet. From a similar perspective, Rothwell (1979) found that in the case of the United Kingdom, the relatively efficient agricultural sector bought its more innovative and sophisticated machinery from foreign sources.

The few more general empirical studies in this area – in particular the work of Franko and Davidson mentioned above, although suggestive and interesting – have in our view not yet convincingly demonstrated the existence of a clear international specialisation pattern of innovation based on relative factor scarcities. Apart from identifying a truly representative sample of innovations, the most severe problem in these studies – and in particular in Davidson's work – is the difficulty of identifying systematically and accurately the specific factor-saving bias in a country that stimulated various classes of innovation. In particular, has the stimulus to innovation in machinery – where Germany has a particularly strong position – been towards capital- or labour-saving, or both? Was the stimulus for the development of oxygen steel-making in Austria and Japan towards capital-, energy-, labour- or materials-saving, or all four? Was the stimulus to microelectronics innovations in the United States capital- or labour-saving, or was it induced by a large, technically demanding and protected defence market? The answers to these questions are not easy to find, and remain to some extent arbitrary. They will, however, determine the conclusions of any analysis.

Since Schmookler's pioneering work, a number of studies have suggested that the most successful innovations are stimulated by 'demand-pull' rather than by 'science-push'. Perhaps the most influential has been the study by Marquis and Myers (1969) of 567 innovations in five industries, which concluded that more than three-quarters of the innovations resulted from 'demand-pull'. However, on the basis of historical example, Rosenberg (1976, p. 268) has argued that innovative activity depends not only on demand, but also on the underlying science and technology that determines the ease (and/or costs) with which the demand can be met: 'It would not require a very lively imagination ... to compile an extensive list of "high priority" human needs which existed for many centuries, which would have constituted highly profitable commercial activities, but yet remained unsatisfied.'

Mowery and Rosenberg (1979) later cast doubt on the conclusions that can be drawn from the studies, stating that innovation is demand-determined. They point out that, in many of these studies, little distinction is made between the roles of science and technology-push and demand-pull in triggering innovative activity, and their roles in full-scale implementation. Thus, while Marquis and Myers found that only 21 per cent of their sample of innovations had been initially stimulated by technical opportunity, Mowery and Rosenberg point out that 83 per cent required inputs of scientific and technical information for successful implementation. They conclude that few of the studies carried out enable one to specify whether an innovation was brought forth by a shift in market demand, or by a shift in science and technology supply.[3]

One reason for this is that most of the studies make no clear distinction between the recognition by innovators of actual and of potential demand. Freeman *et al.* (1980) have argued that, with the emergence of large R&D-intensive firms, entrepreneurs, in their innovative activities, have begun to anticipate as well as to respond to market demand.[4] They found what might be described as 'counter-Schmookler' trends at certain times in the chemical industry, with growth in inventive (and sometimes scientific) activity preceding market development in plastics and dyestuffs and drugs in the 1920s, and continuing throughout the depression in the 1930s. Similar anticipatory inventive and innovative activity abounds today in electronics and biotechnology, where a combination of radical scientific breakthroughs and rapidly improving technology enables entrepreneurs to anticipate future applications and demands.

One striking example is provided by Cape (1980), a co-founder and chairman of the Cetus Corporation in biotechnology. He describes the founding of the company by a group of scientists in California in 1971 as follows:

There had been 20 years of incredible advances in molecular biology, a couple of dozen Nobel Prizes, and not a single practical or commercial application had been made ... we became determined to make a business out of this ... (entrepreneurs) don't sit back as global economists, find a need and then fill it ... entrepreneurial energy comes from what they know they can do, and then they go out and try to figure out where they fit in (p. 70).

Coming back to the three contributions with which we commenced this chapter, it will now be clear that Vernon is indeed correct in assuming that the entrepreneurial function consists mainly of the deliberate search to match technological opportunity and market needs. Such activities involve high levels of uncertainty and conflict, and may require inputs from individuals with particular talents.[5] Over time, and as illustrated in a variety of technological proxies (such as patenting activity), firms have progressively become the dominant source of invention and innovation. However, Vernon also assumes that the direction of innovative activities is determined entirely by market signals, whether present or anticipated. As Mowery and Rosenberg (1979) have pointed out, it is a truism that a successful innovation must reduce costs, or improve product performance per unit cost as compared to existing techniques. It does not necessarily follow, however, that the only triggers to firms' innovative activities are real or anticipated changes in market signals, or that such changes necessarily elicit an appropriate change in technology. Different technologies have different rates of development at different times. In some cases, rapidly improving technologies can themselves open up possibilities for innovation without any change in market signals. In other cases stagnant or difficult technologies mean that glaringly obvious market opportunities cannot be exploited.

Furthermore, it would be wrong to assume that technological knowledge consists of mainly scientific principles. Lindbeck is correct in assuming that such knowledge is very specific to applications. In most advanced countries, at least 60 per cent of 'R&D' expenditures are on 'D', namely expenditures geared to the development of specific products or production processes (National Science Board, 1984). In industrial firms the distribution of the costs of innovation − excluding normal investment in plant and equipment − is roughly as follows: research, 10−20 per cent; development, 30−40 per cent; production engineering, 30−40 per cent; market launch, 10−20 per cent (Kamin *et al.*, 1982). Depending on the assumptions made, this distribution of expenditures predicts that between 10 and 30 per cent of the inputs to industrial technology come from outside industry (mainly from universities and government laboratories), with the remainder coming from within industry itself. This also emerges from a number of studies that have tried to identify the institutional sources of knowledge inputs into industrial innovations (Langrish *et al.*, 1972; Gibbons and Johnston, 1974; Townsend *et al.*, 1981; Wyatt and Bertin, 1985; Pavitt, 1984).

This pattern reflects the existence of highly differentiated ranges of techniques and related technological knowledge. These cannot easily be derived from, or reduced to, scientific principles; they depend on a range of acquired skills, practices and sub-theories (or rules of thumb). The acquisition of technology is always involved when a firm moves from one vintage of production technique to another, or from one product to another. Such acquisition involves not only written information (e.g. patents, blueprints, operating instructions), but also person-embodied skills and know-how, and the adaptation of techniques to local operating conditions and markets.

Rosenberg (1976) has described how US firms in the nineteenth century accumulated skills related to metalworking that enabled them to move from the production of textile machinery to machine tools, firearms, sewing machines, bicycles and motorcycles, and eventually to automobiles. Firms probably followed a similar process in Sweden (Granstrand, 1979), moving upstream and downstream from the processing of raw materials into more sophisticated technologies and high growth markets and, in Switzerland, diversifying from textiles into special machinery and into dyestuffs and other fine chemicals. Given their dependence on the accumulation of skills, these innovative movements into new areas are neither easy nor automatic. In his study of the strategy, structure and performance of more than 200 large US firms between 1949 and 1969, Rumelt (1974) found that firms with the strongest financial performance were those that diversified into related areas. Successful diversification depended on the skill base of the firm. His findings, and those of Rosenberg, suggest that skills and technologies in chemical products, electrical and electronic equipment, and metalworking are those that have most readily enabled diversification into new areas.

In order to disentangle these complex links between market conditions, the nature of the technologies and patterns of innovation, one needs a deep understanding of the nature and determinants of technological activities. We will discuss these issues in the following sections.

4.2   Technological paradigms and trajectories

Over the past twenty years, various analyses have been made of the process of innovation and technical change, with the purpose of giving a satisfactory account of the relationship between economic forces, and the relatively autonomous momentum that technical progress appears to maintain. These analyses, which can be classified under the broad heading of 'Innovation Studies' (Griliches, 1984), include those of Abernathy and Utterback (1975 and 1978), Freeman (1974), B. Klein (1977), Nelson and Winter (1977 and 1982), Rosenberg (1976 and 1982), Sahal (1981 and 1985), and also some of our own: Dosi (1982 and 1984), Pavitt (1979 and 1984), and Soete (1979). The analytical aims of these authors differ, and the contributions are heterogeneous. None the less, they all point towards the explanation of some common phenomena which, in our view, are of crucial importance in understanding the process of technological change.

First, as illustrated in the preceding section, the innovative process has some rules of its own which, at least in the short and medium term, cannot be described as simple and flexible reactions to changes in market conditions. It is the nature of technologies themselves that determines the range within which products and processes can adjust to changing economic conditions, and the possible directions of technical progress.

Second, scientific knowledge – even though it might account for only a fraction of the input in the innovative process – plays an increasingly crucial role in opening up new possibilities of major technological advances.

Third, the increasing complexity of research and innovation activities militates in favour of institutional organisations (R&D laboratories, design offices, government laboratories, universities, etc.) as opposed to individual innovators, as the typical environment for the production of innovations.

Fourth, in addition to the previous point, and in many ways complementary to it, a significant amount of innovation and improvement happens through 'learning by doing', and is generally 'embodied' in people and organisations (primarily firms). The same can be said for R&D, which is generally incorporated in, and linked with, the productive activities of the firms.

Fifth, notwithstanding the increasing institutional formalisation, research and innovative activities maintain a highly *uncertain nature*. The technical (and, even more so, the commercial) outcomes of research activities are difficult to predict *ex-ante*.

Sixth, technical change does not occur randomly for two main reasons: (i) in spite of considerable variations with regard to specific innovations, the directions of technical changes are often defined by the state-of-the-art of the technologies already in use; and (ii) the probability of technological advances by firms, organisations and even countries is, among other things, a function of the technological levels already achieved by them.[6] In other words, technical change is to a large extent a cumulative activity.

Elsewhere (Dosi, 1982 and 1984), one of us has suggested that, just as modern philosophy of science suggests the existence of scientific paradigms (or scientific research programmes), so there are *technological paradigms*. Both scientific and technological paradigms embody an *outlook*, a definition of the relevant problems, a pattern of enquiry. A 'technological paradigm' defines contextually the needs that are meant to be fulfilled, the scientific principles utilised for the task, the material technology to be used. In other words, a technological paradigm can be defined as a 'pattern' of solution of *selected* problems based on highly selected principles derived from prior knowledge and experience. A *technological trajectory* (Nelson and Winter, 1977) can then be defined as technological progress along the economic and technological trade-offs defined by a paradigm. Moreover, the technological paradigm also defines the boundaries of the inducement effects that changing market conditions and relative prices can exert upon the directions of technical progress.

One can take as fairly evident examples of such paradigms the internal combustion engine, oil-based synthetic chemistry, or semiconductors. A closer look at the patterns of technical change, however, suggest the existence of 'paradigms' and 'trajectories' with different levels of generality, in several industrial sectors. Whatever name is chosen, this concept points to interpretations broadly consistent with Rosenberg's 'focussing devices' (Rosenberg, 1976) or Sahal's 'technological guide-posts' (Sahal, 1981 and 1985). The crucial hypothesis is that innovative activities are strongly *selective*, *finalised* in quite precise directions, and often *cumulative*.

This concept of technology is very different from the equation of technology with information that is generally applicable and easy to reproduce and re-use (Arrow, 1962a), where firms can produce and use innovations mainly by dipping freely into a general 'stock' or 'pool' of technological knowledge. Instead, we have firms producing things in ways that are differentiated technically from things in other firms, and making innovations largely on the basis of in-house technology, but with some (and varying) contributions from other firms, and from public knowledge. Under such circumstances, the search processes of industrial firms are *not* likely to cover the whole stock of technological knowledge before making their technical choices.[7] Given its highly differentiated nature, firms will instead seek to improve and to diversify their technology by searching in zones that enable them to use and to build upon their existing technological base. What the firm can hope to do technologically in the future is heavily constrained by what it was capable of doing in the past.

Two major implications follow from this argument. First, while we thoroughly acknowledge the general characteristics of *imperfect* and *asymmetric information* of economic activities, we also suggest that it is misleading to reduce differences in innovative capabilities to the information domain. Rather, *companies and countries* are also differentiated in terms of *knowledge* and (somewhat tacit) *competences* which pre-exist information processing, yet determine the degree of technological and economic success. Second, and as a consequence, we depart from any microeconomic representation of innovation as an 'equilibrium' outcome of 'rational' forward-looking decisions of symmetric agents. Rather, our 'microeconomic foundations' rest in highly differentiated agents embodying diverse and asymmetric competences (Dosi, 1984).

The cumulative nature of innovative activities in firms is reflected in empirical studies. Successful innovations are more closely related to firms' existing ranges of technological and marketing skills than are unsuccessful ones (Cooper, 1983; Maidique, 1983), and innovations in product fields approximate to firms' existing activities entail initial learning costs that are recovered later as a consequence of cumulative improvements in product performance and in wider market applications (Teubal, 1982; Rothwell and Gardiner, 1984).

Lindbeck himself almost recognises the cumulative nature of technological development and innovative activities:

> ... if a country at a certain point in time has some specially trained people, such as engineers in a specific field, say a part of the chemical industry, one may perhaps dare to predict that the country in question will be successful also in the future in industries that use those types of skills. On the other hand, such a statement may be no more than an assertion about a certain *inertia* over time in the production structure. (1981, p. 394)

Once the cumulative and firm-specific nature of technology is recognised, its development over time ceases to be random, but is likely to be constrained to zones that are closely related technologically to existing activities. If those zones can be identified, measured and explained, it is possible in principle to predict likely future patterns of innovative activities in firms and countries.

This does *not* imply any irrelevance of the inducement mechanisms upon changes of techniques stemming from the levels and changes in relative prices (in particular the price of labour to the price of machines[8] and also to the price of energy) or from changing demand conditions.

On the contrary, these factors are likely to be fundamental ones, influencing both the rate and direction of technical progress *within the boundaries* defined by the nature of the technological paradigms. The main point is that the new techniques are likely to be superior to the old ones irrespective of relative prices.

In order to illustrate the point, which finds empirical corroboration in the study by A. Carter on the evolution of the technological coefficients in the American economy,[9] one might consider a simple case of a process innovation and its link with relative prices. Suppose that at time zero a firm uses a certain technique which is characterised by a factor combination *A*, as in Figure 4.1. Suppose also that this is an 'equilibrium' combination, at least in the weak sense, i.e. that at the prevailing relative prices the particular firm does not have a direct stimulus to change the existing technique. Let us now assume a change in relative prices, thus stimulating a change in the factor combinations in production. In traditional theory, the fact that all changes in techniques are *search processes*, the directions of which depend on the knowledge associated with the technique in use,[10] is neglected. However, the firm reasonably 'knows' only about the neighbourhood of point *A* (Figure 4.1) and its search cost will increase in relation to the distance from it.[11] That, together with the permanent existence of national innovative opportunities, is generally going to induce the discovery and exploitation of techniques that are unequivocally more efficient and that, with higher

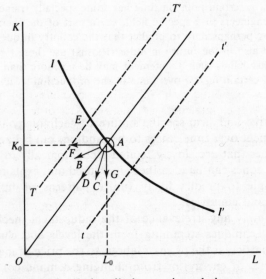

Figure 4.1 'Induced' changes in techniques

probabilities, are also 'similar' to past techniques, in terms of relative input intensities.

In this respect, the first question we must ask is, then, *where* will the firm search? Clearly, if the search cost associated with any probability of a given saving in the factor which has become more expensive is the same along the notional isoquant II′ as well as on 'better' isoquants, the firm will always choose the latter. In other words, it will always follow the rule (which we may call the 'innovative rule'): 'search within the K_0AL_0O area and *not* along the notional isoquant defined by the existing state-of-the-art'. The reason is obvious: the more expensive factor can be saved without increasing the use of the other one(s) proportionally. Even if we allow the search costs of the two rules to differ, the firm will still search in some direction F, B, D, C, or G as long as the *technological opportunity* is sufficiently high to guarantee a proportionally higher total cost saving. This is reinforced by the four following considerations:

1. If the nature of the search is *local*, then search outcomes are likely to be serially correlated (cf. Atkinson and Stiglitz, 1969; Nelson and Winter, 1982, pp. 175–84; and Arthur, 1985). Thus the probabilities of going from a low-intensity combination of inputs to another ('better') low-intensity combination are higher than the probabilities of going to a high-intensity one, etc.

2. The movement to unequivocally better techniques is in a sense an insurance against the uncertainty of the future: if relative prices will reverse some time in the future, any technique B, D, C, F or G might still be viable, while a technique on the isoquant (e.g. technique E) certainly will not be.

3. All the strategies within the *innovative search rule* combine an adaptive reaction to the macroeconomic environment (here, the change in relative prices of inputs) with 'Schumpeterian behaviour' in terms of intraindustry (i.e. interfirm) competition. In other words, the success of the innovative search rule may mean, simultaneously, an efficient reaction to a changing environment combined with differential profits stemming from a technological advantage over the other firms in the industry. On the other hand, the 'neo-classical search rule' (i.e. 'search along the notional isoquant defined by technique A') might in the long term mean disappearance from the industry, if some other firms are successful in their Schumpeterian behaviour.

4. There are generally strictly technological limits to straightforward substitution. They stem from the nature of the technological paradigms and the constraints they place on the nature of processes and products.[12] To use trivial examples, the ideas of substituting labour

for fuel in the operation of internal combustion engines, or increasing the mechanisation of production by simply increasing the content of steel of machine tools, are obviously nonsensical. In other words, the nature of the technological paradigms and trajectories are likely to define the outer boundaries of the possible input ratios (say, TT' and tt' in Figure 4.1). If these boundaries are rather tight, this is an additional factor pushing towards the 'innovative rule'.

One can see that the 'neo-classical rule' ('search along the present notional isoquant') becomes that limit case wherein technological opportunities disappear, i.e. technical change no longer occurs. In this case, static changes in input combination will indeed become the only possible adaptive rule to changing environments. In the real world, one may imagine a continuum of possibilities: sectors with high technological opportunities are likely to be dominated by 'innovation rules', with a rapid fall in both capital/output and labour/output ratios (that is, changes within the OK_0AL_0 area),[13] while in less dynamic sectors, technological changes might have lower degrees of innovative freedom so that the direction of change might be somewhere above F or to the right of G in Figure 4.1.

Qualitatively similar considerations apply to *product* innovations. In this case, technological changes have to be described with reference to the performance characteristics and costs of the products: 'innovative rules' of adjustment to possible changes in market signals (e.g. changes in demand patterns) imply straightforward improvements in the trade-offs implicit in the relevant dimensions related to each specific technological paradigm (e.g. in automative technology, increasing speed without any additional fuel consumption).

Cumulativeness of technological advantages, localised learning, firm-specific and technology-specific forms of knowledge do not exhaust the description of the features of the process of change in techniques and products. Another fundamental characteristic relates, for example, to the forms and degrees of private *appropriability* of technological advances. As suggested by the classical and − even more so − Schumpeterian traditions, varying degrees of private appropriation of the benefits of the innovation are both the incentive to, and the outcome of, the innovative process. In other words, each technology embodies a specific balance between its public good aspects and its private (i.e. economically appropriable) features (Nelson, 1984). As a consequence, 'market structure and technological performance are endogenously generated by three underlying sets of determinants: the structure of demand, the nature and strength of opportunities for technological advance and the ability of firms to appropriate the returns from private investment in research and development'.[14]

Nelson and Winter (1982) develop an evolutionary model whereby these features of technology affect the rates and patterns of change in industrial structures and performance. Elsewhere, one of us (Dosi, 1984) also analyses the role of these variables as entry and mobility barriers. Appropriability conditions clearly differ between technologies: Levin *et al.* (1984), for example, study the different empirical relevance of patents, secrecy, lead times, and superior sales and service efforts as 'appropriation' devices. On the basis of their results, Levin *et al.* (1984) draw the conclusion that lead times and learning curves are relatively more effective ways of protecting process innovations, while patents are a relatively better protection for product innovations.[15] Moreover, there is significant interindustrial variance in the importance of the various ways of protecting innovations, and in the overall degrees of appropriability, with around three-quarters of the industries surveyed in the study claiming the existence of at least one effective means of protecting process innovation, and more than 90 per cent of industries claiming the same for product innovations.[16]

The changing conditions of cumulativeness, opportunity and appropriability depend, in our view, partly on the nature of the various technological paradigms and partly on the outcome of the strategic choices and competitive interactions between firms over time. Technological paradigms not only determine the boundaries of the possible directions of progress (the technological trajectories), they also shape the range of notional degrees of appropriability and the ease of technological advances. The degrees of strategic freedom within these boundaries are filled by the specific histories of technological accumulation, patterns of competitiveness, behavioural regularities – which are company-specific, industry-specific and country-specific.

In other words, there are two fundamental dimensions. One is related to the nature of the main technologies and applies across countries and across firms within the same technology and/or industry. The second dimension (related to strategies, context conditions and more generally to 'history') varies with companies and countries, while it may well apply across technologies (within the same country or the same company). Moreover, technology-specific and country-specific aspects of opportunity, cumulativeness and appropriability of technological advances affect both the *intersectoral* distribution of sources and uses of innovations and the *international* distribution of technological advantages/disadvantages. It is to these that we now turn.

4.3　Intersectoral differences

In addition to the mechanisms of appropriability, there are also marked differences among sectors in their importance as sources and as users of technology, in the size distribution of innovating firms, and in the sectoral distribution of technological activities according to firms' core businesses.

In nearly all OECD countries, the major source of new technology – R&D activities funded by business enterprises – is heavily concentrated in manufacturing, with just five sectors (chemicals, non-electrical machinery, electrical and electronic products, instrumentation, and automobiles) accounting for more than 80 per cent of the total. Similar sector patterns emerge from studies of the sectoral distribution of patenting and of significant innovations.[17] These studies also show that other sectors of the economy benefit from the impact of technological advance in these core sectors of high technological opportunity, through a dense network of interindustry purchases and sales of equipment, materials and components. Table 4.1 shows the considerable similarities between the United Kingdom and the United States in their sectoral patterns of production and use of technology. A high proportion of innovations emerging from the mechanical, electronic and chemical sectors

Table 4.1　Comparison of sectoral patterns of technology production and use in the United Kingdom (1970–9) and the United States (1974)

	Percentage of all technology produced		Percentage of all technology used	
	United Kingdom	United States	United Kingdom	United States
Core sectors	68.3	62.8	18.3	18.8
Secondary sectors	20.6	23.9	16.4	12.7
Other manufacturing	8.3	12.0	26.0	11.4
Non-manufacturing	2.9	1.3	39.4	57.1
All group	100.0	100.0	100.0	100.0

Notes:
- Sectoral groups: core sectors include chemicals, machinery, mechanical engineering, instruments and electronics.
- Secondary sectors include metals, electrical engineering, shipbuilding/offshore engineering, vehicles, building materials, rubber and plastic goods.
- Other manufacturing includes food, aerospace, textiles, paper, printing.
- Non-manufacturing includes agriculture, mining, construction, utilities, transport, business, R&D, other services, health care, defence, other government services, final consumers.

Source: Robson *et al.* (1988).

are pervasive in their use across many sectors, with mechanical technology finding a relatively high proportion of applications within manufacturing, and electronics and chemicals also a high proportion outside. Both studies show that, although an insignificant source of technology, non-manufacturing sectors are a major user of technology originating elsewhere.[18]

Numerous studies have also shown similarly large and consistent variations among sectors in both the distribution of innovative activities according to firm size, and the related degree of concentration of such activities (Scherer, 1965; Mansfield, 1968; Soete, 1979; Pavitt *et al.*, 1987; Acs and Audretsch, 1989). High technological opportunity is associated with heavy concentration of innovative activities in large firms in chemicals, electrical and electronics, and transport; at the same time, there is a much more dispersed pattern, and greater involvement of small firms, in machinery and instrumentation.[19]

A third dimension of sectoral diversity in technology is in the scope and direction of firms' technological activities (Archibugi, 1986; Jaffe, 1989; Kodama, 1986; Pavitt *et al.*, 1989). In general, firms are active technologically in zones close to their core production activities and, as might be expected, small firms are technologically more specialised than large ones. However, large firms in chemicals and electronics tend to concentrate on product innovations emerging from synergies in their R&D-based technologies, while process technologies tend to be a stronger focus of attention in sectors based on assembly production or continuous processes.

On the basis of this evidence, let us now bring together some of the analysis of the nature of technology and technical change to reinterpret the various taxonomies of the sources, uses and mechanisms of technology generation, already suggested elsewhere (Townsend *et al.*, 1981; Pavitt, 1984). The evidence presented so far can be summarised as follows.

In the market economy, the rate and direction of technical change in any sector will depend on three features: *first*, the sources and nature of the technological opportunities; *second*, the nature of users' requirements and, more generally, of actual or potential markets; and *third*, the possibilities for successful innovators to appropriate a sufficient proportion of the benefits of their innovative activities to justify the research effort invested in such activities.

There are a number of possible sources of technology. Inside firms, there are R&D laboratories and production engineering departments. Outside firms, there are suppliers, users, and government-financed research and advice. Similarly, users' requirements can vary. For standard structural or mechanical materials, price is of major importance once certain performance requirements are met. For machinery and equipment used in modern and interdependent systems of production, performance and reliability will be given a higher premium than price.

The methods used by successful innovators to appropriate the benefits of their activities compared to those of their competitors also vary. Process innovations can be kept secret; some product innovations can be protected by natural and lengthy technical lags in imitation (e.g. aircraft), while others cannot and thus require patent protection (e.g. pharmaceuticals); and both product and process innovations may be difficult to imitate because of the uniqueness of the technological knowledge and skills available in the innovating firm.

These ingredients are summarised in Table 4.2, where column 1 defines the categories of firm, column 2 enumerates typical core sectors for such firms, columns 3–5 describe the determinants and the nature of the technological trajectories of the firms, and columns 7–10 identify some of the measured characteristics of these trajectories. The nature of these trajectories allows us to distinguish four main groups of firms/ industries: supplier-dominated; scale-intensive; specialised suppliers, and science-based. The scale-intensive and specialised suppliers will be discussed under the common heading production-intensive.

Supplier-dominated

Supplier-dominated firms can be found mainly in traditional sectors of manufacturing, in agriculture, housebuilding, informal household production, and many professional, financial and commercial services. They are generally small, and their in-house R&D and engineering capabilities are weak. They appropriate less on the basis of a technological advantage than on the basis of professional skills, aesthetic design, privileged access to a resource (such as fertile land), trademarks and advertising. Within their technological trajectories, reducing costs is a fundamental aim, but they make only a minor contribution to their process technology. Most innovations come from suppliers of equipment and materials, although in some cases large customers and government-financed research and development services also make a contribution. Technical choices more closely resemble those described in Salter's vintage model, the main criterion being the level of wages compared to the price and performance of exogenously developed capital goods.

In sectors made up of supplier-dominated firms, we would expect that a relatively high proportion of the process innovations used in the sectors are produced by other sectors, even though a relatively high proportion of innovative activities in these sectors are directed to process innovations. According to data on the sectoral patterns of production and use of technology compiled by Scherer (1982) for the United States, and Robson *et al.* (1988) for the United Kingdom, the following sectors have such characteristics: textiles; printing and publishing; agriculture; and construction.

Production-intensive: scale-intensive and specialised suppliers

A second set of sectors consists of two groups of what one could call 'production-intensive' firms. Adam Smith described some of the mechanisms associated with the emergence of production-intensive firms, namely the increasing division of labour and simplification of production tasks resulting from an increased market size, and enabling a substitution of machines for labour and a consequent lowering of production costs. Improved transportation, increased trade, higher living standards and greater industrial concentration have all contributed to this technological trajectory of increasing large-scale fabrication and assembly production. Similar opportunities for cost-cutting technical change exist in continuous processes producing standard materials, where the so-called 'two-thirds engineering law' means that unit capacity costs can potentially be decreased by 1 per cent for every 3 per cent increase in plant capacity.

The technological skills to exploit these latent economies of scale have improved steadily over time. In fabrication and assembly, machines have been able to undertake progressively more complex and demanding tasks reliably as a result of improvements in the quality of metals and the precision and complexity of metal forming and cutting, and in power sources and control systems. In continuous processes, increased scale and high temperatures and pressures have resulted from improvements in materials, control instrumentation and power sources.[20]

The economic pressures and incentives to exploit these scale economies are particularly strong in firms producing for two classes of price-sensitive users: first, those producing standard materials; second, those producing durable consumer goods and vehicles. In reality, it is difficult to make these scale-intensive processes work up to full capacity. Operating conditions are demanding, with regard to equipment performance, controlling physical interdependencies and flows, and the skills of operatives. In such complex and interdependent production systems, the costs of failure in any one part are considerable. If only for purposes of 'trouble-shooting', trained and specialist groups for 'production engineering' and 'process engineering' have been established. As

Table 4.2 Sectoral technological trajectories: determinants, directions and measured characteristics

1	2	Determinants of technological trajectories			Technological trajectories	Measured characteristics			
Category of firm	Typical core sectors	3	4	5	6	7	8	9	10
		Sources of process technology	Type of user	Means of appropriation		Source of process technology	Relative balance between product and process	Relative size of innovating firms	Intensity and direction of technological diversification
Supplier-dominated	Agriculture Housing Private services Traditional manufacture	*Suppliers* Research and extension services Large users	Price sensitive	Non-technical (e.g trademarks, marketing advertising aesthetic design)	Cost-cutting	Suppliers	Process	Small	Low vertical
Production-intensive Scale intensive	Bulk materials (steel, glass) Assembly (consumer durables and autos)	Production engineering supplier: R&D	Price sensitive	Process secrecy and know-how Technical lags Patents Dynamic learning economies	Cost-cutting (product design)	In-house	Process	Large	High vertical

	Machinery: instruments	*Design and development* Users	Performance sensitive	Design know-how Knowledge of users Patents	Product design	In-house Customers	Product	Small	Low concentric
Specialised suppliers									
Science-based	Electronics/ electrical Chemicals	R&D Public science PE*	Mixed	R&D know-how; patents Process secrecy and know-how Dynamic learning economics	Mixed	In-house Suppliers	Mixed	Large	Low vertical High concentric

*Production Engineering.

Rosenberg (1976) has shown, these groups develop the capacity to identify technical imbalances and bottlenecks which, once corrected, enable improvements in productivity. Eventually they are able to either specify or design new equipment that will improve productivity still further. Thus, important sources of process technology in production-intensive firms are production engineering departments.

Adam Smith also pointed out that process innovations are also made '... by the ingenuity of the makers of machines when to make them became the business of a peculiar trade'.[21] The other important sources of process innovations in production-intensive firms are the relatively small and specialised firms that supply them with equipment and instrumentation, and with whom they have a close and complementary relationship. Large users provide operating experience, testing facilities and even design and development resources for specialised equipment suppliers. Such suppliers in turn provide their large customers with specialised knowledge and experience as a result of designing and building equipment for a variety of users, often spread across a number of industries. Rosenberg (1976) describes this pattern as 'vertical disintegration' and 'technological convergence'. He draws his examples from metalforming machinery. The same process can be seen at work today in the functions of production monitoring and control performed by instruments, in robots in CAD (computer-aided design), and in applications software. These specialised firms have a different technological trajectory from their users. Given the scale and interdependence of the production systems to which they contribute, the costs of poor operating performance can be considerable. The technological trajectories are therefore more strongly oriented towards performance-increasing product innovation, and less towards cost-reducing process innovation.

The way in which innovating firms appropriate technological advantages varies considerably between the large-scale producers and the small-scale equipment and instrument suppliers. For the large-scale producers, particular inventions are not in general of great significance. Technological leads are reflected in the capacity to design, build and operate large-scale continuous processes, or to design and integrate large-scale assembly systems in order to produce a complex final product. Technological leads are maintained through know-how and secrecy around process innovations, and through the inevitable technical lags in imitation, as well as through patent protection. For specialised suppliers, secrecy, process know-how, and lengthy technical lags are not available to the same extent as a means of appropriating technology. Competitive success depends to a considerable degree on firm-specific skills reflected in continuous improvements in product design and product reliability, and in the ability to respond sensitively and quickly to users' requirements.

Finally, one of us has argued elsewhere that one of the major revolutionary effects of the electronics revolution is the emergence of an 'information intensive' technological trajectory, similar in many ways to the 'production intensive' trajectory, but with information being processed through software engineering in service activities, rather than materials being processed through mechanical engineering in manufacturing activities (Pavitt *et al.*, 1989). Large users play a major role in developing their own complex, interdependent and idiosyncratic systems for processing information (on financial services, see Barras, 1986). This involves a symbiotic link between strong in-house technical expertise (often embodied in a 'Systems Department') and clusters of small suppliers of specialised software services.

Science-based

The last category, namely science-based firms, was also foreseen (if not observed) by Adam Smith who spoke of the contribution to technical progress of '... those who are called philosophers or men of speculation, whose trade it is not to do anything, but to observe everything; and who, upon that account, are often capable of combining together the powers of the most distant and dissimilar objects'. From the data on innovations described above, science-based firms are to be found in the chemical and electronic/electrical sectors. In both of them, the main sources of technology are the R&D activities of firms in the sectors, based on the rapid development of the underlying sciences in universities and elsewhere.

As Freeman (1974, Freeman *et al.*, 1982; Freeman and Soete, 1987) in particular has shown, the development of successive waves of products has depended on *prior* development of the relevant basic science: in particular, of synthetic chemistry and biochemistry for the chemical industry; and of electromagnetism, radio waves and solid-state physics for the electrical/electronic industry. Synthetic chemistry has enabled the development of a wide range of products, with useful structural, mechanical, electrical, chemical or biological characteristics, ranging from bulk materials replacing wood, steel and natural textiles, to specialised and expensive chemical and biological agents for medical or other uses. Post-War advances in the fundamentals of biochemistry are enabling the extension of these skills and techniques into biological products and processes.

Advances in electromagnetism, radio waves and solid-state physics have enabled products and applications related to the availability of cheap, decentralised and reliable electricity, communications and (now) information processing, storage and retrieval. Applications in electricity vary from huge transformers to small motors within mechanical systems, in communications from expensive radar and satellite tracking systems to cheap transistor radios, and in information from huge computers to electronic wristwatches. This pervasiveness has dictated the technological trajectories of firms in the science-based sectors. The rich range of applications based on underlying science has meant that successful and innovative firms have grown rapidly on the basis of product innovations,[22] and have had little incentive to look for innovative opportunities beyond their principal sector. Given the sophistication of the technologies and underlying sciences, it has been difficult for firms outside the sectors to enter them. The pervasive applications have also meant a wide variance in relative emphasis on production and process technology within each of the sectors, reflecting the different cost/performance trade-off for consumer goods, standard materials and specialised professional applications.

In the science-based group, firms appropriate their innovative leads through a mix of methods (i.e. patents, secrecy, natural technical lags, and firm-specific skills). Patent protection is particularly important in fine chemicals, with specific high-grade applications, where the predominant product innovations can be quickly and cheaply imitated.[23] In addition, dynamic learning economies in production have been important barriers to the imitation in continuous process technology, large-scale assembly and – over the past twenty-five years – in the production of electronic components.

4.4 Explaining national rates and directions of technological accumulation

How do the cumulative, specific and sectorally differentiated properties of technology, so far described, help to explain the marked international differences in the volume, trends and sectoral patterns of technological activities? Ergas (1984) has tried to answer this question, under the title: 'Why do some countries innovate more than others?' On the basis of admittedly imperfect evidence, he identified the most important variables as: the differences in the size of local markets; the supply of skills (from the shop-floor to basic research in universities); the degree of interfirm rivalry; and the ease of entry and exit. These variables have important effects on countries' rates of innovation. However, they are only part of the complex links between the technological opportunities, capabilities and economic signals on the one hand, and entrepreneurial decisions on the other, that explain international differences in 'innovativeness'. In order to push the analysis further, we shall distinguish between those factors which influence the incentives and the constraints on innovative activities in *all* firms in a country, and those factors which are likely to be *firm-* or *sector-specific*.

The nature and extent of the differences between countries is summarised in Table 4.3 (comparing countries' business R&D as a proportion of output), and Table 4.4 (comparing countries' sectors of relative technological strength and weakness). These show:

- the high level and strongly upward trend in aggregate technological activities in Japan, coupled with particular sectoral strength in electronics and automobiles;
- the relatively poor performance of the United States in terms of aggregate business-financed R&D, coupled with the growing relative strength of US-based firms in defence- and natural resource-based technologies;
- marked differences in aggregate technological activities within Western Europe, with high levels in the Federal Republic of Germany, Sweden and Switzerland co-existing with low levels and weak trends in the United Kingdom and the Netherlands.[24]

Table 4.3 Trends in industrial R&D as a proportion of industrial output in some OECD countries: 1967–85

	Total			Industry financed		
	1967	1975	1985	1967	1975	1985
Japan	0.92	1.28	2.11	0.90	1.26	2.07
United States	2.35	1.84	2.32	1.15	1.18	1.54
France	1.36	1.36	1.78	0.75	0.87	1.24
Federal Republic of Germany	1.31	1.65	2.42	1.07	1.30	1.99
Italy	0.43	0.61	0.92	0.41	0.55	0.71
Netherlands	1.45	1.45	1.50	1.31	1.30	1.22
Sweden	1.29	1.64	3.03	0.94	1.48	2.64
Switzerland	na	na	na	na	na	na
United Kingdom	2.01	1.72	2.01	1.34	1.08	1.32
Western Europe	1.27	1.35	1.81	0.92	1.00	1.37

Notes:
1. Industry-financed R&D excludes that funded by government.
2. Western Europe is defined as the seven European countries listed above plus Belgium, Denmark and Ireland. Total R&D and industrial output for Europe has been calculated by first transforming each country's data into US dollars on the basis of purchasing power parities and then aggregating.

Source: Pavitt and Patel, 1988.

Table 4.4 Sectoral patterns of relative advantage in total US patenting for some OECD countries: Revealed Technology Advantage Index

	Chemicals Fine	Other	Mechanical	Motor vehicles	Raw materials	Defence	Electrical machinery	Electronics Cons.	Capital
Japan									
1963–8	3.01	1.38	0.77	0.65	0.51	0.35	1.10	1.37	1.80
1981–6	0.87	0.96	0.81	2.08	0.40	0.11	1.11	1.71	1.86
United States									
1963–8	0.89	0.94	1.01	0.95	1.08	0.99	1.01	0.99	1.01
1981–6	0.86	0.98	1.01	0.68	1.21	1.16	1.00	0.92	0.94
France									
1963–8	1.95	0.96	1.02	1.89	0.54	1.10	1.12	1.04	0.80
1981–6	1.45	0.94	0.99	0.80	0.84	1.66	1.08	1.10	0.86
Federal Republic of Germany									
1963–8	1.11	1.41	0.96	1.37	0.61	1.03	0.82	1.25	0.88
1981–6	1.17	1.24	1.12	1.48	0.67	1.14	0.90	0.60	0.54
Italy									
1963–8	1.21	1.66	0.95	1.01	0.76	0.78	0.68	0.64	0.36
1981–6	2.23	1.02	1.16	1.15	1.07	0.95	0.69	0.64	0.40

Netherlands									
1963–8	1.72	1.40	0.70	0.17	1.00	0.15	1.16	1.36	2.22
1981–6	0.63	1.05	0.75	0.36	1.69	0.30	1.10	1.44	1.59
Sweden									
1963–8	0.92	0.69	1.20	1.05	1.03	2.35	0.97	0.90	0.57
1981–6	0.59	0.61	1.47	0.75	1.38	2.07	0.95	0.55	0.24
Switzerland									
1963–8	2.18	1.72	0.89	0.45	0.51	1.44	0.90	0.43	0.48
1981–6	2.02	1.30	1.00	0.44	0.73	1.01	0.98	0.55	0.32
United Kingdom									
1963–8	0.88	1.00	1.06	1.55	0.65	1.28	1.04	1.06	1.09
1981–6	2.00	1.00	1.01	0.97	0.86	1.02	0.97	0.89	0.68
Western Europe									
1963–8	1.30	1.24	0.99	1.29	0.66	1.15	0.94	1.05	0.91
1981–6	1.44	1.11	1.08	1.07	0.86	1.18	0.94	0.76	0.62

Notes:
1. Revealed technology advantage index is defined as a particular country's share of US patents within a sector divided by that country's share of total US patents. Thus a value of greater than 1 shows the relative strength of a country in a sector and vice versa.
2. The definition of the sectors is based on an aggregation of three-digit US patent clauses, the precise correspondence being available from the authors.

Source: Pavitt and Patel, 1988.

More generally, four characteristics of countries' technological activities emerge from more detailed sector-based and firm-based analysis (Soete, 1987; Pavitt, 1985b; Patel and Pavitt, 1988).

1. As might be expected, smaller countries are clearly technologically more specialised, as measured by the standard deviation of each country's sectoral distribution of revealed technological advantage.
2. There is considerable stability in each country's sectoral pattern of technological advantage over time, reflecting the cumulative nature of technological activities.
3. In accordance with Lindbeck's observations mentioned earlier in this chapter, each country has a very different sectoral pattern of technological advantage, once one moves beyond broad aggregates.
4. In all countries, technological activities in R&D-intensive sectors (chemicals, electrical-electronics, aerospace) and in automobiles are heavily concentrated in a few firms, while in machinery and instrumentation they are spread among many. The technological strategies of a few firms in the concentrated sectors have marked effects on countries' sectoral and aggregate technological activities.

Aggregate technological activity: myopic versus dynamic systems

On the basis of the above evidence, one of us has argued elsewhere (Patel and Pavitt, 1988) that the observed international differences in aggregate levels and trends in technological activities reflect the degree to which national systems take into account the cumulative, irreversible and uncertain nature of technological activities. In 'myopic' systems that do not recognise these properties, technological activities are evaluated like an ordinary investment, namely, on the basis of their prospective rate of return in responding to an existing and precise market demand, and including stiff discounts for time and risk. In 'dynamic' systems that do recognise these properties, the evaluation of technological activities also includes the prospect of creating new market demands, and of accumulating, over time, firm-specific knowledge that opens up further applications and opportunities in the future.[25] There are four (not necessarily independent) reasons why firms and national systems tend to be myopic rather than dynamic.

First, the system providing funds for business may evaluate mainly on the basis of short-term financial performance, in which case the strictly cumulative dimensions of technology will either be ignored or seen as a cost. More concretely, there is evidence that technology-based diversification into related product markets entails both greater short-term costs and greater longer-term benefits than incremental innovations in existing product markets (Pavitt, 1986b). Short-term horizons and risk aversion are thus likely to lead to both underinvestment in technology and to diminishing returns.

Second, as argued by Abernathy and Hayes (1980), the strict application of the managerial principles of M-form organisation may stifle entrepreneurial activities, through the joint effects of short-term financial evaluations of divisions' performance, coupled with rigid definition of each division's 'business', which effectively exclude opportunities that cut across divisional boundaries.[26]

Third, there is the nature of technological expectations in the firm. As Atkinson and Stiglitz (1969), Rosenberg (1982), David and Olsen (1984), Ireland and Stoneman (1986), Silverberg, Dosi and Orsenigo (1988) have pointed out, technological expectations are just as important as market expectations for firms' decisions. Expectations can be incorrectly formulated – and sometimes are – because of inappropriate technological inputs into decision-making, or simply because they are based on inappropriate 'strategic rules'.

Fourth, there are the more general organisational and technical skills of management and the workforce. The dynamic and cumulative benefits of technology are not automatic, but depend on the learning capacities of firms, which in turn depend on the levels of skill and on effective communication, both inside and outside the firm.

To sum up, we expect international differences in levels and rates of growth of technological activities to be a function of the general education context, the science and engineering competence of management, the skills of the workforce, the nature of the financial system, and the characteristics of large firms. Especially organisational studies have shown that these factors do vary among countries and do influence dynamic efficiency (e.g. Pratten, 1976; Pavitt, 1980; Prais, 1987; Mansfield, 1968).

Sectoral patterns of technological accumulation

The differences among sectors in the sources and directions of technical change have one major implication: specific inducement mechanisms have differing effects, depending on the sector. *Supplier-dominated* sectors resemble those represented in the capital-embodied models of accumulation à la Salter:[27] firms make relatively homogeneous products; process technology is generated exogenously; and technical advances will be influenced by the capabilities of the adopters of the new equipment, relative input prices and the performance/price character-istics of capital goods.[28]

Supplier-dominated firms rarely accumulate technology beyond the ability to operate and improve marginally on the production systems based on exogenously generated inputs. However, the production equip-ment that they choose, or are expected to choose in the future, influences innovative activities and technological accumulation in the firms that supply them. Long-term trends in the relative price of machines to labour are thus likely to influence *both* the technological trajectory of the equipment producers, focussing their innovative efforts in the direc-tion of a higher mechanisation/automation of productive processes, and the technical choice of the supplier-dominated firms.

In addition to such product technology, relative factor prices will also influence the trends in process innovations within *scale-intensive and science-based* firms. However, here it will not be primarily a matter of 'choices' as in the case of the supplier-dominated firms. Instead of being exogenously generated, process technology advances will now be a con-sequence of investment and production in the firms themselves, through some of the mechanisms described by Schmookler (1966; i.e. investment-induced innovation in capital goods), Arrow (1962b; i.e. learning-by-doing in production), and Rosenberg (1982; i.e. learning-by-using capital goods). Such process technology is cumulative and firm-specific. With respect to such 'localised' technical progress, 'history is' indeed 'very important':[29] the techniques used and the technology accumulated will be a function of the firm's earlier activities, primarily in production (learning-by-doing) and in investment, design, develop-ment and production engineering (innovation in capital goods). As a consequence, powerful irreversibilities are likely to be built into the process of technological change.

In scale-intensive firms and related specialised suppliers of capital goods, international differences in relative input prices will still affect international differences in the rate and direction of change in their process technologies. However, the effects of such differences in process technology are likely to be outweighed by international differences in past activities in production, investment, design and development, and production engineering. Similar effects will be felt in science-based firms, except that firm-specific R&D activities will play a relatively bigger role compared to firm-specific design and development and production engineering activities.

Table 4.5 summarises the factors likely to lead to international differ-ences in the rate and direction of innovative activity and technological accumulation in various categories of firms. Relative input prices influence most types of innovative activity, albeit within the boundaries

Table 4.5 Factors affecting international differences in patterns of product and process innovation in different categories of firms

Category of firms	Type of innovation	Relative factor costs	Volume of production	Factors influencing and influenced by entrepreneurial expectations		
				Accumulated investment and production	Production engineering and design	Research and development
Supplier-dominated	Product	×				
	Process	×				
Scale-intensive	Product	×		×	×	×
(Production-intensive)	Process		×	×	×	×
Specialised suppliers	Product	×		×	×	×
	Process				×	
Science-based	Product	×	×	×	×	×
	Process	×				×

of particular technological trajectories (see Section 4.2 above). Levels of production determine the degree to which scale-intensive and science-based firms accumulate in technologies characterised by economies of scale in production. Together with the level of expenditures on investment, production engineering, design and development, and on R&D activities, they also determine the rate and direction of 'localised' technological accumulation.

Thus, levels of innovative activity are not set automatically by firms in response to external market signals. They reflect both past accumulated technology, and expectations about future technology, markets and input prices. The former is firm-specific and differentiated, while the latter is uncertain and involves technical and economic judgements. Levels of innovative activity can therefore vary among firms in part as a function of different levels and directions of accumulated experience, and differing entrepreneurial expectations about the future.

Furthermore, international differences in patterns of investment can help to explain international differences in the rate of technological accumulation in 'upstream' sectors, supplying specialised production equipment. In Table 4.2 the linkages between scale-intensive manufacturing firms and their specialised suppliers is emphasised. Case studies have shown similar linkages between technological accumulation in capital goods suppliers and investment in coal mining (Townsend, 1980), in agriculture (Andersen *et al.*, 1981), and in a variety of public and private investment programmes in newly industrialised countries (Lall, 1980).

An attempt at synthesis

Thus, differences in national rates of technological accumulation are influenced by strictly country-specific factors such as: differences in the economic signals that agents face; differences in the technological and institutional context; and differences in the macroeconomic and social environment. The various industries will be linked by stimuli and constraints which are both technology- and country-specific. Perroux (1973) defines these patterns of interdependence in terms of commodity flows; changing productivities (and by implication input costs); and investments (and thus the technologies 'embodied' in them). National (or even regional) systems of interdependence show relatively easily identifiable sub-sets of activities which present a higher 'inner' intensity of commodity, technology and information flows. In French literature, these are called 'filières',[30] a concept which can probably be best approximated in English as 'webs' or 'clusters'.[31] In so far as the inter-linkages within a 'filière' can be adequately represented by input requirements, prices, and commodity flows the concept of 'filière' simply summarises the existence of structured sub-sets of activities, together with the 'effets d'entraînement' (pulling effects) that they embody on the demand side.

In our view such an interpretation is unduly restrictive. A 'filière' will also embody powerful patterns of technological complementarities, untraded technological interdependencies, and information flows that are not entirely captured in the flows of commodities. In this sense, they represent a structured set of technological and informational 'externalities' which act as 'focussing devices' (Rosenberg, 1976), and as a collective asset to that group of industries within each national economy. These technological externalities affect the dynamics of innovation and imitation in each individual sector, and the overall pattern of technological accumulation in each country.

Of course, one must also assume, as we explicitly do, that these externalities are highly specific to particular spatial and institutional contexts; that they reproduce, or even increase over time (Arthur (1990)); and that they are dynamically-coupled with microeconomic decisions on, for example, investment locations, R&D efforts, etc.

The different patterns of technical change characteristic of each sector, their different degrees of technological opportunity, appropriability, cumulativeness and complexity imply that, within each sub-set of activities (each 'filière'), there are likely to be technologies that are crucial in defining the pace and direction of innovative advances for the whole. As an example, one may think of the role of steel and machine tools in the 'mechanical filière', especially in the second half of the last century, or the role of microelectronics' components within the present 'electronics filière'.

The uneven effects of different technologies and sectors is twofold. First, each sector shows a different intensity of 'forward' and 'backward' linkages in terms of the demand flows it activates in the input/output matrix.[32] Second, and more importantly, the different intensities of the 'pull' and 'push' that each technology exerts upon the related sectors highlight the special role played by the equipment sectors (e.g. machine tools). As Rosenberg (1976) and Mistral (1983) have pointed out, these sectors shape to a considerable extent the rate and direction of technical progress in the sectors to which they are an input. Even within a static framework, it can be shown formally that the total (direct and indirect) effect of a productivity-increasing rate of technical progress is higher when the latter is generated in the capital-goods sector (Strassman, 1959).

Within each filière, the search activity that characterises innovation and imitation can draw, to different degrees, on the learning and problem-solving experiences of other interrelated sectors. This technological interrelatedness might well be totally independent of the traded input/output relationships: for example, it may concern two similar processes related to commodities that do not enter into each other's production (e.g. chemical and food processing). None the less, clusters of interrelated sectors will also mean clusters of interrelated demand flows. One can also appreciate here the role of domestic demand (final demand and, probably more importantly, demand of reproducible inputs). The structure of input–output, as well as the untraded technological interdependencies of each economy, can be regarded as a huge feedback machine that amplifies, transforms or smooths technological and demand impulses generated in any one part of the economy, transmitting them to the rest of the system in ways which are both sector-specific and country- (or region-) specific.

Other factors affecting the patterns of 'national' technological accumulation relate to the different intensities of stimuli that are none the less common to all countries. Rosenberg (1976) identified three main factors that focus and direct technological advances: technological imbalances between interdependent processes; 'labour-saving'; and sudden, and somewhat exogenous, shocks to accustomed sources of supply. Among these, the effects of wage rates and income distribution upon labour-saving are probably the most controversial. As we mentioned at the beginning of this chapter, there is no formal way of demonstrating the necessity of a labour-saving trend in technical progress by means of a competitive neo-classical model. However, in the evolutionary world described here, there are powerful reasons to assume so.

First, as Rosenberg (1976) himself – and long before him Marx – pointed out, 'machines do not strike'. In more general terms: in societies that are structurally characterised by industrial conflict over income and power distribution, it is plausible to assume a powerful trend towards labour substitution.[33]

Second, there is a straightforward economic argument that is often neglected. Suppose that within the technological–economic trade-offs defined by a given technological paradigm, the cost of a reduction of X per cent in the capital productivity associated with a certain new machine is expected to be identical to the same X per cent reduction in unit labour cost with an alternative new machine. Suppose also for simplicity that the cost of capital per unit of output is identical to the unit cost of labour. Under these circumstances in static terms a 'rational' entrepreneur must be entirely indifferent – on strictly economic grounds – between the two forms of advances. However, there is a fundamental difference between capital inputs and labour inputs. As regards the former, 'bygones are bygones', as Salter (1969) has reminded us: the capital stock is acquired and paid once-and-for-all. Once a machine is acquired, it also determines the labour coefficients of production. For these coefficients, however, the price of labour (the wage rate) might change in the future and there is bound to be uncertainty about its future level. Thus, it is easy to predict that for equivalent costs of alternative labour-saving and capital-saving technical advances and for expectations of non-decreasing (or, *a fortiori*, increasing) wage rates, labour-saving advances will be preferred by risk-averse entrepreneurs. The historical trends towards the increase in real wages, at least in this century, represent a powerful objective basis for these expectations and will reinforce the trend towards labour substitution.

To repeat the point made at the beginning of this sub-section, even though these factors may be common to all countries involved in the manufacturing of a common set of commodities, the *intensity of these stimuli is likely to vary across countries.*

More generally, we suggest that the cumulative nature of innovative activities, jointly with the country-specific nature of incentives and capabilities, explain both (i) the relatively uniform patterns which technical change shows within sectors and across countries, and (ii) the lags/leads among companies and countries. The effect of environment-specific 'focussing factors' will vary according to the position which countries and firms occupy vis-à-vis the existing technological frontier. For example, countries with strong technological accumulation in traditional production technologies are likely to be able, through cumulative processes, to integrate and exploit the new electronics technologies. One should not therefore be surprised by the relatively rapid rate of development, production and use of robots and related technologies in Sweden, Japan and Germany (OECD, 1983): nor, for similar reasons, should one be surprised if Swiss companies, given their traditional strengths in chemical synthesis and fine chemicals, turn out to be strong in product markets emerging from synthetic biotechnology.

Within the framework proposed here, technological leadership is not just a function of innovative responses to the most critical scarcities. The latter or, conversely, the favourable conditions produced by *abundance* of primary inputs, will be only one of the possible factors conducive to technological accumulation. Relative technological latecomers, for example, *can* catch up or overtake the leader(s) through high rates of investment and growth, coupled with heavy expenditure on production engineering, design and development, and R&D: this appears to have been the case in post-war Japan, especially in steel, electronics and automobiles.

More generally, the rates of technological accumulation of each country can be said to be affected by the *intensity* of economic stimuli, which may well touch all countries but to different degrees (e.g. the pressure to substitute labour for machines) or may be limited to any one country (such as the abundance or scarcity of particular inputs); the features of the various clusters of inter-related sectors (filières) defined by strong commodity – and knowledge – flows and technological complementarities; and the conditions and trends in the home markets.

The 'context' conditions are distinguishable from the strictly economic factors in that they relate to a set of technological opportunities, capabilities and stimuli which do not have a proper 'market', but represent the *learning universe* within which economic processes take place. From a dynamic point of view, innovative capabilities, capital accumulation and labour productivity growth are linked in

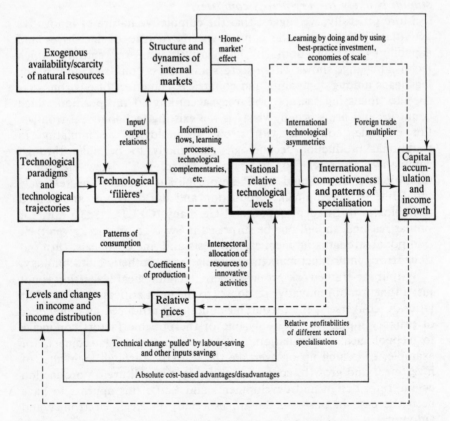

Figure 4.2 National technological levels and their determinants

positive feedbacks whose intensity shows irreducible firm- and country-specificities.

Figure 4.2 summarises some of the major feedback loops which affect the national dynamics of technological accumulation and link it to the overall socio-economic 'tuning' of the system. As argued at greater length elsewhere by one of us (Dosi and Orsenigo, 1988; and Dosi, 1988), country-specific institutional factors have a role of paramount importance in that 'tuning', through their effect on the knowledge accumulated in companies' R&D facilities, universities, etc.; the forms of organisation of labour, commodity and financial markets; the social/cultural determinants of the baskets of consumption, and, of course, direct forms of political intervention related to innovation policies and, more generally, to economic management.[34]

Notes

1. Habakkuk (1962). See also Temin (1966), David (1975).
2. In this respect, cf. the discussion which followed Hicks' hypothesis on the link between relative prices and biases in technical change (Hicks, 1932; Fellner, 1961; Salter, 1969; Olsson, 1982; von Weizsäcker, 1965; Kennedy, 1964; Samuelson, 1965). It must be noted also how strictly the arguments put forward in this discussion depend on highly restrictive assumptions of the 'pure' neo-classical model: see Field (1982), who can demonstrate quite different propositions by simply abandoning some of them and assuming linear production models. He formally shows that higher land abundance in the United States and higher profit/interest rates may have been a powerful stimulus to capital saving and techniques characterised by relatively fast depreciation.
3. We discussed these issues at greater length in Dosi (1984).
4. Cf. *Ibid*.
5. See, in particular, the discussion by Freeman (1974), Part Two.
6. Nelson and Winter (1982).
7. For a thorough argument along these lines, cf. Nelson and Winter (1982).
8. On this point, cf. also Sylos Labini (1984).
9. Among other things, she shows (a) the univocal superiority of 1958 coefficients with respect to 1947 coefficients; and (b) the dominance of labour-saving upon other variations of input coefficients and determinants of structural change. Cf. A. Carter (1970).
10. The property is thoroughly argued by Nelson and Winter (1982). A similar point is argued by Atkinson and Stiglitz (1969), David (1975) and Arthur (1985).
11. See again Nelson and Winter (1982).
12. This is consistent with Sahal's hypothesis that each technology requires an internal 'technological balance'. See Sahal (1981) and (1985).
13. For some evidence on electronics as compared to other sectors, cf. Soete and Dosi (1983).
14. Levin *et al.* (1984), p. 1.

15. *Ibid.*, p. 33.
16. *Ibid.*, p. 20. For detailed discussions of appropriability mechanisms, see also Taylor and Silberston (1973), von Hippel (1978), (1982) and Buer (1982).
17. See Townsend *et al.* (1981), Scherer (1982) and Robson *et al.* (1988). In some countries, R&D in the aerospace sector is of major importance, but most of this is funded by government for the development of weapons.
18. This is not true of software technology which finds major applications in service products, and often originates in service firms.
19. Studies based on counting innovations show that statistics of measured R&D activities grossly underestimate technological activities in firms with fewer than 1,000 employees, the small size of which often does not justify the establishment of a specialised and separately accountable R&D department (Kleinman, 1975; Feinmann and Fuentevilla, 1976; Pavitt *et al.*, 1987). This leads to a considerable underestimation of the volume of innovation activities in machinery and instrumentation.
20. See Levin (1977) for well-documented examples.
21. A. Smith (1937).
22. See, for example, the research of Rumelt (1974) on the growth and diversification of US firms.
23. See the empirical studies of Taylor and Silberston (1973) and Levin *et al.* (1984).
24. Table 4.4 also yields results that are generally consistent with what we know from conventional wisdom and expert opinion about the technological strengths of different countries: for example, the Netherlands in electronics, Switzerland in fine chemicals, Sweden in mechanical engineering, and Germany in chemicals, mechanical engineering and automobiles.
25. This distinction is not original; Atkinson and Stiglitz said as much in 1969, and Stiglitz (1987) recently returned to the subject. It is also observed and analysed by industrial practitioners; see European Industrial Research Management Association (1986).
26. The importance of continuous revision of organisational boundaries is confirmed by a recent study, showing that about 40 per cent of the significant innovations in divisionalised UK firms between 1945 and 1983 have been developed outside the principal three-digit activity of the innovating divisions (see Pavitt, Robson and Townsend, 1989).
27. Cf. Salter (1969).
28. Hayami and Ruttan (1971) and David (1975) have shown that these last two factors account for the technological trends in agriculture, within the United States and in international comparisons.
29. Atkinson and Stiglitz (1969), p. 577; see also Arthur (1985).
30. For a critical review, see Toledano (1978) and for an application to electronic components, Pastre and Toledano (1975). On their long-term dynamics, see Lorenzi, Pastre and Toledano (1980). In the economic literature in English, several illuminating works by Rosenberg show historical examples of such interrelatedness. See Rosenberg (1976), (1982) and also Yan and Ames (1965). Similarly, as regards complementarities in the innovative process, cf. Freeman (1974).
31. The concept is somehow overlapping with Sraffa's 'sub-systems' (Sraffa, 1960) or Pasinetti's 'vertically integrated sectors' (Pasinetti, 1981). The

analytical purpose of the latter two theoretical models, however, is different: while the idea of filière tries to capture the intensity of inter-relations between a whole group of sectors, 'sub-systems' try to disentangle the entire (direct and indirect) input requirements of a final item of demand. The former concept is appropriate to study the 'micro' structure of technological dynamics, while the latter helps in finding a more 'systematic' measure of the overall impact of technical change and links it to macroeconomic dynamics, as in Pasinetti (1981). For an interesting development along these lines, see Momigliano and Siniscalco (1984).

32. Cf. Hirschman (1958).
33. For case analyses related to contemporary history of technology, see also Noble (1977), Coriat (1979) and (1983).
34. The specific pattern of consistency or mismatching between institutional, economic and technological variables in each phase of development is analysed at length by the French 'Regulation school' (see, in particular, Aglietta, 1976; Boyer and Mistral, 1983, 1984). We discuss these issues in relation to macroeconomic theory in Dosi and Orsenigo (1988) and in relation to industrial policies in Dosi (1985). See also Perez (1983).

5

Interfirm and international differences in technology: A theoretical interpretation and some tests

5.1 Introduction: innovation, imitation and diversity

We now have most of the necessary ingredients for the explanation of some of the 'stylised facts' identified in Chapter 3, related to the international distribution of innovative activities and their evolution through time. A first implication is the general existence of *asymmetries*[1] between firms and between countries in technological capabilities, technical coefficients and product performance. In other words, there exist unequivocal differences in product and process technologies, which can be ranked as 'better' or 'worse' independent of any knowledge of relative prices. This property stems from the very nature of technology, organised around technological paradigms and trajectories, and characterised by varying degrees of opportunity, cumulativeness, appropriability, local learning, and (in general) high levels of irreversibility in the pattern of technological advance.

This point can hardly be overstressed. It implies a *theory of production* that is an alternative to the familiar theory based on production possibility sets.[2] In the latter, 'free-good' technologies and uniformity between firms are core hypotheses. Conversely, here, the fundamental hypotheses are firm- *and* technology-specific forms of knowledge and widespread differences between firms. As already mentioned at the end of Section 4.1 in the previous chapter, the theory of technology and production implied by traditional, general equilibrium analysis, now becomes a particular case of our approach, when technical change is non-existent and the industrial world collapses into 'entropy' and uniformity.

A more realistic representation of the world includes the coexistence of 'better' and 'worse' firms, characterised by different technological and economic performances, compared to the technological frontier. Thus, in representing the technological structure of production of an industry at any one time in an n-dimensional space defined by n inputs, one would find a discrete set of points more or less ordered along a ray departing from the origin. The nature of the technological paradigms defines the n inputs and the direction of the ray (the 'trajectory'). The distance between the outer points and the one nearest to the origin defines the technological gaps between firms (that is, the *degree of technological asymmetry* of the industry). From a dynamic point of view, *innovation* and *diffusion* processes are the core mechanisms of change. To be more specific, all innovations, whether related to products or processes, represent an *asymmetry-creating* mechanism which, *ceteris paribus*, increases the technological and performance gaps between firms, and – as we will discuss in the next chapter – between countries. Conversely, diffusion processes can be regarded as *mechanisms of convergence*.

In this evolutionary world, one may of course still draw *ex-post* gradients departing from the points representing best-practice techniques, and call these 'production possibility sets'. However, such a procedure is more likely to obscure the difference between two fundamentally different theories of production: namely the neo-classical based on the idea of substitutability between inputs and the concept of technology as a set of 'blueprints', and the one put forward here, based on irreversibility, a limited number of techniques corresponding to the technological frontier, cumulativeness of technological advances, and changes in techniques as the result of processes of innovation, imitation and diffusion.

Along a relatively well-established technological trajectory, the evolution of an industry can then be described by two dynamic features. First, the changing balance between innovative and imitative efforts in relation to the 'set of basic design parameters, which guides and constrains engineers and innovators in the design of a range of products and their related processes of production', shared 'by all firms in a given technological area'.[3] Second, the competition between specific design configurations, which in Metcalfe's words 'relate to specific products and processes and is to be identified and mapped in terms of the performance characteristics, input coefficients and product attributes which embody a particular constellation of the basic design parameters'.[4] The development of what we called here technological trajectories is then again in Metcalfe's words 'determined over time by three interdependent processes: the selection process, the diffusion process and the inducement process'.[5] In other words, the evolutionary pattern of any one industry will be characterised by both mechanisms of 'Darwinian' selection and 'Lamarckian' learning/adaptation/imitation,[6] intertwined with major discontinuities in the technologies generally associated with the emergence of new technological paradigms.

5.2 Product innovations: innovation, competition, diffusion

Let us first consider an industry where technical change only takes the form of product improvements. For simplicity, suppose that this industry produces a set of products which can be unequivocally ranked by their performance characteristics. In Figure 5.1, it is assumed that the performance features of the product, weighted by the cost of production, can be represented synthetically by the index θ. Thus, technical progress is assumed to be entirely represented by the increase in the θ index. Conversely, the x-axis represents an indexing of the firms in the industry, weighted by their share in production, μ. Suppose that at time $t = 0$ the broken line AA' represents the distribution of firms according to their technological performance (measured by θ). The *degree of asymmetry*, which is an inverse measure of the diffusion in production of best-practice products, will then be related to the slope of the AA' line. For simplicity, we will also assume that the θ index is not only cost-weighted, but that the products of different 'technological vintages' are in a loose sense homogeneous, in such a way that the structure of demand becomes irrelevant: 'backward' producers, if they want to sell, will have to charge prices corresponding to lower profits.

In this stylised representation, firms will continue to innovate and/or imitate in 'best-practice' products. The lines BB' and CC' represent two possible developments over time. BB' shows a trend towards *increasing asymmetry* while the CC' line points towards a *tendency to convergence*. What determines these possible alternative trends? Part of the answer stems from some of the features of technology discussed above:

1. The higher the cumulativeness of technical progress, the higher the probability that the best-practice firms will maintain/increase their lead. Similar considerations apply to the degrees of appropriability of innovations.
2. Conversely, the easier it is to 'watch and learn', do reverse engineering, etc., the greater, other things being equal, the degree of diffusion (cf., for example, the CC' line).
3. The issue of cumulativeness relates clearly to that of *capabilities*: each agent's *present* technological performance is one of the determining factors of its *future* performance.

Moreover:

4. The diffusion of any one vintage of innovations may well never reach 100 per cent, at any one point in time, being superseded by 'better vintages'.
5. More generally, one of the determinants of the degree of asymmetry (which, to repeat, is an inverse measure of the degree of diffusion) is the rate of technical progress. The higher the technological opportunity, other things being equal, the higher the degree of asymmetry.
6. In addition to technological cumulativeness, other factors which are asymmetry-inducing are economies of scale in production/research/marketing; various forms of 'externalities' (for example, a special user–producer relationship enjoyed by virtue of location); and the availability/absence of particular skills, services, etc.
7. The degree of asymmetry is directly linked with *entry* and *mobility barriers* within each industry. Interfirm differences in technological capabilities (among existing producers and between producers and potential entrants) act as structural barriers to intra- and interindustrial mobility. An implication[7] is that, other things being equal, the *level* of profit margins (for the leaders as well as for the industry)

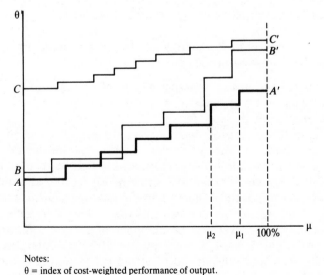

Notes:
θ = index of cost-weighted performance of output.
μ = firm's index in relation to output shares.

Figure 5.1 Technological asymmetries, innovation and diffusion

and the variance in the margins will be a positive function of the degree of technological asymmetry of the industry.

8. From a behavioural point of view, the existence of technological asymmetries will at the same time act as an entry barrier and as an incentive to innovate – by virtue of the differential profits and market-shares that technological upgrading generally yields. Which one of the two effects will prevail, depends again on the nature of the technology (cumulativeness, appropriability, opportunity, etc.) compared with the technological capabilities of 'backward' producers and potential entrants.

To summarise, both the pattern of diffusion in production and the long-term rate of technological change are a function of the interaction between some of the intrinsic features of each technological paradigm and the endogenously generated set of stimuli/constraints which the moving sequence of leads/lags poses to each firm.

5.3   Innovation and diffusion of capital-embodied innovations

Let us now consider the opposite case of a 'user industry' (in the terminology of Section 4.2, a 'supplier-dominated' industry) that utilises, for example, as capital inputs those product innovations which have just been analysed.

The general features of technology and technical change discussed so far suggest the following propositions:

1. All technical progress (and especially product innovations) in the capital goods sector expands the population of *potential adopters* of the innovation in the user sector.
2. The rate of technical progress influences the *actual* rate of diffusion positively, both by improving performance in the capital goods sector and by the fall in the performance-weighted relative price.
3. The size and rate of change of final demand, on the other hand, is likely to exert a positive influence on the *rate of technical change* in the supplying sector (we can call this the 'Schmookler effect').[8]
4. The technological level and requirement of the user industry (its degree of sophistication, the complexity of its products, etc.) will generally exert an 'inducement effect' on the technological level of the supplying industries (see the discussion in Section 4.3).
5. The existence of technological bottlenecks, unsolved technical and organisational 'puzzles' in the user industry, represents, as

Rosenberg (1976) puts it, a powerful 'focussing mechanism' which will influence the technological trajectory of progress in the capital goods industry.

6. The nature of the pattern of technological progress in the innovation-producing sector, on the other hand, will generally exert a powerful influence on the trend in technical progress for users and even on the nature of their products.

Taken together, these considerations allow one to draw a first overview of the mechanisms affecting technological diffusion in user sectors.

First of all, the process of diffusion of an innovation (say, a new machine) in a user sector is, in essence, a process of innovation and technological change for the user itself. In other words, far from being simply a decision of buy-and-use, diffusion will involve a process of *learning, modification of the existing organisation of production* and, often, even a *modification of products.* An important consequence is that the process of adoption of innovations is also affected by the technological capabilities, production strategies, expectations, and forms of productive organisation of the users. One can find here the first reason why the empirical evidence shows relatively slow diffusion patterns over time: quite apart from any kind of 'non-optimising behaviour' or 'information failure' – as sometimes suggested by the literature – the 'pecking order' in the adoption process is influenced by the technological asymmetries in the user sector. Other things being equal, one would therefore expect a rate of diffusion of any one innovation or cluster of new technologies to be higher than the pre-existing technological levels of the users. [9]

The pattern of actual diffusion of 'new machines' and the change over time of the potential adopters in an ideal industry are represented in Figure 5.2. The asymptotic line A moves upward as a function of time and of θ (the same 'technical progress index' as in Figure 5.1, representing here the performance of the machinery). One implication is that the empirically observed pattern of diffusion, say the line OP (Figure 5.2) is now the joint outcome of a movement *along* the diffusion curves and a movement *of* the curves themselves (say from ll' to dd', gg', etc.). [10] Moreover, the *slope* of each of the notional curves ll', dd', etc. (and thus also the slope of the actual OP diffusion curve) will be affected – as mentioned above – by the technological capabilities of the adopters. Even if we assume that the new technology would be *ideally* profitable for all of them, the pattern of asymmetry in their technological capabilities, the degree of uncertainty associated with the new technologies and the particular search strategies of each firm will influence their pace of adoption (Silverberg, Dosi and Orsenigo (1988)).

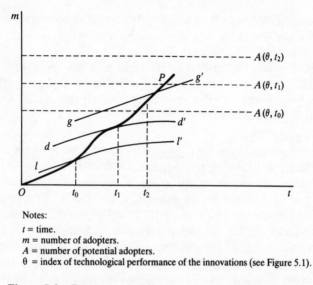

Notes:

t = time.
m = number of adopters.
A = number of potential adopters.
θ = index of technological performance of the innovations (see Figure 5.1).

Figure 5.2 Patterns of diffusion of new technologies in a 'supplier dominated' sector: an illustration

In other words, it may well be that the adoption of any one innovation is economical for a certain population of potential adopters and that all of them *know* about its existence and its main features. However, most of these potential adopters may well not utilise the innovation for the simple reason that they do not have the technological/organisational capabilities for doing so. To put it simply, they do not adopt because they do not know *how* to.

In turn, the pattern of diffusion shapes the performance of each firm in the sector. Figure 5.3 illustrates such a case. The pattern of adoption of the new technologies determines the pattern of asymmetry in the industry concerned, as expressed here by production cost differentials. Through time, the rate of *best-practice* technical change (as expressed by the movement down from A' to B', C', etc., in Figure 5.3) jointly with the *pattern of diffusion* of new technologies (reflected in the slope of the lines AA', BB', CC', etc.) determines the moving sequence of asymmetries in the performance of firms. Some of the formal aspects of this process are discussed elsewhere (Soete and Turner, 1984). Suffice it to suggest here a few implications of this approach. First, it is interesting to observe how interfirm (and, by extension, international) asymmetries play a double role. *Asymmetries* in *capabilities* provide an explanation for the differentiated pattern of diffusion. Correspondingly, *asymmetries* in the *degrees* of *diffusion* determine differentiated perform-

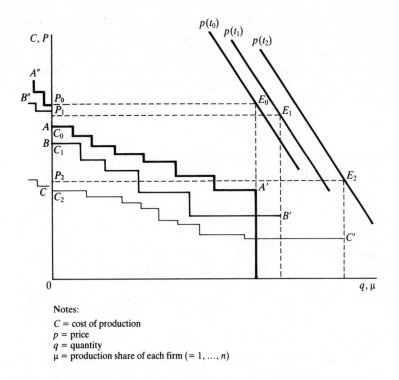

Notes:

C = cost of production
p = price
q = quantity
μ = production share of each firm ($= 1, ..., n$)

Figure 5.3 Diffusion of process innovations and technological asymmetries

ances (as shown by the slope of the *AA'*, *BB'*, *CC'* lines, in Figure 5.3). Second, by extending the analysis to would-be entrants, it is easy to see how the pattern of asymmetry in the adoption of new technologies provides the structural foundation for both *entry* and *mobility barriers*, and thus the structural ground for an explanation of the variance in profitability between firms (compare, for example, in Figure 5.3 the gross profit margin of the 'leader', at $t = 0$, equal to the segment $E_0 A'$, with that of the inframarginal firm, equal to the segment $P_0 C_0$). A corollary to this is that, once given any pricing rule, the higher the asymmetry in diffusion (i.e. the higher the slope of the lines *A"AA'*, *B"BB'*, etc.), the steeper the 'profitability gap' between leaders and followers. Conversely, the neo-classical conditions of 'pure competition' and identity between firms can be considered only when technical progress tends to stop and diffusion reaches its asymptotic limit.

Finally, these evolutionary patterns of change bring to the forefront two endogenously determined mechanisms of diffusion (cf. Iwai, 1981;

Nelson and Winter, 1982): the increase in the number of the actual adopters within the population of potential ones, and the increase in the relative size (and thus market share) of the fastest adopters. It is clear that the relative balance between these two processes at the national, and even more so at the international, level will shape the trend in industrial *concentration*.[11]

5.4   Choice of techniques, technical progress and irreversibility

A synthetic way of representing the dynamics of evolving industries is through movements of both the best-practice and the average wage–profit frontiers associated with the various techniques (Soete and Turner, 1984). This applies to intranational interfirm changes in techniques as well as to international changes. It is important to explore the likely trends in the wage–profit frontiers associated with the features of innovation/diffusion discussed so far. Let us recall the following properties of a model characterised by reproducible capital goods and non-decreasing returns in production:[12]

1. The choice of techniques is not influenced by variations in the wage rate as long as the rate of profit does not change.
2. Conversely, *international* differences in wage rates do not influence the choice of techniques, if every country is characterised by an identical rate of profit and has access to the same techniques.[13]
3. Even when the relationship between wages and profits matters, the latter influence the choice of techniques only in so far as they influence the relative price of machines. In other words, it is the ratio between the price of labour and the price of machines which is the relevant one.[14] As regards the price of machines, one may reasonably assume an approximately unique international price.

In addition to these theoretical properties, let us also make explicit the following hypotheses, consistent with some of the 'stylised facts' about technical change summarised in Chapter 3:

4. From an empirical point of view, international differences in the profit rates appear in any case to be more limited than international differences in wage rates.
5. One of the fundamental characteristics of the technological trajectories of progress is the trend towards mechanisation/automation of production and the substitution of 'machines' for labour.
6. The same process occurs both in the use and the manufacture of

the 'machines' themselves. Moreover, product innovations in the 'machine' sector tend to increase their productive capacity in physical terms continuously. Thus, labour-saving in the machine-producing sector represents capital-saving in all sectors using machines (including, of course, the machine sector itself).

7. As already mentioned above, any technical 'state-of-the-art' is likely to be associated with one or very few techniques; in other words, instead of the traditional continuous isoquants, there are likely to be only groups of very few points clustered near each other. Conversely, these groups, corresponding to different generations of technological innovations, are likely to be roughly ordered along a ray starting from the origin of the axes (cf. Figure 4.1).

Taken together, these assumptions have the following important consequences:

1. The nature of technical progress and the patterns of income distribution are such that, in general, capital/output ratios are *roughly* constant, or at least do not exhibit any strong trend, both over time and across countries. [15]

2. Technical progress generally brings about techniques showing *superior* wage–profit frontiers, irrespective of relative prices.

These properties are illustrated in Figures 5.4 and 5.5. Harrod neutrality of technical progress implies that increasing mechanisation of production (as expressed by increasing capital/labour ratios, in Figure 5.4) corresponds to proportional increases in labour productivity, with constant

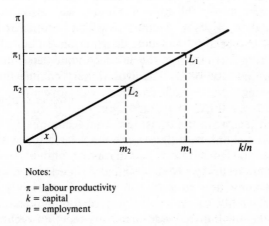

Notes:

π = labour productivity
k = capital
n = employment

Figure 5.4 Labour productivity and mechanisation/automation of production

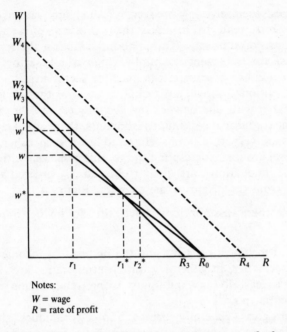

Notes:
W = wage
R = rate of profit

Figure 5.5 Technical progress and wage–profit frontiers

capital/output ratios. Moreover, 'new' techniques are unequivocally superior to 'old' ones.[16] Suppose technical progress leads to a new (more mechanised) technique ($m_1 > m_2$) yielding a higher labour productivity ($\pi_1 > \pi_2$); at the same time, the new technique will also define a wage–profit frontier (e.g. W_2R_0 in Figure 5.5) which is superior to the old one (e.g. W_1R_0), irrespective of income distribution. In our illustration, for any given profit rate (e.g. r_1), the new technique determines the wage rate ($w' > w$), and *vice versa*. The evolutionary changes in both best-practice and average wage–profit frontiers, will normally take the form of a transition from W_1R_0 to W_2R_0 or, even, to W_4R_4.[17] In such cases, the retardation factors in the transition from technique 1 to technique 2 will have a crucial link with those variables related to capability, learning, knowledge and uncertainty, as discussed above. In other words, even if the new technique is *economically* superior it may well be that firms do not know how to master it, exploit it efficiently or do not have the necessary skills to run it and/or provide maintenance. In our view, this also lies behind the widespread existence of technology gaps in production processes among OECD countries and, even more so, among all industrialising countries.

Obviously, one cannot, *a priori*, rule out cases such as those depicted by technique W_3R_3 (Figure 5.5), whereby the new technique is 'superior' only for high wages. We would maintain, though, that, even when this occurs, processes of innovation in capital-goods production, learning-by-doing and changes in relative prices will tend to push the *WR*-line outwards, thus making 'irreversible' the transition to the new technology.

Consider now this same process of technical change from the point of view of intersectoral technology flows. Suppose there are two sectors, one producing a final good and the second producing machines – for itself and for the consumption sector. Suppose also that a change in relative prices induces a demand for 'new' machines so as to save labour. Recalling Figure 4.1, imagine that product innovations in the machine sector yield new techniques for the consumption sector represented by a point somewhere between *E* and *F*. In other words, technical progress is labour-saving and capital-using in the Harrod sense. However, if the new machines are also adopted in the machine-producing sector, this will reduce the unit price of machines, thus reducing correspondingly the capital/output ratio in the machine-using sector.

Whenever the rates of technical progress in the two sectors do differ, because the rate of product and process innovation in the input-producing sectors is higher, as for instance in the case of microelectronics, our hypothesis on the univocal superiority of new techniques will apply even more strongly. In this case, technical progress is such that labour productivity will increase, while the capital/output ratios may even fall.[18] The wage–profit frontier of the new techniques is no longer determined by a clockwise rotation of the old one around an unchanged maximum rate of profit, but by an outward movement which may also increase the maximum rate of profit corresponding to the intersection of the wage–profit frontier with the *x*-axis (e.g. a movement from W_1R_0 to W_4R_4, in Figure 5.5).

Conversely, suppose that two different techniques (say, W_1R_0 and W_2R_0 in Figure 5.5) belong to two different countries. At any given time, for an identical profit rate, the less advanced country has an 'inferior' technique, characterised by lower mechanisation, lower productivity, lower wage rates and an identical capital/output ratio. The 'stylised facts' discussed above tend to suggest that this might well be the *general case*.

The process of development and catching-up acquires, in this framework, an unequivocal meaning: it is the process of diffusion of strictly superior techniques. At the same time, though, the less advanced country may well find a competitive advantage in the commodity to which the two techniques refer, whenever wage rate differentials more than compensate for the absolute technological advantage of the more advanced country.[19]

This argument on the irreversibility of technical change and the unequivocal inferiority/superiority of techniques, it should be stressed again, does not imply any irrelevance of relative prices.

First, changes in relative prices might be important focussing and triggering mechanisms which stimulate innovation (see Section 4.1). Second, even when a new technique is unequivocally superior to another one, the *differential* profitability of adopting it (and thus the incentive to do so) will still bear a relationship with income distribution and relative prices under conditions of 'bounded rationality'. Take, for example, techniques W_2R_0 and W_1R_0 in Figure 5.5. Other things being equal, the profitability gain of adopting the better one is proportionally much greater for a country which happens to have a wage rate, say at w, than for a country with a wage rate at w^*. We shall return to this point when we try to explain the different patterns of technological accumulation in the different OECD countries.

5.5 Evolutionary patterns of industrial change

The two stylised models of innovation and diffusion of 'products' and 'processes' discussed so far are obviously extreme 'ideal types': as shown earlier, one observes in reality different combinations of product and process innovations, different balances between embodied and disembodied technical progress, different weights of internally generated innovations as opposed to innovations acquired from other industries and/or firms, etc.

However, all processes of innovation *and* diffusion are *search processes*: linked to the opportunities of technological advance – whether generated endogenously within the firm, opened up by advances in pure science achieved in non-profit institutions, or generated in other industrial sectors – driven by the perspective of (partial) appropriation of the economic benefits, and based on the specific (and differentiated) technical and organisational capabilities of each firm.

However, there are important specificities of the innovation/diffusion processes, which stem from the following:

(a) the knowledge base on which technical advances can draw;
(b) the nature of the technology and the techno-economic dimensions of progress;
(c) the intersectoral distribution of both technological opportunities and search capabilities;

(d) the sources, means, and degrees of appropriability;
(e) the nature of the interactions between users and producers of innovations (whenever they are different economic agents) and the characteristics of the product markets.

Clearly, the evolutionary world described here is characterised by continuous disequilibrium, in a static allocative sense. A wide range of more and less efficient methods of production continuously coexist within each industry (within each national industry and even more so within world industry). Even in a hypothetically closed but evolving economy:

> ... not only the fittest but also the second, third, fourth ... indeed a whole range of less fit will survive in the long run. The forces of economic selection working through the differential growth rates among firms with different unit costs is constantly outwitted by the firms' imitation activities and intermittently disrupted by the firms' innovation activities.[20]

Only under particular circumstances, will

> the processes of growth, imitation and innovation interact with each other and work ... to maintain the relative structure of industry's state of technology in a statistically balanced form in the long run.[21]

We must wonder whether there are particular *paths* which any one particular industry will follow. That is, whether there are 'evolutionary equilibria', whereby the balance between innovative mechanisms and diffusion mechanisms will keep a relatively ordered pattern of transformation of the industry.[22]

A simple example of such evolutionary equilibria is discussed in Nelson (1985). Suppose there are two firms (or groups of firms): an innovative one and an imitative one. Suppose also that all 'Schumpeterian behaviours' (related to innovation and imitation) are expressed by the R&D efforts of the firms. Following Nelson, $(R/S)_{IN}$ is the ratio of R&D to Sales; P is the price of output; C_{IN} are the total costs for the innovator(s); $\Delta A/A$ is the total cost-saving stemming from innovative activities; L is the time lag after which the imitator can learn from the innovator's advances, with an R&D cost which is a fraction (λ) of the original innovator's cost. In addition to Nelson, let us add the possibility of differential profits of the innovator (ψ), which we assume to be linear to the degree of asymmetry (i.e. the gap in technological capabilities) between the two groups of firms. Then an 'evolutionary equilibrium' will be defined by the condition:

$$\psi\left[\left(\frac{R}{S}\right)_{IN} \cdot P + C_{IN}\right] = \lambda\left(\frac{R}{S}\right)_{IN} \cdot P + \left(1 + \frac{\Delta A}{A} \cdot L\right)C_{IN} \quad (5.1)$$

This condition states, for example, that an industry will not be in 'evolutionary equilibrium' if the reward of imitation is in excess of that of innovation, when compounded by the maximum differential profitability that the innovator can enjoy due to the differential capabilities it embodies, etc. One can find a straightforward link with the features of technology discussed earlier on: the values of the parameters λ and L (the relative cost of imitation and the lag of the imitator, respectively) are functions of the degrees of appropriability and cumulativeness of technological advances; (R/S) and $(\Delta A/A)$ can be taken to measure the technological opportunities and the degrees to which they are exploited via formalised R&D.[23] In the long term, innovative and imitative processes also change the values of the parameters, and with that also the technology gaps between leaders and followers (that is, the degree of asymmetry implied by each 'evolutionary equilibrium'), the opportunities of advance and the degrees to which they are exploited by the economic agents. Admittedly, in the interpretation of trade patterns presented here and despite our emphasis on oligopolistic forms of market organisation and widespread product differentiation, we almost entirely neglect any explicit account of purposeful *'strategic'* interactions among different firms on the world market. Our analysis is, however, quite complementary to investigations such as Cantwell's (1989) focussing on the dynamic links between firm-specific characteristics of multinational enterprises, national/regional context conditions and technological learning. In any case, the perspective of this book rests on the conjecture that, *in a first approximation*, diverse national constraints and opportunities shape technological and economic performances of firms irrespective of any detailed reconstruction of their particular strategic behaviours.

5.6   International patterns of evolution

The analysis developed so far finds a direct application not only to the structure and evolution of industries within each country, but also to the differences between countries in technology and economic performance, which were identified among the main 'stylised facts' of Chapter 3.

If technical progress is cumulative not only at the company level, but also at the country level, the relative advantage of one country vis-à-vis others does not stem from any 'original endowment' but from differential technological knowledge, experience, etc., which are reproduced through time. In many ways, these differential advantages will be jointly produced with the production of the commodities themselves. From such a perspective, one can easily point to the possibility of the existence of 'virtuous circles' and 'vicious circles' in the patterns of international technological advantages/disadvantages.

Cumulative processes have a technological dimension (the nature of the technological trajectories), an economic one (the profitability signals which stem from technological asymmetries between firms, sectors and countries, and – as we will see in Chapter 6 – may be re-enforced by the trends in international specialisation), and, finally, a behavioural one (the different search and learning capability, different efficiency and different incentives of firms placed in different positions vis-à-vis the technological frontier and facing different relative profitability patterns).

While the positive feedbacks associated with virtuous circles imply that, other things being equal, 'success breeds success', there is a fundamental way in which 'past success constrains the future'. Past technological success is indeed also embodied in the stock of existing capital equipment, the particular structure of skills and the behavioural commitments of past successful firms to what may have become old technologies.

These factors are likely to become important during the process of substitution of a new technological paradigm to an old (and competing) one. In these circumstances, a leadership in the old paradigm may be (although it is not always) an obstacle to a swift diffusion of the new one, especially owing to the interplay between the constraint posed by the old capital stock to a readjustment of productive activities and the behavioural trends in 'old' companies which may embody differential expertise and enjoy high market shares in 'old' technologies. In some previous work, one of us (Soete 1981b, 1985) has stressed how the change in international technological leadership is generally associated with the transition from one fundamental paradigm to another. This is a convergence mechanism, which might also apply to interfirm diffusion and competition in the domestic context.

More generally, there are a number of factors which tend to induce *convergence* and the *international* diffusion of technology.[24] Among these are the following:

(a) the 'free' international diffusion of codified scientific and techno-logical knowledge (e.g. publications, qualified scientists, engineers and technicians, etc.);
(b) traded transfers of technology (licensing, transfer of know-how, etc.);
(c) processes of technological imitation (e.g. reverse engineering) by late-coming companies and countries (both 'spontaneous' and government-induced processes of imitation);[25]
(d) direct foreign investment in 'late-coming' countries, by companies

which own – among their company-specific advantages – differential technological capabilities;

(e) international trade in capital goods and intermediate components.

In general, there appear to be three factors that encourage international diffusion of both technology and production, namely international differences in variable costs (primarily international differences in wage rates); 'specificity' of local markets (including everything which goes under the heading of 'market imperfections', such as the advantage enjoyed by local manufacturing due to: proximity-to-the-market; forms of government intervention; tariff and non-tariff barriers; transport costs; etc.); and the autonomous efforts in the catching-up countries at technological accumulation (reflected in investments, indigenous R&D efforts, the development of skills, improvements in organisational sophistication and complexity).

It must be stressed that these diffusion mechanisms are highly complementary. As Sahal puts it,

> ... a characteristic feature of technical know-how is its lack of permeability: it is often acquired in bits and pieces, and is fractioned to a far greater extent than is commonly believed.
>
> Moreover, advances in technical know-how generally depend on accumulation of *hands-on experience* in the design and production activities. Thus, the relevance of technological learning is often bounded by a particular system of doing. It is context-dependent. Unlike pure scientific knowledge, which is freely available to all, technical know-how is largely product and plant specific ... . Technology transfer can never be a total substitute for independent R&D activity ... the development and transfer of technology ought to be regarded as a part and parcel of the innovative activity from the very beginning.[26]

A synthetic way of summarising the forces of innovation and diffusion in the international context consists of rewriting equation (5.1) so as to take into account explicitly the international differences in wage rates (call these proportional differences ω). Moreover, for simplicity, call the R&D intensity of the industry,

$$N = \left(\frac{R}{S}\right)_{IN} \cdot P$$

Thus:

$$\omega \cdot g = \frac{(\psi - \lambda)N + \psi C_{IN}}{C_{IN}} \tag{5.2}$$

The technology gap of the imitative companies (country) is $g = (1 + \Delta A / A \cdot L)$, while their cost (i.e. wage) advantage, at current exchange rates, is expressed by ω.

Equation (5.2) implies a relationship between technology and wage gaps as illustrated in Figure 5.6. The interpretation is straightforward: at the international level, an 'evolutionary equilibrium' will exist whenever the differential cost of innovating first (as opposed to imitating) and the differential profits allowed by the differential technological capabilities (summarised by $\psi - \lambda$) just corresponds to the technology gap vis-à-vis the imitators, discounted by the cost (= wage) advantage of the latter.

Suppose we start from the 'evolutionary equilibrium' defined by the pair (ω_1, g_1). All improvements in the technological capabilities of the imitative company (country) will decrease the actual gap. Suppose also that the wage gap shrinks. The company will then follow, say, the trajectory t_1. On the other hand, the direction and speed of the shift in the locus of the evolutionary equilibrium (say to $g''g''$ or to $g'g'$) will depend on the evolution of the conditions of appropriability (expressed by λ) and of the technological opportunities (which link N and $\Delta A/A$).

It can be easily seen that the evolution over time of the *relative competitiveness* between the two groups of companies (i.e., in an extreme simplification, the two countries) depends on the pace of change of the technological capabilities and the wage conditions relative to the pace of change of the structural parameters defining the conditions of opportunity and appropriability of the technology. For example, every loss in opportunity makes any given 'lead' more expensive to achieve, and thus

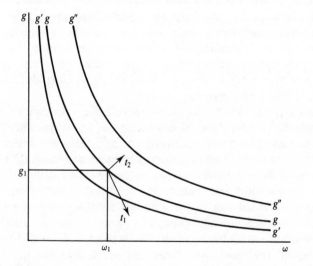

Figure 5.6 Technology gaps and wage gaps in 'evolutionary equilibria'

shifts the locus of evolutionary equilibria to the top right (say to $g''g''$): being an imitator 'costs less' in terms of wage gaps. Conversely, any increase in appropriability makes imitation more difficult and thus shifts the gg line to the bottom left, say to $g'g'$. Finally, the higher the differential profitability that the innovator tries to achieve (as expressed by ψ), the easier it is for the imitator to carve a niche in the international market.[27]

In general, in this interpretation the international patterns and dynamics of competitive advantages/disadvantages entail underlying microeconomic processes of innovation/imitation/diffusion which, in turn, are shaped by the characteristics (e.g. opportunity, appropriability, knowledge base, etc.) of each technology and by country-specific variables (wage rates, market features, public policies affecting technological capabilities and market signals, etc.).

5.7 What is left of product cycles?

From this perspective, one can also see that product-cycle accounts of the evolution of technological and productive advantages over time are only a *particular case* of a wide range of possible patterns.

The product cycle, as proposed by Vernon (1966), and later elaborated by Abernathy and Utterback (1975), implicitly assumes that processes of technological accumulation over time are the same for all product groups. In its appealing simplicity, it is not surprising that the product-cycle concept cannot help to explain and predict firm and country patterns of innovative activities, for two sets of reasons.

First, patterns of technological opportunity, appropriability, and accumulation of innovative activities in firms are not necessarily the same over every product life cycle (see Walker, 1979, Gort and Klepper, 1982 and Gort and Konakayama, 1982).

Second, even if the typical product-lifecycle S-curves can be empirically demonstrated in the national production of broad product classes such as steel, bulk chemicals or consumer durables, these may only reflect the changing degrees of appropriability and/or changing demand elasticities over different ranges of per capita income, rather than the autonomous acceleration and then deceleration of product innovation. Furthermore, as pointed out in some recent studies, when supposedly technologically mature product groups such as colour television and automobile manufacturers began in the 1960s to shift their locus of production to Japan, the result was a marked acceleration in the rate of product and process innovation (Peck and Wilson, 1982; Altshuler *et al.*, 1984).

Conversely, the model presented here can generate quite diverse patterns of international location of innovation and production, according to the nature of the various technologies and the features of technological accumulation. We will now turn to the interpretation of possible regularities in the levels and changes of national technological advantages/disadvantages, either in the form of different production efficiencies or in the form of different capabilities of generating new products.

5.8   Innovativeness, capital accumulation, labour productivities: intersectoral and international differences

Sectoral/technological specificities also affect the link between the leads and lags in innovativeness, the degree of capital accumulation, and labour productivity. As is well known, there is a great deal of literature and a highly controversial debate on the 'sources of productivity growth', which we cannot tackle here. Suffice it to present apparent empirical regularities, based on, admittedly crude, indicators and estimates which, however, appear broadly consistent with other more detailed investigations (cf. Fagerberg, 1987; Patel and Soete, 1987).

In Table 5.1 a summary is presented of the results of the econometric estimates obtained through linear and log-linear[28] regression analysis of the form:

$$\pi = \alpha_1 + \beta_1 P + \mu_1 \tag{5.3}$$

$$\pi = \alpha_2 + \beta_2 P + \sigma_2 M + \mu_2 \tag{5.4}$$

$$\pi = \alpha_3 + \sigma_3 M + \mu_3 \tag{5.5}$$

$$\pi = \alpha_4 + \beta_4 M + \tau_4 S + \mu_4 \tag{5.6}$$

$$\pi = \alpha_5 + \tau_5 S + \mu_5 \tag{5.7}$$

where π is labour productivity (value added per employee at constant prices and exchange rates), P is the degree of technological innovativeness (approximated here by the cumulative number of patents registered by each country in the United States over the period 1963–77), M is the degree of mechanisation of production (approximated by the investment/labour ratio), S is capital intensity of production (approximated by the investment/output ratio), and the μs are the error terms. The estimates were run on a cross-country (OECD) basis for some thirty-nine industrial sectors.

The desire to undertake a relatively disaggregated analysis forced one

Table 5.1 Labour productivities, innovativeness, capital intensities: the significant results

	Degrees of innovativeness (patents per head) (a)	Degrees of mechanisation (investment/labour ratios) (b)	Capital intensity (investment/output ratios) (c)	Best fit Adj. $R^2 > 0.50$ $F > 5$ (d)
1. Food products	+	++		*
2. Textile products	++	++		*
3. Industrial organic chemicals	+			
4. Inorganic chemicals	+	++	−	
5. Plastic and synthetic resins	++	++	−	*
6. Agricultural chemicals	+	++		
7. Soap, detergents, cleaning toilet preparation				
8. Paint, varnishes, lacquers and allied products		++		
9. Miscellaneous chemicals	++	++	−	*
10. Drugs				*
11. Rubber and miscellaneous plastic products	++	+++		*
12. Stone, clay and glass	++	+++		*
13. Ferrous metals	++	+++	−	*
14. Non-ferrous metals	++	+++	−	*
15. Fabricated metal products	+	++	+	*
16. Engines and turbines			−	
17. Farm and garden machinery and equipment	++	++		*
18. Construction, mining, material				*
19. Metal working machinery	+	+		*
20. Office, computing and accounting machinery	+		−	*
21. Special industrial machinery	+	+		*
22. General industrial machinery	++	+		*
23. Refrigeration and service machinery	+	+		*

Sector					
24. Miscellaneous (non-electrical machinery)	+				*
25. Electrical transmission and distribution equipment	++	++			*
26. Electrical industrial apparatus	++ / ++	++			*
27. Household appliances					
28. Electrical lighting and wiring equipment	++	++		−	
29. Miscellaneous electrical equipment	++	++		−	
30. Radio and television receiving equipment	++	++			*
31. Electronics components and communication equipment	++	++			
32. Motor vehicles and parts	++	++			* *
33. Ships and boats	+	−			
34. Railroad equipment	++	++			
35. Motorcycles, bicycles					
36. Miscellaneous transport equipment	++	++		−	
37. Missiles, space vehicles	++				
38. Aircraft and parts	++				*
39. Professional and scientific instruments	++	++			*

Notes:

1. The dependent variable is always labour productivity (i.e. value-added per employee).

2. Column (d) reports all cases (*) whereby the R^2, adjusted for the degrees of freedom, is greater than 0.50 and the F statistics are greater than 5 in at least one of the sectoral estimates.

3. The dependent variables have been tested against (a), (b) and (c) in simple regression and against (a) and (b) and, (a) and (c). Relatively high multicollinearity prevented the joint use of (b) and (c).

4. The symbols stand as follows:
   One sign (e.g. − or +): the variable is significant at 10% or more in at least one estimate with positive (+) negative (−) sign.
   Two signs (e.g. − − or + +): the variable is always significant at 10% or more in all attempted estimates.
   Note that nowhere did different estimates yield results with opposite signs and both significant signs within the same sector. With only 4 exceptions, the cases corresponding to one sign only (− or +) represent a variable which was significant in simple regression estimates and stopped being so with multiple regression analysis.

5. Sector 11 (petroleum and coal products) has been omitted due to the low reliability of productivity data.

6. For the sources of the variable used, cf. Appendix, Chapter 6.

to use 'heroic' proxies for both the capital/output and capital/labour ratios: constrained by the available data we had to use a two-year average in the investment/output and investment/labour ratios. (For more details on the data used, see Appendix to Chapter 6).

These 'heroic' approximations undoubtedly introduce much imprecision into the estimates. However, there is no reason to believe that a bias will have been introduced. The approximations by themselves will in any case not determine the nature of the results.

The analysis is econometrically very simple and does not amount to a comprehensive test of the various causal relationships of the model discussed in the preceding section. We would argue, however, that the results fulfil the weaker requirement of consistency with the theoretical framework proposed above.[29] The degrees of mechanisation and automation of production appear to be powerful factors in determining the levels of labour productivity. Moreover, productivity also appears to be influenced by our approximation of technological innovativeness which might not be directly embodied into physical equipment (if it is, it would also be capital-saving in addition to being labour-saving).

Three 'reasonable' interpretations can be drawn from the results.

First, the country-specific and sector-specific levels of technological innovativeness, which, at least in the short term, are statistically independent of the patterns of capital accumulation,[30] have a significant impact upon productivity levels within each sector. This result illustrates the broad complementarity between disembodied and embodied forms of technological progress and points to the importance of both in explaining international differences in levels of labour productivities. This applies to the majority of industrial sectors, irrespective of their average capital intensity.

Second, both patterns of accumulation and increasing mechanisation of the productive processes appear to be characterised by the absence of any capital-using bias (in the Harrod sense, i.e. in terms of capital/output ratios). In other words, technical progress appears to correspond broadly to an assumption of 'neutrality'. The relationship between labour productivity and the proxy for the capital/output ratio, when significant, always appears to have a negative sign, either when used alone or in conjunction with the innovativeness variable. This result might be interpreted as pointing to some of the higher capital-saving capabilities of the most high-technology countries. The pattern of technical progress is such that higher degrees of automation and higher capital/labour ratios are also likely to be associated with innovations in capital equipment and processes, thus increasing the physical productivity of the equipment and lowering its unit costs. In other words, countries showing the highest labour productivity, which one may expect to also be the most advanced and the most capital 'endowed' countries, will also be those which show the lower capital intensity (in terms of output).

One could consider this to be the domestic counterpart of the so-called Leontief 'paradox': the most advanced countries are the most efficient not only in the use of labour but also in the use of capital. This result, as Pasinetti (1981) has observed no longer amounts to a 'paradox', as soon as one takes into account the dominant characteristics of *learning and progress* in modern economies. However, the evidence presented in Table 5.1 can also be interpreted as highlighting some of the fundamental features of the appropriation and irreversibility of technological advance, as discussed in the preceding section. With regard to irreversibility, it is obvious that any technique with both a higher labour productivity and a lower capital/output ratio is a 'superior' one. If such a technique is not adopted 'world-wide', this is because the technology is not a free good, but is often privately appropriated within individual economic units (possibly within individual countries) and requires complex processes of learning.

Third, the degree of mechanisation of production appears to be particularly important in some of the 'scale-intensive' and science-based sectors, such as most of the chemical sectors, food, construction materials, radio and TV equipment, and motor vehicles.

Innovativeness, as measured here, captures two phenomena: process innovations and product innovations, appearing in different relative proportions in the different sectors. One may reasonably expect the former to influence labour productivity *directly*. Conversely, new products are likely to show, if anything, a direct impact on market performance, while retaining an indirect or even ambiguous effect upon productivity.[31] Furthermore, on the grounds of the sectoral taxonomy set out above, one may expect a differentiated impact of technical change on productivity depending on the nature of innovations (product vs. process), but also on the sectors of origin and use. More specifically, and as illustrated in the results reported in Table 5.1, the technology variable is likely to perform well in those sectors where it can be expected to take the form mainly of process innovations, either generated within the sector or purchased from other sectors (such as in food products, textiles, stone, clay and glass, non-ferrous metals, etc.). The technology variable, on the other hand, is likely to perform poorly when it takes, essentially, the form of 'pure' product innovations, such as in the drug industry. Finally, within the group of sectors belonging to non-electrical and electrical engineering, innovativeness will have a statistically significant impact, as illustrated in the results, because product innovations and process innovations are overlapping in so far as 'new machines' and 'new components' will also be used within the sectors from which they originated.

These broad results are more or less complementary to other analyses on the relationship between R&D expenditures and productivity. These studies generally point to the positive impact of direct R&D and total R&D (direct plus indirect via input-output flows) upon productivity changes.[32]

With respect to the analysis of trade flows carried out in the following chapter, the results reported here illustrate the determinants of one source of *absolute advantage*, i.e. international productivity differentials, stemming from both 'disembodied' technological progress and capital accumulation. Of course, the dynamics of these lags and leads in production efficiency, together with the others more directly related to product innovations, depend on the rates at which the various domestic companies from any one country learn, innovate, imitate, and, in turn influence the evolution of international competitiveness, by sector and by country. We shall now turn to these issues.

Notes

1. We discussed this concept at length in Dosi (1984).
2. For a similar argument, see Winter (1982).
3. Metcalfe (1985), p. 7.
4. *Ibid.*, p. 7.
5. *Ibid.*, p. 9.
6. For a thorough formalisation of these processes, cf. Nelson and Winter (1982), Winter (1984), Iwai (1981).
7. For more details see Dosi (1984).
8. Cf. Schmookler (1966).
9. For an illustration of this argument in relation to the diffusion of microelectronics in 'downstream' sectors, cf. Pavitt (1984c), and for a model of this process, Silverberg, Dosi and Orsenigo (1988).
10. On this point see also Metcalfe (1985).
11. The relative balance between these two mechanisms of innovation and diffusion clearly depends also on the nature of technological paradigms, on the degrees of appropriability and cumulativeness of technological advances, etc. For a discussion of the implications of different 'technological regimes', see Winter (1984).
12. Points (1) and (2) which follow are discussed in more detail by Pasinetti (1981).
13. Cf. *ibid.* pages 195–7. Note that by 'identical techniques', one also means the import content associated with each of them and the related terms of trade.
14. This is thoroughly argued by Sylos Labini (1982) and (1983–4).
15. Over the post-War period and with the exception of electronics, there seems to be some evidence of a capital-using bias of the rate of technical

change, with the 'real', physical capital/output ratio increasing in most sectors (see Soete and Dosi, 1983, for more details). However, relative prices are likely to move in the opposite direction, since we may expect gross margins to increase in sectors whose 'physical' capital intensity increases. Thus, we would probably find relatively smaller changes in the capital/output ratio at *current* prices, which is the relevant indicator in our discussion here. For some comparative evidence on capital/output ratios, cf. OECD (1983) and (1984). These works show a relatively small variation over the last twenty years, with some increase after 1973 for the United States, United Kingdom, France, Canada and a fall in Germany and Japan. After adjusting for capacity utilisation and accelerated scrapping, however, that increase − it is suggested − is likely to disappear (OECD (1983a), pp. 65–6).

16. For a discussion of all the notional possibilities in the choice and change in techniques, see Schefold (1976) and (1979). For an analysis of the micro and 'macro' measures of technical progress, cf. Soete and Turner (1984) and, for a discussion of the measurements of the possible biases in technical change, cf. Steedman (1985).

17. In this case, technical progress is not only labour-saving, but also strictly capital-saving. The transition to either W_2R_0 or W_4R_4 is strictly consistent with the 'innovative search rules' discussed earlier on (cf. Section 4.1). Formally, these 'search rules' fulfil the conditions for the Okishio theorem to hold (cf. Okishio, 1961; Bowles, 1981): the new techniques will generally imply a straightforward saving of some inputs without a compensating increase in others, so that, the theorem shows, even after allowing for the appropriate changes in relative prices, the new techniques will be associated with a higher profit rate, once given the wage rate, or vice versa.

18. For more general formalised analyses of technical change, see Pasinetti (1981). See also Le Bas (1982), Spaventa (1970) and Opocher (1986).

19. Identical conclusions can be drawn from Pasinetti's model: see Pasinetti (1981), Chapter IX.

20. Iwai (1981), Part I, p. 26.

21. *Ibid.*, pp. 26–8.

22. This issue is discussed at greater length in Dosi and Orsenigo (1986).

23. For detailed empirical research on the innovative processes in Italy, showing, among other things, that the higher the technological opportunity, the higher is its exploitation through *formal internalised* R&D (as opposed to other mechanisms of production of innovation), see Momigliano (1985).

24. More detailed discussions of the convergency/divergence issue, by the authors, can be found in Pavitt (1979) and (1980), Soete (1982) and (1985), Metcalfe and Soete (1984).

25. By 'late-coming' companies/countries here we do not only refer to LDCs, but also to developed countries (and NICs) which happen to lag behind the technological frontier on any particular technological trajectory.

26. Sahal (1982), pp. 138–9.

27. A case of interest is that situation whereby g and ω are both in the neighbourhood of 1. While in all other circumstances the attribution of competitive advantages to different groups of companies is dominated in the short term by technological conditions (the size of the technological gaps) and macroeconomic conditions (the wage gaps), in this case more

behavioural considerations tend to come in the forefront: that is, even in the short term, all (nearly equal) firms will be able to 'choose' their competitive position, according to their strategic rules in relation to uncertainty, profitability, 'being first' or 'early second', etc. In fact, this particular case tends to be privileged in the economic literature by e.g. game theoretical analyses.

28. The results summarised in Table 5.1 refer to the log-linear estimate which proved to yield a systematically better fit.

29. Thus, we cannot answer on *econometric grounds*, objections of possible simultaneity, etc., between the variables. However, we feel rather confident on the directions of the causal links for theoretical and empirical reasons related to the pattern of technical change. For example, it is clearly absurd to imagine that 1977–8 productivity levels feed back upon the 1963–7 number of patents. Even with regard to a possible relationship running from productivity to degrees of mechanisation or to capital/output ratios, one may think only of rather indirect links via changes in rates of return and relative prices.

30. Note that the multicollinearity between innovativeness and mechanisation is, on average, rather low (the simple average between the correlation coefficients across the thirty-nine sectors is 0.08 while they reach 0.50 in only three sectors).

31. The fact that a positive correlation appears only in a sector characterised by relatively low 'technological opportunity' is also meaningful. As suggested above (Section 4.1), the process of increasing mechanisation of production is likely to tend towards 'static' substitution only when the opportunity of genuine technological advances decreases.

32. See Terleckyj (1974), (1980) and (1982), Griliches and Mairesse (1984), Clark and Griliches (1984), Griliches and Lichtenberg (1984).

6

Technology gaps, cost-based adjustments and international trade

As we have observed, particularly from the broad literature review in Chapter 2, the century of economic discussion which focussed on the allocative optimality for given and identical technologies has somewhat obscured the importance of differences in techniques between countries, and has neglected the analysis of their origin and their effects. As we illustrated in the preceding chapter, it is quite plausible that the wide international differences in per capita income might be due primarily to differences in the degree of capital accumulation and differences in technology rather than just differences in relative prices.

The investigation of these phenomena has, however, developed separately from trade theory, which, until recently, did not take technology gaps as one of the fundamental facts from which to start theorising. This applies, as we saw in Chapter 2, in different ways to both neo-classical and classical theories. The former have generally excluded from the core of the model the implications of straightforward inferiority/superiority of techniques and products between countries for the validity of the most general theorems (such as international factor price equalisation or even the demonstration of the gains from trade) to hold. The latter, in principle, allows the existence of such international technological differences, but takes a rather general and agnostic view, describing the equilibrium specialisations irrespective of the specific nature of the techniques available in each country.

The recent literature on technology-gap explanations of international trade – as we also saw in Chapter 2 – has developed quite independently from the classical (e.g. Ricardian) analysis of the relationship between absolute and comparative advantages. A few syntheses have been attempted between technology-gap models and traditional factor endowment theories, the so-called 'neo-technology' theories, whereby the number of primary factors is increased to include some technology-related ones also.

The hypothesis put forward here, though, is that technology-gap explanations of trade flows are essentially accounts of the impact of different absolute advantages upon competitiveness which can be reconciled within a classical framework of cost-based adjustments. At the core of our explanation are the *technological differences* between countries which as we will attempt to illustrate, also determine the boundaries of the universe of all cost-based adjustments.

In other words, the analysis starts from the opposite assumption to that of the prevailing neo-classical theory. The latter, in its standard form, assumes technological identity between countries. We, by contrast, assume technological differences between countries as the main 'stylised fact' from which we begin theorising. Empirical and theoretical arguments for this choice have already been put forward in the preceding chapters. To name a few: against any 'revisionist' use of neo-classical trade theory, there are the inner logical flaws of factor-endowment theories (cf. the famous Cambridge debate on capital theory), the lack of empirical support for the theory (by any standard the so-called Leontief 'paradox' should be understood as a falsification of the theory), and, perhaps even more important, the evidence about technology and technical change, discussed in Chapter 4, which suggests that the international distribution of innovative activities is uneven.

As we then argued in Chapter 5, technology gaps can be more adequately represented by unequivocal differences (i.e. superiority/ inferiority) in techniques and in products, which are not in any direct sense an endowment, but closely related to the process of capital accumulation, the outcome of processes of discovery, learning, imitation and improvement.

Here we shall suggest an interpretative model of trade flows based on international and intersectoral technological differences. In Section 6.1 we shall consider the interplay between technology gaps, wage gaps and national comparative advantages. In Section 6.2 we explore further the notion of *competitiveness*, distinguishable from comparative advantages and related to the participation of each country to international trade flows. The effects on competitiveness of absolute advantages, wage differences and different forms of industrial organisations will be analysed. In Section 6.3 we present an empirical analysis of the determinants of export performances by sector and by country. Finally, in Section 6.4, we discuss some evidence on the dynamics of technological advantages, cost-based competitiveness and export trends.

6.1 Technology gaps, wage gaps and comparative advantage

A number of implications can be drawn immediately from the analysis of technical change in Chapters 4 and 5.

First, widespread technological asymmetries between countries relate in the first instance to the capability of some countries to produce innovative commodities (i.e. commodities which other countries are not yet capable of producing, irrespective of relative costs) and to use process innovations more efficiently or quickly in the reduction of input coefficients.

Second, the nature of technical progress is such that processes of factor substitution are of minor importance at any given level of technological knowledge.

Third, international differences in labour productivity appear to express adequately technology gaps in relation to techniques that can often be unequivocally ranked as superior and inferior (more/less efficient) independent of input prices.

Fourth, the relationship between wages and productivity is generally a good measure of those factors of competitiveness which are related to costs and prices. In other words it can be considered as an approximation of the 'Ricardian' adjustment process, taking place on the basis of given international technological asymmetries (stemming from different innovative and imitative capabilities).

These points can easily be illustrated by re-interpreting the international 'evolutionary equilibria' discussed in Chapter 5. Take the simple case of when the intrasectoral, international technological gap is determined only by process innovations, affecting labour productivity while leaving the capital/output ratio unchanged. Figure 6.1 represents a hypothetical industry whose world demand is *DD*. For simplicity, we assume that there are only three countries and each national industry is characterised by only one firm.

As a first (but empirically reasonable) approximation – which we consider to be not that far from reality – assume that in the short term techniques are fixed and that there is no actual choice of technique: each country will stick to the best technique that it is able to master. This best technique is defined primarily by the country's technological competence and is, in this first approximation, independent of relative prices. This also implies that there are techniques which are unequivocally more efficient but are not used by every country, except the technological leader, due to asymmetric competence.

Such technological asymmetries induce international differences in labour productivity (without, however, affecting capital/output ratios).[1]

Country 1 is the most advanced country, while country 3 is the most backward one. If each country had the same wage rates (expressed in international currency) as country 1, the line C_3^*CKBHA would represent unit variable costs for countries 3, 2 and 1, respectively. At an identical international price equal to P, country 3 could not even produce economically ($C_3^* > P$). However, wages vary across countries. The broken line C_3NMLHA, representing the actual unit wage costs, illustrates an extreme case of competitiveness reversal due to such differentials, which more than compensate for the technological asymmetries. The most advanced country is also the least competitive ($C_1 > C_2 > C_3$).

The relationship between technological levels and wage rates

Figure 6.1 illustrates how international competitiveness is determined by the relationship between sectoral absolute technological advantages and wage rates. It is impossible to deal here in any satisfactory depth with the theory of income distribution which implicitly underpins such a model of trade.[2] Let us just mention the hypothesis that, given the country-specific institutional factors which affect the determination of wages and profits (such as the modes and levels of industrial conflict, the nature of the labour markets, the patterns of competition, etc.), wages in terms of international currency are determined by the relationship between domestic rates of macroeconomic activity and the average technological advantages/disadvantages vis-à-vis foreign economies in the tradeable sector.[3] We would even adopt a more restrictive hypothesis and take the view that in the long term for each economy or – in broad international comparative terms – between countries, the pattern of absolute average technological levels is the dominant factor explaining the trends (and the international differences) in wage rates (see also Chapter 7, below).[4]

One can now reinterpret the example illustrated in Figure 6.1 in the following way: owing to the *functional dependence of wage rates* (in international currency) *on average absolute technological advantages/ disadvantages* (average of the tradeable sector as a whole), the diagram represents an extreme case where the *comparative* advantage (as expressed by the relationship between sectoral and average technological advantages) takes over from the pattern of competitiveness determined by sector-specific technological lags and leads.

Figure 6.2 illustrates possible forms of such a relationship between technological advantages and wage rates. Let us imagine a continuum of countries (ordered in relation to wage rates represented on the x-axis). The corresponding labour productivities are represented on the y-axis.

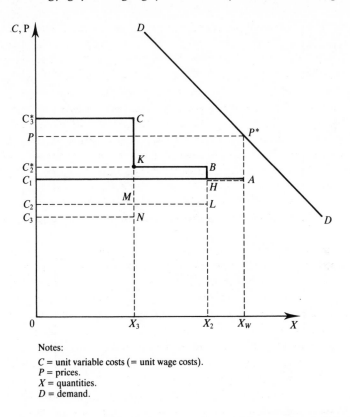

Notes:

C = unit variable costs (= unit wage costs).
P = prices.
X = quantities.
D = demand.

Figure 6.1 Technological asymmetries and international differences in wage rates

All the points below the 45° line show unfavourable competitiveness and vice versa. The lines AA', BB', CC', DD' correspond to hypothetical sectors. In sector A the countries with higher productivity and higher wages are also the least competitive. The opposite applies to sector B. Finally, sectors C and D show higher levels of competitiveness in the intermediate groups of countries. Which case will apply depends on the relationship between degrees of international technological asymmetries and international wage differences. So, for example, the line AA' describes a sector characterised by relatively low asymmetries (say, due to low appropriability of technological advances) in a world characterised by relatively higher wage gaps. Conversely, in the sector represented by BB', appropriability is relatively high, technological asymmetries are large and technology gaps dominate over wage advantages. Of course, the corresponding line for a hypothetical sector with

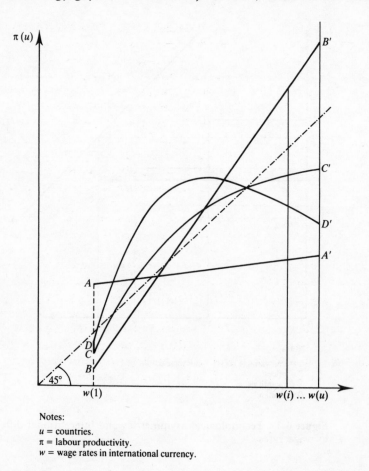

Notes:

u = countries.
π = labour productivity.
w = wage rates in international currency.

Figure 6.2 Productivity and wages in a 'continuum of countries'

sectoral technological gap/lead for each country identical to the country's average gap/lead would also run the 45° line cutting the quadrant, and no country would display a 'comparative advantage' in that activity.

It is easy to extend the analysis to a variety of different firms in each country. As we argued in Chapter 5, interfirm technological asymmetries are an essential feature of each country's industry. Suppose for simplicity that technological coefficients are normally distributed across firms in each country. Then, the input coefficients of each country are averages of a distribution whereby there can always be a 'tail' of highly competitive firms in an 'uncompetitive' national industry, and *vice versa*. Hence, one can also account for the empirically observed lack of complete specialisation in activities characterised by national comparative advantages.

Comparative advantages

The argument so far can be directly linked to the Ricardian approach to intersectoral specialisation. The analysis in Chapters 4 and 5 can be seen as an interpretation of the origins and evolution of sectoral and national absolute advantages/disadvantages. The relationship between wage rates (in international currency) and *average* technological levels of each country determines the borderline between sectors of comparative advantage and those of comparative disadvantage.[5]

In the simplified framework adopted so far, it can readily be shown that such a borderline is determined by the relationship between relative 'physical' labour productivities and relative wages. Suppose that the wage in any one country (w_j) and the rest-of-the-world wage (w_t) are determined according to

$$w_j = \sigma_j \sum_i \pi_{ij} s_{ij} \tag{6.1}$$

and

$$w_t = \sigma_t \sum_i \pi_{it} s_{it} \tag{6.2}$$

where the πs are labour productivities, the ss are the sectoral shares in output, the σs are the 'distributive coefficients' linking wages and average productivities, and the suffixes i, j, t stand for the sectors, the countries and the world respectively.

The sectors of national advantage/disadvantage will then be ranked according to

$$\frac{\pi_{ij}}{\pi_{it}} > \dots > \frac{w_j}{w_t} > \dots > \frac{\pi_{nj}}{\pi_{nt}} \tag{6.3}$$

where the wage of country j relative to the world wage (w_j/w_t) represents the border line between comparative advantages and disadvantages.

So far, our analysis simply shows how in principle an *evolutionary microstructure*, continuously yielding interfirm and international asymmetries, can be directly linked to a classical (Ricardian) approach of comparative advantage: any country will find its comparative advantage in the sector where its technological gap is proportionally smaller (or the lead greater) and vice versa.

6.2 National trade performance: absolute advantages and absolute measures of competitiveness

We now address the question of the extent to which the role of *absolute* technological advantages is limited to determining the wage rate and comparative advantage. We shall argue that absolute advantages have different, even more important, effects.

Some public good features of absolute advantages

Consider the (more complex and more realistic) case where different pieces of technological knowledge and different inputs enter the production process of each tradeable commodity. Given the discussion in Chapter 4 on some of the cross-industry and cross-technology interdependencies, it will come as no surprise that most technological capabilities have some *public good* (or 'externality') features, which are essential to the organisation of production and innovation. One can think of the (maybe trivial) technological capability of making machines work or handling electricity supplies: irrespective of comparative advantages, every nation and firm must rely on these capabilities. Similarly, in the division of labour between individuals, coordination and administrative activities have analogous public input features, irrespective of the set of activities which are undertaken within an organisation.

At a higher level of abstraction, *dominant* technologies play a similar role in that they shape the technological and productive efficiency in a wide set of sectors, no matter what the comparative advantages are. In all these cases, as highlighted by MacDonald and Markusen (1985), the sole knowledge of comparative advantages (either between individuals or between countries) is not a sufficient predictor of actual (or 'optimal') allocations. As they point out:

> ...it is not persuasive that the employee with the highest comparative advantage in management should become president. Indeed it is plausible that the presidency assignment will have something to do with absolute advantages; alternatively a person with poor management skills will not be chosen even if he is relatively worse at every other task in the firm. Further, in academic economics, generally poor economists will not be chosen as department chairman even if they have a comparative advantage in these activities relative to research and teaching .... . A prediction that follows from Ricardian and Heckscher-Ohlin comparative-advantage models is that identical economies will not trade. Yet, that countries with apparently similar technologies and factor endowments seem to trade large volumes of manufactured goods with one another can

be taken as evidence that assignments do not depend entirely on comparative advantages. Indeed, trade arising from scale economies in models with identical countries, is now referred to as 'non-comparative advantage trade'... . That specialisation may be optimal independent of differences in comparative advantages is a special case of a more general failure of the comparative advantage principle to predict assignments. (MacDonald and Markusen, 1985, pp. 278–9)

In terms of the analytical framework presented here, the implication is that whenever there are strong technological interdependencies, hierarchical links between technologies and externalities (in terms of cross-sectoral fertilisations, spill-overs, etc.), the pattern of absolute advantage in these dominant technologies, skills or capabilities will have to be taken as an autonomous determinant of international competitiveness, independent of the pattern of comparative advantage.

Moreover, 'comparative advantage will tend to be a poor proxy for optimal assignment when differences in absolute advantages are large relative to differences in comparative advantages'.[6] Recalling the empirical analysis in Chapter 3, this is, generally speaking, the case for most contemporary economies: the *intersectoral intranational* differences in technological capabilities, although significant, tend to be of smaller orders of magnitude than international differences.

The notion of absolute advantage requires a redefinition of *competitiveness*. Clearly, in a Ricardian or Heckscher–Ohlin world, every country, by definition, must be relatively competitive in something. Competitive in this sense amounts, however, to little more than a tautology: being competitive might simply mean that anyone is bound to be less bad in something and worse in something else. Conversely, the externality features of absolute advantages (in the form of country-specific technological capabilities and institutional arrangements) imply that:

> The competitiveness of a national economy is more than the simple outcome of the collective 'average' competitiveness of its firms; there are many ways in which the features and performance of a domestic economy viewed as an entity with characteristics of its own, will affect in turn the competitiveness of the firms. (OECD 1985, p. 6)

Absolute competitiveness and comparative advantage

A direct impact of absolute advantages upon competitiveness requires something like an absolute notion of competitiveness. According to

Cohen, Teece, Tyson and Zysman:

> International competitiveness at national level is based on superior productivity performance and the economy's ability to shift output to higher productivity activities, which in turn can generate high levels of real wages ... . It is not just a measure of the nation's ability to sell abroad, and to maintain a trade equilibrium. The very poorest countries in the world are often able to do that quite well. Rather it is the nation's ability to compete internationally in those commodities and services likely to constitute a larger share of world consumption and value added in the future. (Cohen, Teece, Tyson and Zysman, 1984, p. 2)

Similarly, Mistral argues that

> ... competitiveness is the expression of a global property (both micro and macroeconomic) specific to each national economy – the efficiency with which each country mobilises its factorial resources and, in so doing, modifies the technical and social characteristics of industrial activity. At the same time, competition on world markets as a whole (domestic and foreign) reveals the success of those national performances relative to each other: the more advanced and competitive economies then exert an external constraint on the others through the pattern of foreign payments balances. (Mistral, 1983, p. 2)

Mistral calls this feature of national economies 'structural competitiveness'.

The two concepts of 'structural' (or absolute) competitiveness and that of 'relative' (intersectoral) comparative advantage point to some tangled and rather complex issues of economic analysis.

The core of trade theory has generally attempted to answer the question: 'What explains comparative advantages?' and the complementary question: 'Are there gains from trade?' An answer to these questions has traditionally also meant an answer to another question, namely: 'What explains the international composition of trade by country, i.e. the participation of each country in trade flows?' In the classic Ricardian example, the analytical identification of the two questions is straightforward: comparative advantages and specialisation explain the entire amount of trade occurring between England and Portugal in wine and cloth. In the simplest case, trade even yields absolute specialisations. This line of thought, and even more so in the neo-classical approach, puts the main emphasis on the question of the gains from trade.

Our analysis on the other hand suggests that the two questions must be theoretically separate. Take two countries of comparable size but with different degrees of technological and economic development: the advanced country will generally show a higher participation in world trade in the sectors of comparative disadvantage than will the backward country in the sectors of comparative advantage.[7] It is certainly interesting to understand why the world-market share of country 1 in product x is, say, 10 per cent, while it is 11 per cent in product y. However, it is also interesting (and certainly more relevant to macroeconomic issues) to understand why country 1 has that 10 per cent share in product x while another country, n, has only a 0.1 per cent share in the same product, despite the fact that the sector might well be one of 'comparative advantage' to country n, whose product y only has 0.05 per cent of the world market. The concept of absolute competitiveness relates to the explanation of issues such as: Why has country 1 a market share of 10 per cent in product x (and, not, say, 5 per cent or 20 per cent)? or: Why has country 1 an average world-market share of, say, 10.8 per cent? Conversely, the concept of comparative advantage relates to issues (more familiar to economists and a little awkward to practitioners) such as: Why is the revealed comparative advantage of country 1 in product x equal to $10/11$ of that in product y?

Our hypothesis is thus that absolute advantages *dominate* over comparative advantages as determinants of trade flows. Their dominance means that they account for most of the composition of trade flows by country and by commodity at each point in time and explain the evolution of such trade flows over time.[8]

This dominance takes two forms. First, absolute advantages/disadvantages are the fundamental factors which explain sectoral and average competitiveness, and, thus, market shares. Second, they also define the *boundaries* of the universe within which cost-related adjustments take place. As we saw in the preceding chapters, intersectoral, intranational differences in technological levels are of an order of magnitude smaller than intrasectoral, international differences. Thus, the boundaries of the adjustments linked to comparative advantages and relative sectoral profitabilities are rather tight: *a fortiori*, the dominance argument applies.

Adjustments in market shares and adjustments in sectoral specialisation

The distinction between the two concepts relates in the first instance to different *adjustment* mechanisms at work within each economy and in the world markets. Let us consider these in some detail.

Suppose we start from an international set-up whereby each industry is on an international evolutionary equilibrium, as defined in Chapter 5. Each national foreign account − assumed for simplicity to be equal to the trade account − is balanced; each national wage is proportional to the average technological level of the tradeable part of the economy; and there is some unemployed labour in each economy.[9] Suppose that, due to some innovative success, any one country j improves its relative productive efficiency (limited here to labour productivity) in sector i, while all others remain unchanged.[10] In other words, we have an increase in the absolute advantage (or a decrease in the absolute disadvantage) for country j in sector i. What will happen?

First, an increased technological capability in sector i, relative to foreign competitors, will lead to an increase in the world-market shares of country j in that sector.

Second, the average technological level of country j improves approximately by:

$$\frac{\Delta \pi_{ij} s_{ij} + \pi_{ij} \, \Delta s_{ij}}{\sum_i \pi_{ij} s_{ij}}$$

Wages (in international currency) will consequently tend to adjust correspondingly. This will occur in three ways: (a) through the effect that higher world-market shares have on domestic growth via foreign-trade multipliers and the resulting impact of higher growth on the domestic labour market; (b) through the effect of the higher competitiveness on the exchange rate; and (c), finally, through the institutional mechanisms which in most contemporary economies link productivity growth and wage increases.

Third, the domestic allocation of investment and employment will lead to a relative increase in investment and employment in sector i and an absolute increase in all employed resources. This will be the joint result of the increased competitiveness of sector i vis-à-vis the rest of the world and an increase in the relative profitability of sector i vis-à-vis the other domestic sectors.

Fourth, there *might* be some changes in the price of product i relative to other products (this is more likely to occur if country j is large in relation to the world).

Strictly speaking, the comparative advantage mechanisms of adjustment relate to the intersectoral changes in the allocation of resources, pulled by changed profitabilities and relative prices. Conversely, competitiveness-related mechanisms of adjustment also have macroeconomic dimensions, such as changes in the *absolute* amount of employed resources, rate of growth, wage rates and exchange rates.

At the end of these various adjustment processes, country j will have a higher world-market share in i; a higher rate of macroeconomic activity and higher wages; somewhat lower world-market shares in sectors other than *i*; a higher revealed comparative advantage (or lower revealed comparative disadvantage) in *i*; and a higher average world-market share for the country as a whole. As an illustration of this last point, imagine as an extreme case that all mechanisms of adjustment just mentioned occur, except that wages (in international currency) do not adjust upwards (recall that we have assumed the general existence of unutilised labour). In this case we will eventually see a higher world-market share for country *j* in sector *i* and *unchanged world-market shares* in all other sectors. More likely will be the case where the 'gains of competitiveness' will be distributed between higher growth and higher wages. This will, however, not alter our conclusion: the higher share in sector *i* will more than compensate for the fall in the other sectors.

We leave the more formal analysis of the relationship between technology, trade, specialisation and growth to Chapter 7. Here it is important to note how the foregoing example highlights the distinct roles of absolute advantages and absolute competitiveness, on the one hand, and revealed comparative advantages (more rigorously – revealed relative allocations) on the other. The former is reflected by the link between international technological asymmetries in sector *i* and national market shares in that same sector, and the link between average national technological asymmetries and average national shares in world markets. Conversely, relative intersectoral allocations result from the intersectoral differences of these sector-specific gaps and leads.

In the illustration given above it is easy to see how these two questions are fundamentally different. Consider in the foregoing example, the post-adjustment pattern of revealed comparative advantages. As we saw, this was the result of an absolute increase in the technological level of sector *i*, leaving all others unchanged. However, the same pattern of revealed comparative advantage could also have been achieved as a result of a *fall* in the technological level (compared to other countries) in all sectors except *i*, that is, through a general fall in competitiveness, market shares, and rates of growth. Finally, consider the case of a proportional improvement of technological levels in all sectors. Here we do not have any comparative advantage effect. Instead, the export market shares will grow in all sectors and the country-wide increase in competitiveness will result in higher growth and higher wages.

The reader might recall the analogy between this case and our interpretation of the argument by 'heretic' trade theorists, reviewed in Chapter 2: adjustment to changing country-specific absolute advantages leads to changes in competitiveness, market shares and real incomes, irrespective of the pattern of comparative advantage. More generally, this leads to the proposition that: the international pattern of sectoral absolute advantages/disadvantages is a fundamental determinant of sectoral competitiveness as expressed by the sectoral market shares of each country.[11]

The latter are influenced by comparative advantages only in so far as the differences between sectoral and average gaps and leads affect the relative cost structures and profitabilities of each sector. However, we suggest that the main adjustment mechanism to changes in the pattern of absolute advantages/disadvantages (under normal conditions of non-decreasing returns, reproducible capital inputs and less than full employment of world labour) does not occur through changes in relative quantities and relative prices in each economy, with unchanged levels of macroeconomic activity, but through changes in world-market shares and (relatedly) in the total level of employed resources and in the levels and rates of growth of incomes and wages. As we shall see in Chapter 7, this argument can easily be linked with a Keynesian open-economy model.

This proposition can best be illustrated with reference to the famous Ricardian example of trade in wine and cloth between England and Portugal. Our reformulation of the technology-gap model, based on some of the patterns of technical change analysed in Chapter 4, explains why the Portuguese coefficients of production are 'better' than the English ones, and uses this difference to explain both the participation of each country in trade and the pattern of revealed comparative advantage. Our hypothesis is that the former is primarily explained by absolute advantages. In other words, and staying with the Ricardian example, a major part of the explanation of the pattern of international production and trade in, say, cloth, can be simply inferred by looking at the size of the technology gap in cloth between Portugal and England. Conversely, comparative advantage only accounts for that part of the international distribution of production and trade stemming from the difference between sectoral and average technology gaps for each country.

A comparative advantage mechanism, based on relative prices and relative profitabilities is still undoubtedly at work and will contribute to the explanation of relative specialisations. However, as is implicit in technology-gap theories, the dominant effects run from technology gaps to domestic levels of production, exports, and income. In other words, any absolute measure of the international competitiveness of a country or industry is primarily based on its absolute advantages/disadvantages in terms of product technology and labour productivity. This property finds an intuitive corroboration in the 'stylised facts' presented in Chapter 3. There it was found that long-term changes in the export market shares of each country were often general to all or most sectors.

Our model suggests that these changes are in fact due to country-wide changes in absolute advantages/disadvantages.

A technology-gap model of international competitiveness

Formally, one can specify sectoral trade performance as a function of both technological absolute advantage (T_{ij}) and variable costs (C_{ij}):

$$X_{ij} = f(T_{ij}, C_{ij}) \tag{6.4}$$

where X_{ij} is some indicator of international competitiveness (related to the size of exports in sector i for each country j); T_{ij} represents an indicator of technological levels (both product and process technologies in the same sectors i for each country j) and C_{ij} represents a proxy for variable costs e.g. labour costs (as we shall see, either wage rates or unit labour costs, depending on the specification of the model).

Even if the income distribution between wages and profits is neglected in this simple relationship, we suggest that the latter can nevertheless be taken to represent the proximate determinants of international competitiveness fairly well. This hypothesis can be justified on the basis of our earlier analysis in Chapter 5 on the choice and change in techniques. To recall, we showed there that technical progress tends to be more or less Harrod-neutral. It should be clear that we are not claiming that technical progress is precisely neutral – through time or across countries. For our purposes here, it is sufficient that its possible international or intertemporal biases are of an order of magnitude smaller than international gaps in labour productivity and technological innovativeness,[12] and that there is no *a priori* reason to expect the capital intensity biases to be systematically correlated with degrees of technological development.[13] This is also supported by the fact that capital goods tend to have a (nearly) unique international price; that international differences in profitability are indeed of an order of magnitude smaller than differences in wage rates[14] and that they also do not appear to show any correlation with degrees of development or relative capital endowments.[15]

Taking all these considerations together, one may safely conclude that in all sectors which do not have a high intensity of natural resources (such as minerals, energy, etc.), differences in wages will mostly capture those international differences in input prices which do not stem directly from varying degrees of technological efficiency.

Equation (6.4) can therefore be considered to capture the effects of both sectoral absolute technological gaps (through the variable T) and 'comparative advantages' (through the variable C, specified as unit labour costs) on 'absolute' competitiveness (approximated, for example, by world market shares or per capita exports).

In order to illustrate this, let us suppose that each country is in what one could call a 'macroeconomic' foreign-balance equilibrium: given a certain average (for the tradeable sector as a whole) technological gap vis-à-vis other countries, the relationship between the levels of wages, the exchange rate and the rates of macroeconomic activity is such that their foreign accounts exactly balance. For simplicity, suppose also that there is no capital account and that all external trade is in manufactures.

As mentioned earlier, if we had an industrial sector representative of the average technological gap of every country, this sector would show identical unit labour costs in international currency for all countries (see Figure 6.2 in Section 6.1).[16] Thus, such a 'representative sector' would present productivity gaps equal to wage gaps in every country (see equations (6.1) and (6.2)) and unit labour costs would be identical across countries. The sector would therefore also represent the border line between sectors of revealed comparative advantage and disadvantage. However, other sectors may well still show international differences in unit wage costs. If adjustment processes are not instantaneous and if, as is likely, the sectoral input coefficients and technological levels are averages of distributions between different firms, we can expect the sectors of comparative advantage to show relatively lower unit costs (compared to other countries in the same sector), and *vice versa* for sectors of comparative disadvantage.

One can imagine a plausible situation in which each economy is permanently in a state of microeconomic disequilibrium: technical change takes place all the time; technological diffusion processes are rather slow; and demand lags in response to international price changes are significant. In some way, one is always in the middle of an adjustment process. Under these circumstances, the effects of intersectoral patterns of comparative advantage can be detected without the knowledge of the notional pre-trade values of the variables.[17] A country will find an incentive to expand its export in those sectors where it has a relative cost-based advantage, and vice versa.

Let us now relax the assumption of a macroeconomic foreign balance equilibrium. For a given average technological gap, each country is allowed to have 'disequilibrium' wage rates, expressed in international currency (or, which is the same, disequilibrium exchange rates), yielding an across-the-board competitive advantage for some countries and disadvantage for others. In this case, the 'representative sector' would also show international differences in unit wage costs, while in all other sectors the unit wage cost differences would be increased/reduced by a proportion expressing the degree of macroeconomic disequilibrium. In the model presented here, the unit wage cost variable will therefore capture two effects, both stemming from cost-related adjustments; first, the degree of comparative advantage/disadvantage of each country in each individual sector; and second, the cost-based general advantage/disadvantage each country experiences through what could be called an undervalued/overvalued currency.

Forms of industrial organisation and international competitiveness

Let us now go back to equation (6.4). As it stands, it captures the proximate determinants of international competitiveness, as revealed by export performance. However, the discussion so far has been based on the simplifying assumption that forms of industrial organisation are neutral in relation to the effect on competitiveness of given technology gaps and wage gaps. In reality this will rarely be the case.

On theoretical grounds, as one of us has argued elsewhere (Dosi, 1984), the *history* of technological and economic development of an industry and of each individual company has an important influence upon the present competitive position of each company (and, by implication, each country), independent of present relative technological capabilities and present cost conditions. More precisely, the history of the technological development of a company and – in general – the history of its relative competitive success vis-à-vis other companies is also the history of market shares, market power, geographical diffusion, distribution networks, accumulation of goodwill, and diversification and differentiation of production.[18] All these variables affect *present* competitive performances on both domestic and international markets in ways which may be partly independent of present relative technological capabilities and relative costs.

The role of industrial organisation becomes even more important when one introduces international investment. In other words, present national and international industrial organisation forms are a reflection of the *cumulative result* of past technological advantages/disadvantages and of the ways in which firms have exploited their behavioural degrees of freedom throughout their competitive history. As a striking illustration, one may take, at least until recently, the competitive performance of a firm such as IBM (and, through it, of the United States) in computers. A good part of the reason for this performance rests in its present technological and cost advantages. However, its history of international penetration, its organisation, industrial market power, etc., also play an important part.

The non-neutrality of the forms of industrial organisation with respect to the amount, composition and even direction of trade flows is a relatively robust result which is also obtained from neo-classical models, whereby either firms enter into strategic price/quantity interactions of the Cournot type, or the market is characterised by imperfect (Chamberlinian) competition.[19] *A fortiori*, we would expect this non-neutrality to apply to the complex evolutionary world that we are analysing here, where firms differ not only in size but also in technological capabilities, and where the past has a strong inertial effect upon the present and the future since it is sedimented in organisational structures, behavioural rules, fixed investments, etc.

In this context, it is interesting to observe a couple of empirical facts. First, export propensities often appear to be directly related to firms' sizes for reasons which do not show a straightforward link with *technological differentials*;[20] second, the abundant evidence on intra-industry (and intrafirm) trade, indirectly at least, points to the role of international oligopolistic competition and market structures in shaping trade patterns;[21] and third, the evidence, as contradictory as it may seem about the export-complementarity vs. the export-substitution effects of foreign investment, also highlights the non-neutrality of this form of international industrial organisation with respect to trade patterns.[22]

From a dynamic point of view, industrial organisations are of course the essential actors in technological accumulation, innovation and imitation. This also means that both industrial structures and technological gaps/leads are endogenous to the competitive dynamics of each country but that they evolve along patterns which cannot generally be expected to show a simple linear relationship to each other.[23]

Within a dynamic context, the influence of industrial organisations on a country's international competitiveness emerges even more strongly. As suggested by Cantwell (1983), on the basis of Dunning's (1981) eclectic approach, international investment is one of the forms of adjustment by firms which aim strategically to exploit privately appropriated absolute advantages. The important point for our discussion here is that the form of exploitation (direct investment vs. export) influences both the evolution of competitiveness – on a country-basis – and the pattern of national technological accumulation. Current investment decisions with respect to the location of production, R&D, etc., influence the national patterns of trade but also the technological capabilities (and, over large numbers) the cost conditions of each country. In turn, all this influences both the general competitiveness of 'parent' and 'host' countries and also the future locational advantages/disadvantages. Nothing, of course, prevents, *a priori*, these dynamic loops between corporate strategies and national/regional characteristics entailing either 'virtuous' or 'vicious' loops (Cantwell and Dunning, 1986).

The long-term effect of inward and outward multinational investment on export competitiveness depends in the last resort on whether foreign production and exports are substitutes or complements. This is a tangled controversy which cannot be discussed in any detail here. Suffice it to say that the model of technical change developed earlier (Chapter 4) implies that complementarity is more likely to occur when appropriability of technological advances is high, and/or when user–producer linkages are internalised within single firms. In this case, when marketing networks represent some kind of common asset for local production and exports, the 'crowding-out' of local firms resulting from foreign investment will be high and economies of scale (in either R&D, production or sales) will be significant. Under these circumstances, foreign direct investment is likely to pre-empt the foreign markets and, often, reproduce through time the initial pattern of country-specific advantages/disadvantages[24] (see Dosi, 1984, for a more detailed discussion of this issue).

A general model of the determinants of international competitiveness

In view of these considerations, equation (6.4) above must be modified in order to account for the additional effect that the forms of industrial organisation have upon international competitiveness.

Let us rewrite equation (6.4) as follows:

$$X_{ij} = f(T_{ij}, C_{ij}, O_{ij}) \tag{6.5}$$

Ideally, the independent variables should capture the set of technological advantages/disadvantages (T_{ij}); international differences in variable costs – primarily labour costs – (C_{ij}); and the sectoral forms of industrial organisation (O_{ij}), e.g. the domestic market structure, the degree and forms of participation in international oligopolies, whenever they exist, etc. In other words, O_{ij} stands for that set of organisational specificities (in terms of size, degrees of internationalisation, etc.) of each national industry as compared to foreign competitors in the same sector.

At each point in time, the international competitiveness of each economy in each sector (e.g. export shares or exports per capita) is determined by the technological gap/lead of that economy, by its wage gap and by the forms of *industrial organisations* which are, in a sense, the structural result of the past history of relative innovativeness and relative competitiveness.

A priori, we may expect the relative impact of these three variables to differ between sectors. Those sector-specific features which affect the process of generation and diffusion of innovations discussed earlier (see

Chapter 4), also determine the size of the international technological gap and the way the organisational structures influence trade flows.

In science-based and specialised supplier sectors, for example, we would expect international innovative gaps to be critical to competitiveness and, thus, the *T*-variable to be of overwhelming importance. In scale intensive sectors (e.g. cars) various kinds of economies of scale, product technology, labour productivity and organisational forms can be expected to be important. Finally, in supplier-dominated sectors with relatively simple, readily available technologies (e.g. textiles), we would expect international competitiveness to be determined essentially by labour costs (that is, by the relationship between capital embodied technology and wage rates).

A way of reformulating the foregoing discussion is by reference to Figure 6.2 above. In Section 6.1 we analysed the link between technology gaps and wage gaps in so far as it determined national revealed comparative advantages. From Figure 6.2 it appeared that country *i* had a comparative advantage in the sector represented by *BB'*, and that country 1 had a comparative advantage in *AA'*. However, the question addressed here is different. We now ask what determines international competitiveness – as reflected by market shares or export per capita within, say, sector *BB'* or *AA'*. Equations (6.4) and (6.5) account for these determinants of competitiveness. It is now possible, and indeed likely, that country *i* will also have a higher market share than country 1 in sector *AA'*, its sector of comparative disadvantage.

Let us consider this sector in more detail, and assume for realism that on the *y*-axis of Figure 6.2 we represent both product-related and process-related technological asymmetries. We know that in sector *AA'* country *i* has a technological lead (although not a big one) and a cost disadvantage vis-à-vis country 1. Equation (6.5) tells us how much the technological, organisational and cost advantages count in determining international competitiveness (and, thus, world-market shares).

The taxonomy discussed above (see Chapter 4) allows for some predictions in this respect. For example, in sector *AA'*, which can be taken to represent supplier-dominated industries, cost of production (and thus cost advantages/disadvantages) are likely to be important. The opposite would apply to science-based sectors.

The general structural (in Mistral's definition) competitiveness of each economy can also be represented by:

$$X_j = F(T_j, C_j, O_j) \tag{6.6}$$

where the variables without the *i*-suffix are the sum of, or weighted, averages across each country. In a notional state of macroeconomic equilibrium (defined earlier in this chapter) the C_j variable — when expressed in terms of unit labour costs — will tend to be identical across countries, while overvalued or undervalued currencies would be reflected in differences in the C_js. Still, the wide international differences in the absolute technological advantages and in the forms of industrial organisation determine the wide variance in the levels of competitiveness of each economy (measured by market shares or per capita exports). In a sense, the specific functional form of the relation between competitiveness, on the one hand, and technological accumulation, capital investment, process-efficiency and organisational structure, on the other, expresses the degree of fitness of each national economy to the prevailing international pattern of growth and trade (Mistral, 1982 and 1985).

In other words, revealed comparative advantage (that is, the actual distribution of exports between sectors) is the ratio of two absolute measures of competitiveness, namely sectoral competitiveness and competitiveness for the economy as a whole. That is:

$$RCA_{ij} = \frac{f_j(T_{ij}, C_{ij}, O_{ij})}{F(T_j, C_j, O_j)} \tag{6.7}$$

where RCA_{ij} is the index of revealed comparative advantage of country j in sector i and the variables T, C and O have the same meaning as in equation (6.5). Thus, equation (6.7) a more analytical expression of the usual formula:

$$RCA_{ij} = \frac{X_{ij} / \Sigma_j X_{ij}}{\Sigma_i X_{ij} / \Sigma_i \Sigma_j X_{ij}}$$

Under competitive conditions, the variable (O) would become irrelevant. Similarly, if absolute advantages/disadvantages between countries tended to disappear, the variable (T) would lose much of its importance in explaining sectoral and country-wide competitiveness. Recalling that the wages that appear in the numerator of unit costs (C) are a function of average productivity (cf. equations (6.1) and (6.2)), equation (6.7) would tend to shrink to:

$$RCA_{ij} = f_i \left(\sigma_j \frac{\Sigma_i \pi_{ij} s_i}{\pi_{ij}} \right) \tag{6.8}$$

This is equivalent to the formula we obtained earlier with respect to comparative advantage (equation (6.3)), illustrating that the determination of comparative advantage and of sectoral competitiveness become one and the same thing only under competitive conditions *and* with technological similarity between countries.

The dynamics of international competitiveness

Equation (6.5) above represents the determinants of international competitiveness at any given time. From a dynamic point of view, however, the dependent and independent variables interact with each other: different levels of international competitiveness affect the evolution of industrial organisations, their capability to innovate/imitate, the exploitation of economies of scale and of learning curves, etc. In other words, industrial organisations have to be treated dynamically as endogenous variables within the international competitive process. Furthermore, the time profile of the technology gaps will also depend on some of the forces affecting the relative rates of innovation and diffusion and, thus, also on the changing levels of opportunity, cumulativeness and appropriability that each technology presents. Finally, labour costs depend essentially on macroeconomic factors, related to the evolution of average technological levels, rates of macroeconomic activity, and institutional features of the labour market and industrial conflict.

In other words, there will be an entire *set* of paths that the dynamic counterpart of equation (6.5) might follow, of which product-cycle evolutions of international competitiveness and widening technological gaps are the two extreme cases: which path is actually followed will depend on country-specific conditions (such as the rates and directions of the patterns of national technological accumulation, trends in wage rates, capital accumulation, etc.) as well as on sector-specific conditions (such as changes in the degrees of opportunity, appropriability, complexity, etc., of each technology).

Following Silverberg (1987) and re-interpreting it in relation to the present model we suggest the following dynamic process, derived from equation (6.5):

$$\dot{X}_{ij} = A(E_{ij} - \bar{E})X_{ij} \tag{6.9}$$

where the dots stand for the rates of change; X_{ij} are world-market shares; E_{ij} encompasses the factors of competitiveness T, C, O; and $\bar{E}$ is the weighted 'competitiveness' of the world market ($= \Sigma_i X_{ij} E_{ij}$).

In general the long-term trade performance of each country is determined by the dynamics of its E_{ij} as compared to the world average. Consider in particular the T-components of E (i.e. technology-related variables) and suppose that they are summarised by a vector μ_{ij} with $E_{ij} = E(\mu_{ij})$. Hence, country-specific and sector-specific dynamics of competitiveness depend on the transition probabilities in the μ_{ij}: $P[(\mu_{ij} + \varepsilon) | \mu_{ij}]$. But what explains these transition probabilities and their differences across countries and across sectors? Here one can see the full importance of the interpretative categories discussed in

Chapter 4 in relation to technical progress. It is precisely the different degrees of opportunity, cumulativeness, appropriability of technical advances which account for different rates of change in competitiveness across countries and across sectors. For example, one can infer that, if technical progress is very cumulative, for any two pairs of countries 1 and 2:

$$P[(\mu_{i1} + \varepsilon)\,|\,\mu_{i1}] \geqslant P[(\mu_{i2} + \varepsilon)\,|\,\mu_{i2}] \qquad \textbf{(6.10)}$$

for $\mu_{i1} \gtrsim \mu_{i2}$

Success in this case tends to breed success and the process will lead to diverging trends in competitiveness, formally similar to those cumulative processes analysed in Arthur (1985) and (1988). Similar conclusions hold for high levels of appropriability of innovative capabilities. The opposite holds for low cumulativeness and appropriability. In these cases the model predicts a more likely convergence in the levels of competitiveness of the various countries and also less unevenly distributed market shares.

Finally, high technological opportunities imply, other things being equal, a relatively high rate of change in the μ_{ij}s and thus in E_i, with an effect on the dynamics of distribution of the E_{ij} (i.e. on the dynamics of international asymmetries). That, again, depends on the cumulativeness of technological advances, the easiness of imitation, reverse engineering, technological transfer, possibilities of 'leapfrogging', etc.

Rigorously, equation (6.5) and its dynamic counterpart (6.9) should represent the state (and/or change in) of the variables on the right-hand side with regard to both each industry in question and the vertically integrated sector which directly or indirectly enters the production of the exportable commodity X_i (see in more detail Momigliano and Siniscalco, 1984). As in our earlier discussion (Chapter 4) of the complex thread of technological flows between sectors, this should come as no surprise: input–output and technological interdependencies transmit the effects of absolute advantage/disadvantage well beyond the industry where they originated. In a sense, these interdependencies are a fundamental link between sectoral competitiveness and the general competitiveness of each economy as a whole. It is not possible to pursue that issue further here, but there seems to be no *a priori* reason why the foregoing interpretative framework could not be extended to a model that explicitly accounts for intersectoral commodity flows.

To summarise: equation (6.5) can be interpreted as the joint account of the effects on international competitiveness of absolute technological and organisational advantage/disadvantage, and, only in a second instance and indirectly, of comparative advantage (as revealed by relative variable costs). In other words, when one measures sectoral competitiveness (say, sectoral market share in world exports), this is an 'absolute' measure of competitiveness (it is certainly relative to other countries, but independent from other sectors within the same country). It is also the relevant variable which one needs in relation to the analysis of macroeconomic growth (Harrod's multipliers, etc.). This measure of competitiveness depends, we argue here, on technology, on costs and on forms of industrial organisation.

Comparative advantages, on the other hand, depend on the intersectoral comparisons of the technology and organisational gaps, within the same country. Thus, the sectoral ('absolute') measure of competitiveness can be notionally divided into two parts: that part which is common to all tradeable sectors (the 'average' gap) and that part which is sector-specific. A country can be bad in everything and a bit less bad in something, or vice versa. Moreover, there is a sectoral specificity of the importance of technology, wage costs and organisations. In some sectors, wage gaps may compensate (or more than compensate) for the technological gaps and this may determine a relatively high international competitiveness. In other sectors, the international market might put a high premium on innovativeness, quality, product and process sophistication, so that even a unit cost advantage, in the presence of a technological gap might still be reflected in a low level of international competivitiveness. Similarly, in some sectors (which we grouped under the heading 'scale intensive'), size, international investments, worldwide marketing networks, differential capabilities of managing complex structures of production and service will represent the most powerful sources of competitive advantage. Within other sectors (especially the so-called 'specialised suppliers' sectors), flexibility, location-related externalities and user–producer linkages are likely to provide the organisational advantages.

Trade theory has generally focussed on the (intranational, intersectoral) comparative aspects of trade flows. Here we have suggested that one should really start by explaining the origins and effects of the absolute gaps/leads which are sector-specific and are the core element in explaining trade flows. Comparative advantage is in some sense a residual result – although an important one since it generates those intersectoral signals (relative profitabilities, etc.) which contribute to shaping the allocation of resources.

Patterns of demand and patterns of trade

A final set of comments concerns the relevant world and domestic demand conditions. The model suggested above is essentially a supply-side one, in the sense that it attempts to give an explanation for sectoral and country-wide competitiveness in the world market, on the basis of the differential supply conditions that each country is confronted with in each sector (and as a whole). On the other hand, the structure of demand, domestically and as between trading partners, is an important factor in explaining average import propensities and the geographical destination of trade flows. This is one of the main approaches of trade theories, along the lines of Linder and Barker.[26] *A priori* there is no inconsistency between the technology-gap model discussed above and these demand-based models. The latter tend to explain the size and growth of each sectoral market and its geographical distribution between countries (which is taken to be a function of income per capita, product characteristics, etc.). In our approach, on the other hand, these markets are taken as 'given', and it is the international distribution of supply in terms of the technological, cost and organisational characteristics of the various national industries within the same sector which is explained.

Dynamically, the link between the two models is close: as we saw in Chapters 4 and 5, the demand and supply factors behind the diffusion of innovations are not at all independent; the conditions of each domestic market influence the patterns and rates of technological accumulation; user–producer and, more generally, input–output links influence the generation and diffusion of innovation throughout the economy. Thus, Andersen *et al.* (1981) present evidence that domestic demand conditions can induce technological advantage in supplying sectors.[27]

At a more macroeconomic level, the evolution of national competitiveness is influenced by the evolution of sectoral patterns of demand. Let us recall equation (6.6). The total export share of each country is a weighted average of each sectoral share. The change over time of such total country-shares is the result of the effects of sectoral gaps/leads upon sectoral competitiveness, but also of changing sectoral weights. In turn, the change in these sectoral weights depends on the evolution of patterns of world demand and of relative prices.

National relative specialisations (which determine the sectoral weights in each country) have an important effect on the long-term evolution of competitiveness in so far as they determine the degree of consistency between national points of strength and weakness and changing world demand conditions.[28] In the last resort, this depends on the world income elasticities of the various commodities, relative to national specialisations. Consider, for example, the following, rather extreme example. Suppose we have two countries, Portugal and England, which export wine and cloth. At time zero, Portugal exports $8 of wine out of a world exports total of \$10 and \$2 of cloth out of a world exports total of \$20. Conversely, England exports \$1 of wine and \$9 of cloth. Obviously, the sectoral competitiveness and the patterns of specialisation differ between the two countries, but their country-wide competitiveness measured by their world-market shares is identical: $(8 + 2)/(10 + 20) = (1 + 9)/(10 + 20) = 1/3$. Suppose now that at time 1 the sectoral competitiveness of Portugal in wine increases, so that it exports, say, \$9 out of an unchanged world market of \$10, while the English competitiveness falls to a market share of

$$\frac{\$0.5}{\$10}$$

Conversely, suppose that the Portuguese share in cloth grows: say it exports \$21 out of an increased world-market value of \$200, while the English one falls slightly, with exports growing only to \$85. From this sectoral evidence, it would appear that English competitiveness has fallen and Portuguese competitiveness has increased. However, due to very different patterns of world demand, the total English market share has now grown to

$$\frac{0.5 + 85}{10 + 200} \approx 41 \text{ per cent}$$

while the Portuguese one has actually fallen to

$$\frac{9 + 21}{10 + 200} \approx 18 \text{ per cent}$$

As Lafay (1981) points out, it is this dynamic implication of the patterns of specialisation which makes them analytically important, well beyond the once-and-for-all gains in efficiency that openness and specialisation generally bring about in the usual static context of trade theory.[29] Thus, following Rothschild (1985) and to some extent in analogy with our discussion on technology gaps, one could define the 'structural demand-determined gap' as the (positive or negative) difference between actual world export growth and that notional world export growth which would have resulted if world exports had kept the same intercommodity weights as the country in question.

When we allow for the possibility of intersectoral shifts in the composition of world demand, and, at a finer level of disaggregation, the possibility of intrasectoral shifts among products with different characteristics, quality, etc., the path followed by the country-wide counterpart of equation (6.9) may well lead to diverging national trends in the C-variable (representing unit labour costs), with constant average technological gaps. Other things being equal, one country may still gain in overall competitiveness, even with rising average unit labour costs, to the extent that this is associated with a movement towards inter- and intrasectoral specialisation characterised by higher quality and sophistication, higher value added per physical unit of output and/or higher income elasticity of demand.[30] The opposite may apply to countries with a worsening quality of their pattern of specialisation.

6.3   Some tests on the determinants of export performance

A complete empirical test of the model outlined in the preceding section, both in its cross-sectional and dynamic forms would require a relatively wide set of data that are not generally available. Thus, with respect to equation (6.4), one would need comparable sectoral and country data for a number of technologies or technological performance indicators (product-embodied technology, process technology, labour productivity, input efficiencies, etc.); some sectoral measures of labour costs per physical unit of homogeneous output; and a variety of 'market structure' indicators, ranging from firm size, concentration, degrees of foreign ownership, levels of internationalisation, etc., again all specified at the sectoral level. Such data are not yet available. The approach chosen here thus aims, in the first instance, at providing a broad set of empirical tests and results – much constrained by available statistical data – which could form the basis for further empirical research in this area based on more complete and reliable statistical data.

Technology and trade patterns: some evidence

Let us first consider a set of tests of the form

$$X_{ij} = f(T_{ij}) \tag{6.11}$$

where the Ts stand for a number of proxies related to sectoral and country-specific technological advantages/disadvantages. The econometric evidence reported here is based in the first instance on some earlier empirical research by one of the authors (see Soete, 1980 and 1981a), interpreted here, however, in the light of the theoretical framework developed above and in the preceding chapter.

As we already saw earlier (Chapter 3) patenting in the United States appears to be a reasonably good indicator of the innovative performance of each country within single sectors. We use this variable here as a proxy for the sectoral innovativeness of a country. Variations in export performance across the various OECD countries[31] (X_{ij}, where $j = 1$–22) will be regressed on variations in innovativeness (P_{ij}) for each of forty 3-digit industrial sectors $i(i = 1-40)$. The choice of sectors was dictated by the US patent data source.[32] The testing procedure (across countries within each industry) is analogous to that pioneered by Leamer (1974) and Lacroix and Scheuer (1976).

Moreover, in the estimates we shall consider some variables also used by these authors, namely population, GDP, the country-wide capital/labour ratio and a 'resistance' variable, i.e. a distance proxy from export markets. Our interpretation of these variables is different, however, from theirs. On the grounds of the foregoing discussion we shall consider these variables (with the exception of 'distance') as proxies for a set of country-specific absolute advantages which tend to affect, to different degrees, all sectors in any one particular country. In other words, in our interpretation population will tend to capture the potential economies of scale that can be achieved on the domestic market; GDP on the other hand will be a more mixed indicator of size and degree of development, whereas the capital/labour ratio is assumed to be a proxy for the degree of capital accumulation and thus also of the automation or mechanisation of production achieved in the economy at large.[33]

Multicollinearity problems between the population and the GDP variable on the one hand,[34] and the GDP and patent variables on the other hand,[35] forced us to drop the GDP variable. A regression equation where the dependent variable is weighted by GDP (equation (6.13) below) was, however, also estimated. The following four sets of regression equations were estimated for each of the forty industries i:

$$\ln\ XSHA_{ij} = \beta_{0i} + \beta_{1i}\ \ln\ PSHA_{ij} + \beta_{2i}\ \ln\ KL_j + \beta_{3i}\ \ln\ Pop_j$$
$$+ \beta_4 D\ is\ t_j \tag{6.12}$$

$$\ln\ RCA_{ij} = \beta_{0i} + \beta_{1i}\ \ln\ PSHA_{ij} + \beta_{2i}\ \ln\ KL_j + \beta_{3i}\ \ln\ Pop_j$$
$$+ \beta_{4i} D\ is\ t_j \tag{6.13}$$

$$\ln\ \frac{(X_{ij})}{(M_{ij})} = \beta_{0i} + \beta_{1i}\ \ln\ PSHA_{ij} + \beta_{2i}\ \ln\ KL_j + \beta_{3i}\ \ln\ Pop_j$$
$$+ \beta_{4i} D\ is\ t_j \tag{6.14}$$

$$\ln\ \frac{(X_{ij})}{(GDP_j)} = \beta_{0i} + \beta_{1i}\ \ln\ PSHA_{ij} + \beta_{2i}\ \ln\ KL_j + \beta_{3i}\ \ln\ Pop_j$$
$$+ \beta_{4i} D\ is\ t_j \tag{6.15}$$

where,

$XSHA_{ij}$ = share of each country's j exports of industry i (X_{ij} in total OECD exports of industry i ($\sum_{j=1}^{22} X_{ij}$)

$$RCA_{ij} = X_{ij} \bigg/ \sum_{j=1}^{22} X_{ij} : \sum_{i=1}^{40} X_{ij} \bigg/ \sum_{i=1}^{40} \sum_{j=1}^{22} X_{ij}$$

and

$$X_{ij} = \text{exports of country } j \text{ for product } i;$$

$$\Sigma_{j=1}^{22} X_{ij} = \text{OECD exports (excluding Iceland) for product } i$$

$X_{ij}/M_{ij} = $ ratio between the exports of country j for product i and the imports of country j for product i (M_{ij})

$X_{ij}/GDP_j = $ share of exports of country j for product i in the gross domestic product of each country j

$PSHA_{ij} = $ share of each country's j 1963–77 US patents in industry i (P_{ij}) in total OECD (including the estimated US figure (see Chapter 3) 1963–77 US-registered patents in industry i) ($\Sigma_{j=1}^{22} P_{ij}$)

$KL_j = $ gross fixed capital formation divided by total employment for each country j

$Pop_j = $ population of each country j

$Dist_j = $ Linnemann's distance proxy (1966, p. 186, Table 7.4, using I_i (0.8)) which is a proxy for the physical distance of various countries from some assumed 'world centre'.

In so far as these empirical tests aim in the first instance at providing more corroborative evidence of some of the structural characteristics of trade among OECD countries, the particular year chosen is not of real importance to the analysis presented here. In order to allow for some comparison with the analyses carried out previously by one of us (Soete, 1980, 1981a), all variables have been calculated for the same year, 1977. However, to avoid large variations in annual numbers – for some countries the number of annual patents granted in particular industries will be extremely small – the patent variable was calculated for the period 1963–77. Our analysis, in other words, does not make any claim to be updated; its aim is not to provide an explanation of the most recent trade patterns following recent changes in competitiveness. Rather, it provides a picture of what have been the major determinants of trade competitiveness in the post-War period, in this case the mid-1970s.

The best results were obtained for regression equation (6.12). This is not surprising: it is in terms of export shares (i.e. competitiveness) that one would expect to find the clearest indication of the effects of the various sector-specific and country-specific advantages. In terms of revealed comparative advantage indices, where the commodities' export shares are being weighted by the overall export share, one might expect a far less clear picture to the extent that interindustry variations in export performance are being introduced in the dependent variable. Nevertheless, the results for equations (6.13), (6.14) and (6.15), while less significant overall, are similar to the results presented in Table 6.1.

A number of interesting features emerge from these results:

1. Overall non-significant results (non-significant F values) were obtained for three industries: food, agricultural chemicals, and petroleum and natural gas – all industries where one might assume that natural resource endowments play a crucial role. Because no such variable was included in equation (6.12), the non-significant results obtained for these industries should come as no surprise.

2. As regards the capital/labour ratios, their country-average is clearly an imperfect proxy for sectoral capital intensity. The lack of significance with regard to this variable should again come as no surprise. Nevertheless, the significance of this variable in some of the continuous-process industries where one would expect process technology and capital equipment to be important for competitiveness (see plastics and synthetic materials, petroleum and natural gas, non-ferrous metals) is striking.

3. Population, as used here, captures both the size and scale effects of large countries. It is interesting to note that most significant results are obtained for stone, clay and glass products, fabricated metal products, refrigeration and service machinery and motor vehicles – all industries in which *economies of scale* play an important role.

4. As noticed by Gruber and Vernon (1970), proximity to the major foreign markets is still a crucial advantage in many industries. The distance variable performs relatively well in most industries.

5. Last but not least, the results in Table 6.1 bring to the forefront the crucial role of the technology variable in explaining the intercountry variations in export performance in a large number of industries. With the exception of the 'natural resource intensive' industries (food, petroleum, agricultural chemicals and stone, clay and glass) and a number of industries where *patented* innovations can be expected to be less of an appropriate proxy for innovativeness (such as textiles, ships and boat building, motorcycles and bicycles), significant results are obtained for all other industries.

Furthermore, a ranking of the industries by their estimated 'technology' elasticities (β_1) reveals a number of interesting facts.[36] First, as illustrated in Table 6.2, the ranking of the various industries is relatively independent of the equation chosen. While the estimated technology elasticities for equations (6.13) and (6.14) are in general less significant,

Table 6.1 Estimates of regression equations explaining OECD countries' export shares for forty industrial sectors[*]

Dependent variable ln $XSHA_{ij}$ for industries j:	β_0	β_1 ln $PSHA_{ij}$	β_2 ln KL_i	β_3 ln Pop_i	β_4 $Dist_i$	$\bar{R}^2$	$F(4, 17)$
1. Food products	-5.01 (2.69)	0.099 (0.147)	0.402 (0.588)	0.368 (0.255)	0.004 (0.003)	0.32	3.52
2. Textile mill products	-12.90* (2.19)	0.145 (0.117)	-0.337 (0.551)	0.631** (0.230)	0.011* (0.003)	0.73	15.15*
3. Industrial inorganic chemicals	-8.10** (2.97)	0.488** (0.197)	-0.128 (0.849)	0.522 (0.393)	0.003 (0.004)	0.78	19.53*
4. Industrial organic chemicals	-8.66* (2.63)	0.238 (0.114)	0.712 (0.539)	0.776** (0.262)	0.013** (0.004)	0.82	25.37*
5. Plastic materials, synthetics	-2.55 (1.99)	0.305* (0.098)	1.143** (0.477)	0.344** (0.225)	0.008* (0.003)	0.91	51.16*
6. Agricultural chemicals	-11.36 (8.24)	0.256 (0.385)	0.457 (1.607)	0.939 (0.785)	0.009 (0.009)	0.20	2.34
7. Soaps, cleaners, toilet goods	-0.49 (3.65)	0.325** (0.158)	1.261 (0.656)	0.382 (0.334)	0.009** (0.004)	0.69	12.67**
8. Paints and allied products	-0.69 (3.79)	0.214 (0.164)	1.585* (0.538)	0.478 (0.338)	0.010** (0.004)	0.68	12.15*
9. Miscellaneous chemical products	-4.33 (2.83)	0.226 (0.137)	0.743 (0.627)	0.492 (0.289)	0.006** (0.004)	0.67	11.61*
10. Drugs	-5.22** (2.57)	0.340* (0.108)	0.164 (0.495)	0.278 (0.252)	0.011* (0.003)	0.77	11.41*
11. Petroleum, natural gas	3.22 (7.76)	-0.151 (0.362)	3.581** (1.363)	1.071 (0.827)	0.009 (0.008)	0.36	3.96
12. Rubber and miscellaneous plastic products	-7.63* (2.11)	0.441** (0.121)	-0.038 (0.573)	0.424** (0.210)	0.009* (0.002)	0.86	33.38*
13. Stone, clay, glass and concrete products	-11.58* (1.88)	0.220 (0.113)	-0.129 (0.489)	0.679* (0.191)	0.009* (0.002)	0.81	23.97*
14. Primary ferrous metal products	-4.71** (2.32)	0.417** (0.146)	0.577 (0.842)	0.514 (0.265)	0.005** (0.003)	0.84	28.69*

Continued

Table 6.1 *(Continued)*

Dependent variable ln $XSHA_{ij}$ for industries j:	β_0	β_1 ln $PSHA_{ij}$	β_2 ln KL_i	β_3 ln Pop_i	β_4 $Dist_i$	$\bar{R}^2$	$F(4,17)$
15. Primary and secondary non-ferrous metals	0.94 (2.02)	0.262** (0.118)	1.154** (0.533)	0.316 (0.234)	0.001 (0.002)	0.81	23.36*
16. Fabricated metal products	-7.68* (1.81)	0.346* (0.090)	0.107 (0.468)	0.502* (0.180)	0.008* (0.002)	0.88	40.34*
17. Engine and turbines	-4.71 (3.32)	0.473** (0.213)	1.250 (0.765)	0.843** (0.382)	0.008** (0.004)	0.31	23.52*
18. Farm and garden machinery equipment	-3.37 (3.98)	0.657* (0.223)	0.704 (1.022)	0.530 (0.349)	0.005 (0.004)	0.78	19.52*
19. Construction, mining material handling machinery equipment	-7.44** (2.74)	0.512* (0.154)	0.117 (0.749)	0.527 (0.257)	0.007** (0.003)	0.84	28.31*
20. Metalworking machinery and equipment	-8.93* (2.74)	0.650* (0.133)	-0.562 (0.709)	0.287 (0.293)	0.009* (0.003)	0.34	28.35*
21. Office, computing and accounting machinery	-7.95 (6.36)	0.392** (0.320)	-0.509 (1.591)	0.238 (0.630)	0.014** (0.007)	0.65	10.90*
22. Special industry machinery	-4.49 (2.80)	0.676* (0.146)	-0.051 (0.729)	0.191 (0.264)	0.007** (0.003)	0.86	33.60*
23. General industrial machinery	-6.09** (2.67)	0.494* (0.112)	0.340 (0.642)	0.494** (0.232)	0.009* (0.003)	0.87	36.72*
24. Refrigeration and service machinery	-8.30** (2.94)	0.513* (0.146)	0.618 (0.629)	0.858* (0.271)	0.006 (0.003)	0.84	28.46*
25. Miscellaneous machinery excluding electrical	-0.37 (2.97)	0.930* (0.166)	-0.248 (0.768)	-0.211 (0.301)	0.007** (0.003)	0.87	36.67*
26. Electrical transmission and distributing equipment	-3.14 (2.93)	0.672* (0.174)	-0.230 (0.797)	-0.230 (0.334)	0.008** (0.003)	0.81	23.03*
27. Electrical industrial apparatus	-1.39 (3.32)	0.615* (0.190)	0.134 (0.878)	0.040 (0.401)	0.004 (0.004)	0.78	19.18*

					R^2	F
28. Household appliances	-4.68 (2.46)	0.501* (0.132)	0.109 (0.618)	0.184 (0.248)	0.004 (0.003)	0.78	20.09*
29. Electrical lighting, wiring equipment	-3.37 (3.47)	0.509** (0.219)	0.373 (0.992)	0.245 (0.488)	0.009** (0.004)	0.77	19.05*
30. Miscellaneous electrical equipment supplies	-4.71 (2.27)	0.412* (0.119)	0.702 (0.551)	0.578** (0.264)	0.006** (0.003)	0.88	40.76*
31. Radio, TV receiving equipment	-5.58 (4.48)	0.503 (0.254)	-0.97 (1.185)	0.170 (0.580)	0.009 (0.005)	0.61	9.13*
32. Communication equipment, electronic components	-8.29** (2.59)	0.463** (0.172)	0.009 (0.862)	0.499 (0.343)	0.010* (0.003)	0.80	22.36*
33. Motor vehicles and equipment	-9.45* (2.88)	0.456** (0.162)	0.732 (0.724)	1.027* (0.310)	0.007** (0.003)	0.86	32.85*
34. Ship, boat building, repairing	1.15 (5.68)	0.529 (0.348)	0.808 (1.388)	0.089 (0.582)	0.003 (0.006)	0.38	4.21**
35. Railroad equipment	-14.95** (5.49)	0.133 (0.239)	1.154 (0.988)	1.557** (0.542)	0.015** (0.006)	0.62	9.71*
36. Motorcycles, bicycles and parts	0.54 (6.63)	0.530 (0.282)	1.898 (0.998)	0.575 (0.599)	0.012 (0.007)	0.60	8.87*
37. Miscellaneous transportation equipment	6.29 (4.12)	0.799* (0.199)	1.186 (0.764)	-0.189 (0.404)	0.011** (0.004)	0.80	21.51*
38. Ordnance, guided missiles, space vehicles and parts	-5.09 (5.79)	0.900* (0.277)	-0.982 (1.118)	-0.108 (0.570)	-0.001 (0.006)	0.53	6.88*
39. Aircraft and parts	1.09 (4.50)	1.262* (0.242)	-0.206 (0.891)	-0.307 (0.449)	0.009 (0.005)	0.91	22.67*
40. Instruments	-6.94 (3.53)	0.743* (0.184)	-0.611 (0.944)	0.109 (0.343)	0.010** (0.004)	0.80	22.82*

Notes:
* Significant at the 1% level.
** Significant at the 5% level.
The figures in parentheses are the estimated standard errors of the coefficients.
For the SIC-definition of these industries and their conversion into SITC product codes see Soete (1981).

Source: Soete, L. (1981).

Table 6.2 Ranking of the technology variable's elasticities β_1

Industries[a]	Equation			
	6.12	6.13	6.14	6.15
Aircraft	1.26	0.97	0.87	1.19
Miscellaneous machinery	0.93	0.67	0.73	0.83
Ordnance and guided missiles	0.90	0.77	0.52	0.82
Office equipment	0.89	0.64	0.52	0.83
Miscellaneous transportation equipment	0.80	0.54	0.76	0.73
Instruments	0.74	0.47	0.57	0.67
Special industry machinery	0.68	0.43	0.64	0.62
Electrical transmission and distributing equipment	0.67	0.38	0.54	0.58
Farm and garden machinery	0.66	0.38	0.57	0.57
Electrical industrial apparatus	0.62	0.40	0.55	0.55
Metalworking machinery	0.57	0.41	0.43	0.49
Ship, boat building[b]	0.53 [+]	0.30 [+]	0.32 [+]	0.47 [+]
Motorcycles and bicycles[b]	0.53 [+]	0.32 [+]	0.33 [+]	0.47 [+]
Refrigeration and service machinery	0.51	0.27	0.35	0.43
Construction and mining machinery	0.51	0.24	0.39	0.43
Electrical lighting, wiring equipment	0.51	0.30 [+]	0.27 [+]	0.40
Radio and TV receiving equipment[b]	0.50 [+]	0.27 [+]	0.17 [+]	0.41 [+]
Household appliances	0.50	0.25	0.38	0.41
General industrial machinery	0.40	0.30	0.40	0.43
Industrial inorganic chemicals	0.42	0.25 [+]	0.48	0.43
Engines and turbines	0.47	0.28 [+]	0.46	0.40
Communications equipment and electronics	0.46	0.17 [+]	0.35	0.39
Motor vehicles	0.46	0.18 [+]	0.32 [+]	0.39
Rubber and plastics products	0.44	0.14 [+]	0.33	0.37
Ferrous metal products	0.42	0.24 [+]	0.32 [+]	0.33
Miscellaneous electrical supplies	0.41	0.21	0.31	0.34
Fabricated metal products	0.35	0.09 [+]	0.26	0.28
Drugs	0.34	0.18	0.25	0.26
Soap, cleaners	0.33	0.14 [+]	0.18 [+]	0.27
Plastic materials	0.31	0.08 [+]	0.22	0.25
Non-ferrous metal products	0.26	0.14 [+]	0.13 [+]	0.19 [+]
Agricultural chemicals[b]	0.26 [+]	0.03 [+]	0.28 [+]	0.18 [+]
Industrial organic chemicals[b]	0.24 [+]	0.08 [+]	0.13 [+]	0.17 [+]
Miscellaneous chemicals[b]	0.23 [+]	0.06 [+]	0.14 [+]	0.17 [+]
Stone, clay and glass[b]	0.22 [+]	−0.08 [+]	0.05 [+]	0.14 [+]
Paints[b]	0.21 [+]	0.01 [+]	0.18 [+]	0.15 [+]
Textiles[b]	0.15 [+]	−0.12 [+]	−0.10 [+]	0.07 [+]
Railroad equipment[b]	0.13 [+]	−0.06 [+]	−0.05 [+]	0.05 [+]
Food[b]	0.10 [+]	−0.16 [+]	−0.14 [+]	0.02 [+]
Petroleum products[b]	−0.15 [+]	−0.25 [+]	−0.13 [+]	−0.22 [+]

Notes:
[a] Industries ranked by the technology variable's elasticity in equation (6.12), as given in Table 6.1.
[b] Overall *not* significant at the 10% level (t-statistic).
[+] *Not* significant at the 10% level (t-statistic).

Source: Soete (1981a).

their ranking is very similar to the estimated elasticities for both equations (6.12) and (6.15).

Second, in contrast to Lacroix and Scheuer's findings (1976), the ranking of the technology elasticities suggests – with some important exceptions – a relationship with 'technology intensity': not so much R&D-intensity, but some measure which also gives weight to the technological performance of the various machinery industries, such as patent-intensity. This corresponds to what one would expect *a priori*. Any increase in a country's relative – as compared to its competitors – technological performance will be more rewarding in terms of its relative export performance, or even relative comparative advantage index, in technology-intensive industries than in non-technology-intensive industries (for a discussion of the classification of the various industries in the two groups, see Chapter 3). With respect to the industries with relatively low and/or non-significant technology elasticities, one could argue that basic technology has been essentially diffused,[37] and that the patents relate primarily to less 'important' improvement innovations.

Third, it could be argued that the relatively good results for some of the 'miscellaneous' industries illustrate the crucial impact of industrial innovation on trade performance in some of these highly heterogeneous and ill-defined 'other' industries, where new products and industries eventually emerge.

Technology gaps and wage gaps

Introducing a more comprehensive specification of the set of sector-specific absolute advantages and the inclusion of a proxy for wage costs has its statistical price: we have comparable sectoral wage data for only fourteen OECD countries. The general form of the tests will be:

$$X_{ij} = f(T_{ij}, C_{ij})$$

As above, one of the proxies for the set of technology-related variables, will consist of numbers of patents granted in the United States. However, we will extend the model in order to take into account other sources of absolute advantages (i.e. different degrees of mechanisation and/or, more generally, productive efficiency, expressed by different sectoral capital/labour ratios and/or labour productivities) and in order to explore at a more detailed level the relationship between cost-based processes of adjustment and absolute advantages.[38]

The dependent variable is, as already discussed above, an absolute measure of competitiveness, i.e. independent of the competitiveness of other sectors within the same country. *A priori*, one could have chosen export shares on the world market (as in equation (6.12)) or exports per capita. The drawback of the former measure is that it depends very much on the sheer size of each country, and thus requires a size-proxy on the right-hand side of the estimating equation. Exports per capita, on the other hand, eliminate the direct country size effect, but do not eliminate the possible effect that size might have on a country's export propensity: high for small, and low for large countries. Throughout the estimates that follow, the dependent variable will be the exports of country j in sector i normalised by the population of country j (XPC_{ij}).[39] The innovativeness proxy is again the cumulated 1963–77 number of patents registered in the United States in sector i by country j, but normalised by the population of j (PPC_{ij}). The degree of mechanisation of production (K_{ij}), was approximated by the two-year average of the fixed investment/labour ratio;[40] labour productivity (Q_{ij}/L_{ij}) by the two-year average of the value-added/employment ratio; and the capital/output ratio (I_{ij}) by the two-year average of the fixed investment/value-added ratio, all at current prices and exchange rates. Finally, the proxy for wage costs consisted of the two-year average of the remuneration per employee (R_{ij}) or the two-year average of the ratio of employees' remuneration to value-added (VLC_{ij}).[41]

The following equations were estimated:

$$\ln XPC_{ij} = \beta_{0i} + \beta_{1i} \ln PPC_{ij} + \beta_{2i} \ln ULC_{ij} \qquad \textbf{(6.16)}$$

$$\ln XPC_{ij} = \beta_{0i} + \beta_{1i} \ln PPC_{ij} + \beta_{2i} \ln R_{ij} + \beta_{3i} \ln K_{ij} \qquad \textbf{(6.17)}$$

$$\ln XPC_{ij} = \beta_{0i} + \beta_{1i} \ln \pi_{ij} + \beta_{2i} \ln R_{ij} \qquad \textbf{(6.18)}$$

$$\ln XPC_{ij} = \beta_{0i} + \beta_{1i} \ln PPC_{ij} + \beta_{2i} \ln K_{ij} + \beta_{3i} \ln VLC_{ij}$$
$$\textbf{(6.19)}$$

$$\ln XPC_{ij} = \beta_{0i} + \beta_{1i} \ln PPC_{ij} + \beta_{2i} \ln I_{ij} + \beta_{3i} \ln VLC_{ij}$$
$$\textbf{(6.20)}$$

$$\ln XPC_{ij} = \beta_{0i} + \beta_{1i} \ln PPC_{ij} + \beta_{2i} \ln I_{ij} + \beta_{3i} \ln K_{ij} \qquad \textbf{(6.21)}$$

Single regression tests of the dependent variable ($\ln XPC_{ij}$) against each of the independent variables were also carried out. Table 6.3 presents the results of the estimates obtained from equation (6.19). Table 6.4, on the other hand, presents a summary of all the results obtained from equations (6.16)–(6.21) as well as from the single regressions.

A first outcome is the corroboration of the importance of the innovativeness variable in the majority of sectors and a demonstration of its robustness. In view of the different functional form of the dependent variable (in per capita terms) and the exclusion of some of the very small or less developed OECD countries (such as Iceland, Greece,

Table 6.3 Export performance, technological levels, degrees of mechanisation of production, wage-costs; regression analysis, forty sectors, log-linear estimates

Sector	Constant	Patents per head	Investment per employee	Wages on value added	$\bar{R}^2$	F
1. Food products	-4.355 (-2.407)**	-0.080 (-0.247)	1.231 (2.359)**	-0.021 (-0.029)	0.403	2.02
2. Textile products	-3.870 (-2.436)***	0.038 (0.246)	0.321 (0.586)	-1.944 (-0.995)	0.204	0.77
3. Industrial inorganic chemicals	-3.397 (-2.965)***	0.505 (4.642)****	0.900 (1.893)**	0.654 (1.091)	0.709	7.29
4. Industrial organic chemicals	-1.879 (-1.921)**	0.818 (5.644)****	0.683 (1.585)*	0.606 (1.168)	0.789	11.24
5. Plastics & synthetic resins	-2.990 (-2.354)***	0.429 (4.776)****	1.488 (2.990)	0.790 (0.773)	0.847	16.67
6. Agricultural chemicals	-5.610 (-0.620)	0.300 (0.279)	0.721 (0.284)	0.198 (0.085)	0.047	0.15
7. Soaps, detergents cleaning & toilet preparations	-0.019 (-0.013)	0.565 (4.389)****	0.027 (0.067)	2.122 (2.965)***	0.762	9.61
8. Paints, varnishes lacquers & allied products	-3.616 (-1.791)*	0.199 (0.957)	0.426 (0.861)	1.244 (1.156)	0.265	1.08
9. Misc. chemicals	-1.482 (-1.294)	0.486 (4.188)****	0.354 (0.717)	1.353 (1.997)**	0.752	9.10
10. Drugs	-0.102 (-0.102)	0.753 (5.006)****	0.362 (0.947)	1.781 (2.862)****	0.776	10.41
11. Petroleum, natural gas, petroleum refining	-2.099 (-0.590)	0.341 (0.702)	0.360 (0.233)	0.345 (0.398)	0.079	0.26
12. Rubber & misc. plastic products	-4.050 (-2.446)***	0.160 (1.119)	1.265 (1.727)*	0.453 (0.305)	0.751	9.04

Continued

Table 6.3 (*Continued*)

Sector	Constant	Patents per head	Investment per employee	Wages on value added	$\bar{R}^2$	F
13. Stone, clay & glass	-3.630 (-1.710)	0.131 (0.905)	0.649 (1.100)	0.511 (0.245)	0.316	1.39
14. Ferrous metals	-0.344 (-0.176)	0.421 (2.009)**	-0.087 (-0.089)	0.287 (0.313)	0.437	2.33
15. Non-ferrous metals	-0.835 (-0.338)	0.507 (2.332)***	0.752 (0.859)	1.084 (0.694)	0.590	4.32
16. Fabricated metal products	-2.426 (-4.639)****	0.227 (3.539)****	0.697 (2.358)***	0.463 (0.773)	0.760	9.50
17. Engines & turbines	-3.311 (-7.275)****	0.409 (9.062)****	0.741 (3.976)****	-0.466 (-1.651)*	0.984	180.13
18. Farm & garden machinery & equipment	-4.044 (-2.024)**	0.409 (2.013)**	0.933 (1.083)	-1.027 (-0.721)	0.733	8.24
19. Construction, mining, material handling machinery	-3.732 (-5.904)****	0.175 (2.010)**	0.911 (1.940)**	-1.185 (-2.815)***	0.913	32.42
20. Metal working machinery	-3.689 (-3.096)****	0.347 (1.607)*	0.202 (0.356)	-1.688 (-1.315)	0.596	4.43
21. Office, computing & accounting machinery	-2.187 (-1.837)**	0.354 (2.472)***	-0.195 (-0.533)	0.254 (0.456)	0.585	4.22
22. Special industrial machinery	-2.104 (-2.369)***	0.466 (3.518)****	0.270 (0.988)	-0.394 (-0.479)	0.866	19.33
23. General industrial machinery	-4.342 (-7.004)****	0.205 (2.380)***	1.317 (2.733)***	-1.324 (-2.662)**	0.935	43.43
24. Refrigeration & service machinery	0.304 (0.087)	1.235 (2.865)***	-0.447 (-0.628)	2.291 (0.592)	0.591	4.34
25. Misc. (non-electrical) machinery	-7.235 (-4.676)****	0.121 (0.649)	2.946 (3.617)****	-0.445 (-0.482)	0.871	20.32

26. Electrical transmission & distribution equip.	-2.203 (-1.455)	0.342 (2.545)****	-0.049 (-0.133)	0.475 (0.222)	0.615	4.79
27. Electrical industrial apparatus	-2.030 (-1.827)**	0.351 (3.494)****	0.015 (0.053)	0.777 (0.485)	0.722	7.81
28. Household appliances	-1.252 (-1.502)	0.556 (5.365)****	0.311 (0.692)	0.728 (0.711)	0.765	9.75
29. Electrical lighting & wiring equipment	-2.408 (-2.473)***	0.380 (3.048)****	-0.093 (-0.174)	2.645 (2.250)***	0.610	4.70
30. Misc. electrical equipment	-2.675 (-3.791)****	0.427 (4.966)****	0.165 (0.625)	0.999 (1.475)	0.764	9.71
31. Radio & TV receiving equipment	-3.726 (-1.785)*	0.151 (0.731)	0.270 (0.285)	0.189 (0.105)	0.117	0.40
32. Electronic components & communication equip.	-2.389 (-2.955)***	0.272 (3.305)****	0.205 (0.442)	0.764 (0.928)	0.699	6.97
33. Motor vehicles & parts	-2.810 (-1.290)	0.345 (1.467)	0.498 (0.567)	-1.825 (-1.191)	0.638	5.29
34. Ships & boats	-3.119 (-1.556)*	0.243 (0.928)	1.784 (1.230)	-1.362 (-0.639)	0.288	1.21
35. Railroad equipment	-3.893 (-4.373)****	0.458 (3.204)****	0.160 (0.859)	-0.449 (-0.405)	0.667	6.00
36. Motorcycles, bicycles	-4.221 (-1.169)	0.196 (0.587)	0.086 (0.045)	0.610 (0.254)	0.076	0.25
37. Misc. transport equipment	-3.228 (-0.871)	0.672 (1.358)	0.465 (0.580)	-0.661 (-0.240)	0.424	2.21
38. Missiles, space vehicles, ordnance	-0.517 (-0.177)	0.756 (1.951)**	-0.391 (-0.447)	3.350 (1.222)	0.311	1.35
39. Aircraft & parts	0.030 (0.012)	0.915 (2.622)***	-1.101 (-2.425)***	0.077 (0.029)	0.582	4.18
40. Professional & Scientific instr.	-2.377 (-3.303)****	0.415 (4.073)****	-0.533 (-1.037)	-0.516 (-0.861)	0.725	7.90

Technological levels approximated by patents per head.
t-Statistics in parentheses. **** significant at the 1% level; *** at the 5% level; ** at the 10% level; * at the 15% level.

Table 6.4   A tentative taxonomy of the factors affecting export performance, by sector

(1) Sector	(2) Technological innovativeness as expressed by patenting	(3a) Process-related technological advantages as expressed by labour productivity	and/or by	(3b) degree of mechanisation of production (capital/labour ratios)	(4) Cost-based competitiveness	(5) Other factors not identified by the model
1. Food products		X		X		
2. Textile products		X				*
3. Industrial inorganic chemicals	X					
4. Industrial organic chemicals	XX					
5. Plastics and synthetic resins	X	X		X		
6. Agricultural chemicals					(a)	*
7. Soaps, detergents, cleaning and toilet preparations	XX					*
8. Paints, varnishes, lacquers and allied products						
9. Miscellaneous chemicals	XX				(a)	
10. Drugs	XX				(a)	
11. Petroleum, natural gas, refining						*
12. Rubber and miscellaneous plastic products	X	X		X		
13. Stone, clay and glass	X	X				
14. Ferrous metals	X	X				*
15. Non-ferrous metals	X	X				*
16. Fabricated metal products	XX			XX		

Item					
17. Engines and turbines	XX	X	X		
18. Farm and garden machinery and equipment	X	XX			
19. Construction, mining, material handling machinery	XX	X	X	X	
20. Metal working machinery	XX			X	
21. Office, computing and accounting machinery	XX	X			
22. Special industrial machinery	XX	X			
23. General industrial machinery	XX	X			
24. Refrigeration and service machinery	XX	X	X	X	
25. Miscellaneous (non-electrical) machinery	X	X			
26. Electrical transmission and distribution equipment	X	X	XX		
27. Electrical industrial apparatus	XX			X	
28. Household appliances	XX	XX		X	
29. Electrical lighting and wiring equipment	XX	XX			
30. Miscellaneous electrical equipment	X	X		(a)	
31. Radio and television receiving equipment	X	X			*
32. Electronic components and communication equipment	XX				
33. Motor vehicles and parts	X	X	X	X	*
34. Ships and boats	X	XX			

Continued

Table 6.4 (*Continued*)

(1) Sector	(2) Technological innovativeness as expressed by patenting	(3a) Process-related technological advantages as expressed by labour productivity	and/ or by	(3b) degree of mechanisation of production (capital/labour ratios)	(4) Cost-based competitiveness	(5) Other factors not identified by the model
35. Railway equipment	XX	X			X	*
36. Motorcycles, bicycles		X				
37. Miscellaneous transport equipment	X	XX		X	X	
38. Missiles, space vehicles, ordnance	XX	(a)			X	
39. Aircraft and parts	X			(a)		
40. Professional and scientific instruments	XX	X			X	

The following conventions have been adopted:

X: The variable is significant (at 10% or more) in at least one regression estimate.

XX: 'dominant variable'. It always appears significant (at 15% or more) in all attempted estimates; whenever introduced alone as an independent variable yields an R^2 (adjusted for the degrees of freedom) higher than 0.30; there is at least one estimate where it is significant at 1% level.

*: None of the estimates yield an R^2 (adjusted for the degrees of freedom) higher than 0.50.

(a): The variable is significant at least once but the sign is opposite to that predicted.

Column (4) refers to the ratio of employee remuneration to value added and/or to remuneration per employee with a negative and significant value. Note that in sector 37 it is remuneration-to-value-added which appears significantly negative in one estimate, while remuneration-per-employee is significantly positive in another one.

Ireland, Turkey, etc.) from the sample in Table 6.3, this feature is certainly worth observing.[42] Compared to Table 6.1, the results obtained for the innovativeness variable in Table 6.3 illustrate that in the majority of cases (thirty-four out of forty), the results are indeed stable: the patent variable is either non-significant or significant in both estimates.[43] In only three cases does a previously significant estimate become insignificant (rubber and plastic miscellaneous products, miscellaneous non-electrical machinery, and motor vehicles and parts), while in three other cases (industrial organic chemicals, miscellaneous chemicals, railway equipment) the opposite occurs.

Furthermore, the results presented in Tables 6.3 and 6.4 highlight the significance of the technology variable in a number of sectors: in chemical sectors characterised by relatively high degrees of process and product innovation such as organic chemicals, detergents, miscellaneous chemicals and, even more so, pharmaceuticals; in mechanical engineering, in practically all sectors (machine tools, special and general industrial machinery, construction and mining machinery, engines and turbines); and in the majority of electrical/electronic sectors with a significant rate of technological innovation (electronic components and communication equipment, office and computing machinery, electrical industrial apparatus, professional and scientific instruments, space and missile equipment).

The picture is less clear with respect to the sectors producing consumer durables and various kinds of transport equipment. Many of these sectors belong to what we referred to as scale-intensive sectors. As we discussed at greater length in Chapter 4, these sectors are, generally speaking, characterised by international oligopolistic structures, reflecting the adoption of innovations produced in other sectors and embodied in capital equipment; mass production and various kinds of economies of scale; the successful management of complex production systems; and product design and performance, all of which are not fully patented. One should not therefore be surprised to find, in some of these sectors, that the technology proxy used does not capture the full complexity of the innovative process.[44]

It is difficult to separate the effects of innovativeness, strictly defined, from labour productivity and the degree of mechanisation. As already discussed in Chapter 5, these variables are all correlated through 'virtuous circles' of innovation, capital accumulation, the adoption of best-practice equipment, etc. Table 6.3 only presents results for the mechanisation variable, while Table 6.4 also provides a summary of some of the other tests. The labour productivity variable results are, by and large, similar to the mechanisation variable results.[45]

Overall, labour productivity and mechanisation/automation of production appear to be relatively important within the mechanical engineering group and appear to be broadly complementary to straightforward innovativeness (as measured by patents) in several scale intensive sectors (e.g. in miscellaneous transport equipment, farm and garden machinery) and in one supplier-dominated sector (fabricated metal products), where one would expect technical progress to be embodied in equipment and machines. Generally, labour productivity, capital/labour ratios, or both, appear to be important in sectors which are strongly affected by innovations acquired through input–output flows instead of, or in addition to, own internally produced innovations.

The long-term complementarity of these two processes of technological change is obvious: straightforward innovativeness, equipment-related technological advances, increasing degrees of mechanisation/automation of production are all factors which determine absolute advantages of some countries vis-à-vis others in that they yield better products and/or univocally superior techniques of production.

In relation to these technology gaps, we must also assess the role of the wage-related variable. We have already argued above that in a world generally characterised by non-decreasing returns and freely reproducible capital and intermediate inputs, the greatest source of international variance in input prices is likely to be the international difference in wage rates. The proxy for unit wage costs used in Table 6.3 is the wages to value-added ratio. The results presented in Tables 6.3 and 6.4 suggest that the cost-related variable used here performs rather poorly, and is more often than not the opposite sign to what one would expect (i.e. positive).

A possible explanation for the positive sign is that the wage variable stands for different degrees of skill of the labour force. However, this cannot be the only explanation; a closer look at the results shows that the coefficient is negative precisely in those sectors where we would expect labour-embodied skills to be of crucial importance (such as in the machinery sectors), whereas positive, significant results are obtained for two process industries (soap and detergents and miscellaneous chemicals) where it could be considered of less importance.

Despite the empirical and statistical shortcomings of the above tests, the results presented in Tables 6.1, 6.3 and 6.4 provide support for the hypothesis of the dominance of univocal technology advantages over cost-related factors in shaping international competitiveness: in a good number of sectors, the international composition of trade (within each sector) is explained by the sector-specific patterns of technology gaps/leads, and in particular by different degrees of innovativeness. This holds even when we introduce into the estimate a proxy for wage cost-related factors.

Before proceeding to a dynamic analysis of absolute advantages and relative costs, it is worth mentioning the role of the capital/output ratios in the explanation of export flows. The proxy for the possible bias in capital use does not show any evident correlation with export performance, either if used alone or in conjunction with our technology gap and cost variables.[46] In other words, the tests do not appear to conflict with our hypothesis that technological advantages are associated with a more efficient use of both labour and capital which dominates over static interfactoral substitution,[47] irrespective of the capital intensity of the sectors.

6.4   The dynamics of international technological advantage and competitiveness

Technological innovation creates technology gaps and is a fundamental source of absolute advantages/disadvantages between countries. Conversely, international technological diffusion tends to reduce technological gaps. Here, we are interested in how changing patterns of competitiveness depend on the overall balance between the two processes, and on their relation with the trend in unit labour costs. In a hypothetical world tending to technological convergence, intracountry mechanisms of specialisation (related to relative prices, income distribution and, ultimately, comparative advantages) are likely to become the fundamental factor in explaining patterns of international competitiveness and the world distribution of exports within each sector. The opposite will apply to a world where technological asymmetries are increasing: technological gaps between countries within each sector would become the major determinant of international market shares.

We have attempted in the above to illustrate the dominant role of technological advantages in a 'static' cross-country analysis of international competitiveness. We will now look more closely at the dynamic aspects of such competitiveness patterns. The results presented so far are, by and large, consistent with those findings from time-series estimates of cost or price elasticities of exports showing an unexplained trend[48] or even a long-term 'perverse' relationship between the evolution of cost advantages and export market shares. The latter finding is sometimes referred to as the 'Kaldor paradox',[49] whereby countries which improved their export performance the most are also found to be those countries whose cost-related competitiveness deteriorated the most and vice versa.

Some evidence on the trends in exports, innovativeness and costs

It is not possible, because of the lack of the appropriate data on productivity and wages, to test the dynamic version of the model presented above at the level of sectoral disaggregation used so far. We will confine our analysis here to rates of change in the manufacturing sector as a whole.

At this level of aggregation, the performance indicator (rates of change in exports) is inevitably the outcome both of changing country-wide absolute advantages and changing patterns of specialisation. However, we can still explore the relative importance of average absolute technological advantage as compared to cost-related changes in competitiveness.

Table 6.5 shows some estimates of the relationship between changes in competitiveness, costs and technological indicators (innovativeness – measured by patenting – and labour productivity).

A comparison between the estimate under 1 and the estimates under 2 and 4 broadly corroborate the previous hypothesis of the dominance of the trends in technological asymmetries over cost-related factors as determinants of trade flows. Over the longer period (1964–80), unit labour costs generally acquire the correct negative sign, but the values are statistically insignificant. Relative trends in technological innovativeness, on the other hand, differ substantially from these trends in unit labour costs, and explain a good part of export changes. In other words, in the long term, unit labour costs adjust to the underlying trends in innovativeness and productivity, but play a relatively small role in determining long-term trade performance.

It should be stressed that here we are considering costs expressed in international currency (dollars): in the relationship between international technological asymmetries, levels of domestic absorption, domestic income distribution and exchange rates, the latter will adjust costs in dollars near those levels consistent in the long run with the changing pattern of international technology gaps.

Certainly, our variables do not capture the entire set of factors affecting trade. In particular, the innovativeness variable used here may not be entirely adequate to represent the process of technological innovation and international diffusion of technology when these do not involve patented innovations; we do not have any variable representing the changing average degree of participation of each national industry to the international oligopolies, inward and outward flows of international investment, changing domestic structures of supply, and so on;[50] and our estimates do not include any proxy for the quality – in terms of income elasticities – of the sectoral patterns of export specialisation of each country (see the section on patterns of demand and trade on p. 164).

Bearing these limitations in mind, the reader may appreciate the powerful impact of the changes in the technology variables, either expressed by patenting or by a variable highly correlated with it, namely labour productivity (cf. estimate 3) on trade performance.

Similar to the trends in productivity (cf. Chapter 5 above), a 'catching-up effect' has been at work, so that countries with relatively low levels of wages have been able, other things being equal, to enjoy a somewhat higher growth in exports (see estimate 6).[51] Our interpretation of this phenomenon is that, since the Second World War, processes of technological diffusion have outpaced the domestic growth of wages, thus creating a 'buffer of competitiveness' which has allowed high rates of growth of exports in most OECD countries which were catching up with the United States and started from relatively low wage levels. Conversely, in the most recent period, the 'catching-up effect' appears to have faded away within the group of fully industrialised OECD countries to which our tests refer (cf. the period 1970–80 in estimate 3).[52]

The importance of the technological factors appears also in relation to the trends in trade balances (approximated here by the growth in exports minus the growth in imports), although with less force (compare estimates 8 and 9 with 4–6).

As already mentioned, the goodness of fit of our estimates decreases considerably when the sub-period 1970–80 is examined alone. Our own hypothesis – which cannot be tested adequately here – is, that this has not been the result of the decreasing importance of the role of innovativeness and technology in international competitiveness, but primarily the result of changing macroeconomic policies. Exchange rates in the 1970s have been heavily managed from a perspective other than trade policy, including the control of domestic inflation. In a sense, this might have led to 'disequilibrium' values in the long-term relationship between technological asymmetries, wage-costs and exchange rates, since the various countries have shown widely differing emphasis upon the objectives of growth, and of the control of inflation.[53] Two countries in particular are 'out of line' in the estimated functions, namely the United States and the United Kingdom. As regards the latter, the 1980 exports might not yet fully account for the full impact of a revalued pound. In general, the shorter period of the 1970s is likely to be more sensitive to 'disequilibria' in the international market produced by discrete jumps in the exchange rates which take time to be fully accounted for in terms of trade flows.[54]

Table 6.5   The determinants of trade competitiveness, aggregate manufacturing, regression analysis, 1964–80 and 1970–80

Dependent Variable	Period	Constant	ULC	RPAT	RWAGE	LW	PH	$\bar{R}^2$	F	Form of the Estimate
EXP 1.	64–80	12.078 (2.268)***	-0.064 (-0.043)					0.002	0.02	lin
	70–80	3.828 (3.080)***	0.590 (1.297)					0.063	1.68	lin
EXP 2.	64–80	8.924 (14.471)****		1.230 (6.710)****				0.815	45.03	lin
	70–80	4.255 (7.853)****		1.023 (2.312)***				0.303	5.35	lin
EXP 3.	64–80	2.945 (1.350)			0.029 (0.981)		3.520 (4.010)****	0.624	9.31	lin
	70–80	2.150 (1.543)			0.163 (0.616)		1.556 (1.175)	0.355	3.76	lin
EXP 4.	64–80	2.240 (11.884)****	-0.028 (-0.184)	0.376 (6.396)****				0.796	20.65	log
	70–80	1.301 (7.035)****	3.445 (2.003)**	0.233 (2.003)**				0.375	4.00	log
EXP 5.	64–80	8.512 (3.593)****	0.116 (0.181)	1.231 (6.341)****				0.793	20.11	lin
	70–80	2.411 (2.253)***	0.607 (1.923)**	1.081 (2.777)***				0.464	5.32	lin
EXP 6.	64–80	15.609 (3.805)****	-0.919 (-1.214)	0.938 (4.220)****		-0.018 (-1.989)**		0.849	19.68	lin
	70–80	4.102 (1.632)	0.355 (0.757)	0.811 (1.503)*		-0.002 (-0.748)		0.432	3.54	lin

						R^2	F	
BAL	7.	64–80	0.496 (0.089)	1.245 (0.945)	−0.252* (−1.630) −0.476 (−1.080)...	0.108	0.03	lin
		70–80				0.016	1.17	lin
BAL	8.	64–80	−2.297 (−1.769)* −1.440 (−2.710)***		0.800 (2.073)** 1.144 (2.636)***	0.248	4.30	lin
		70–80				0.373	6.95	lin
BAL	9.	64–80	−1.817 (−0.364) −0.203 (−0.174)	−0.135 (−0.600) 1.407 (1.177)	0.798 (1.950)** 1.105 (2.593)***	0.155	1.92	lin
		70–80				0.399	4.31	lin

**** significant at the 1% level; *** at the 5% level; ** at the 10% level; * at the 15% level.

Variables:

EXP = percentage change in exports (current values in $).

BAL = percentage change in exports minus percentage change in imports.

ULC = percentage change in unit labour costs at current exchange rates (wage rates in international currency divided by labour productivity at constant prices and exchange rates).

RPAT = percentage change in the number of patents registered in the USA.

RWAGE = percentage change in hourly worker remuneration, (in $).

LW = levels of hourly workers remuneration at the initial year.

PH = percentage change in hourly labour productivity (output per manhour at constant prices).

The 11 countries of the estimates are the same as in Table 3.6.

Sources: Elaborations on unpublished data from the US Bureau of Labor Statistics, Confederation of Swedish Industries and national sources.

6.5 Conclusions

In this chapter we have analysed the relationship between technological gaps/leads and international competitiveness and their implications. Processes of 'circular causation' are particularly difficult to disentangle and our attempt has to be considered as a tentative exploration. However, despite the statistical and data difficulties, the results obtained are consistent with the proposed model: technological gaps, in terms of asymmetries in the techniques of production and product-technologies, are the dominant feature of an international economic system characterised by technological learning, innovation and imitation along technological trajectories of progress that continuously bring about a more efficient use of both labour and capital, and add new or improved products to production baskets.

A first consequence is that the international composition of trade flows is primarily explained by the pattern of technological lags and leads. The latter, we argued, broadly correspond to Ricardian absolute advantages. On the grounds of these absolute advantages, cost-related adjustments will undoubtedly take place: each country gains a relative specialisation in those sectors which, given the patterns of costs and income distribution, yield relatively higher profitabilities.

However, as we discussed in Chapter 5, the intranational intersectoral differences in comparative advantages are generally much smaller than international gaps in technology: in terms of our model, this implies that the boundaries within which 'Ricardian' processes of adjustment take place (i.e. processes of intersectoral allocation through relative prices and relative profitabilities) are rather tight. The model developed in this chapter predicts that in these circumstances the main adjustment mechanism in the international markets will run from sectoral (and country-wide) technological gaps/leads to sectoral (and country-wide) market shares in world exports. This interpretation allows a clear and, we would claim, rigorous distinction between three different concepts: 'competitiveness', 'comparative advantage', and 'relative specialisation'.

'Competitiveness' is an 'absolute' concept, in the sense that it is independent of intranational comparison of the activities in which a country is 'better' or 'worse', although it obviously compares one country with the rest of the world. In the model developed here, the various degrees of national competitiveness are the outcome of an adjustment mechanism linking absolute advantages and market shares (and, through that, domestic rates of activity, incomes and wages). Conversely, 'comparative advantage' relates, as is common in trade theory, to relative efficiencies: that is, to the intersectoral, intranational comparison of technological lags/leads. These comparative advantages lead to a 'Ricardian' adjustment process, based on intersectoral differences in profitabilities.

Finally, relative specialisation is in a sense the revealed outcome of both market-shares adjustments and Ricardian adjustments. In the simplest case, where no interdependencies between technologies and sectors exist, relative specialisation mirrors comparative advantage. In the more complex and realistic case, when some absolute advantages/disadvantages act as externalities and semi-public goods, absolute advantages will shape the intersectoral allocations of exports in ways which are likely to show only indirect links with comparative advantages, as shown by MacDonald and Markusen (1985).

Notwithstanding the difficulty in finding adequate indicators of the factors underlying both absolute and comparative advantages, the evidence presented here is consistent with the hypothesis that absolute advantages are a dominant factor in explaining trade flows. A similar concept of 'dominance' applies to the dynamic relation between the technological innovativeness of each country as a whole and relative costs: the trends in the former appear to have a much greater impact than changes in the latter as determinants of long-term variations in the competitive position of each country. The paradox pointed out by Kaldor who showed the worsening trade performance of countries whose 'competitiveness' in terms of costs was improving, is confirmed here and in some sense explained: the long-term trends in trade performance of each economy are essentially determined by their different degrees of innovativeness and technological dynamism.

These results can be easily linked with the analysis of the effect upon international competitiveness of the level and changes in the patterns of specialisation, in terms of the income elasticities of exports, i.e. the 'structural gaps' discussed in Section 2 of this chapter (see also Lafay, 1981; CEPII, 1983; Rothschild, 1985).[55] The importance of both technology gaps and demand-related gaps highlights the fundamental role of structural factors (that is, factors related to the long-term characteristics of the pattern of technological and capital accumulation) which shape the varying levels of adaptation of each country to the world economy, and, thus, also their differing degrees of success in terms of market shares, growth possibilities (consistent with the foreign balance constraint) and wage growth. In the next chapter we attempt to draw these strings of the analysis together, with the help of a simple formalised model showing the relationship between technology, demand elasticities of export and growth.

Appendix

A methodological note

The data on investment, productivity, employees' remuneration, etc., used in Tables 6.1 to 6.4 are based on unpublished OECD data for sixty-six manufacturing sectors at 2-, 3-, 4-digits of the ISIC classification-level, supplemented by the *UN Yearbook of Industrial Statistics* and national sources. Export data are from the OECD, *Trade by Commodities*, various years.

The 'innovativeness' variable is approximated by the number of patents registered by each country in the United States in each of the forty sectors considered. These sectors have been built around OTAF attributions of patents to SIC classes. The concordance between patent (SIC) classes and trade (SITC) classes is described in Soete (1981a). At this level of aggregation, there is no strict correspondence between these forty sectors and the various industrial performance indicators (such as investments, productivity, employees' remuneration, etc.) expressed in the ISIC categories at the disaggregation allowed by OECD data and/or national sources. Thus, we are sometimes forced to attribute to any one of the forty sectors a performance indicator belonging to an ISIC class of which the former is a sub-set. Moreover, quite a few countries had gaps in their data. We therefore assumed that the relative values of the relevant ratios (e.g. value added per employee, investment per employee, etc.) compared to a reference country (e.g. the United States) was the same in the missing sector as for the more aggregate sector for which the data were available.

Table 6A.1 shows the correlation matrix of the independent variables of estimates 6.12–6.15.

As mentioned in the text, the 'capital' variables of the estimates 6.14 to 6.19 have been approximated by two-year (1977–8) averages in the ratio of gross fixed investment to total employment (K_{ij}) and to value added (I_{ij}), at current prices and exchange rates. Similarly, labour productivity is approximated by the two-year (1977–8) ratio of value added to employment.

The two capital proxies are certainly far from perfect. As we briefly discuss in Dosi (1984), the investment/value-added ratio (I_{ij}/Y_{ij}) is linked to the 'true' capital/value-added ratio (K_{ij}/Y_{ij}) by the formula:

$$I_{ij}/Y_{ij} = [\sigma_1(g_{ij}) + \sigma_2(a_{ij})] (K_{ij}/Y_{ij}) \tag{A6.1}$$

where g_{ij} is the sectoral rate of growth and a_{ij} is the rate of scrapping. Similarly, the investment/employment ratio (I_{ij}/N_{ij}) is linked to the

Table 6A.1 Correlation matrix of the independent variables

	ln Pop	ln GDP	ln KL	ln RDSH[b]	Dist
ln Pop	1.00				
ln GDP	0.90	1.00			
ln KL	−0.17	0.21	1.00		
ln RDSH	0.60	0.87	0.57	1.00	
ln Dist	−0.15	−0.04	0.25	0.14	1.00
ln PSHA[a] $i =$ 1	0.48	0.77	0.60	0.94	0.18
2	0.51	0.79	0.60	0.96	0.23
3	0.55	0.82	0.62	0.90	0.26
4	0.54	0.80	0.54	0.90	0.22
5	0.56	0.81	0.58	0.93	0.30
6	0.53	0.78	0.53	0.94	0.25
7	0.54	0.77	0.48	0.88	0.24
8	0.68	0.83	0.39	0.88	0.15
9	0.53	0.79	0.58	0.88	0.20
10	0.55	0.80	0.49	0.92	0.23
11	0.69	0.88	0.41	0.89	0.14
12	0.43	0.76	0.71	0.92	0.16
13	0.46	0.77	0.68	0.92	0.11
14	0.52	0.81	0.65	0.91	0.12
15	0.54	0.82	0.62	0.88	0.15
16	0.38	0.72	0.74	0.91	0.15
17	0.63	0.86	0.53	0.92	0.16
18	0.38	0.72	0.73	0.91	0.15
19	0.40	0.73	0.74	0.91	0.17
20	0.50	0.81	0.65	0.95	0.15
21	0.46	0.76	0.67	0.96	0.18
22	0.40	0.73	0.72	0.90	0.20
23	0.39	0.71	0.70	0.93	0.18
24	0.47	0.76	0.60	0.94	0.20
25	0.46	0.78	0.67	0.96	0.16
26	0.51	0.81	0.65	0.95	0.17
27	0.53	0.81	0.62	0.90	0.28
28	0.47	0.78	0.66	0.96	0.16
29	0.60	0.87	0.59	0.94	0.22
30	0.55	0.82	0.59	0.93	0.21
31	0.59	0.86	0.58	0.96	0.20
32	0.48	0.79	0.69	0.93	0.21
33	0.51	0.80	0.63	0.93	0.14
34	0.53	0.79	0.60	0.89	−0.01
35	0.63	0.85	0.43	0.94	0.12
36	0.67	0.83	0.32	0.90	0.10
37	0.61	0.83	0.46	0.94	0.13
38	0.59	0.83	0.48	0.93	0.13
39	0.58	0.82	0.51	0.93	0.14
40	0.42	0.75	0.72	0.93	0.18

[a] i are the industries identified in SIC-terms and listed from 1 to 40 in Table 6.3.
[b] RDSH stands for the share of country j R&D expenditures (BERD) in total OECD R&D expenditures (BERD).

Source: Soete (1980).

'true' degrees of mechanisation of production (K_{ij}/N_{ij}) by

$$I_{ij}/N_{ij} = [\sigma_1(g_{ij}) + \sigma_2(a_{ij})] (K_{ij}/N_{ij}) \tag{A6.2}$$

For the purposes of our tests, however, our proxies keep an economic meaning. More specifically, I_{ij}/Y_{ij} is used to test whether there is a significant effect of 'static substitution' (of the production function type). We know that international differences in labour productivities are quite high (cf. Chapter 3): were they essentially explained by movements along the same production functions, the variance in (K_{ij}/Y_{ij}) should be high enough to dominate statistically over the 'noise' introduced by the variance associated with internationally different rates of growth of output and rates of scrapping. A similar argument applies to the use of (I_{ij}/N_{ij}). A more general discussion of the meaning of capital/labour ratios in dynamic economies – whose conclusions we broadly share – is given in Pasinetti (1981).

Notes

1. We also assume constant returns to scale and the absence of any variable input other than labour.
2. For more detail, see Chapter 7.
3. See Pasinetti (1981) whose model of economic growth embodies a similar link between wage rates and average technological levels of each economy.
4. This argument is consistent with Pasinetti's account of the relationship between structural change and international trade (cf. Pasinetti, 1981).
5. For somewhat similar Ricardian analyses, see Dornbush, Fisher and Samuelson (1977), Henner (1983, 1984), Wilson (1980). See also Chapter 7.
6. *Ibid.*, p. 291.
7. Obviously, with the exceptions of products linked to the only actual 'endowments' we know of, such as mineral endowments, sunshine, etc.
8. We owe the original definition of 'dominance' in this context to Luigi Orsenigo.
9. The latter hypothesis appears to us more reasonable than the opposite one of full employment.
10. Note that the argument related to a product innovation would be conceptually identical.
11. A similar adjustment process, within a Marxian framework of analysis, is analysed by Shaikh (1980). One might also wonder why in our model, characterised by non-decreasing returns, international adjustments do not lead to total specialisations, but to market sharing. There are four complementary reasons, namely (a) the products of each sector may well be imperfect substitutes of each other in ways which correspond to the different locations of production (see Isard, 1977; Armington, 1969); (b) each sector may be composed of groups of homogeneous products, manufactured with different efficiencies in the different countries (Petri, 1980); (c) the groups of products of each sector may differ in their perform-

ance and technological sophistication (Shaked and Sutton, 1984); (d) as we saw, the sectoral technological levels of each country are averages of distributions across different firms, so that there are always likely to be several pairs of products/firms for which the international location of production is indifferent (i.e. these firms, located in different countries and producing an identical product are an 'evolutionary equilibrium').

12. Clearly, for other theoretical purposes, such as the intertemporal analysis of income distribution or of the macroeconomic rates of activity, even small changes in the capital/output ratio are important.

13. See Chapter 4 for some sectoral evidence.

14. Cf. Haitani (1970) and Chapter 3 above.

15. See Chapter 3.

16. One also requires Harrod-neutrality of technology, identical rates of profit, etc.

17. One needs to assume non-decreasing returns and no scarce factor. These are likely to correspond to the normal conditions of developed economic systems (see Chapter 5).

18. See Caves, Porter and Spence (1980), Caves (1985).

19. See Dixit and Norman (1980), Brander (1981) and Krugman (1979a), Helpman (1984a), Eaton and Kierzkowski (1984), and, for a critical survey, Caves (1980).

20. Cf. Glejser, Jacquemin and Petit (1980).

21. See, among others, Grubel and Lloyd (1975), Giersch (1979), Helleiner and Lavergne (1979), Caves (1982) and Helleiner (1981). For a critical overview, cf. Onida (1984).

22. Cf. for example, the analysis by US Tariff Commission (1973).

23. See Nelson and Winter (1982).

24. This view is supported by the findings at firm-level by Lipsey and Weiss (1981), and Lipsey and Kravis (1985), showing a significant complementarity between exports and local production abroad by US firms.

25. A similar point on the sector-specificity of trade analysis is made by Leamer (1974).

26. Cf. Linder (1961), Barker (1977), Vona (1979).

27. In particular, with regard to a group of engineering products, they find rather robust links for the United States, Germany, Netherlands, Denmark, Norway, some (but weak) links for Japan, Italy and Sweden and non-significant/non-existent correlations for the United Kingdom, France and Belgium. Similarly, they identify a few engineering products which, in cross-country analysis, show rather close correlations between national specialisations and 'backward' linkages on the home markets (see Andersen *et al.*, 1981).

28. See the important analyses of Lafay (1981), and CEPII (1983).

29. On this point see Kaldor (1980) and Pasinetti (1981).

30. An interesting model, which is consistent with this proposition, is in Shaked and Sutton (1984): different product qualities are demanded at different income levels while unit variable costs rise with quality but less than proportionally. The model is important also in other respects: it introduces something like a 'hierarchical order' in the patterns of demand and studies market structures stemming from different combinations of demand schedules and production technologies. For a discussion and some evidence on

diverging unit labour costs among OECD countries, see Ghymers (1981).

31. Excluding Iceland, because of lack of export data at the level of disaggregation required for the analysis; and grouping Belgium and Luxembourg.

32. Data on patenting in the United States have been reclassified (here, as well as in the estimates presented earlier on labour productivities – cf. Table 3.5) into US Standard Industrial Classification (SIC) groups by the Office of Technology Assessment and Forecasting (OTAF) of the US Patent and Trademark Office. Standard International Trade Classification (SITC) correspondence problems forced us to group together 'ordnance' and 'guided missiles, space vehicles and parts', reducing the number of sectors to forty. Details concerning SIC-definition, SITC-correspondence and some of the problems involved are given in Soete (1981a).

33. That this is not an indicator of 'revealed endowments' should be clear from our discussion of technical progress in Chapter 5: when 'production functions', so to speak, are different across countries, capital/labour ratios do not reveal anything of the capital intensity of production processes (in terms of output) but simply their degrees of mechanisation.

34. The sample being limited to the OECD countries only. This is to be expected.

35. The complete correlation matrix between the various independent variables is given in Table 6A.1 of the appendix.

36. I.e. the degree to which a notional 1 per cent increase in a country's foreign (US) patent share would lead to an increase in that country's OECD export share.

37. An interesting explanation in terms of the importance of multinational corporations in the export performance of some countries (Belgium, Canada and Ireland in particular), in some of the industries with low technology elasticities shown in Table 6.2 has been suggested by John Dunning. Our patent data do indeed only take into account endogenous technological performance.

38. The results that follow are based on Dosi and Soete (1983).

39. In order to test the stability of the results whenever different size-related propensities to export are accounted for, in some estimates not shown here, we added 'population' to the set of independent variables: the results remained quite stable (in terms of significance, although clearly not in terms of values of the coefficients).

40. For more details on the sources of the variables, see the appendix.

41. The reader should note that the variable falls short of being a unit wage cost measure. It would be so if we had a proper 'physical' productivity measure at the denominator. As we are forced to use value added at current prices and exchange rates, the ratio of wages to value added is a mixed measure of unit wage costs and income distribution. However, it maintains an economic significance, in the sense that processes of adjustment related to relative prices are ultimately based on relative profitabilities. Were technology perfectly neutral (in the Harrod sense), that ratio would be an inverse monotonic function of the profit rates.

42. The only 'low-development' OECD country in the smaller sample is Portugal.

43. Within countries which are well below the technological frontier, one would expect innovativeness, as measured by US patenting, to play a rather minor role and, thus, misrepresent their technological levels.

44. Out of the twenty-three sectors which maintain the significance in both samples, ten decrease their level (on the t-test) and four improve it. The only rather surprising result is the fall in the significance of patenting, from 1 per cent to 15 per cent in the estimates given in Table 6.3. However, this is due to an abnormally high multicollinearity between the three independent variables.

45. Our analysis also excludes several traditional sectors (clothing, footwear, wood products) where patenting is negligible.

46. Note that the degree of multicollinearity between degrees of mechanisation and patenting is, on average, low, while this is not so for patenting and productivity (cf. Chapter 5).

47. Used alone, capital/output ratios are positive and significant (at 5 per cent or 1 per cent level) in only one case, negative and significant in two cases. Whenever used together with patenting and a cost variable they are significant in five cases, three with a positive sign and two with a negative one. Moreover, when net balances are used as dependent variables, capital/output ratios come out significant (at 5 per cent or more), with a negative sign in six cases: if anything, this indirect measure of 'comparative advantage' is sometimes associated with capital-saving technical progress.

48. See, in particular, Fetherson, Moore and Rhodes (1977), Modiano and Onida (1983), and, for an extensive analysis of the estimates of price elasticities, see Stern, Francis and Schumacher (1976).

49. Cf. Kaldor (1978).

50. On the importance of these factors, see Section 6.2 above.

51. Moreover, note that estimate 6 may well underestimate the catching-up factor, in so far as the latter is overlapping with an above-average growth of patented innovations, already accounted for by the RPAT variable.

52. For the list of countries considered in the estimates of Table 6.5, see Table 3.6.

53. In general, the floating exchange rates of the 1970s have been affected by factors different from manufacturing competitiveness, e.g. short-term capital movements due to interest rate differences, changes in oil prices, etc.

54. Notably, the sensitivity of the estimates is very low if the initial or final year is changed over the period 1964–80. The opposite applies to the 1970s taken alone.

55. Rothschild (1985) shows that a 'catching-up' effect has also been at work through the 1960s and 1970s in terms of export composition, and that this has had a relevant effect upon differential income growth of the European OECD countries. The data on which the calculations are based, however, are rather aggregate and approximate income elasticities with percentage growth of world exports.

In the more complex analysis by Lafay (1981), the conclusions on 'catching-up' are less straightforward. However, the main point holds: differences in the patterns of specialisation according to their demand dynamism are a crucial ingredient of the explanation of why the competitive success differs between countries. On these points see also Chapter 7.

7

Technology gaps in open economies

The main thrust of the analysis so far has been towards a better understanding of the international patterns of technical change and their influence on international trade patterns. The focus of the analysis has been largely microeconomic, in the sense that the prime objects of enquiry were individual sectors or groups of sectors. In this chapter, we turn to some of the macroeconomic implications of our analysis and findings. We shall in particular address the following question: What is the relationship between the pattern of technological change, on the one hand, and the pattern of macroeconomic growth on the other? In keeping with the spirit of this book, the investigation will be of an exploratory nature, given the relatively primitive state-of-the-art of economics in this area: most neo-classical growth models rule out *ex-hypothesi* all the problems in which we are most interested, such as international technological gaps, whereas the more 'classical' (post-Keynesian) growth models are of limited use, in so far as they are generally based on closed-economy and steady-state assumptions.[1] The most recent 'new' growth contributions (Romer, 1986, 1989, Lucas, 1988), particularly when concerned with open economy issues (see e.g. Grossman and Helpman, 1989, 1990a, b and c), clearly follow similar lines of concern. However, their treatment of technological change remains as yet rather traditional and, in our view, somewhat remote from the process described by many authors of the economics of technological change and summarised in Chapter 4.

Our aim in this chapter is not to develop a complete open-economy multisector model embodying the most relevant features of technical change, but, rather, to bring to the forefront the set of relationships which one might expect between the nature of technological change among countries, and the stimuli and constraints that each national economy faces in its growth process.

It was suggested in the preceding chapter that absolute advantages in the form of product and process-related technological asymmetries are likely to be dominant upon comparative advantage mechanisms as determinants of each country's participation in world trade. Here we shall take – as the case of the broadening of 'new' trade theory to 'new' growth theory – the question a step further and ask whether a similar concept of dominance applies to the relationship between technology and macroeconomic growth in an open economy. The main assumptions of the preceding chapter will be maintained: technology is not a free good, but shows varying degrees of appropriability at the company and country level; one can identify relatively 'ordered' patterns of technical change that will allow technologies to be ranked as economically superior and inferior irrespective of income distribution; and, finally, the absolute advantages such technological advantages generate are likely to be a fundamental force shaping trade patterns. When considering the growth process of each economy, these properties of technical change have a number of important implications.

Let us start from three evident facts. First, the growth possibilities of each economy are technically limited by its production coefficients. Second, in open economies the patterns of production do not depend solely on the nature of domestic consumption and production coefficients, but also on the factors shaping international specialisation and international terms of trade. Third, if one economy buys commodities from another, it has got to be able to pay for its imports by means of its exports. Technology, as we shall see, affects all these variables in ways which contribute to the determination of both the constraints and the stimuli to growth.

It is not only the absolute technological levels of each economy that determine the maximum attainable per capita income and rate of accumulation, but also the relative technological levels between countries which affect growth possibilities through the balance of payment constraint. We shall first analyse a very simple case of two economies characterised by different production coefficients and a Ricardian mechanism of specialisation, taking into account the joint effect of international specialisation and the balance of payment constraint upon the growth possibilities of each economy (Section 7.1). We shall then expand the discussion to a dynamic framework and investigate the effects of technological innovation and imitation (Section 7.2). In Section 7.3, a more detailed consideration will be given to the overall pattern of interdependence brought about by the existence of international trade: in particular the possibility of processes of circular causation and virtuous and vicious circles in the patterns of growth. Finally, in Section 7.4 we shall discuss some of the empirical evidence on the relationship between technological change, trade and growth.

7.1 International specialisation, trade balances and growth possibilities: a simple model

In the following we shall present a highly simplified formal framework which is meant to be a sort of 'theoretical abacus' highlighting some linkages between technology gaps, patterns of specialisation and macroeconomic rates of activities. Further developments of the basic model can be found in Cimoli, Dosi and Soete (1986), Cimoli (1988) and Cimoli and Soete (1988).

Let us define two groups of commodities. The first group, which we call Ricardian commodities,[2] is traded solely on the grounds of the relative cost of production. A second group of commodities, innovative commodities, are produced and exported only by one country, where the product innovation occurred, irrespective of production costs. For the time being we shall focus on the former group. Let us start from the reformulation of a Ricardian model of trade provided by Dornbush, Fisher and Samuelson (1977) and assume a continuum of properly ordered commodities. There are two countries, A and B.

Simplifying the picture to the extreme, we start by assuming no inputs other than labour. Denote labour input coefficients as $a_1, a_2, ..., a_n$ for country A and $a_1^*, a_2^*, ..., a_n^*$ for country B. Commodities are conveniently indexed so that relative unit labour requirements are ranked in order of diminishing home country comparative advantage (advantages of country A in our definition).[3] This ranking is such that, in a discrete representation:

$$a_1^*/a_1 > ... > a_i^*/a_i > ... > a_n^*/a_n \qquad (7.1)$$

Calling z each commodity, a function can be defined on a conventional continuum, say $[0,1]$:

$$A(z) = \frac{a^*(z)}{a(z)} \qquad (7.2)$$

with

$$A'(z) < 0$$

International specialisation for each commodity in A or B will depend on relative unit labour costs (denominated in a common measure):

$$a(z) \cdot w \lessgtr a^*(z) \cdot w^* \tag{7.3}$$

i.e.

$$\omega \lessgtr A(z)$$

with

$$\omega \equiv \frac{w}{w^*}$$

where w and w^* are the wage rates in countries A and B respectively. Commodities will be produced in A or B depending on which one is cheaper at current wage rates and labour productivities. The borderline commodity, separating those produced in A and B, respectively, will be

$$\tilde{z} = A^{-1}(\omega) \tag{7.4}$$

with $A^{-1}(\omega)$ as the inverse function of A. The process of specialisation is visualised in Figure 7.1. For a wage ratio (w/w^*) equal to ω, country A specialises in the set of commodities from 0 to $\tilde{z}$ and country B in commodities from $\tilde{z}$ to 1.

It will be clear from Figure 7.1 that an increase in the domestic wage relative to the commercial partner will reduce the set of commodities which that country can competitively produce, and vice versa.

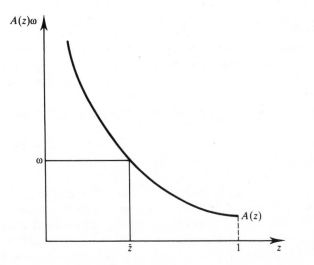

Figure 7.1 Specialisation with a continuum of 'Ricardian commodities'

It can be shown that the same result also applies in those cases where there are capital inputs and positive profits, provided that there is no 'reswitching of commodities'. This will be the case when:

(a) the rate of profit is identical across commodities and across countries;
(b) the capital/output ratios for each commodity are identical in A and B;
(c) all capital goods are domestically produced with labour inputs only.

Assumptions (a) and (b) seem to conform to much empirical evidence (cf. Chapters 3 and 4). Assumption (c), on the contrary, is very unrealistic. Below, we shall briefly discuss the properties of an economy where all capital goods are imported.

Under assumptions (a)–(c), the price equations for each final commodity are:

$$p_i = c_{ki}p_{ki} (1 + r) + wa_i \tag{7.5}$$

$$p_i^* = c_{ki}^* p_{ki}^* (1 + r) + w^* a_i^* \tag{7.6}$$

where the cs are capital ('machine') inputs per unit of final output, the p_ks are the prices of the machines and r is the rate of profit. The prices of the capital goods ('machines') are:[4]

$$p_{ki} = l_{ki}w \tag{7.7}$$

$$p_{ki}^* = l_{ki}^* w^* \tag{7.8}$$

Define the capital/output ratios as h and h^*.[5] Now, the condition of international specialisation is given by

$$p_i/p_i^* \lessgtr 1$$

However, rewriting (7.5) and (7.6) as functions of h and h^* and rearranging:

$$p_i/p_i^* = \frac{w \cdot a_i \ [1 - h_i^*(1 + r)]}{w^* \cdot a_i^* \ [1 - h_i \ (1 + r)]} \tag{7.9}$$

If $h_i = h_i^*$, the condition is reduced to that of equation (7.3) above:[6] specialisation still depends only on labour productivities and wage rates.

Dornbush, Fisher and Samuelson (1977), whose model forms the basis of the above formulation, proceeded to close the model by imposing labour market-clearing conditions and by assuming homotheticity (such as Cobb–Douglas) of the demand functions. We shall radically depart from that approach in order to account for what we consider to be five fundamental properties of modern economic systems, namely:

1. Different commodities show a wide range of price and income elasticities.
2. In normal circumstances the rate of growth of each economy is not constrained by the supply of labour but by the requirement of balancing the foreign accounts.[7]
3. For a given state of technology, the rate of utilisation of the labour force is determined by the levels of macroeconomic activity.
4. Wage rates are also determined by institutional factors which grant them some degree of freedom vis-à-vis the prevailing labour market conditions.
5. Microeconomic processes of technological change are highly 'rational boundedly', diverse among firms, and generally full of mistakes. Thus, the rates of technological change cannot be 'inferred back' from the properties of theoretical steady-states, assuming 'representative agents' with 'rational technological expectations'. (Incidentally one may note that this is the spirit of many of the recent equilibrium growth models with endogenous technical change, such as Romer (1990).)

By bringing these hypotheses into the picture we will now be able to provide a link between the conditions for international specialisation and a 'Keynesian' determination of the levels of activity.

Let us start with the demand function. In the first instance we are interested in that portion of demand which goes to imports because in our two-country model that is what counts in determining the trade-balance constraint of each economy.[8] The latter can be written as:

$$Y^* \cdot \int_0^{\bar{z}} \theta^*(z) \, dz = Y \cdot \int_{\bar{z}}^1 \theta(z) \, dz \qquad (7.11)$$

where the demand functions $\theta(\,)$ and $\theta^*(\,)$ are taken to be different from each other due to the different income and price elasticities with respect to each commodity, z.[9] The income of country B multiplied by its import propensity must equal that of country A times the latter's import propensity. That is:

$$Y/Y^* = \frac{\psi^*(z,\omega)}{\psi(z,\omega)} \qquad (7.12)$$

where $\psi(\,)$ and $\psi^*(\,)$ stand for the integrals from equation (7.11). In the simplest case, where labour is the only input, each income will be:

$$Y = wN \qquad (7.13)$$

$$Y^* = w^*N^* \qquad (7.14)$$

with

$$N \leqslant L \text{ and } N^* \leqslant L^*$$

where N and N^* are the employment levels, less than or equal to the supplies of labour L and L^*, respectively.

In the more complex case with capital inputs and positive profits, equations (7.13) and (7.14) can be rewritten as:

$$Y = (1/s)wN \tag{7.13.1}$$

$$Y^* = (1/s^*)w^*N^* \tag{7.14.1}$$

where s and s^* are the shares of wages in national income.[10]

The system of four homogeneous equations (7.3), (7.12), (7.13) and (7.14) leaves four degrees of freedom in the determination of the seven unknowns (two levels of income, Y and Y^*, employment N and N^*, the wage rates w and w^*, and the border-commodity in the pattern of specialisation, $\tilde{z}$).

The system defines the boundaries of all possible price-related and income-related adjustments, determined by:

(a) technological conditions;
(b) the composition of the demand baskets; and
(c) an interdependence constraint via trade balances.

Let us illustrate this point with the help of Figure 7.2. The S-line through the top left quadrant is the locus of the ratios between wages (w) which guarantee a certain specialisation commodity $\tilde{z}_0$.[11] For that same commodity the TB line is the locus of equilibrium points for the trade balance.[12] In the simplest case of $Y = wN$, the angle (α) between any f-line and the w-axis is a straightforward measure of employment in country A and so is the angle (α^*) between any f^*-line and the w^*-axis, for country B.[13]

As an illustration, assume now a pair of wages, w_m and w_m^*. These wages must be feasible in the sense that they must be (in terms of own-produced commodities) equal to or less than the average labour productivity of the economy for any given specialisation as given by the S line in Figure 7.2.[14] In particular, suppose that w_m is the minimum socially acceptable wage in country A which equals average productivity of the economy with specialisation $\tilde{z}_0$ defined by w_m/w_m^*.[15]

Moreover, suppose (for simplicity, although by no means analytically necessary) that economy A is at full employment, defined by the line f_r. The corresponding equilibrium income for country A is Y_T, the maximum income level. For country B, however, it is Y_T^*. This may correspond to less than full-employment income in country B. Say, B-

full-employment income is defined by the line f_T^*: when B specialises in commodity $\tilde{z}_0$. However as illustrated in Figure 7.2 this cannot be achieved, given the trade-balance constraint. At point R, country B will suffer significant unemployment given by the line f_m^*.

It is important to note that despite unemployment in B, the pair w_m-w_m^* yields an equilibrium position in the sense that the specialisation is 'efficient' in static allocative terms: it satisfies equation (7.4) and thus corresponds to the dividing line between comparative advantages and comparative disadvantages. Let us call this microeconomic criterion of efficiency 'Ricardian efficiency'.

As can be seen from Figure 7.2, there is an entire set of points which

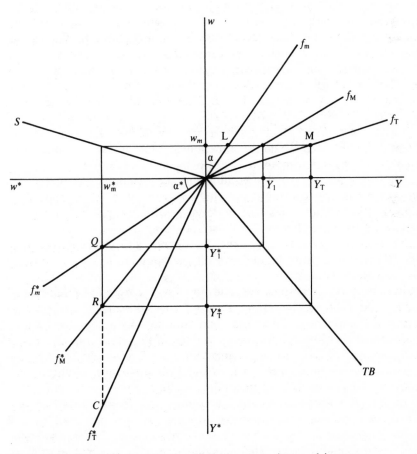

Figure 7.2 Specialisation, foreign balance constraints and income possibilities: an illustration

satisfy these equilibrium conditions while yielding less than full employment rates of activity in both economies: for example, incomes Y_1 and Y_1^* correspond to less than full employment in A (as defined by f_M) and an even lower level of employment in point Q in country B (as defined by f_m^*). The interdependence properties of trading economies are, in other words, such that their 'size' is reciprocally constrained by their trade balance for any given technological and demand condition. Thus, the set of notional equilibrium points between what could be called maximum acceptable unemployment, illustrated in Figure 7.2, for instance by the employment line f_m in country A and f_m^* in country B, and full employment or maximum employment consistent with the trade balance corresponds to the segment LM for country A and QR for country B (see Figure 7.2).

Given the state of technology and demand, we may try other feasible combinations of the wage rates in the two countries (say some $w > w_m$ and $w^* < w_m^*$). The latter are relative wage rates, meaning that in our limited two country world, they cannot both increase. The S-line will turn clockwise, thus increasing the number of commodities produced by B. The TB line will do the same, since the import propensities have now increased in A and decreased in B. The LM line will move upwards while the QR line will move to the right.[16] Wages per worker and workers' average productivity in A are now higher, but that country faces a tighter foreign-balance constraint because it has specialised in a smaller number of commodities but it must import more.

By trying all the possible equilibrium combinations consistent with the trade-balance constraint and characterised by 'efficient' specialisation, we thus obtain the set of notional equilibrium points for each of the two economies. Figure 7.3 illustrates this.

One boundary to this set is the one defined above in Figure 7.2, as the full employment, minimum socially acceptable wage w_m in country A, and the accompanying wage in country B, w_m^*. The specialisation pattern S_T and foreign-balance condition TB_T correspond to that pair of wages. At that specialisation, suppose for sake of illustration that country B happens to be at the maximum socially acceptable level of unemployment Q on the employment line (f_m^*) whereas country A is at full employment E on the employment line (f_T). Conversely, for the wage pair w_M-w_M^*, yielding specialisation S_T^* and trade-balance condition TB_T^*, country A happens to be at maximum acceptable unemployment (point C on line f_M) whenever B is at full employment (point M on line f_T^*). These two extreme boundaries are defined on the one hand by full employment in either or both economies, and on the other side by social and institutional factors, the maximum socially acceptable level of unemployment and/or the minimum acceptable wage in each of the two

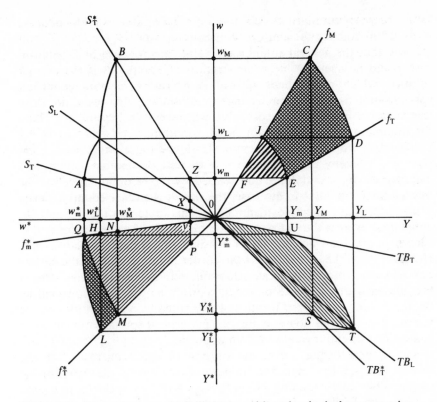

Figure 7.3 Wage–income possibility sets, with technological asymmetries and foreign balance constraints

economies. Within these boundaries, the range of acceptable specialisations lies between S_T and S_T^*. In the simplest case, when all income consists of wages and prices are equal to wage costs, the function mapping the pair of wages into an efficient specialisation is described by the curve AB in Figure 7.3.[17]

As regards the trade-balance constraint, the equilibrium points consistent with rates of activity equal to or below full employment are defined by the area $OSTU$.[18] For each economy, the possible equilibrium points which are technically feasible yield efficient specialisations, balance the foreign accounts, and are domestically acceptable, corresponding to the areas $FEDC$ in country A and $QLPV$ in country B. However, some of these points might not correspond to acceptable situations for the *other* country, in the sense that they might correspond to rates of unemployment which are too high, or wages which are too low. The set of equilibrium points which is acceptable to both countries is $EDCJ$ in country A, and QLM in country B.

Note that the general equilibrium point (in the sense of Dornbush, Fisher and Samuelson) in the illustration of Figure 7.3 is that corner solution which corresponds to full employment in both countries, specialisation S_L and foreign balance condition TB_L. However, note also that such a point might not exist at all, whenever its achievement violates the minimum socially acceptable wage condition.

The points on the lines DC and QL define those equilibrium combinations whereby the maximum rate of macroeconomic activity and employment in A and B are constrained by the 'economic size' of the international system – in our case, the size of the other country – even if the latter is at full employment. To see this, note that the CD and QL curve lines express the 'maximum' combinations of wages/incomes that each economy can achieve under feasible 'Ricardian' specialisations. However, with the exceptions of the corner points L and D, the corresponding rates of activity entail below-full-employment incomes. This is because each of the two economies, 'constrains' the other through its limited import capability. In other words, the income intensities of the various commodities do not match the patterns of specialisation so as to guarantee full employment in both countries.

Let us now define a criterion of *growth efficiency* related to the income intensity (in a dynamic framework, the income elasticity) of the commodities corresponding to any given pattern of specialisation, and thus to the levels of foreign demand they generate. The foregoing example highlighted the general possibility of mismatch between Ricardian (static allocative) efficiency and growth efficiency. As a parenthesis, it is worth noting that from a normative point of view this also illustrated the possibility of trade regimes which were different and better, in terms of growth possibilities, than free trade.

The line ED for country A and LM for country B, in Figure 7.3 correspond to the set of equilibrium combinations whereby the full employment constraint is met before the foreign-balance constraint: it is the domestic economy which puts a ceiling on world development via its own 'size', and thus its capacity to absorb exports from the rest of the world. Another way of saying the same thing is that there is an 'over-competitiveness' of the domestic economy which tightens the foreign-balance constraint for the rest of the world.[19]

The *position* of the AB line depends in a straightforward manner on the absolute technological levels of each economy. Holding the relative technological gap between the two economies constant, the higher the absolute technological levels (i.e. in our case, the higher average labour productivities), the more 'outward' the AB line will be: this illustrates the obvious fact that steady technical progress throughout the world allows for (but, as we shall see, does not necessarily determine) higher wages and higher incomes in all countries, even if we hold the pattern of specialisation constant. To see this, recall that any point on the AB line expresses a ratio between w and w^* and that that ratio must be equal to the productivity ratio $a(z)/a^*(z)$. If both $a(\ )$ and $a^*(\ )$ fall (hence, productivity grows), both w and w^* can proportionally increase. Thus, the AB line moves outward. Technical progress in A only pushes the AB line upward, thus improving the income possibilities (i.e growth possibilities in a more realistic formulation) of A for an unchanged wage rate or the wage possibilities for unchanged levels of macroeconomic activity. Note that in this case, $a(z)$ falls while $a^*(z)$ remains unchanged. Hence the S_T^* line moves clockwise. The symmetric opposite applies to wages and incomes in B, for domestic technological improvements in B. Thus, an increase in the 'technology gap' between the two economies allows for, other things being equal, an increase in the wage and income gaps between the two countries, without, however, necessarily implying an absolute fall in wages and incomes in the country falling behind.[20]

Any change in the income intensity of the commodities, which is the result of varying income and price elasticities, will cause a shift in the position of the $OSTU$ area, thus relaxing or tightening the foreign-balance constraint of each trading partner in favour of the country producing commodities with a higher income intensity, for any given specialisation.

Finally, the length and the slope of the AB line can be taken to represent the scope of cost-related and specialisation-related adjustment processes for any given state of technology and demand. The length depends on two factors: first, the intracountry variance in labour productivity, which determines the sensitivity of the patterns of specialisation to changes in wage rates, and, second, the socially determined boundaries to the variations in wages and unemployment rates. The slope depends on the relative degrees of homogeneity in the production coefficients across countries and across commodities.

By *homogeneity* of each country we mean the degree of similarity in the productivity leads or lags between the various commodities it produces (i.e. the similarity in the commodity-specific absolute advantages/disadvantages).[21] Different degrees of homogeneity also determine the sensitivity of the patterns of specialisation to changes in wage rates. In the case depicted in Figure 7.3, for example, country B requires a relatively small change in wages to achieve large shifts in specialisation as compared to country A.

We may now start to appreciate more fully the meaning of

technological dominance over comparative advantage mechanisms of specialisation as a determinant of income and wage levels. If each economic system is relatively *tight*, in the sense that:

(a) it has relatively stringent constraints in terms of its maximum unemployment rate and minimum wage;

(b) it is confronted with a relatively sharp discontinuity between the average technology gap/lead in the group of commodities it exports and those that it imports;[22] and

(c) its production structure is relatively homogeneous (so that the *inter-commodity variance* in the labour productivity gaps vis-à-vis the partner regarding domestically produced commodities is low);

it will be more likely that the range of the country's possible equilibrium points is *relatively limited*: the AB line is short while the f_m and f_T lines are close to each other, as are the f_m^* and f_T^* lines. In this tight case, only technical progress will be able to induce significant improvements in incomes and wages for any configuration of the international system.

It must be stressed that the model developed so far is concerned with the boundaries of the set of points consistent with efficient microeconomic specialisation (in a static allocative sense) and with the macroeconomic requirement of balancing the foreign account. It does *not* tell us at which point each economy will settle. This will be a function of the domestic mechanism of demand formation and its international interdependence via import and export flows. In other words, we can identify the areas $JEDC$ for country A and QLM for country B as the areas of feasible specialisations and acceptable Keynesian adjustment processes.

More precisely, taking the simple model presented here as an illustration of a more general one, accounting also for investments, profits, etc., we can read any horizontal movement in the country A- set and any vertical movement in the country B-set as a *Keynesian process* of change in equilibrium income. Conversely, any vertical movement in the A-set and horizontal movement in the B-set can be defined as a *Ricardian process* of change in equilibrium specialisation. Both processes can operate only under strong interdependence requirements, so that there must be an international symmetry in the movements of wages and incomes. Disequilibrium variations may of course occur: macro-economic – via the exchange rate and variations in 'absorption' – and microeconomic adjustment processes – via changes in the competitiveness of each commodity and intercommodity mobility of capital – will react to every imbalance. The time profile of these adjustment processes will determine the actual path followed by each country.

There is, however, an important difference between these Keynesian and Ricardian adjustment processes. The former are straightforward positive- (or negative-) sum games: everyone gains as, for example, in the movement from J towards D in country A and from H to L in country B, or everyone loses, as in the case of movements in the opposite direction. Ricardian processes, on the other hand, do involve trade-offs: there is certainly a trade-off between domestic and foreign wages, sometimes also a domestic trade-off between wage and income levels – in the case of country A for example, for wages between w_L and w_M; in country B, for wages between w_L^* and w_M^*.[23]

We may to some extent interpret these Ricardian adjustment processes as the real microeconomic counterpart of devaluation/revaluation adjustment mechanisms. In essence, each devaluation is a downward change in the domestic real wage vis-à-vis foreign wages.[24] Taking a closer look at Figure 7.3, one can appreciate how this simply shifts possibilities of growth from one country to another. Take, for example, any downward adjustment of wages in A from point w_M: if income is not correspondingly increased along the CD line, the expansion of country A's income (from Y_M to somewhere short of the income corresponding to the CD line) is 'paid for' with less than full employment rates of activity in B. More generally, the model and framework presented here brings together three sorts of economic analysis which have traditionally been kept separate from each other:

(a) the 'Keynesian' account of macroeconomic levels of activity in open economies;
(b) the microeconomic processes of specialisation; and
(c) the effects of technological differences between and within countries.

The greater the degree of 'tightness' of each economy – as defined above – the more the technological dominance will apply to both Ricardian and Keynesian processes of change from one equilibrium position to another; in other words, only the outward movements of the CD and QL frontiers are likely to disentangle unfavourable (sub-optimal) set-ups of any economy. This is even more so if one thinks of the way Ricardian and Keynesian adjustment processes are related. Suppose country A tries to increase competitiveness by decreasing its real wage starting from wage w_M and income Y_M: more often than not, a 'Keynesian process' (deflation) is used to achieve the 'Ricardian' result. If the trade partner is also forced to use the same instrument, being very sensitive to the foreign-balance constraint, the resulting path may closely follow the CF

line downwards in country A and push from M towards N in country B. In other words, *everyone* may end up in a *worse* position in terms of employment or income or both. This particular case highlights a general characteristic of the international system: while it requires a high degree of symmetry and synchrony in the process of change, it does not automatically provide any functional mechanism which guarantees it. We shall return to this question below.

Before analysing the functional mechanisms which determine the *actual* combinations between wages, specialisation, income, and employment level at greater length let us mention some other interesting properties of the system to conclude this section:

1. It may well be that full employment specialisation for one of the two countries can be achieved only for wage rates *below* the minimum acceptable level (or even below the subsistence level in the case of a technologically backward country). This result is more likely if a country is confronted with a very wide domestic productivity gap between a few modern sectors and the rest of its tradeable commodities or if the income intensity in the world market of the commodities in which it specialised, is very low.[25]
2. Allowing for profits and investments and relaxing the simplifying hypothesis that all capital goods are domestically produced yields some further interesting results. Let us start from the opposite case and assume that all capital goods are produced by country A. Consider now the position of country B. Any given downward change in country B's wages has a lower or even perverse effect upon the country's pattern of specialisation (the S-line) and trade-balance constraint (the TB-line). In fact, capital inputs have now to be paid for at a higher real price, while the terms of trade have deteriorated. If the capital/output ratios in B are sufficiently high,[26] it may well be that a decrease in the domestic real wage (e.g. through a devaluation) yields a *tighter* trade-balance constraint with a *lower* number of commodities efficiently produced.

On a more speculative note, one might even suggest the following hypothesis: the sensitivity of both the pattern of specialisation and the trade-balance constraint to Ricardian adjustment processes is proportional to the degree of self-sufficiency (or, more generally, the net trade balance) in the sectors producing capital goods.[27] If this were to hold true in general, then adjustments based on relative wage and exchange rates are easier (and less painful) for relatively developed countries than for less developed ones, whose capital goods sector is generally small or non-existent.

7.2 Technological dynamics: the changing patterns of specialisation and international distribution of growth possibilities

In the preceding section, we discussed some of the effects of technological innovation on the set of equilibrium incomes and wages in two countries A and B. Suppose now that country A – the North – is the more advanced (innovative) country and B – the South – the less advanced one. We illustrate this particular case in Figure 7.4, using the same terminology as in Figure 7.3. Absolute productivities of the 'North' are always higher than of the 'South' – so that the A^1B^1 line always rests above the 45-degree line cutting the w-w^* quadrant. Moreover, the income-intensities (i.e. dynamically, the income elasticities) of B-exports into A-incomes are relatively low: so, the $OS^1T^1U^1$ area remains relatively near the x-axis. Finally, we assume that in country A the maximum-wage/minimum-employment is f_m^1 and the full employment line is f_T^1. In country B, the minimum socially acceptable employment is f_m^{1*} and the full employment is f_F^{1*}. Given the efficiency gap between the two countries and the demand patterns, full employment in B is unattainable even when country A is indeed at a full-employment income (say, at Y_T^1). The area $K^1L^1M^1$ is, as depicted in Figure 7.4, located within the boundaries given by f_m^{1*} and f_F^{1*}. Keeping technology constant, how could the position of B notionally improve? One possibility would have been a bigger 'size' of country A: other things being equal, a larger 'advanced' country would imply a clockwise turn of the f_T^1 line, greater absorption of imports from B and, hence, higher income and employment possibilities for B, holding B-wages constant. Conversely, one can imagine a clockwise rotation of the lines TB_T^1 and TB^{1*}: that is, a relative increase of the intensity of B-export in A-income (or, on the contrary, a decrease in the intensity of A-exports in B-incomes). As a consequence, the income and employment possibilities would increase (the lines f_T^{1*} and f_F^{1*} would turn anti-clockwise), leaving an unchanged income for country A and also an unchanged pair of 'efficient' wages (w_T^1 and w_T^{1*}). It is obvious though, as discussed in the previous section, that all innovation processes which increase labour productivity in A will widen the gap in income and wages between the two countries, even if they leave their absolute levels in the 'backward' country unchanged. Conversely, all technological imitation and/or technology transfer to country B will decrease the gap between the two countries by increasing wages and incomes in B relative to A. In other words, and as discussed at greater length in Chapter 5, we now assume a situation whereby innovative processes induce divergence and all imitation processes induce convergence between two countries A and B. The

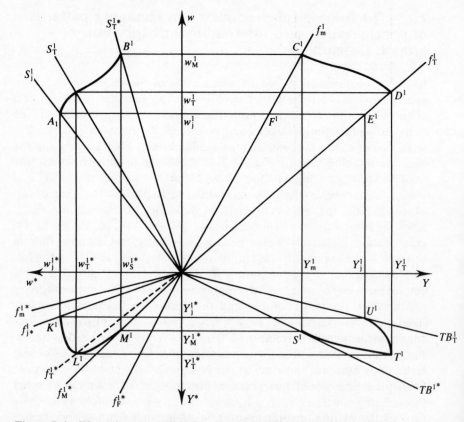

Figure 7.4 Wage–income possibility sets: a North–South illustration

model will account for a straightforward link between technology gaps and income (and wage) gaps between countries.[28]

We will also bring into the picture the innovation commodities, neglected so far in the analysis for the sake of simplicity. The innovative commodities can be produced only by one country, A, irrespective of relative costs, for the simple reason that only that country knows how to produce these, given its innovative lead. We may therefore re-arrange the 'continuum of commodities' on a range (o, l) as shown in Figure 7.5. The range between o and r_0 covers innovation commodities, the range from r_0 to l the Ricardian ones. As regards the latter, the diagram simply highlights what has already been stated above: process innovations (i.e. across-the-board increases in productivity) in A shift the R_0R_0' line to R_1R_1', thus allowing for a wider specialisation (from $\tilde{z}_0$ to $\tilde{z}_1$) for a given wage ratio (ω_0) or a higher wage for an unchanged specialisation ($\tilde{z}_0$).

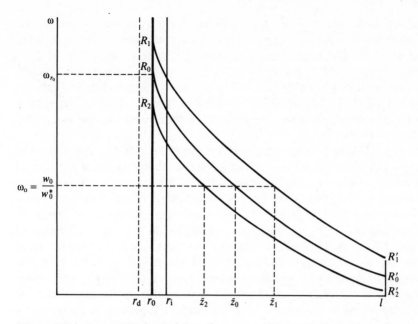

Figure 7.5 International specialisation with a continuum of 'Ricardian' and 'Innovation' commodities

The opposite applies to process imitation as depicted by the shift to $R_2 R_2'$.

The introduction of innovative commodities into the formal analysis, developed in the preceding section, brings to the forefront a number of additional interesting features.

First, there is now a clear limit to wage-induced changes in specialisation, i.e. to the Ricardian adjustment process. This is given by r_0, the borderline commodity between the innovative and Ricardian commodities. It can be easily seen from Figure 7.5 that any increase in ω (e.g. any decrease in country B's wages) above w_{r0} does not have any effect on specialisation but only worsens the terms of trade for B.[29] In terms of Figure 7.4, no downward change in w^* will turn S_T^{1*} and TB^{1*} clockwise. The only effect such change will have is to move the equilibrium combination towards lower levels of macroeconomic activity for *both* countries. If some gain in employment is achieved in B, this is paid for by lower wages, possibly even with a lower aggregate income as a result.

This is an interesting case in other respects also. Country B, in order to achieve full employment without falling in the trap of 'immiserizing growth', is in the last resort dependent on a 'Keynesian process' occurring in A, i.e. on the willingness of the latter to push macroeconomic activity towards the *CD* line (Figure 7.3). However, even if this occurred, the more advanced country (*A*) might *not* be able to achieve full employment because it is limited by the low capability of *B* to absorb commodities produced in *A*: it may well meet the foreign-balance constraint below its full employment level. Interestingly, *A* might be at full employment only in a disequilibrium set-up whereby it finances a steady balance of payments *deficit*, while at the same time wages in *B rise*.[30]

Second, there is some similarity between the case just discussed and unequal exchange theories[31] in the sense that there may be a correlation between the gap in wages (between *A* and *B*) and the respective terms of trade, so that there may be a notable difference between the level of *B* wages (and *B* output) as measured in terms of the basket of commodities produced in *B*, and the same variables, as measured in terms of demand baskets. However, the causal link runs precisely in the direction opposite to that suggested by 'unequal exchange' theories. It is not unequal exchange which causes backwardness, if anything it is the other way round: the technological gap of *B* is ultimately the cause of both low wages and unfavourable terms of trade. Moreover, as we have just seen, there may not be any objective interest in country *A* to keep wages in *B* down: quite the contrary, the latter may limit the levels of country *A*'s macroeconomic activity via the trade-balance constraint.

Suppose now product innovations increase the total number of commodities produced in the system (thus pushing *l*, in Figure 7.5, to the right), while at the same time moving the borderline commodity between the innovative and Ricardian commodities, from r_0 to r_i. Conversely, all product imitations move the borderline commodity to the left, say to r_d.

Let us first consider the effects of *product imitation*. The latter increases the space of the 'Ricardian' adjustment processes and turns *S* and *TB* (Figure 7.3) in favour of the imitating country. Suppose the commodities which shift (from 'innovative' to Ricardian) happen to be proportionally distributed along the entire *RR'* range of Figure 7.5. Then, product imitation will always improve both the pattern of specialisation and the balance of payment constraint for *B*, even if $\bar{z}$ happens to be within the range of Ricardian commodities already. As regards product innovation, the opposite applies.[32]

The presence of innovative commodities tends to relax the link between wages, productivity and prices as implied in the wage–income possibility sets illustrated in Figures 7.2, 7.3 and 7.4.[33] As far as 'Ricardian' commodities are concerned, Ricardian adjustment mechanisms always check the limits of the variation of wages vis-à-vis productivity growth, and of prices vis-à-vis unit costs, since any excess will be paid with loss of specialisation. When we allow for product innovations, the picture becomes more blurred and the contours of the *JEDC* area (Figure 7.3) cannot be rigorously defined any longer. This is not only the effect of an index number problem (how can we reasonably say when income is 'the same' if it is also made of new and 'better' commodities that did not exist before?), it is also the reflection of an important characteristic associated with product innovations: the major competitive force checking the cost/price relation for these commodities is now domestic oligopolistic competition between the firms producing it.[34]

From the point of view of international adjustment mechanisms, one can see that the higher the share of innovative commodities in production and income, the lower will be the sensitivity of the system to wage/price (i.e. Ricardian) adjustment processes. In the extreme case when all the commodities produced by *A* are innovative commodities, the international distribution of the 'growth possibilities' is essentially determined by the levels and dynamics of the income intensity of demand for the various commodities,[35] and, dynamically, by the relative rates of innovation and imitation.[36] Under these circumstances, holding technology constant, the *S*-line will be fixed, whereas the position of the *TB* line will depend on the income intensities and the only adjustment process from one equilibrium to another will be a Keynesian one (east/westward for country *A* and south/northward for country *B*, in terms of Figure 7.3). Conversely, only innovation/imitation can change the international pattern of specialisation, jointly with the shape of the balance of payment constraint.

From a more normative point of view, in such a world any one country which happens to fall below full employment may only rely, in the short run, on 'international Keynesianism' (or domestic Keynesianism and import protection), and, in the long run, on imitation/innovation policies, whereas cost-related adjustments may be perverse in so far as they backfire on the terms of trade, leaving specialisation unchanged. From this perspective, one may even account for a couple of extreme cases whereby an improvement of both the balance of payment constraint and the domestic possibilities for growth are achieved through a revaluation of the exchange rate and the domestic real wage (see, e.g. van der Ploeg, 1989).

7.3 Technological conditions, foreign balances and effective demand

So far, the analysis has focussed on the 'outer boundaries' of the various equilibrium combinations which are consistent with a balanced foreign account and yield efficient specialisation. The question as to which one of these points is actually achieved is partly addressed in this section. In order to do so, one must also account for the factors which determine levels of domestic macroeconomic activity.

Let us start with the old-fashioned macroeconomic identity:

$$Y = C + I + X - M \qquad (7.15)$$

where Y equals income, C consumption, I investment, X exports, and M imports.[37]

We already have the analytical expressions for exports and imports.

$$X = \psi^*(\ ) \cdot Y^*$$

$$M = \psi(\ ) \cdot Y$$

The consumption function will be assumed to be stable with average (= marginal) propensity of consumption equal to c. For analytical purposes it is useful to differentiate, following Kaldor and Pasinetti, between consumption from wages (c_w) and consumption from profits (c_k). In the extreme case of $c_w = 1$, equation (7.15) can be rewritten as:[38]

$$Y = c_k Y + (1 - c_k)W + I + \psi^*(\ ) \cdot Y^* - \psi(\ ) \cdot Y \qquad (7.15.1)$$

where W is the total wage bill. Total employment in the economy N is equal to Y/π, with π equal to the weighted average of labour productivities in the production of each commodity z (in the range between 0 and $\bar{z}$) and in the production of the corresponding capital goods.[39] Since $W = wN$, substituting and rearranging gives:

$$Y = \frac{1}{[1 + \psi(\ ) - c_k - (1 - c_k)(w/\pi)]} [\psi^*(\ ) \cdot Y^* + I] \qquad (7.16)$$

This is an alternative formulation of the Keynesian multiplier, where exports and investments are taken to be, as usual, the two 'autonomous' demand items.

The same equation can be written for country B:

$$Y^* = \frac{1}{[1 + \psi^*(\ ) - c_k^* - (1 - c_k^*)(w^*/\pi^*)]} [\psi(\ )Y + I^*] \qquad (7.17)$$

To the extent that the usual trade-balance constraint applies to both countries:

$$Y/Y^* = \psi^*(\ )/\psi(\ )$$

The system, however, maintains some degrees of freedom,[40] which account for both a somewhat institutional determination of wage rates (and thus income distribution within each country) and the interdependence condition between the sizes of the two economies. Dependent on the initial conditions and the adjustment paths of the endogenous variables, the system may well fluctuate within the shaded areas of Figure 7.3, possibly following paths characterised by (nearly) balanced trade, (nearly) efficient specialisation and *below full employment* rates of macroeconomic activity. A study of these paths requires the introduction of additional stylised facts with regard to the *relative intensity and speed* of the adjustment processes which are beyond the scope of this book and would most likely require an explicit formalisation of some evolutionary microfoundation of macrodynamics.[41] Some qualitative considerations might, however, give an indication of how this will occur.

As regards changes in wages (expressed in terms of an internationally comparable 'real' measure), one may reasonably assume that they tend to adjust to imbalances in both foreign trade and the labour market. Within the present framework — which is strictly real — exchange rate variations are directly expressed as variations in the domestic real wage, as are the effects of different unemployment rates. In other words, these are the 'Ricardian' adjustments to foreign imbalances, and what we could term 'classical' adjustment processes to the labour market. Wages, on the other hand, enter the determination of the domestic rate of activity via the multiplier: any downward adjustment of wages — in the stylised framework presented here — implies, other things being equal, a decline in endogenously generated aggregate demand. In other words, they affect 'Keynesian' adjustment. Thus, the system exhibits a clear duality in the role of wages. On the one hand, the wage level bears a negative relationship with the trade-balance constraint and, as a consequence, has a negative effect on employment levels. On the other hand, wages appear in the multiplier to have a positive effect proportional to their real level and, as a consequence, a positive effect on employment.[42]

A particular case is that whereby the system may tend to overshoot in the reaction of wages (via exchange rates) to imbalances in foreign trade, thus depressing aggregate demand at home and, indirectly, abroad. This is more likely to apply if the patterns of specialisation are slower to adjust to trade imbalances than wages and income levels. The more this is the case, the more the behaviour of the system will approach that of a purely 'Keynesian' one, with rates of activity determined primarily by autonomous investments and by rather sticky foreign-trade multipliers.

The duality in the role of wages is likely to define relatively narrow adjustment paths, both within each economy and in the world as a whole, limited as they will be by trade-balance constraints on the one hand and macroeconomic demand depression on the other.

Finally, it may be noted that, for any given pattern of income intensity for the various commodities, wages bear a close relation to the average technological levels of each economy:[43] in a more realistic formulation, to the technological levels of the vertically integrated sectors generated by the set of tradeable commodities that each economy produces: see Pasinetti for further details (1981). In some loose sense, these average technological levels define the 'centre of gravity' around which the adjustment processes take place. International wage differentials are, in other words, related to the average technological gap/lead between countries.

With respect to investment, the assumption about its strict exogenous nature can now be abandoned. Investments can then be subdivided into the following three parts:

(a) an induced part, via the familiar accelerator-stock adjustment mechanisms;
(b) a part related to the changes in specialisation: a gain in commodities will require a related investment in new capacity, and, vice versa, a loss in commodities will imply a related disinvestment; and
(c) an exogenous part, stemming from innovation opportunities in each economy.

The difference between the *actual* level of income, i.e. that level of income endogenously determined by the autonomous items of demand and the multiplier, and full employment income, can be referred to as the *Keynesian gap*. Technology plays a crucial role on both sides of this gap. On the one hand, it determines in a straightforward manner the full employment income, once given the supply of labour (L), as $Y_{max} = \pi L$, where π is labour productivity. On the other hand, it affects the *actual* rate of macroeconomic activity in two separate ways: first, technology gaps and leads determine, as we saw in Section 7.1, to a large extent the international distribution of growth stimuli and constraints via import and export schedules; and second, there is the determination of the innovation opportunities associated with 'autonomous' investment.

As one of us has argued elsewhere (Dosi and Orsenigo, 1988), there is no *a priori* guarantee that these dual effects of technology will yield actual levels of income equal or close to the maximum ones.

A similar set of considerations to the ones suggested in the preceding section on the possible dominance of technological conditions over the boundaries of the notional equilibria applies *a fortiori* to the actual paths achieved. If (a) the technology gaps/leads are relatively homogeneous for each economy (so that the space for changes in specialisation related to 'comparative advantages' is low), (b) the income intensities of the various commodities differ widely, and (c) the proportion of innovative to Ricardian commodities is high, then the two countries will be, so to speak, stuck in their respective positions, despite any possible Ricardian adjustment mechanism at work. Only technical change can then redefine the pecking order in terms of wages and incomes while in the short term exogenously induced 'Keynesian processes' (e.g. through fiscal policies) will be limited by the interdependence of the international system.

7.4 Technological progress and economic dynamics: an overview

From what has been said so far, it will be clear that technical change superimposes some dynamic mechanisms of paramount importance on the 'stationary' Ricardian and Keynesian adjustment processes ('stationary' in that one theoretically assumes them to operate on the grounds of given technologies and demand preferences).

In Section 7.1 we saw how technological innovation and imitation improved the trade-offs implicit in the relation between wages, income and international competitiveness, and moved the boundaries of the set of notional macroeconomic equilibria that one country can achieve. We now discuss the effects of technical change on the *actual* levels of income (and the correlated growth patterns). For the sake of simplicity, we will stick to the dichotomy between process and product innovations: these two 'ideal types' help in highlighting the economic effects of the process of technical change which can be placed on a continuum ranging from pure productivity increasing to pure additions to the basket of intermediate and consumption commodities.[44]

Let us first consider productivity-increasing innovations. We know from the preceding sections that they expand the boundaries of the growth possibilities of the economies concerned. The movement of the maximum feasible income for a given labour force is obviously defined as $\dot{Y} = \dot{\pi}$ where the dots stand for rates of change. The *actual* percentage change in income (starting from an equilibrium position) will be:

$$\dot{Y} = \dot{E} + \dot{A} \qquad (7.18)$$

where $\dot{E}$ is the percentage change in the multiplier, as in equation (7.16), and $\dot{A}$ is the change in the autonomous items of demand. In the simplest case when all domestic expenditure is endogenous and income is written as a straightforward function of export levels and import propensities ($Y = 1/mX$), the elasticity of income to productivity will be a function of the export and import elasticities to the same productivity change.

With sticky baskets of consumption, it is interesting to note that whenever such pure productivity-increasing innovations do not lead to any increase in real wages and do not influence the domestic investment propensity, their sole positive effect upon income levels stems from the gains in foreign competitiveness.[45]

A pure process innovation increases the efficiency of labour inputs, decreasing the total labour force required to produce a certain amount of physical output and, thus, the size of the multiplier which also operates by means of workers' consumption. In a closed economy, the compensation effect may well be rather weak. In traditional, general equilibrium models, such a compensation is generally guaranteed by three hypotheses. First, prices of commodities and primary inputs are assumed to change contextually to imbalances in any market. Second, there must be at least substitution in consumption between different commodities (and possibly also substitution between techniques of production). And third, all this supposedly occurs via adjustment processes that, to be fair, have never been fully specified in their dynamics.

This is not the place to criticise these various hypotheses in any detail.[46] Suffice it to say that, as opposed to these hypotheses, the analysis presented in this book starts from the view that (a) prices are rather close to costs of production under conditions of constant or increasing returns; (b) there is only a very limited number of techniques available at any one time, which can generally be ranked as superior or inferior irrespective of relative prices (as argued in Chapter 4); (c) that demand for consumption commodities follows Engel-like patterns, with relatively limited price-induced substitution; and (d) that economic processes are by nature sequential and irreversible:[47] 'disequilibrium' decisions have effects which spread over the future.

These features of the economic system also constitute the 'microeconomics' of a Keynesian adjustment process: quantities adjust to variations in the direct and indirect effects of the autonomous elements of demand in a way whereby wages play the double role of being an item of costs (and thus a determinant of prices and competitiveness) and an essential item of aggregate demand generation through the multiplier.[48]

Consider again the particular case of a pure process innovation when real wages remain constant, so that prices in terms of international currency fall (cf. equations (7.5) and (7.6)). The $A(z)$ schedule in Figure 7.1 will shift — due to a changed 'productivity gap' between the two economies — and so will the borderline commodity $\tilde{z}$.

The net effect on income of the process innovation will stem from the relative impact of (a) positive specialisation and in a more general model, the price elasticity effects on exports and imports; and, (b) extending beyond the model of Section 7.3, the negative effect on the domestic generation of demand, as a consequence of the reduced consumption capabilities of a reduced employed labour force. Two properties are worth noticing.

First, a fundamental difference with Ricardian adjustment (i.e. the devaluation case) lies in the fact that improved competitiveness must not be paid for in terms of falling wages: the latter may remain stable or even increase slightly. However, in analogy with the devaluation case, there is a beggar-my-neighbour element, in so far as the entire increase in domestic income (if any) could lead to a deteriorating competitiveness and possibly even lower growth possibilities for the trading partner.[49]

Second, we suggest that there is no endogenous force which guarantees that *in general* the potential level in income (that implicit in $\dot{Y} = \dot{\pi}$) will be achieved: in other words, the *Keynesian gap* between potential and actual rates of growth may widen.[50] If this occurs, the trade balance of the trading partner will become tighter and trigger off a process of international feedbacks which might even lead to an international growth rate lower than the pre-innovation rate. Conceptually identical considerations apply to pure process imitations.

Generally speaking, irrespective of what might happen to the absolute value of the growth rates of each economy, the *relative* rate of growth of the country undertaking the process innovation will always increase as compared to the other economy. In other words, the argument relating all innovative processes to *diverging* growth tendencies does not only apply to the boundaries of the potential equilibrium; it also applies to *actual* incomes (and rates of growth).

Let us now consider the case of a pure product innovation: a straightforward addition to the basket of consumption goods. Its impact upon foreign competitiveness will clearly be positive. The introduction of such a commodity will also be associated with an increase in autonomous investment. Thus, domestic income will increase. As a consequence, imports, too, will most likely increase.[51] At the end of the day, both incomes of the two countries (or, for that matter, both rates of growth) might have increased, although the increase in the innovative country (say, country A) will be higher than in B. In other words, the product innovation (at least, partly) will have *paid for itself*: while it increased country A's exports, relaxing its balance of trade constraint, at the same time it pulled up both country A's income (via the joint effect of autonomous investment associated with that innovation and increased exports) and country B's income (via increased import absorption in A and, thus, a stronger foreign-trade multiplier in B).[52] Considerations of a similar nature apply to product imitations in B.

These two ideal types of innovation – purely productivity-increasing or purely additional to the consumption basket – are highly unrealistic.

The overwhelming majority of innovations contain features of both. The foregoing discussion, however, helps in bringing to the forefront the different impact of a simple increase in the efficiency of the economic system on the one hand, and the generation of new investment and new market opportunities on the other. Since the characteristics of technical change do not allow one to put forward, *a priori*, any hypothesis of constancy in the relative balance between these two fundamental properties, one may also expect long-term variations in the endogenously generated rate of growth and in the *Keynesian gap* between the actual growth rate and the maximum rate which would guarantee full employment of the labour force, reflecting shifts in the balance between product and process innovation.

We now have all the elements for a synthetic account of the growth process under conditions of technical change. Reconsider equation (7.2). We may define the rate of productivity-increasing innovation in country A as:

$$\alpha = \frac{d(a(z))/dt}{a(z)} \tag{7.19}$$

whereas the rate of productivity-increasing imitation/diffusion in B is:

$$\alpha^* = \frac{d(a^*(z))/dt}{a^*(z)} \tag{7.20}$$

The change in specialisation among the 'Ricardian' commodities, as expressed by the change in $\tilde{z}_t$, will be a function of the change in wages in both countries, relative to their rate of process innovation and imitation:

$$\frac{d\tilde{z}}{dt} = Z(\dot{w}, \dot{w}^*, \alpha, \alpha^*) \tag{7.21}$$

The pattern of specialisation will not change through time if:[53]

$$\dot{w} - \dot{w}^* = \alpha - \alpha^* \tag{7.22}$$

Or, in other words, an 'imitative' country willing to increase its wage at the same rate as the 'innovative' country without 'de-specialising' has to sustain a rate of technological imitation (i.e. productivity improvement) equal to the rate of innovation of the 'leader'. Clearly, that same country may catch up if its rate of productivity growth is higher than that in the leading country (see Figure 7.4).[54] In each country, the maximum technically feasible rate of growth will be:

$$\dot{Y}_{max} = \dot{\pi} + \dot{L} \tag{7.24}$$

and

$$\dot{Y}^*_{\max} = \dot{\pi}^* + \dot{L}^* \tag{7.25}$$

These are Harrod's 'natural' rates, with $\dot{\pi}$ equal to labour productivity growth and $\dot{L}$ equal to the rate of growth of labour supply. However, in the long run, each economy will be able to grow only at the maximum rate consistent with the balance of payment constraint: Y_T^*.[55]

Differentiating equation (7.11) with respect to time, we get:[56]

$$\dot{Y}_T - \dot{Y}_T^* = T(\dot{w}, \dot{w}^*, \dot{\alpha}, \dot{\alpha}^*, \, \mathrm{d}r/\mathrm{d}t) \tag{7.26}$$

where $\dot{Y}_T$ and $\dot{Y}_T^*$ stand for these maximum growth rates and $\mathrm{d}r/\mathrm{d}t$ stands for the change in the set of innovative commodities. The exports of the two countries are a function of the patterns of specialisation within the Ricardian commodities and of the net flow of innovative commodities.[57]

In the extreme case where B is specialised in all the Ricardian commodities with very sticky baskets of consumptions, the function is reduced to:

$$\dot{Y}_T - \dot{Y}_T^* = T\left(\frac{\mathrm{d}r}{\mathrm{d}t}\right) \tag{7.28}$$

Equation (7.26) shows that convergence or divergence in the rates of growth compatible with the trade-balance constraint is essentially a function of the relative rate of productivity growth and the relative rate of product innovation and imitation.

Note that equation (7.26) does *not* show the *actual* rates of growth in each economy, but only the *relative* rates in A and B, consistent with the foreign accounts.

We may now consider the extreme (but not entirely implausible) case in which the international system is economically 'hierarchical': the endogenously generated growth of the leader (country A) is of paramount importance in determining the world growth rate. Suppose that the growth in A is essentially based on the flow of new products and new market opportunities (i.e. 'autonomous' investment undertaken in A). The international system can then be closed by:

$$\dot{Y} = \lambda\left(\frac{\mathrm{d}r}{\mathrm{d}t}\right) \tag{7.29}$$

This crude over-simplification accounts for a fundamental Schumpeterian property of the dynamics of the international system, namely the role of innovations in the form of new product development and the associated autonomous investment, undertaken by the technological leader(s), as well as – in a more realistic formulation – imitators, as an *engine of growth*. This is the case, because such new product innovations expand export possibilities, while at the same time compensating for them with higher levels of endogenously generated demand, higher incomes and thus higher levels of imports. Purely productivity-increasing innovations, on the other hand, increase the *possibility* of growth of the international system, but at the same time might not generate an aggregate demand sufficient to achieve the notionally possible rate of growth.[58]

The model allows one to define a series of dynamic trade-offs. Particularly important is the dynamic property which states that, for any given rate of growth consistent with the balance of payment constraint, the higher the rate of product innovation in country *A*, the higher its relative wage growth (in other words, country *A* can afford to lose Ricardian commodities to country *B*); conversely, the higher the rate of imitation in *B*, the higher its rate of wage growth. The same argument can be repeated allowing the rates of growth to vary for some given rates of increase in wages.

Moreover, the model clarifies the difference between 'stationary' adjustment processes (i.e. holding technology constant) and 'dynamic' ones (i.e. related to technical change). A first stationary adjustment is based on the behavioural tendency at the microeconomic level towards minimum-cost/maximum-profit activities: at best, this induces a once-and-for-all increase in the short-term efficiency of the international location of productive activities.[59] This is what we have referred to as a *Ricardian adjustment process*. The other adjustment process at work, holding technology constant, refers to the property by which open economies 'pull' each other's demand via imports, while at the same time constraining each other's size and possibilities of growth via the need to balance the foreign accounts. We have called this a *Keynesian adjustment process*.

Certainly, even under conditions of no technical change, the system could undergo quantitative expansion by means of expanding investment and capital accumulation. In reality, however, growth is intimately interlinked with technical change. It is technical change which is of paramount importance in shaping the inner dynamism of the international system by (a) expanding the possibilities of growth; (b) *stimulating* that same growth via new or expanding international markets; and (c) continuously redistributing the relative possibilities of growth between countries.

In other words, technical change provides a *transforming* and *expanding* universe within whose boundaries 'stationary' adjustment processes take place at each given point in time.

In an open economy, the *relative* rates of innovation and imitation also define the moving thread of stimuli and constraints that each economy faces, thus determining also the relative dynamics of interdependent systems. In particular, if the relatively fast technological innovator fails to fill the 'Keynesian gap' between maximum and effective growth rates, the burden of adjustment will fall upon the 'slower innovator' who will have to adjust income growth to the foreign-balance constraint. This will also lower the growth possibilities of the fast innovator, who will, in turn, tighten the foreign-balance constraint of the slower innovator even further. The overall net result might even be a *lower* rate of growth of income than would have occurred without the new technologies, and a lower level of employment.

Whenever the 'slow' economy fails to increase its rate of technological progress, there appear to be three alternative results: (a) the country with the highest innovation speed is ready to finance the trade deficit of its partner(s); (b) protectionist barriers are erected by the slow-innovation country; and (c) the slow country is ready to accept lower rates of growth of its real wages in the hope that Ricardian processes of specialisation, jointly with favourable price elasticities of exports and imports, will neutralise, at least for some time, the increasing technology gap.

In open economies, technical change has the dual property of being labour-saving (in the simplest sense that it decreases the labour input requirements per unit of output), and at the same time competitiveness-increasing. This may determine a quite narrow growth path between the need to satisfy the foreign account and its effect upon domestic employment. Boyer and Petit (1980) describe this property with the metaphor of Scylla and Charibde. An increase in the relative rate of productivity growth of any one country presents a greater potential for growth for that same country, which, however, may not be entirely exploited by the endogenous creation of aggregate demand stemming from the augmented foreign competitiveness. On the other hand, a failure in innovating and thus, also, in increasing productivity, bears as a consequence the tightening of the foreign-balance constraint which will reduce growth possibilities.

The nature of the international equilibrium which is actually reached depends on the international distribution of the burden of adjusting foreign account imbalances and on the actual history of these adjustments. We can compare these international interdependence conditions with the properties of a tandem. *A priori*, there is an infinite range of velocities at which two or more people bicycling on a tandem can go. The interdependence between the cycling speed of each person, however, is rigidly fixed. It is relatively difficult to change velocity, especially to accelerate, unless there is a high level of coordination between them with respect to both effort and timing. Lacking such coordination, either the strongest cyclist must be powerful enough to pull the other(s) at the velocity he/she desires, or the velocity of the tandem will adjust close to that of the weakest one. The analogy also appears to be quite adequate in that the condition of international interdependence has often been fulfilled throughout the history of capitalist economies by means of the dominant position of one country which dictated the pace, and the rules of the game of international patterns of growth (cf. Mistral, 1982).

However, unlike the tandem analogy, where the distance between the partners is fixed, in the international system one or more economies may well fall behind or cluster nearer to each other, through patterns of divergence or convergence, as discussed above.

On a theoretical level, the approach suggested here presents some analogy with the family of models following on from Kaldor and Thirlwall, whereby the long-term rate of growth of each economy is determined by that maximum rate consistent with the balance of payment constraint.[60] The joint outcome of both 'stationary' adjustments and technical change could lead to the 'synthetic' formula (as in Thirlwall, 1980) expressing the dynamic foreign-trade multiplier:

$$\dot{Y}_B = \frac{x_t}{Y_m} \tag{7.30}$$

where $\dot{Y}_B$ is the rate of growth of income, x_t is the rate of export growth and Y_m is the income elasticity for imports. However, the foregoing analysis implies that this is likely to be an approximate, albeit sometimes empirically robust, historical regularity.

A summary of the main causal chains, linking innovation and income growth, are depicted in Figure 7.6. Some of these links depend on the nature of technological trajectories and on the direction and intensity of the positive feedbacks between growth and technical change (see the links 1–6 and 19 in Figure 7.6). We could call this set of links the *technological 'regime'*.

Some other links relate to the effects of innovation upon competitiveness (see links 1, 10–13 and 18). We may call this set of relationships *the regime of insertion in the world economy* (see Mistral, 1985). Yet another set of links refers to the relationship between the tradeable and the non-tradeable sectors of the economy (the former being approximated here by manufacturing) (see links 15 and 16 in Figure 7.6). In a way, this is an expression for both the degree of openness of an economy and the degree to which its growth is based on the productivity of tradeable commodities.

One last set of relations highlights the *regime of macroeconomic*

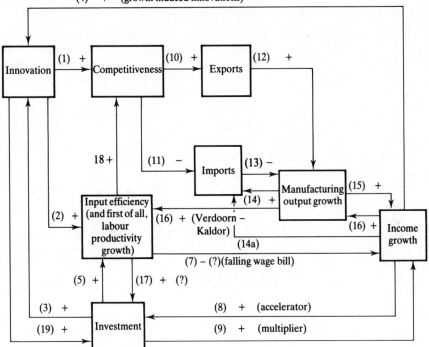

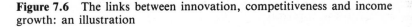

Note: The (+) and (−) signs stand for the likely direction of the effect

Figure 7.6 The links between innovation, competitiveness and income growth: an illustration

demand formation (see link 19), which overlaps with the nature of the 'technological regime' (see links 7–9, 14a and 17 in Figure 7.6).

The Kaldor–Thirlwall formula is a synthetic formulation of links 12–16. On the grounds of our earlier discussion, we can predict that it presents an adequate representation of international differences in growth patterns, whenever both the technological regimes and the regimes of macroeconomic demand formation are stable through time, when they are relatively similar across countries, and when the institutional set-ups and policies are rather similar (so that the role of non-tradeables in each economy, i.e. links 15 and 16, follow similar patterns). One can see that these conditions broadly correspond to the period of high growth following the Second World War.

In general, however, the relationship between the innovative process and patterns of growth depends on the *tuning* between the intensities and directions of causal loops which have:

- a *technological dimension*: the nature of technological paradigms and trajectories; the degrees of appropriability of technologies; their labour-saving impact as compared with their demand creating effect; the sensitivity of competitiveness with respect to technological gaps, etc.;
- a directly *economic dimension*: the pattern of capital accumulation linked to the multiplier/accelerator; the effect of income distribution on investment propensities; the role of wages in aggregate demand formation; the foreign-trade multiplier, etc.; and
- a *social/institutional dimension*: the forms of organisation of commodity, labour and financial markets; the effects of public policies, etc.

Each major phase of economic development can be regarded as a particular configuration of these dimensions involving specific socio-economic tuning between the (positive and negative) feedback loops discussed so far (see Boyer and Mistral, 1984; Dosi and Orsenigo, 1988; Perez, 1985).[61]

7.5 Conclusions

The account of the moving thread of international technological gaps/leads between countries and the strong interdependence condition brought about by the foreign-balance constraint brings some important conclusions to the forefront.

First, the importance of the fact that each economy is 'open' lies in the link between technological dynamism, competitiveness, dynamism of demand patterns and accumulation rather than in a problem of short-term efficient allocation of given resources. Thus, whereas Ricardian adjustment processes (as defined above) are always at work, checking the (varying degrees of) allocative efficiency of the international system, the main impetus to international growth stems from the creation of new markets and new opportunities of accumulation, and the tendency toward increasing efficiency of used inputs.

Second, the model sketched in the first part of this chapter defines the conditions of international convergence/divergence in income and wages as ultimately dependent on convergence/divergence in technological levels and innovative capabilities.

Third, within interdependent economies, each characterised by some of the technological features described in Chapters 4 and 5, the satisfactory outcome of Keynesian processes of reciprocal adjustment in aggregate demand is likely to depend either on high levels of international coordination or a highly hierarchical international system. In turn, technological gaps and the commodity composition of national specialisations shape the international competitiveness of each economy, and, thus, also the degrees of 'fitness' of each country to the prevailing regime of international growth.

Admittedly, a fully developed model of growth with endogenous technological change would require a thoroughly formalised 'microfoundation' (as qualitatively discussed in Chapters 4 and 5) based on 'evolutionary' processes of learning and market selection. This ambitious task cannot be performed here. However, 'synthetic' representations of sector-specific and country-specific technological change, jointly with empirically plausible macroeconomic relations, allow a promising link between the analysis of aggregate growth patterns and the underlying features of innovative activities.

The perspective outlined here is also quite different from approaches to similar interpretative issues based on some equilibrium properties of steady-state dynamics. For example, like Romer (1986) or Lucas (1988), we ask 'why are productivities and per-capita incomes systematically different across countries?'. However, unlike their analysis, we reject – on both micro and aggregate evidence – the underlying ideas that:

(a) microeconomic activities of innovation correspond, on average, to 'correct' predictions of technological opportunities and appropriability conditions;
(b) individual agents are identical in their capabilities of accessing and exploiting public information and human resources;
(c) market-clearing conditions intertemporally hold.

In our view, departing from these assumptions entails a more fruitful possibility of joining microeconomic analysis of the patterns of technical change with nowadays 'old-fashioned' (Keynesian–Kaldorian) accounts of aggregate consistency conditions in the growth process. So – we suggest – balance-of-payments constraints, differentiated propensities to invest, diverse labour productivities, below-full-employment rates of growth and diverse rates of innovation/imitation, may all be deeply linked with 'disequilibrium' and country-specific characteristics of technological and organisational change.

The other side of the coin is, of course, that such a perspective, no matter how empirically plausible, has – as we have probably illustrated at length in this chapter – a significant theoretical price: formal modelling can only provide some sort of abacus on a few broad macro relations, without clean 'prediction' or elegant theorems. It highlights, however, the strong interactions of technological change, growth and trade patterns and the need for presenting, despite the complexity, a unified account of the microeconomics of innovation, observed patterns of trade, and the growth process.

Notes

1. Exceptions are Pasinetti (1981) and Nelson and Winter (1982). Other models which bear some similarities to the approach suggested here are Giovannetti (1985), Thirlwall and Vines (1983), Blecker (1985). More generally, what is argued here shows several similarities with the Kaldorian analysis of international growth patterns (see Kaldor, 1966, 1980). The Nelson–Winter model does not explicitly account for international trade. However, as should be clear from the earlier discussion (cf. Chapter 4), an evolutionary microstructure is precisely what is behind our synthetic representation of the determinants of growth patterns in the model that follows.
2. The reader should note that this definition has nothing in common with the 'Ricardian goods' sometimes found in trade literature: an improper name for commodities traded on the grounds of differential endowments of natural resources.
3. Dornbush, Fisher and Samuelson (1977) p. 823.
4. Note that each commodity z has its own specific machine. In equations (7.7)–(7.10) which follow, Pk_i, Ck_i, etc., are the equivalent in a discrete representation of $Pk(z)$, $Ck(z)$, etc., on the continuum.
5. That is $Ck_i Pk_i / P_i$ and $C^* k_i P^* k_i / P_i^*$ respectively.
6. The economic meaning of $h_i = h_i^*$ is simply that the relative backwardness or lead in machine manufacturing and machine product-technology is proportional to the backwardness/lead in the manufacturing of the final product. Making use of (7.5), (7.6), (7.7) and (7.8), the equality of capital/output ratios can be written as:

$$\frac{C_{ki}l_{ki}w}{(C_{ki}l_{ki}w)(1+r)+wa_i} = \frac{C_{ki}^* l_{ki}^* w^*}{(C_{ki}^* l_{ki}^* w^*)(1+r)+w^* a_i^*}$$

Rearranging and simplifying we get

$$\frac{C_{ki}l_{ki}}{C_{ki}^* l_{ki}^*} = \frac{a_i}{a_i^*} \tag{7.10}$$

7. On these first two points cf. Thirlwall (1979) and (1980).
8. In a two-country model the imports of one country are obviously the exports of the other country.
9. The formulation in equation (7.11) still assumes, for convenience, homotheticity within each country. *A fortiori*, the argument that follows will apply to strictly non-homothetic demand functions.
10. In this model national and domestic incomes are identical.
11. The angle between the s-line and the w^*-axis is equal to w/w^* and to $A(\bar{z}_0)$.
12. The angle between the TB-line and the Y^*-axis is equal to Y/Y^* and $\psi^*(\bar{z})/\psi(\bar{z})$. Note that all the variables are taken to be measured in some real quantity, however mysterious that is. In particular, problems arise

with regard to whether income and wages of each country are measured in terms of the commodity basket it produces or the basket it demands. Moreover, when we allow specialisation to change, both output baskets and relative prices must change. Facing all these ambiguities, we shall none the less overlook any index-number problem, confident to be forgiven at least by all those economists who keep using aggregate production functions despite a much more devastating critique of the possibility of measuring aggregate capital.

13. In the more complex case of 7.13.1 and 7.14.1 employment is still linear in Y/w, through the income distribution coefficient $(1/s)$.

14. Each average productivity is a weighted average of the $(1/a_i)$ and $(1/a_i^*)$ between 0 and z and between $\bar{z}$ and 1, respectively.

15. There is an ambiguity in this statement in that an index-number problem is unavoidable; however, cf note 14.

16. The simplest hypothesis which guarantees the feasibility of the new wage pairs (i.e. that they remain equal or in some proportion to the average productivity of each economic system) is to assume that the ranking of the $a(z)$s, in A, and the $a^*(z)$s, in B, are both monotonic in $A(z)$, so that the average productivity of each economic system increases as the number of produced commodities decreases. As already mentioned, we basically overlook any index-number problem involved in the changes of output mix.

17. Relaxing these simplifying hypotheses, the set of acceptable specialisations is defined within the area $AXZB$. Our discussion will generally stick to the simpler case, which also highlights the properties of more complex systems.

18. Note that this area also includes the points that are 'technically' in equilibrium but may be socially unacceptable.

19. The reader may visualise the case by thinking of the recent Japanese experience; cf. Thirlwall (1979) for an empirical argument about the Japanese case along similar lines.

20. In other words, an absolute fall in wages and incomes in the 'slow' country is by no means a necessary consequence since there is no shrinking of the 'outward' boundaries of its equilibrium possibilities. It may, none the less, happen. See below.

21. For a discussion of this feature of national economic systems, see Chapters 3 and 4.

22. Note that this is often the case in developing countries.

23. The reader must be reminded again that the model thus far is concerned with the constraints to domestic income and employment. For all rates of activity below full employment a reduction in wages will also relax the foreign-balance constraint. However, this does not imply that it will yield an improvement in the actual levels of income and employment. Since wages are a crucial component of domestic aggregate demand, the opposite may well occur. See below.

24. Cf. J. Robinson (1974).

25. These conditions somewhat resemble Prebisch's analysis of underdeveloped economies; cf. Prebisch (1950). More generally on the role of income elasticities, see Thirlwall (1980).

26. This is not unlikely: cf. Chapter 5, on the capital-saving nature of technical progress.

27. We have still to accept the possibility of widespread 'reswitching of commodities' for this statement to rigorously apply.

28. The reader should remember that the model is not necessarily confined to a 'North–South' framework but is meant to apply to differences between developed countries as well. In a sense, all countries could be placed on a continuum according to the size of their technological gap vis-à-vis the country showing the highest average technological levels.

19. We are focussing here only on the set of final goods. The reader might have noticed, however, that the brief discussion above on capital-goods only produced by country A implicitly assumed that all capital goods are innovative commodities.

30. One may notice some significant resemblance with the role of the United States vis-à-vis Europe and Japan in the post-War period.

31. Cf. Emmanuel (1969). A critical discussion can be found in Evans (1980).

32. We assume that all new products are also immediately consumed by B. Even if this does not occur, however, the property still holds since the relative intensity of B-product in A-income will necessarily decrease and so the foreign-balance constraint for A will be relaxed.

33. Remember that the absolute levels of wages in each country must bear a relationship to the average productivity of the same economy for any given pattern of specialisation. This is also proportional to the Euclidean distance between any point in the income–wage possibility set and the origin along a given f or f^* line.

34. We discussed it at length in Dosi (1984).

35. Cf. Thirlwall (1980). The case characterised only by product innovation and imitation exhibits some features similar to Krugman's model (cf. Krugman, 1979). However, there are some aberrant properties of the latter stemming from its (unnecessary) choice of a general equilibrium framework. For example, a simple increase in the labour supply in the innovating country worsens its income and terms-of-trade. Moreover, were we allowing process innovations in such a model they would have a detrimental effect on the innovating country (cf. Cole, 1980). These unlikely properties stem from the fact that a general equilibrium set-up allows only a definition of prices and terms-of-trade in relation to relative scarcities under a requirement, *ex-hypothesi*, of market clearing. We hope we have avoided all these drawbacks here, by avoiding a conceptual framework which makes dynamics very difficult to represent.

36. See also similar models developed by Krugman (1979) and more recently by Grossman and Helpman (1990a,b).

37. The analysis that follows will continue to deal with real magnitude despite all index-number ambiguities.

38. By definition, $Y = R + W$ (i.e. the total income is made of wages (W) and profits (R)) so that we can write the total consumption as $c_k(Y - W) + c_w W$. If $c_w = 1$ then the expression equals $c_k Y + (1 - c_k)W$.

39. We stick to the simpler hypothesis that all capital goods are domestically produced.

40. The equations are now (7.3), (7.12), (7.13.1), (7.14.1) and (7.17) with $\bar{z}$, w, w^*, N, N^*, Y, Y^* as unknowns and I and I^* as exogenous variables.

41. We discuss some of these issues in Dosi and Orsenigo (1986). See also Silverberg (1985).

42. It may well happen that a decrease in wages leads to a decrease in income in the domestic economy, let alone the other one. This can be seen by differentiating Y with respect to w in equation (7.16). Calling G the

denominator of the multiplier we obtain:

$$dY/dw = \frac{1}{G}\left\{\left[\frac{1}{G}\left(-d\psi(\ )/dw + \frac{1-c_k}{\pi^*}\right)\right]\right.$$

$$\left.(\psi^*(\ )\cdot Y^* + I) + Y^*(d\psi^*(\ )/dw)\right\} \qquad (7.8)$$

The expression within the square brackets can be positive, so that whenever the relative proportion of exports to investments as an 'engine of demand' is low, the increase in export may not compensate for the fall in the domestic multiplier if the elasticities of exports and imports to changing costs are low. Moreover, a decrease in wages (which can be taken as equivalent in any respect to a devaluation) certainly depresses income of the partner(s). One can see here how the endogenous adjustment process may lead to beggar-my-neighbour results and depress the overall rates of macroeconomic activity. Clearly, a full macroeconomic model should also account for the effect of changing income distribution upon the propensity to invest. This is yet another complex issue. Here we are simply forced to state, without any proof, that – even after allowing the effects of changing distributive shares upon the rate of investment – one may not find a sufficient compensating stimulus for the rates of macroeconomic activities. On this issue, see also Sylos Labini (1984), Dosi and Orsenigo (1988), Boyer and Mistral (1983), Cimoli (1988).

43. For a discussion, see Dosi and Orsenigo (1988).
44. In a more complex framework with input/output interdependencies we could define these ideal types of innovation as (a) innovations which increase labour productivity in any one vertically integrated sector without any change in the nature of the outputs and of intermediate and capital inputs; and, (b) innovations which create new vertically integrated sectors, without affecting the coefficients of the existing ones. On the concept of vertically integrated sectors cf. Pasinetti (1981).
45. This can be seen by differentiating equation (7.16) with respect to (π).
46. Cf. Dosi (1984), and Dosi and Orsenigo (1988).
47. On the sequential nature of 'Keynesian' adjustment processes, cf. Pasinetti (1974).
48. The conditions of dynamic stability of such a system are discussed in Dosi and Orsenigo (1988).
49. More precisely the actual growth of the partner economy will fall if the innovative one does not fully exploit its own expanded growth possibilities, compensating with higher income levels for a lower import propensity and higher export propensity.
50. In Dosi (1982a) we illustrate one such case. Note that this argument is consistent with the evidence of no significant impact of productivity growth (net of the effect of foreign competitiveness) upon domestic growth. See Boyer and Petit (1980).
51. For this to happen (neglecting second order conditions) we must have $\psi \cdot \Delta Y + Y \cdot \Delta \psi > 0$. This will generally be satisfied, since the growth in income is not only due to the improved foreign-trade multiplier, but also to the domestic increase in autonomous investment.
52. This last effect on B-income will not apply only if the introduction of the new commodity significantly changes the income intensity of B-exports as

compared to *B*-imports. If this change is large enough the worsening 'quality' of *B*-specialisations will more than compensate for the positive effect of higher *A*-growth rates upon *B*-exports.

53. Rewriting equation (7.4). In its dynamic form, we get

$$A(\bar{z}(t), t) = w(t)/w^*(t)$$

Differentiating with respect to time

$$\frac{1}{a}\left[\frac{\partial a}{\partial t} + \frac{\partial a}{\partial \bar{z}} \cdot \frac{d\bar{z}}{dt}\right] - \frac{1}{a^*}\left[\frac{\partial a^*}{\partial t} + \frac{\partial a^*}{\partial \bar{z}} \cdot \frac{d\bar{z}}{dt}\right] = \frac{1}{w} \cdot \frac{dw}{dt} \bigg/ \frac{1}{w^*}\frac{dw^*}{dt}$$

$$(7.23)$$

Rearranging, one sees that for $d\bar{z}/dt = 0$, $\dot{\alpha} - \dot{\alpha}^* = \dot{w} - \dot{w}^*$ where α stands for $1/a$ $(\partial a/\partial t)$, etc., and, analogously the dots stand for the rates of change. Moreover, note that we assume here 'balanced' productivity growth across all Ricardian commodities. This is only a simplifying device: the essence of the argument also applies to all cases of 'unbalanced' patterns of technical change.

54. Think of post-War productivity trends in Western Europe and Japan as compared with the United States.

55. Remember that throughout our discussion we are neglecting the possibility of international capital flows so that the balance of payment is identical to the trade balance.

56. Differentiating equation (7.11), and also accounting for the effect of innovative commodities (*r*) upon import propensities, we obtain:

$$1/Y(dY/dt) - 1/Y^*(dY^*/dt) = 1/\psi\left[\frac{\partial \psi}{\partial \bar{z}} \cdot \frac{d\bar{z}}{dt} + \frac{\partial \psi}{\partial r} \cdot \frac{dr}{dt}\right] -$$

$$+ 1/\psi^*\left[\frac{\partial \psi^*}{\partial \bar{z}} \cdot \frac{d\bar{z}}{dt} + \frac{\partial \psi^*}{\partial r} \cdot \frac{dr}{dt}\right] \qquad (7.27)$$

By appropriately rearranging equation (7.23), one gets $d\bar{z}/dt$ as a function of α, α^*, $\dot{w}$, $\dot{w}^*$.

57. Net of product imitation by *B*.

58. They might not, although clearly sometimes they do: this occurs essentially when productivity-increasing innovations are associated with the acceleration of the diffusion of new product innovations. Think of the relation between the fall in the relative price and diffusion of electronic products. The important point, however, is that in all these cases productivity growth and product innovation are part of the same innovative process.

59. See Pasinetti (1981).

60. Cf. Thirlwall (1980) which presents a thorough and convincing discussion of the issue. See also Kaldor (1970), Kennedy and Thirlwall (1979).

61. 'Socio-economic tuning' here is the equivalent of the French 'regulation', meaning those forms of economic organisation, rules of behaviour and institutions which 'channel the long term dynamics ... of an economy during an historical period for a given society' (Boyer and Mistral, 1984, p. 9). For more detailed discussion, see Dosi and Orsenigo (1988).

8

Markets, institutions and technical change in open economies: Some policy implications

Every theory is bound to simplify the variety and complexity of the phenomena that it tries to explain. Indeed, as suggested by modern epistemology, the smaller the number of states-of-the-world that a theory allows, the higher its analytical power (Popper (1968)). However, the adequacy of different abstractions and simplifications also depends on the choice of the phenomena that one wants to explain.

In this respect, the preceding chapters entailed a critique of the dominant approaches to technical change and international trade, with regard to the facts analysed and the assumptions made. There is a subtle − but none the less crucial − border between abstraction and trivialisation; between risking highly improbable predictions about the state-of-the-world and ruling out *ex hypothesi* the possibility of the state-of-the-world that the theory might not explain. On analytical grounds the evidence we discussed and the interpretations we suggested, imply that any model based on technology as freely available information, on maximising behaviour, on equilibrium and on relative factor scarcities can provide, at best, only a partial account of open economic systems, characterised by complex and varied mechanisms of technological learning, uncertainty, reproducibility of capital inputs, non-decreasing returns, bounded rationality and evolutionary processes.

Not surprisingly, the difference between the two approaches also extends to the normative. The most familiar intellectual strategy consists essentially of a reduction of the policy issues to exceptions, anomalies, particular cases of a general framework centered around the equilibrium conditions of the economic system, as postulated by the theory. The impact of policies and institutions is evaluated then on the grounds of a yardstick − the equilibrium which the economic system would achieve if left to itself, under very special and sometimes rather awkward hypotheses, the properties of which yield 'optimal' outcomes. In this perspective, any normative issue, phenomenon or behaviour is compared with the fundamental yardstick, defining the role and impact of economic policies. Thus, economists commonly use such concepts as 'externalities', 'market failures', 'limited information', 'imperfect markets', etc., to categorise the most common 'sub-optimal' features of the empirical world as compared with the theoretical model. In a peculiar reversal of positive and normative judgements, these real world 'imperfections' also delimit the domain of institutional intervention, the effects of which are designed to make the real world more similar to the theory.

The problems related to technological and economic change have generally been treated in a similar fashion: assessing, for example, the degree of 'market failure' associated with technological uncertainty, or the 'market imperfection' stemming from property rights on innovation. The methodology is appealing in its generality, simple enough to be treated in its basic form with undergraduate mathematics, incorporates many common-sense beliefs about the benefits of decentralised markets, and last, but not least, is dominant enough in the professional community to make its acceptance widespread and general.

The leap from the theoretical model on which the welfare theorems are based to the properties of actual economic systems is clearly a large one. Yet the correspondence between the fundamental hypotheses of the model (on behaviours, technology, interactions between the agents, etc.) and the real features of any particular economy is generally treated rather casually.

In contrast, the analyses of the preceding chapters yield the following conclusions which are fundamentally non-reductionist:[1]

1. Behaviours cannot be reduced to the simple and universal rationality of maximising agents.
2. Markets and economic processes occurring within them are institutional set-ups specific to historical periods, cultures and countries.
3. Non-market variables (including policies in the strict sense) are a permanent feature of the constitution of the economic system, and an essential part of the ways in which the economic machine is tuned and evolves.
4. There are particular combinations of institutional variables and decentralised market processes that efficiently fit, or appear to be matched, in terms of some performance yardstick.[2]

A discussion of normative issues, once out of the safe surroundings of market imperfections and anomalies, will, as Nelson and Winter have warned: 'be complex and messy. It is unlikely that one will be able to prove many sweeping normative theorems of the sort that are now contained in our advanced treatises and elementary text'.[3] However, the complexity and possible messiness has to be faced, and tackled, in order to take seriously the normative side of the analysis of technical change, trade and growth undertaken in the preceding chapters. Questions such as: what are 'the architectures', what is 'the pattern of organisation of individuals', in Stiglitz's terminology,[4] that are conducive to technological innovation? What is the role of policy in explaining the different national innovative performances identified in Chapter 4? Is it true that decentralised market processes always yield technological dynamism? What kind of performance yardstick can we use in a continuously changing world? And many more come to mind.

The agenda of normative issues is thus long and would lead us to many entangled questions at the core of the economic discipline. The aim here is more limited. In Section 8.1 we hypothesise on the role of different institutions (which we shall define), different organisational set-ups and different policies in relation to technical change. In Section 8.2 we discuss the implications of the openness of most economies for allocative processes, technological dynamism and growth possibilities. In doing so we shall suggest some performance criteria on which to judge the outcome of market processes in open economies. Finally, in Section 8.3 we present some broad conclusions on the relationship between institutions, technical change, and international regimes of growth.

8.1 Markets and institutions in the innovative process

The variety of the modes and effects of technological progress in different sectors, as analysed in Chapter 4, implies in a parallel variety of institutional arrangements that one can observe in modern non-centrally planned economies, with different degrees of involvement of public agencies in each sector, different market structures, and different patterns of interaction in each sector between private profit-motivated agents. In the following, we shall discuss both the effects of broadly defined institutions and explicitly defined public actions – i.e. 'policies' – in terms of technical change and international competitiveness.

Before getting into a more detailed analysis of the regularities in the observed institutional and policy patterns across countries and across technologies, let us put forward two general propositions: first, the institutional organisation of industries and markets does matter in terms of performance outcomes, no matter how defined; and second, each institutional set-up is partly endogenous to the competitive process and partly determined in the country-specific context.

By institutional set-up, we mean three things: (i) the forms of organisation of the interactions between agents (hundreds of agents bartering in the village market, or General Motors and Ford competing on the US market are two very different forms of interaction); (ii) the fundamental rules of behaviour that agents embody towards their competitors, customers, suppliers, employees, government officials, etc.; and (iii) the forms and degrees of direct exercise of discretionary power by non-market actors, who contribute to the organisation of the patterns of allocation, the rules of behaviour and the performance of market processes (clearly policies come under this heading).

Institutions shaping economic behaviour

As we discussed in Chapter 4, the behaviour of agents is most adequately represented by routines, strategies, metarules and search processes (see the seminal work of Nelson and Winter, 1982). Behaviours cannot be entirely deduced from the economic structure (taken to include the asymmetries in technological capabilities, the nature of the technology, the patterns of economic signals, etc.). A specific case concerns the adjustment processes each firm undertakes in a changing environment.

Take as illustration a firm producing any one particular product. The signals that the firm receives are of three kinds:

(a) the technological opportunities (and expected economic benefits) associated with technical change in that and other products;
(b) the rate of growth of demand in that and other products; and
(c) the changes in costs, prices, quantities and profitabilities in its markets (and possibly other markets).

These signals loosely correspond to three notional adjustment strategies. The first one relates to innovation/imitation/technological upgrading. Let us call it Schumpeterian adjustment. The second one relates to the search for the most promising growth opportunities; call it growth (or, in analogy with the earlier, more macroeconomic, definition, 'Keynesian') adjustment. The third one refers to price/quantity changes on the grounds of an unchanged technology. Let us call it Ricardian or classical adjustment. Most firms will choose varying combinations of all three adjustment processes. However, these will be 'open-exit' choices, the outcome of which cannot be deduced from either the knowledge of the state-of-the-world and/or an unchanging rationality principle.

In our view, the behavioural regularities in the strategies of the economic agents are both the result of selection processes of the environment, and the outcome of norms, attitudes and dominant behaviour which contain an irreducible extra-economic element. This applies to both intertemporal comparisons within the same country and, even more so, to intercountry comparisons. Think, for example, of the specific vision of the world that led to the 'entrepreneurship' strategies in some of the most successful late-coming industrialisers, such as Germany in the last century or Japan more recently. Even if the nature of the economic context might go a long way in explaining such performances, it does not explain the whole 'performance'. More institutional explanations (in the broad sociological sense, including established behaviours and fundamental cultural features) are required in order to account for the emphasis in these countries upon processes of growth and Schumpeterian adjustments, instead of short-term profitability.

Here we see a first fundamental role of non-market variables (including strictly political ones), that are instrumental in shaping and selecting the rules of behaviour and interactions of the economic agents. Policies, implicit social rules, dominant forms of organisation of the links within and between the various groups of economic agents (e.g. between firms and banks, between management and workers, etc.), levels and forms of industrial conflict, are of paramount importance in determining the combination and the direction of microeconomic adjustment processes, for any given set of economic signals and structural conditions.

Institutions organising externalities

Another (and related) set of non-market variables often influencing technological dynamism is the pattern of externalities and unintentional outcomes of market processes. As argued in this book, untraded interdependencies between sectors, technologies and firms are of primary importance in the process of technological change. Technological complementarities, untraded technological interdependencies and information flows which do not entirely correspond to the flows of commodities, common infrastructures, various sorts of dynamic economies of scale, all represent a structured set of technological externalities that are truly a collective asset of groups of firms/industries. In other words, technological bottlenecks and opportunities, experiences and skills embodied in people and organisations, capabilities overflowing from one economic activity to another, will tend to organise context conditions which:

(a) are country-specific, region-specific or even company-specific;
(b) are a fundamental ingredient in the innovation process; and
(c) determine different incentives/stimuli/constraints to the innovation process for any given set of strictly economic signals (i.e. relative prices, income distribution, etc.).

These untraded interdependencies and context conditions are the outcome of decentralised (but irreversible) processes of environmental organisation (one obvious example is the 'Silicon Valley') and/or the result of explicit strategies of public and private institutions (it is in this sense that one can interpret, for example, the strategies of vertical and horizontal integration of electrical oligopolies into microelectronics technologies or the efforts of various governments to create 'science parks', etc.).

In general, technology-related externalities and dynamic increasing returns (Arthur, 1985, 1988; David, 1985), are at the core of every complex economic system: jointly with other externalities linked with indivisibilities or with the asymmetric distribution of information and capabilities (see Stiglitz, 1982, 1984; Nalebuff and Stiglitz, 1983). People learn through their successes and mistakes, and make choices on the grounds of incomplete knowledge about the future, the actions of others, and the outcome of their own actions.[5] In many ways the pattern of Schumpeterian competition, discussed in Chapter 4 and analysed in detail by Nelson and Winter (1982), can be interpreted as a process of (Darwinian) selection and (Lamarkian) construction of specific institutions (firms, markets, rules, etc.) which also organise innovative efforts and establish mechanisms of incentives/penalties/rewards for the activities of technological search. One can now see the endogenous features of these institutions: market structures, forms of corporate organisation, particular routines and forms of expertise – of which particular firms are carriers – are linked with innovation and competition through positive feedbacks (see Nelson and Winter, 1982; Momigliano, 1985; Dosi, 1984; and Chapter 4 above). Successes and failures change both market structures and the forms of interaction between the agents.

Take the case of the computer industry by way of illustration. The increasing size and large market share of IBM over the past thirty years can be explained by its cumulative success. In turn, at any given time, firm's size, capabilities, etc., contribute to explaining the innovative performance of the industry as a whole. Without IBM, the innovative record, the particular kind of 'market discipline' and the technological and market expectations would have been different. Conversely, in a market with a firm such as IBM, the 'selection criteria' of the environment are to some extent the decisions of IBM itself.[6]

However, there are aspects of these institutional set-ups that are not directly endogenous to the competitive process of any one industry. Obvious examples are the effects of the regulatory framework (antitrust, pollution, etc.) upon market structure and industrial change (for a discussion of the US case, see Nelson and Winter, 1982; and Nelson, 1984). Moreover, there are important consequences of the relationships between the main social actors. Schumpeter had this same phenomenon in mind when he emphasised interactions within the triad comprising the inventor, the banker and the entrepreneur. One should, in addition, consider two other major actors, namely the government and the workforce.

To sum up, institutions are a necessary part of the organisation of economic processes in general, and innovative activities in particular. These institutions are partly the result of endogenous processes of learning and market selection, and partly the outcome of broader factors related to the general socio-economic tuning of the economic system, specific to countries and historical periods. The nature of the institutions affects economic performance, and in particular the innovative record of industries and countries.

Institutions supporting technological progress

Within the great variety of institutional set-ups, can one identify some regularities across industries and across countries? In order to provide some tentative answers, let us distinguish between 'normal' technical progress along trajectories defined by an established paradigm, and 'extraordinary' technological advances related to the emergence of radically new paradigms (more can be found on both in Nelson, 1988).

As regards the latter, one of us has tried to show elsewhere (Dosi, 1984; Dosi and Orsenigo, 1988) that market processes are generally rather weak in directing the emergence and selection of radical technological discontinuities. When the process of innovation is highly exploratory, its direct responsiveness to economic signals is rather weak and – especially in this century – the linkages with strictly scientific knowledge are quite strong. Non-market organisations play an important role, providing the necessary conditions for new scientific developments and performing as ex-ante selectors of the explored technological paradigm within a much wider set of potential ones. One can cite, for example, the case of the semiconductor and computer technologies and the influence of both military agencies and big electrical corporations in the early days of the development of these radically new technologies.[7] Somewhat similar cases can be found in the early developments of synthetic chemistry. Non-economic stimuli, conditions and 'selectors' are also prevalent in the development of bioengineering and new material technologies. In the processes of search and selection of new technological paradigms, the institutional and scientific context and existing public policy are fundamental, since they affect (a) the bridging mechanisms between pure science and technological developments;[8] (b) the criteria and capabilities of search by the economic agents; and (c) the constraints, incentives and uncertainty facing would-be innovators.

Thus, when new technologies emerge, the relative success of various countries will depend on the successful coordination between the scientific infrastructure and technological capabilities; the nature of its 'bridging institutions'; strictly economic conditions (relative prices, nature and size of the markets, availability/scarcity of raw materials, etc.); and the nature of the dominant rules of behaviour, strategies and forms of organisation of the economic actors. All these variables are, to different degrees, affected by public policies, either directly (e.g. procurement policies or R&D subsidies which obviously influence the economic signals facing individual firms), or indirectly (e.g. through the influence of the educational system upon scientific and technological capabilities, the effect of taxation policies on the emergence of new firms, etc.).

As regards 'normal' technical progress, one is immediately struck by the great variety in the organisational patterns of innovative activities and in the degree of direct public involvement. First, there is a technology and country-specificity of the balance between what is coordinated and organised through the visible hand of corporate structures and what is left to the invisible hand of the markets. Interestingly, many of the observed patterns bear some close correspondence with the intersectoral taxonomy discussed in Chapter 4.

In science-based industries, Schumpeterian competition tends to result in large oligopolies which also internalise considerable innovative capabilities (e.g. computers, semiconductors, synthetic chemicals, etc.). Similarly, in production-intensive industries, the 'visible hand' of large corporations puts the organisation of technological advances at the core of their strategic behaviour (e.g. automobiles, most other consumer durables, etc.). In the case of specialised suppliers, technological advances are generally organised through the matching between their own specific technological skills and intensive (often arms-length and untraded) relationships with users or component producers. Finally, only in supplier-dominated sectors do the mechanisms of organisation and coordination of technological progress appear to retain some signifi-

cant similarities with the classical view of the 'invisible hand': technological advances are generally available on the market in the form of
new capital goods; there are many firms with generally weak strategic
interactions, etc.

Second, there are significant intersectoral differences in the balance
between public institutions and private organisations in the process
of innovation (cf. Nelson, 1984). Some sectors rely mainly on an
endogenous process of technological advance, while others depend
heavily on public sources. One could even suggest the following
empirical generalisation: the stronger the role of the visible hand of oligopolistic organisations, the weaker the requirement for strictly public
institutions in economic coordination and technological advance. And
vice versa: the nearer an activity is to 'pure competition', the greater the
need for strictly institutional forms of organisation of its 'externalities'
and technological advances. Agriculture is a well-known case in point.
Historically, a significant part of its technological advance, at least in
the United States, has been provided by government-sponsored research
(cf. Nelson, 1984). Conversely, many oligopoly-dominated manufacturing sectors have produced, endogenously, a good part of their
technological advance, and have appeared to coordinate their price/
quantity adjustments rather well.

Some normative implications

The foregoing discussion suggests that, in contemporary mixed
economies, non-market agencies have been major actors in the emergence of new technological paradigms. At the same time, the conditions
of technological opportunity and appropriability have guaranteed sustained rates of 'normal' technical progress endogenously generated
through the visible hand of (mainly) manufacturing oligopolistic corporations. Every Western government has intervened, in forms and
degrees that depend on the sectors and countries, so as to strengthen the
incentives to innovate (both in terms of 'normal' innovations and paradigm changes). Confronted with this variety of organisations, degrees
and forms of public intervention, can one make any normative statement linking institutional forms, degrees of public involvement and
economic performance? Certainly a big change in emphasis from traditional welfare analysis is required.[9] In the changing and complex world
that we are analysing here, one can hardly reach definite conclusions on
'optimal' set-ups. At best, one can define some trade-offs involved in
each organisational configuration.

First, we know that in the innovative process undertaken by profit-motivated agents there is necessarily 'market failure', in a static sense. Varying degrees of appropriability are the necessary incentive to innovate, but imply at the same time 'excess profits' and 'sub-optimal' allocation of resources. Best-practice techniques and better products diffuse through the economy after a lapse of time, and the gap between the technological frontier and the inframarginal techniques also measures the static inefficiency of any pattern of allocation of resources. [10]

Elsewhere (Dosi, 1984, 1988; Dosi and Orsenigo, 1988), one of us has argued that these widespread asymmetries in technological capabilities and economic performance result in an equally uneven pattern of economic signals facing economic agents. The asymmetries in capabilities are a direct consequence of the cumulative, idiosyncratic and partly appropriable nature of technological advances. Thus, a situation of high technological opportunity, associated with a high degree of appropriability, will act as a powerful incentive to innovate, for a company at or near the technological frontier. At the same time, such a situation will be a powerful negative signal (an entry barrier) for a company with a lower technological capability.

On normative grounds, one would like to have 'small' asymmetries from a short-term allocative point of view, and a sustained incentive to innovate, from a dynamic point of view. This is a difficult balance and there is no reason to believe that market selection does the trick. As the explorations of these trade-offs by Nelson and Winter (1982) show, dynamic efficiency and the evolution of market structure are rather sensitive to the initial conditions, and to technology-related features. Even in the definition of performance, one encounters difficulties: for example, is the 'maximum' rate of innovation the most desirable one? How far is one ready to depart from static efficiency in order to achieve a faster rate of innovation?, etc.

A second normative puzzle concerns the multiplicity of organisational set-ups which correspond to quite similar performance outcomes (both in terms of static efficiency and innovative records). For example, comparing Europe, Japan and the United States, one sometimes observes significant differences (even within the same sector) in market structure, forms of state involvement, behavioural rules of the companies and yet, sometimes, somewhat similar performance. [11]

A third normative issue is the method through which each society builds its technological capabilities, and translates them into innovative, entrepreneurial behaviour. Again, one can observe rather wide international variance in both the 'supply of entrepreneurship', and the ways in which it is formed institutionally. The difference between the 'organised entrepreneurship' of Japanese firms, and the self-made-man archetype in the United States, is a typical example; or between the formalised 'production' of technological/managerial capabilities in France (the Ecole Polytechnique, etc.) and the anarchic Italian pattern. Noble (1977) provides a suggestive description of the growth of American technocracy, which highlights the enormous changes that contemporary economies have undergone since the times of the 'classical' protestant capitalist studied by Weber in *Protestant Ethic and the Spirit of Capitalism*. Yet, we need many more international studies on the mechanisms of formation of managers/technocrats/entrepreneurs in order to understand the supply of this crucial factor in innovative activities in the various countries.

A fourth normative issue concerns the possible trade-off between allocative efficiency and flexibility, or, more generally speaking, between fitting into a particular state-of-the-world and the capability to cope with other (and unpredictable) environments. One can detect here an analogy with biological evolution. Extreme optimisation within a given environment might well imply a 'dinosaur syndrome' and inflexibility to change. Conversely, high adaptability is likely to involve waste, 'slack' and suboptimal use of resources. In Pavitt (1984d) the possible trade-offs between efficiency and innovativeness are discussed in relation to the internal organisation of the firm. In Dosi (1988) and Soete and Dosi (1983) the (technology-specific) trade-offs between flexibility and economies of scale are analysed, suggesting that microelectronics-based production processes change the intensity of such a trade-off by increasing flexibility and lowering the minimum throughputs which allow for automated processes. However, the trade-off does not disappear. The very existence of technological paradigms and trajectories, with their local and cumulative forms of learning, imply irreversible processes with 'lock-in' companies and industries in particular forms of technological expertise (Arthur, 1985, 1988).

There is a requirement for variety in capabilities, behavioural rules, and allocative processes which will allow for greater adaptability to uncertainty and change. Eliasson (1984) has shown that disequilibrium – in a static allocative sense – is associated with a smoother absorption of external shocks. [12] To put it another way, one of the greatest strengths that capitalism has shown is its capability of continuously producing redundant resources, of exploring an 'excessive' number of technological trajectories, of producing a wasteful number of technological/ organisational 'genotypes'. Contrary to common beliefs, any advantage of contemporary mixed economies as compared to centrally planned ones, reflects the fact that the former do not achieve an equilibrium of the Arrow–Debreu kind, but are highly imperfect and always characterised by allocative inefficiencies and technological slacks.[13]

The policy questions are consequently – and not surprisingly – complex. How can sufficient 'variety' be continuously generated? To what extent can ex-ante strategies and institutional engineering channel technological evolution? These issues become even more entangled in open economies. It is to this 'openness' issue that we now turn.

8.2 Economic signals and technological dynamism in open economies

It is generally agreed that, under conditions of non-decreasing returns, absence of externalities and given rates of macroeconomic activity, the patterns of allocation stemming from international trade will generally be efficient. In other words, there are gains from trade for all partners based on comparative advantages. We will call this performance criterion allocative (or Ricardian) efficiency. However, we know from Chapters 4, 5 and 6 that the above conditions under which the link between comparative advantages and gains-from-trade holds, are unlikely to occur.

We observe intercountry differences in relative prices, relative productivities and relative gaps/leads in technology, which tend to lead to Ricardian adjustments (see Chapters 6 and 7), induced by the search for the maximum-profitabilities/minimum-cost employments for investments. However, this is not sufficient to allow us to conclude that all trading partners will gain in the short run and, even more so, in the long run.

A first question regards the effect that the pattern of allocation – induced by comparative advantages (and, thus, relative intersectoral profitabilities) on the basis of given technologies – will have on technological dynamism and long-term macroeconomic rates of activity. As before, we shall call the performance criterion related to innovative dynamism 'Schumpeterian efficiency' and that related to the maximum rate of growth consistent with the foreign-balance constraint 'growth' or 'Keynesian' efficiency.

There is nothing in the mechanism leading to Ricardian efficiency (as defined above) that also guarantees the fulfilment of the other criteria of efficiency. The easiest way to see the efficiency gains in a Ricardian (or, for that matter, neo-classical) world is to imagine that each nation, before trade, operates at full-employment rates of activity, and that there are no Keynesian adjustment processes (see Chapter 7) linking absolute advantages, market shares and macroeconomic rates of activity in the transition from autarky to trade.[14] (The latter hypothesis is clearly at the core of the neo-classical model which requires market clearing.) With all the other restrictive assumptions mentioned above, one can easily see the full operation of the theorem of comparative advantage: each trading partner gains from trade, since it gets more commodities of a certain kind from abroad than it would otherwise be able to manufacture domestically, without forgoing any production and consumption of the commodities in which it specialises. It can also be seen how gains from trade of this kind are of a 'once-and-for-all', static nature.

Let us now relax both assumptions and ask what the effect of any given pattern of specialisation might be on the technological capabilities of each country, and what the outcome would be, in the short and long run, in terms of macroeconomic rates of activities, whenever one allows for 'Keynesian' adjustments. It might be useful to recall some of our conclusions from Chapters 4 and 5, in particular the cumulative, (partly) appropriable and local nature of technological advances; the widespread existence of static and dynamic economies of scale; the influence that technological gaps between firms and between countries have upon the economic signals agents face; and the importance of country-specific and area-specific untraded interdependencies. These factors taken together allow for the possibility of significant trade-offs between statics and dynamics. As conjectured by Kaldor (1980), if different commodities or sectors present significant differences in their 'dynamic potential' (in terms of economies of scale, technical progress, possibilities of division of labour, learning-by-doing, etc.), specialisations which are efficient in terms of comparisons of given sets of input coefficients may in the long run become either virtuous or vicious circles of technological advance.

This is more than a special case related to infant industries. It is the general condition of an economic system that technological opportunities vary across products and across sectors. More precisely, within each technology and each sector the technological capabilities of each firm and each country are associated with the actual process of production and innovation in the area. Thus, the mechanisms regarding international specialisation have a dynamic effect, in that they also select the areas where technical skills will be accumulated (possibly), innovation undertaken, economies of scale reaped, etc. However, the potential for these effects differs widely between technologies and sectors. This is another aspect of the irreversibility of economic processes: present allocative choices influence the direction and rate of the future evolution of technological coefficients. Whenever we abandon the idea of technology as a set of blueprints and we conceive technical progress as a joint product with manufacturing, it is possible to imagine an economic system which is dynamically better off than otherwise (in terms of productivity, innovativeness, etc.), if it evolves in disequilibrium vis-à-vis Ricardian conditions of allocative efficiency.

It is rather easy to see how a trade-off between 'allocative efficiency' and 'Schumpeterian efficiency' can emerge. The patterns of specialisation (with their properties of Ricardian efficiency) are determined, for each country, by the relative size of the sector-specific technology gaps (or leads) (see Chapter 6). Whenever the gap is highest in the most dynamic technologies (i.e. those characterised by the highest technological opportunities), allocative efficiency will conflict directly with Schumpeterian efficiency. We would suggest that the likelihood of such trade-offs between Ricardian and Schumpeterian efficiencies is proportional to the distance of each country from the technological frontier in the newest, most dynamic and most pervasive technologies.[15]

A similar argument applies to the trade-offs between Ricardian and growth efficiency. As already mentioned, the analysis of the outcome of the transition from autarky to trade focusses only on the adjustments in relative prices and relative quantities, and is based on the assumption of unchanged rates of macroeconomic activity. However, as we saw in Chapter 6 the main adjustment mechanism links absolute advantages, world-market shares, and, through that, domestic levels of manufacturing output (Chapter 7).

Under these circumstances, the growth efficiency of specialisation based on comparative advantage would always hold, if we assumed identical income elasticities across countries and across commodities, and similar and high price elasticities. However, such differences in elasticities underlie many empirical studies on both domestic demand patterns and long-term trade flows.[16] As a first approximation, let us therefore suppose that price elasticities of world demand of the traded commodities for the corresponding world industry as a whole, are relatively low;[17] and commodities present a relatively wide range of income elasticities which are commodity specific and country specific. We may illustrate the case with the help of an example similar to the one presented in Chapter 6, p. 165.

Suppose that both England and Portugal in autarky conditions have less than full employment rates of macroeconomic activity. National expenditure in both countries is composed of wine and cloth. Moreover, the share in consumption of wine relative to cloth in real terms is stable. Suppose, that in both countries a greater share of expenditure goes to cloth and that the share of wine in the basket of consumption is particularly low for England, since English people notoriously are very sober and do not like to drink more than a glass a day, no matter what the price of wine. Under competitive conditions, we maintain the behavioural assumption that economic agents will tend to move towards those activities yielding the highest profit rates. England will specialise in cloth and Portugal in wine. The constancy-of-activity-rate assumption, however, is hard to maintain. Either country will undergo a relative real growth of aggregate income (as measured in terms of embodied labour, i.e. working hours) compared to the other.[18]

Two opposite approaches to this issue exist in economic theory. The neo-classical approach maintains that international specialisation induces simply an efficient reallocation of resources, while the rates of activity remain — in 'normal' conditions — at full employment levels. Thus, the Portuguese and English levels of income are the full employment ones and the burden of adjustment rests upon the movement of prices and consumption coefficients. Consumption coefficients are then fully endogenous variables, changes in which depend on the theory of utility, consumers' preferences and substitution in consumption. The classical Keynesian approach, on the other hand, suggests that the main adjustment mechanism operates through variations in income. In other words, the constancy-of-activity assumption has to be abandoned and variations in real incomes will adjust activity rates to the flows of imports and exports.

The agnosticism one often finds in the trade and balance-of-payments literature in the choice between the two approaches is — in our view — not really justified. The choice depends on alternative theories of consumption patterns. Following the argument in the preceding chapters about the limited price-related substitution in consumption and the way patterns of demand are essentially related to income levels, long-run trends in income distribution and institutional and social factors, it will be obvious to the reader that we favour the Keynesian approach. In a sense, the classical economists' view of fixed baskets of consumption was a rough, yet workable approximation of the general existence of Engel's curves of consumption for individual commodities.[19] Unfortunately, the same classical economists often forgot the full implications of this view when analysing open-economy situations.

If the constancy-of-activity-rates assumption cannot be maintained, then patterns of specialisation which may be efficient when the assumption holds, may not be so in terms of activity rates of one or some of the trading patterns. We can easily derive from this statement its dynamic counterpart: specialisation which is efficient if the economic systems were to move on a steady growth path, may well not be so in terms of possibilities of growth consistent with the foreign account: for instance, when the income elasticities of world demand are different and the price elasticities too low to compensate for possible imbalances in product markets. We would argue that this is the general empirical case.

Limited price induced substitution between commodities and relatively stable evolution in the baskets of consumption may well imply painful trade-offs between microeconomic mechanisms leading to Ricardian efficiency,[20] and those patterns of production which could yield comparatively higher rates of macroeconomic activity compatible with the foreign-balance constraint.

Under conditions of non-decreasing (often increasing) returns, there is no straightforward way in which markets can relate the varying growth and Schumpeterian efficiencies of the various commodities to relative profitability signals for the microeconomic agents. In other words, microeconomic units may well find it relatively profitable to produce commodities that a decreasing number of people in the world want to buy. Putting the same argument in a language more familiar to the economist, the widespread possibility of trade-offs between Ricardian, Schumpeterian and growth efficiencies arises from the fact that the general case is one of non-convexity of production and consumption possibility sets and non-ergodicity of technological advances.[21]

Table 8.1 illustrates from a microeconomic point of view the different criteria of efficiency which relate to the different economic signals economic agents face.[22] Suppose that there are three commodities, A, B and C. On the grounds of a straightforward static allocative efficiency, microeconomic units seeking the highest rate of profit will choose commodity C. However, from the point of view of the country to which the firm belongs, commodities B or A should be chosen, since they yield the highest dynamism in terms of demand and in terms of technical change, respectively.

The choice of any one of these three commodities corresponds, from a microeconomic point of view, to three different strategies and adjustment processes. The choice of C implies a 'classical adjustment' whereby

Table 8.1 An illustration of the trade-offs between 'Ricardian' efficiency, growth efficiency and Schumpeterian efficiency of specialisation

	$A(\%)$	$B(\%)$	$C(\%)$
1. Short-term obtainable rate of profit	2	5	10
2. Rate of profit of world leaders	20	10	10
3. Rate of growth of world demand	15	20	1
4. Levels of technological opportunity (approximated by the long-term rate of productivity growth)	10	5	3

the strategic criterion is simply the rate of profit on the grounds of techniques readily available to the firm. The choice of *B* implies a growth strategy whereby the strategic criterion of choice is based on the rate of growth of the world market. Finally, the choice of commodity *A* stands for Schumpeterian adjustment, whereby a path of technological imitation/innovation is undertaken in order to reap the differential profits associated with technological leadership in that commodity.[23] Clearly, the more pronounced the trade-offs, the more strategies will be structurally constrained: for example, profit-motivated agents will hardly invest in a growth efficient and Schumpeter efficient commodity, whenever the expected rate of profit within a reasonable future is negative.

Conversely, Table 8.2 illustrates 'virtuous circle' conditions, whereby the 'Schumpeterian' incentive to innovation/imitation is linked in a straightforward manner to profitability signals and growth opportunities. Under these circumstances, no trade-offs between static and dynamic efficiencies emerge: the competitive process delivers signals which are also efficient in terms of innovation and growth. The search for maximum profitability also fosters technological dynamism. These trade-offs between allocative efficiency, growth and technological dynamism may well become one of the crucial determinants of the emergence of vicious and virtuous circles in national patterns of growth. This conclusion is similar to many of the analyses in development theory. However, its determinants do not bear any direct relationship with phenomena specific to developing countries (such as the supposed 'market failures' aspects). For our purposes, developed and developing countries could be placed on some kind of continuum, according to their distance from the technological frontier, and the long-term outcome of the allocative patterns generated endogenously in the market.

Technological leaders will tend to find the pattern of their intersectoral profitability signals pointing in the direction of activities which also lead to the highest demand growth, and the highest potential for future product and process innovations. Conversely, countries well behind the

Table 8.2 An illustration of 'virtuous circle' conditions

	A (%)	B (%)	C (%)
1. Short-term obtainable rate of profit	20	10	5
2. Rate of profit of leaders	20	10	10
3. Rate of growth of world demand	15	10	1
4. Long-term rate of productivity growth	10	5	3

technological frontier may be 'dynamically penalised' by their present pattern of intersectoral allocative efficiency. This property contributes, in our view, to the relative stability of the 'pecking order' between countries in terms of technological innovativeness and international competitiveness, and the relatively ordered ways in which this 'pecking order' changes in the long term (see also Chapter 4). The interaction between present economic signals, patterns of specialisation and dynamics of the sectoral technology gaps provides the basis for cumulative processes.

Major changes in the international distribution of innovative activities and in the international competitiveness of each economy, can, however, be associated with the emergence of new technological paradigms. This occurrence reshapes the pattern of technological advantages/disadvantages between countries, often demands different organisational and institutional set-ups and sometimes presents a unique 'window of opportunity' in Perez's words (Perez and Soete, 1988) for the emergence of new technological and economic leaders.

The foregoing arguments can be summarised as follows. Markets characterised by decentralised decision-making fulfil two fundamental functions. First, they provide a mechanism for coordination between individual economic decisions and, in doing so, they reallocate resources in ways, which – under the conditions specified by the theory – present properties of (varying degrees of) efficiency. Second, whenever we allow technological progress to take place (with its features of search, uncertainty, etc.), markets provide an incentive to innovate through the possibility of private appropriation of some economic benefit stemming from technical progress itself.

As soon as these second functions of markets are taken into account in the theoretical picture, their efficiency properties become blurred and complicated to assess, even in a closed economy: allocative efficiency in a static sense may conflict with dynamic efficiency in terms of incentives to technological progress. Overlapping with, and adding to, the 'Schumpeterian trade-off' of the closed-economy case, there is the possibility of a static versus dynamic trade-off originating from the pattern of economic signals in the international market. In a way, the open-economy case induces a structural distortion in the pattern of signals that would have been generated under autarky. In doing so, they may either overrule the domestic 'Schumpeterian trade-offs' or amplify them. The hypothesis we suggested above is that this depends on the relative distance of each country vis-à-vis the technological frontier in those technologies showing the highest opportunities of innovation and demand growth.

8.3 Technological and economic dynamism: the role of policies

The framework of this book shows that institutions are crucial variables that vary according to sector, country and historical phases of development. These are both 'micro' institutions, e.g. complex corporate structures embodying specific capabilities, rules of behaviours and rationalities; modes of institutional organisation of market interactions, etc., and 'macro' institutions, such as strictly public agencies. Institutional factors appear to shape the constitution, behavioural rules, patterns of adjustment and context conditions under which economic mechanisms operate. There is no really meaningful way of either separating the strictly economic variables from their institutional framework, or assuming that strictly economic variables overdetermine their institutional contexts to such an extent that the latter tend to converge to a unique pattern. It is therefore impossible to reduce all extra-economic elements to 'interferences' or 'exceptional corrections' to a supposedly optimally performing, self-contained and well-tuned economic machine.[24]

As illustrated above, complex normative issues emerge in relation to the trade-offs between different criteria of efficiency or the degree of consistency between institutional set-ups, the nature of the technologies and economic processes.

Let us start with a first classification of the variables upon which institutions and policies may act, with particular reference to technological progress. They can be categorised as follows:

(a) the capability of the scientific/technological system of providing major innovative advances and of organising the technological 'context' conditions;

(b) the capabilities of the economic agents in terms of the technology they embody, the effectiveness and speed with which they search for new technological and organisational advances;

(c) the pattern of signals which depend on interfirm and international technological asymmetries, and, in turn, shape the boundaries of the set of possible microeconomic responses that are economically feasible for agents which – irrespective of their precise strategies – have profitability among their behavioural considerations;

(d) the forms of organisation within and between markets: e.g. the relationship between financial structures and industry, the form of industrial relations, the varying balance between cooperation and competition, the degree and forms of corporate internalisation of transactions, etc.;

(e) the main behavioural regularities characterising agents, within the degrees of freedom allowed for by the pattern of technological asymmetries and economic signals: e.g. the strategies affecting the mix between Ricardian and Schumpeterian adjustments; and

(f) the incentives/stimuli/constraints facing agents in their adjustment and innovative processes: e.g. the degree of private appropriability of the benefits of innovations, the intensity of competitive threats, etc.

Ideally, one would like to develop some 'policy taxonomy' grouping these various categories according to the degrees of technological and economic development of the various countries, as well as according to the stage of development of the various technological paradigms, and to ask whether we can make some useful generalisation.

There are two issues here: a positive one and a normative one. On descriptive grounds there is little doubt that all market economies have (and have had for a long time) various mixtures of policies affecting all the above groups of variables. The analytical task is to make sense of the intertemporal, cross-sectoral and cross-country differences. Conversely, on more normative grounds, one should be able to justify the requirement for policies in relation to some performance yardstick.

The discussion of the patterns of technical change provides two broad grounds for a normative approach. First, the innovative process necessarily embodies a complex and differentiated mixture of private appropriation and public good aspects (see Nelson (1981) and (1984)), and involves an unavoidable 'market failure'. The normative counterpart of this intrinsic feature of the innovative process does not, however, regard the question as *if* but *how* and *to what degree* policies should affect innovative activities.

Second, the existence of possible trade-offs between 'static' efficiency, on the one hand, and growth and Schumpeterian efficiencies, on the other (sometimes amplified by the way technological gaps feed back into market signals in the international market) highlights a wide realm for institutional intervention.

Clearly, in a transforming world, the performance criteria and the link between policies and performance are fuzzy and uncertain. Take, again, the example of the cluster of new microelectronics technologies. Despite rapid growth of world demand, innovation and productivity growth in these sectors, pointing to the dominance of 'growth' and 'Schumpeterian efficiency', one is confronted with complex normative issues. For example, how far should one country depart from static efficiency, whenever the latter conflicts with the dynamic criteria of performance, in order to pursue these new technologies? When is private appropriability too low, so that it hinders private innovative incentives? To what extent, and in what manner, can public efforts efficiently substitute for decentralised innovative processes? Even if varying degrees of intervention are required, what are the most conducive institutional arrangements? Relatively little research has been done in these areas. Yet, even after detailed historical and cross-country investigations, one might have to come up with, at best, sets of possible combinations between policies, institutional arrangements and performances, without any claim to having identified the 'optimal' configuration.

In the light of our discussions in Section 8.2 above, the structural need for policies affecting the pattern of economic signals (including relative prices and relative profitabilities), emerging from the international market, will be greater, the greater the distance of any one country from the technological frontier. Conversely, endogenous market mechanisms will tend to behave in a 'virtuous' manner for those countries that happen to be on the frontier, especially in the newest/most promising technologies. This is broadly confirmed by historical experience: unconditional free trade often happens to be advocated and fully exploited only by the leading countries.

Furthermore, as regards the time profile of technological developments, a distinction can be made between policies related to the emergence of new technological paradigms, and policies to sustain technological activities along relatively established paths. In the former case, policies should provide a satisfactory flow of scientific advances, establish 'bridging institutions' between scientific developments and their economic exploitation, develop conducive financial structures to support the trial-and-error procedures generally involved in the search for new technological break-throughs, and act as 'focussing devices' in the selection processes of the direction of technological development.[25]

As regards 'normal' technical progress, important policy tasks are the maintenance of a relatively fluid supply of techno-scientific advances, coupled with 'balanced' conditions of private appropriability of the benefits of innovating (e.g. through patent policies, etc.). Countries well below the technological frontier may also find it necessary to act directly on both the technological capabilities of domestic companies, and on the appropriability features of the related technologies, in so far as they function as an entry barrier for catching-up companies and countries.

Public policies affect also the fundamental 'rationalities' of the agents (including the ways their expectations and objectives are formed). As an illustration, consider the role of military spending. In addition to its effects upon the composition of demand and the pattern of economic signals, military spending is also likely to shape firms' strategies and managerial outlooks. Almost certainly, public agencies tend to be perceived as a 'guarantee of last resort',[26] while the skills of detecting and influencing procurement authorities are likely to become more important than the capabilities of understanding and anticipating market trends in competitive environments. Clearly, this is only one – possibly the most straightforward – example of a set of influences that the political structure exerts upon the behavioural constitution of market processes.

In reality, in all major Western countries a relatively high degree of intervention takes place. Whereas in terms of financial transfer to the industrial sector, significant differences can be detected between the European countries, the United States and Japan,[27] all countries affect, through their policies, the economic signals, the capabilities of agents, the environmental incentives and the context conditions. What appear to differ significantly across countries are the institutional arrangements and underlying philosophy of intervention.

Regarding the latter, one can identify two extreme archetypes. The first is characterised by a 'liberal' view of public policies, more or less loosely underpinned by neo-classical economics. Typically, intervention is justified on three grounds here, namely a regulatory level (anti-trust laws, etc.); the correction of assumed 'distortions' of market mechanisms (e.g. 'unfair' competition from abroad, etc.); and the existence of 'market failures' (e.g. R&D support, etc.).

In addition, public procurement, including military expenditure, is not meant as an instrument of industrial policy and therefore need not be justified on economic grounds. This view appears to characterise, to different degrees, the United States and a limited number of European countries (above all, the United Kingdom). At the opposite extreme, there is an 'instrumentalist' view of market processes, to which one does not attach any optimality feature: markets are simply viewed in relation to their (varying) effectiveness in pursuing exogenously defined objectives (e.g. the technological modernisation of a country, income growth, national power, etc.). As a consequence, policy instruments are also chosen without much respect for the short-term prescriptions of economic theory. This view appears to characterise Japan, possibly France, and certainly pre-War Germany.

Against this background it is interesting to observe the choice of policies for technological innovation by the major Western countries in the most recent period. At one extreme, consider the example of Japan, especially in relation to the cluster of electronics technologies. Japan appears to have acted comprehensively on all the levels discussed above. In particular, it appears to have succeeded in a difficult 'fine tuning' between 'signal policies' which, as such, risk *shelving* and protecting positions that are inefficient from an allocative point of view, and competition policies which stifle the adjustment processes. In this respect, the Japanese case is almost an archetype: heavy discretionary manipulation of the signal structure (by means of formal and informal protection against imports and foreign investments; an investment policy of financial institutions consistent with growth and dynamic efficiency) recreated the '*vacuum environment*' that is generally enjoyed only by the technological leader(s). However, this has been matched by a pattern of fierce oligopolistic rivalry between Japanese companies, and heavy export orientation, which fostered technological dynamism and prevented any exploitation of protection in terms of collusive monopolistic pricing.

It is tempting to compare this Japanese experience with other, less successful ones, such as those of many European countries, which relied heavily upon one single instrument, i.e. financial transfers (especially R&D subsidies and transfers on capital accounts), leaving to the endogenous working of the international market both the determination of the signals and the response capabilities of individual firms. Certainly there are country-specific features of the Japanese example which are hardly transferable. But the Japanese case, in its striking outcome, points to the general possibility of reshaping patterns of 'comparative advantage' as they would notionally emerge from the endogenous evolution of international markets. At the end of the Second World War, no economist would ever have suggested that electronics would be one of Japan's comparative advantages. Now it certainly is.

The use of comparative advantage criteria as the final grounds for normative prescriptions is a luxury that only countries on the technological frontier can afford: *rebus sic stantibus*, it will not be long before Japanese economists preach Ricardo, Heckscher–Ohlin and general equilibrium analysis, while it might also not be too long before Americans rediscover Hamilton, List and Ferrier. The more general point will be clear. Historically, a successful catching-up effort in terms of per capita income and wages has always been contextual to technological catching-up in the new and most dynamic technologies, irrespective of the initial patterns of comparative advantages, specialisation and market-generated signals.[28]

8.4 Some conclusions

In a world characterised by technical change, technological leads shape the pattern of intersectoral and interproduct profitability signals and, thus, also the pattern of microeconomic allocation. The latter, however, may affect the long-term macroeconomic dynamism of each country, in terms of both rates of growth of income, consistent with the foreign balance constraint, and technological innovativeness.

In the last resort, this happens because the effects of a multiplicity of signals (related to profitability, long-term demand growth and technological opportunities, on microeconomic processes of adjustments) are likely to be asymmetric, entail dynamic increasing returns, and various sorts of what economists call 'path-dependencies', 'non-convexities', and 'externalities'. Whenever trade-offs between different notions of efficiency arise, 'sub-optimal' or 'perverse' macroeconomic outcomes may emerge, if profit-oriented agents privilege processes of allocation biased in the direction of what we call 'static' or Ricardian efficiency. Since the future pattern of technological advantages/disadvantages is also related to present allocative patterns, one is confronted here with a set of dynamic processes which Kaldor called 'circular causation'. Economic signals related to intersectoral profitabilities – which lead in a straightforward manner to comparative advantage and relative specialisation – check the allocative efficiency of the various productive uses, but may also play a more ambiguous or even perverse role in relation to long-term macroeconomic growth.

The 'vicious' or 'virtuous' circular processes discussed above concern the very nature of allocative mechanisms, in so far as each economy is characterised by technical change showing varying degrees of sector-specific opportunity, cumulativeness, appropriability, dynamic technological externalities, and local and idiosyncratic learning.

Furthermore, it was argued that institutional factors – including, of course, policies – are part of the constitution of economic processes: i.e. the ways in which economic activities are organised and coordinated, technical change is generated and used, the dominant behavioural regularities emerge, etc. This clearly is another domain for policies.

A detailed understanding of the pattern of signals, of allocative responses and forms of institutional organisation of the 'economic machine', appears to be particularly important in those phases of transition from an old technological regime to a new one. These historical periods define a new set of opportunities and threats for each country: the patterns of international generation and diffusion of technologies become more fluid and with it international trade flows and relative levels of per capita income. In the process, comparative advantages become the self-fulfilling prophecy of a successful set of institutional actions and private strategies: ex-post, technological and economic success makes 'optimal' from the point of view of the economist what are ex-ante political dreams and/or the partly unintentional outcome of processes of evolution and selection within both the domains of economics and institutions.[29]

Notes

1. In Nelson and Winter's words: 'if the economic world is in continuing flux, as our positive theory suggests is the case, the normative properties associated with competitive equilibrium become meaningless, just as that equilibrium is meaningless a description of behaviour' (see Nelson and Winter, 1982, p. 356). Interestingly, Stiglitz, who has made major contributions to the analysis of the properties of equilibrium models characterised, in one way or another, by imperfect information, concludes that 'the notions of decentralisation associated with neo-classical theory are more akin to a description of a computer algorithm – a description of how one might efficiently go about a complicated maximisation problem that one needs to solve once and for all – than of an institutional structure which is required to adapt and respond to a series of new and changing problems' (Stiglitz, 1984, p. 35).
2. These issues have been discussed at greater length in Dosi and Orsenigo (1988).
3. Nelson and Winter (1982), p. 356.
4. Stiglitz (1984), p. 36.
5. For a broad and fascinating view of these issues by a non-economist, see Luhmann (1975).
6. For an interesting model of the pharmaceutical industry, see Grabowski and J. Vernon (1984).
7. Cf. Katz and Philips (1982), Dosi (1984).
8. Cf. Freeman (1974).
9. See also Nelson and Winter (1982), Mowery (1983), and Nelson and Soete (1988).
10. In this sense, one can interpret the measures of best-practice and average technical progress developed in Soete and Turner (1984).
11. As an illustration, take the example of two rather successful machine tool industries: the Japanese and Italian. The former is characterised by relatively large firms, often vertically integrated, and by a relatively close coordination between the government, the banks and the companies. Conversely, the Italian industry, with three or four major exceptions, is made up of small firms, linked to users and suppliers only by arms-length relationships. Alternatively, consider the semi-conductor industry in Japan and the United States: again, in the former the old electro-mechanical oligopolists have succeeded in becoming major microelectronics producers, while in the United States the industry is essentially made up of Schumpeterian new firms which have grown big through their success (see Dosi, 1984). As argued in Dosi and Orsenigo (1988), one would actually need something like a 'theory of possible worlds', that is, a theory of all feasible combinations between organisational structures, nature of technological paradigms and forms of socio-economic tuning, which yield acceptable allocative patterns and innovative dynamism.
12. Silverberg, Dosi, and Orsenigo (1988) discuss the importance of diverse

(and, possibly, *ex post*, unsuccessful) expectations and strategies for technological diffusion.

13. Interestingly, at the microeconomic level. Gardiner (1984) finds that along any technological trajectory, the designs that are 'robust' and successful in the long term, start by being full of slack and 'non-optimised'.

14. Similar assumptions were implicit in the original treatment of international trade by Ricardo:

> No extension of foreign trade will immediately increase the amount of value in a country, although it will very powerfully contribute to increasing the mass of commodities, and therefore the sum of enjoyments. As the value of all foreign goods is measured by the quantity of the produce of our land and labour, which is given in exchange for them, we should have no greater value, if, by the discovery of new markets, we obtained double the quantity of foreign goods in exchange for a given quantity of ours'. (Ricardo (1951), p. 128)

Since production techniques are given, the 'amount of value in a country' is precisely equivalent to its rates of macroeconomic activity as measured by the degree of utilisation of its labour force.

15. A similar argument applies to the implications of allocatively efficient specialisations for long-term technological learning. If learning tends to be 'local', i.e. associated with actual production and research experiences, cumulative and tacit (cf. Chapter 4), static allocative efficiency may well be a poor guide for the long-term innovative opportunities which various productive activities entail. We argued in Chapter 4 that sectors also differ in terms of opportunities for technological advances. This phenomenon, together with the likely feedbacks between incentives to allocate productive and research efforts in 'comparative-advantage' activities, imply the possibility of 'lock-in' effects along particular trajectories of production and innovation. Analytically, such an environment is described by increasing returns, non-ergodic models (see Arthur, 1985, 1988; David, 1985, 1987) and also 'local learning' models (cf. Atkinson and Stiglitz, 1969; Stiglitz, 1987). Normatively, a general implication is that decentralised processes of market allocation may either involve 'vicious' or 'virtuous' circles – whenever judged on the grounds of long-term innovative performances. Technically, this is equivalent to saying that decentralised processes of allocation *cum* increasing returns, *cum* path-dependency generally imply multiplicity of equilibria that are locally stable, but may well be normatively 'sub-optimal'.

16. Cf. the thorough discussions by Thirlwall (1980) and Lafay (1981). See also Cornwall (1977). Within the literature on development, cf. the classical work by Prebisch (1950).

17. This statement must not be confused with price elasticities for individual countries which might well be higher. In other words, relatively small price changes may induce significant changes in the international competitiveness of individual countries, even when the overall world demand for the corresponding commodity shows a very low price elasticity.

18. In the notional transition from autarky to trade, unchanged levels of macroeconomic activity (and employment) will be maintained only if a number of conditions are fulfilled. First, the 'production functions' of cloth and wine, as conventionally defined, have to exist. Second, these must differ in terms of input intensities, at least for some relative prices. Third,

there is sufficient substitution in consumption in reaction to relative prices. And fourth, input markets display a well-above-zero price elasticity for excess demand. For the sake of an *a fortiori* argumentation of our point, one may as well accept the last assumption. However, our foregoing discussion (especially Chapter 4) implies that the first assumption is not generally corroborated by the evidence. Hence, the conclusion rests entirely on the third assumption – substitution in consumption.

19. A thorough discussion can be found in Pasinetti (1981). Cf. also Dosi (1984). For empirical evidence Deaton and Muellbauer (1980), who are not particularly suspected of any anti-neo-classical bias. More specifically in relation to trade, cf. Houthakker and Magee (1969), and on price elasticities, Stern, Francis and Schumacher (1976).

20. Blejer (1978) shows empirically that the structure of imports and exports by country presents a relatively regular evolution in relation to income per capita whenever the sectors are ranked according to the income elasticity of their products. He also shows that such a regularity cannot be found if the sectors are ranked according to their factor-intensity.

21. On this last point, see Arthur (1985) and (1988).

22. In the example that follows we abandon the hypothesis, rigorously implicit in a Ricardian world, of free competition, and we allow for oligopolistic differences in profit rates. It should be clear that this adds realism to the example, without in any sense being the cause of the trade-offs between the different efficiency criteria.

23. Note, however, that in the real world the last two are likely to be strictly associated: world demand of innovative commodities is likely to grow relatively faster.

24. One of us critically analysed these reductionist approaches with reference to the history of economic thought in Dosi (1988).

25. Cf. Rosenberg (1976).

26. We owe this observation to a discussion with H. Minsky. See also M. Kaldor (1980).

27. For some evidence, cf. Ranci (1983) and Horn (1982).

28. See also Soete, 1985.

29. See, for a somewhat similar point, Perez (1984) and Boyer (1988).

9
Conclusions

Despite the intuitive relevance of technical change for international competitiveness and economic growth, few studies have systematically addressed these issues both from an empirical and theoretical perspective. This book has attempted such an undertaking. We began by setting out some of the – in our view – most characteristic features of technological innovation in modern market economies. We then analysed the impact of these features on the composition of and changes in international trade flows, and tried to establish formally the relationship between innovativeness, trade performance and patterns of economic growth.

Our investigation started with a critical overview, a personal assessment, of the state-of-the-art in the economic analysis of technology and trade (Chapter 2). We discussed whether the neo-classical theory of trade – in its 'canonic' form or in some modified version – could adequately account for technical change over time and differences in technological capabilities between countries. Our conclusion, with the exception of some of the contributions falling under the heading of 'new' trade theory (Markusen, 1985, 1989), was essentially negative. The 'canonic' version of the theory explains trade flows exclusively on the grounds of differences in 'endowments' between countries and identity in their technological capabilities. We reviewed several attempts to relax such an hypothesis and introduce international differences in technology and/or technical change over time. These attempts – we concluded – were generally not satisfactory for three main reasons.

First, whenever some more 'realistic' assumption on technology was introduced into the model, the theory generally showed a striking lack of robustness; most predictions stemming from the 'canonic' model no longer appeared to hold, not even in approximate form. It goes without saying that this is a serious theoretical weakness.

Second, the most relevant properties of technical change could only be introduced into the theory in a piecemeal fashion, one at a time, and with a significant amount of 'adhocry'. It is yet to be demonstrated that any version of a neo-classical trade model can incorporate simultaneously all the main features of innovation.

Third, irrespective of the particular version of the model adopted, the crucial adjustment mechanisms that the theory postulated were based on changes in relative prices and relative quantities linked to relative scarcities. Practically by definition, such assumptions must be questioned, when explicit account is taken of technical change which continuously tends to overcome scarcities and increase input efficiency.

The evidence on the relationship between technological innovation and trade, we concluded, thus demands a different theoretical representation whereby international technological differences, disequilibrium processes, forms of increasing returns, all appear as basic underlying assumptions.

We acknowledged the major contribution of 'new' trade theory in this area, but rather than pursuing on a similar trajectory, set out from the economics of technological change. In Chapter 3, we first tried to identify the main 'stylised facts' which a theory of technology and trade should explain. On the grounds of previous empirical work, we identified some significant regularities in the international and intersectoral distribution of innovative activities.

First, the international distribution of innovative efforts and innovative results appeared far from homogeneous, even within the group of relatively rich OECD countries. The 'club of innovators' comprises not much more than a dozen countries and has remained relatively stable for almost a century – with only one major entry (Japan). It nevertheless showed some interesting patterns of evolution in the internal ranking of countries (e.g. Germany and the United States overtaking England at the turn of the century as the major sources of innovations and very rapid catching-up by Japan in the post-War period).

Second, these differences in innovative capabilities appeared to correspond to equally wide differences in labour productivities. As much as we could infer from very imperfect statistical evidence, these differences did not seem to correlate with analogous differences in capital/output ratios. In other words, differences in 'production function' rather than differences in 'endowments' appeared to be the fundamental feature of the international production system.

Third, the cross-sectoral analysis pointed to a high sectoral specificity in the opportunities and propensities to innovate and patterns of intersectoral distribution of one country's innovative strength which defied traditional explanations (e.g. why was Switzerland strong in pharmaceuticals and Sweden in mechanical engineering?).

Fourth, with regard to trade flows, long-term changes in the pattern of national 'revealed comparative advantage' were often interlinked with country-wide changes in world market shares which occurred in all sectors (e.g. the British general decline or the Japanese overall rise).

Against this background of apparent facts and trends, we then constructed an alternative model of technology and trade, set out in Chapters 6 and 7.

In Chapters 4 and 5, we analysed first, however, some features of the nature, origins and implications of the international and intersectoral differences in innovativeness identified in the preceding chapter.

Technology, we argued, cannot be reduced to freely available information or to a set of 'blueprints'. Following some of the analyses of the process of technical change by Rosenberg, Nelson, Winter, Sahal and many others, we proposed a view of technology embodying specific, local, often tacit, and only partly appropriable knowledge. Each set of technical principles, search procedures, forms of expertise – which we called 'technological paradigms' – would lead from this perspective to relatively ordered cumulative and irreversible patterns of technical change: so-called 'technological trajectories'.

Paradigms and trajectories appeared to differ in different sectors, according to the knowledge base on which they would draw, the strength of their linkages with pure science, the nature of the innovative search processes, the degrees of embodiment of technical advances in capital equipment and the forms of private appropriation of the economic benefits from innovation. On the basis of some of these indicators, we were able to develop a sectoral taxonomy of the patterns of production and use of innovations. We observed some remarkable differences in the contribution of each sector to the innovative output of the economic system, and identified a small set of patterns through which innovation would be 'produced' or adopted within the same sector or other sectors, and some typical market structure forms associated with particular patterns of innovation.

An important implication of our analysis of technical change is the support for a *theory of production* whereby different ('better' and 'worse') techniques, products and firms co-exist at any point in time. The main mechanism of change over time thus appears to consist of an evolutionary process of innovation and diffusion of unequivocally better techniques and products. The model developed in Chapter 5 can account for the continuous existence of technology gaps between firms and between countries and for the conditions of *convergence* or *divergence* in interfirm and international technological capabilities, according to the degrees of opportunity, cumulativeness and appropriability that each technology presents.

From such a perspective, the degree of innovativeness of each country in any one particular technology is explained – as regards its origin – through the complex interplay between (i) technology-related opportunities; (ii) country-specific and technology-specific institutions which foster/hinder the emergence of new technologies; and (iii) the nature and intensity of economic stimuli, which stem from abundance of particular inputs, or, alternatively, critical scarcities, specific patterns of demand and levels and changes in relative prices. In other words, the interpretation suggested accounts for the evidence presented by some of the particular theories of 'market-induced' innovations (e.g. product-cycles, demand-pull, relative-price inducements) and incorporates such theories in what we believe to be a more general view of the innovative process.

There is certainly a wide variety of economic inducements to innovation, but these belong to the necessary, although not sufficient, conditions. Sufficiency is provided by the degree of matching/mismatching between these generic market opportunities and the institutional conditions related to scientific/technological capabilities available in each country, the 'bridging institutions' between pure science and economic applications, the expertise embodied in the firm and the pattern of organisation of the major markets.

Over time, we argued, capital accumulation and technological accumulation are interlinked so that improvements in input efficiencies and search/learning processes feed back on each other. In some respects, our analysis overlaps with the question of 'why growth rates differ'. However, our interpretation is the opposite of the traditional one: instead of explaining differences between countries in terms of differential endowments, we argue that the fundamental international differences relate to the country-specific conditions of technological learning and accumulation.

In Chapter 6, we utilised these insights into the innovative process as the starting point for the development of a model of trade based on the general existence of technological differences between countries. These gaps, we argued, were the equivalent of Smith's 'absolute advantages' and determined two fundamental processes of adjustment between and within countries.

First, intersectoral, intranational differences in technology gaps would lead to a tendency toward relative specialisation in the sectors of 'comparative advantages'. This is the familiar mechanism of adjustment described in the Ricardian (and, under different assumptions, in the neo-classical) literature.

Second, and at least as important, intrasectoral gaps between countries would lead to adjustments in world-market shares. This other adjustment process was, in our view, closely related to the notion of 'absolute' or 'structural' competitiveness of each country. It is an 'absolute' notion in the sense that it does not relate to any intersectoral comparison ('I am relatively better in this or that'), although it obviously has a relative country content ('I am better or worse than country B or C').

The link between absolute advantages and world-market shares, within each sector and for each country as a whole appeared to be empirically quite robust. In our tests, different degrees of innovativeness and productive efficiency appeared good predictors of the international distribution of export flows in more than three-quarters of the forty industrial sectors considered.

Most of the trade literature focusses almost exclusively upon the origins and effects of 'comparative advantages'. In our model, revealed comparative advantages are obtained only as a by-product of both intranational, intersectoral changes in inputs allocations and changes in the *absolute* amount of inputs that each economy employs to produce in response to changing shares in the world market.

This analysis, as we tried to illustrate in Chapter 7, can easily be linked with a 'Keynesian' view of the determination of the rates of macroeconomic activity of each economy. Unlike neo-classical trade analysis – which generally imposes market-clearing – and unlike Ricardian trade models – which generally assume steady-state growth – the trade model in Chapter 6 allows, and indeed requires, changes in the levels of macroeconomic activity of each economy in response to changes in international competitiveness. Thus, the link between absolute advantages and world-market shares is theoretically consistent with a determination of domestic aggregate demand via the foreign-trade multiplier. In Chapter 7, we analysed in detail the relationship between such international differences in technology, intersectoral mechanisms of specialisation, and macroeconomic growth.

With the help of a simple formal model, we illustrated how international gaps in technology would define the various boundaries of both 'Ricardian' processes of adjustment in specialisation and 'Keynesian' adjustment in the rate of macroeconomic activity. From a dynamic point of view, it could be established that it was the evolution in the innovative/imitative capabilities of each country which shaped the trend in the relative and absolute rates of growth of the tradeable sector of each economy.

These theoretical results appeared broadly consistent with the evidence we were able to collect. We found that the links between innovativeness and macroeconomic growth, in cross-country analyses over the past eighty years, were rather strong, although the precise form of that relationship depended on each particular phase of development.

In Chapter 8, we finally discussed, albeit briefly, some of the normative implications of our analysis. Certainly, the interpretative, much more complex framework did not allow us to draw the sort of elegant, if misleading, recipes on 'Pareto optimality' of standard trade analysis. The complexity of the innovative process, the multiplicity of adjustment mechanisms and the variety of institutional frameworks can hardly be judged on simple and immutable yardsticks.

However, our theoretical approach does allow a normative counterpart. We were able to identify some general conditions under which conflicts between 'static' (or 'allocative') efficiency and 'dynamic' efficiency (related to innovative and demand dynamism) could arise. Such conflicts, we argued, would be more likely to occur in countries well below the technological frontier. Any judgement as to the preferred trade regime should therefore also take into account an evaluation of the relationship between technological gaps, market signals and conditions of technological accumulation under the different regimes. One must also distinguish between policies related to the emergence of new technological paradigms and those fostering 'normal' technical progress along established trajectories. Historically, we argued, almost unconditional 'free trade' regimes appeared to be the most suited for technological dynamism and growth within established technological paradigms and particularly in the case of countries near or at the technological frontier.

In retrospect, it is probably fair to say that in focussing on the tacit, firm-specific and cumulative features of technological change and the long-term historical evidence of the OECD countries' trade and growth performance, we might have underemphasised some of the international technology diffusion features which seem characteristic to today's multiplicity of strategic technology alliances and agreements between the largest firms in the OECD area. Maybe but maybe not.

We would rather argue that the significant growth of such international technology agreements between firms is precisely the illustration of the crucial firm- and country-specific technological advantages rooted in skills and knowledge. For firms and countries to access such knowledge simple 'transfer' of knowledge bought at the prevailing market price will, generally, be insufficient. Rather it will involve access to the other firm/country's technological expertise and skills, including the knowledge about the 'foreign' institutional framework, foreign suppliers and users (see also Mowery and Rosenberg, 1989).

The trend towards the internationalisation of science and technology is far from being a negation of the firm- and country-specific nature of much technological advance. In our view, such a 'new' globalisation trend is more a reflection of new ways in which firms are increasingly using to try to overcome the firm- and country-specificity and cumulativeness of technological change.

Bibliography

Abernathy, W. J. and Hayes, R. (1980) 'Managing our way to economic decline', *Harvard Business Review*, July/August, no. 58.

Abernathy, W. J. and Utterback, J. M. (1975) 'A dynamic model of product and process innovations', *Omega*, vol. 3, no. 6.

Abernathy, W. J. and Utterback, J. M. (1978) 'Patterns of industrial innovation', *Technology Review*, no. 80, June/July.

Acs, Z. and Audretsch, D. (1989), 'Small firms and technology', Directorate for Technology Policy, Ministry for Economic Affairs, The Netherlands.

Aghion, P. and Howitt, P. (1989) 'A model of growth through creative destruction', May, mimeo.

Aglietta, M. (1976) *Régulation et Crise du Capitalisme*, Paris, Calmann-Levy.

Aho, C. M. and Rosen, H. F. (1980) *Trends in Technology-Intensive Trade: with Special Reference to US Competitiveness*, Office of Foreign Economic Research, Bureau of International Labor Affairs, US Department of Labor.

Altshuler, A., Anderson, M., Jones, D. T., Roos, D. and Womack, J. (1984) *The Future of the Automobile*, Cambridge (Mass), MIT Press.

Andersen, E. S., Dalum, B. and Villumsen, G. (1981) 'The importance of the home market for the technological development and the export specialization of manufacturing industry', in *Technical Innovation and National Economic Performance*, IKE Seminar, Aalborg, Aalborg University Press.

Andersson, J. O. (1987) *Nordic Studies on Intra-Industry Trade*, Åbo, Åbo Akademy Press.

Archibugi, D. (1986) 'Sectoral patterns of industrial innovation in Italy: an analysis of Italian patenting in the US', Technical Report, Rome, CNR.

Armington, P. S. (1969) 'A theory of demand for products distinguished by place of production', IMF Staff Papers.

Arrow, K. J. (1962a) 'Economic welfare and allocation of resources for invention', in Nelson (ed.), *The Rate and Direction of Inventive Activity*, NBER, Princeton University Press.

Arrow, K. J. (1962b) 'The economic implications of learning by doing', *Review of Economic Studies*, vol. 29.

Arthur, W. B. (1985) 'Competing techniques and lock-in by historical events.

The dynamics of allocation under increasing returns', Stanford, Stanford University, CEPR.

Arthur, W. B. (1988) 'Competing technologies: an overview' in G. Dosi *et al.* (eds.), *Technical Change and Economic Theory*, London, Pinter Publishers.

Arthur, W. B. (1989) 'Competing technologies, increasing returns and lock-in by historical events', *Economic Journal*, vol. 99, pp. 116–31.

Arthur, W. B. (1990) '"Silicon Valley": locational clusters: when do increasing returns imply monopoly?' *Mathematical Social Sciences*, vol. 19(3), June.

Atkinson, A. and Stiglitz, J. (1969) 'A new view of technological change', *Economic Journal*, vol. 78.

Bacha, E. (1978) 'An interpretation of unequal exchange from Prebish-Singer to Emmanuel', *Journal of Development Economics*, vol. 5, pp. 319–38.

Balassa, B. (1963) 'An empirical demonstration of classical comparative cost theory', *Review of Economics and Statistics*, vol. 45.

Baldwin, R. E. (1971) 'Determinants of the commodity structure of US trade', *American Economic Review*, vol. 61.

Barker, T. (1977) 'International trade and economic growth: an alternative to the neo-classical approach', *Cambridge Journal of Economics*, vol. 1.

Barras, R. (1986) 'Towards a theory of innovation in services', *Research Policy*, vol. 15, no. 4.

Basberg, B. (1982) 'Technical change in the Norwegian whaling industry', *Research Policy*, vol. 15, no. 4.

Berglas, E. and Jones, R. W. (1977) 'The export of technology' in K. Brunner and A. Meltzer (eds.), *Optimal Policies, Control Theory and Technology Exports*, Carnegie-Rochester Conference on Public Policy.

Bergstrom-Balkestahl, B. (1979) Efforts on R & D Indicators in Sweden, Second Workshop on the Measurement of R & D Output, OECD, Paris, 5th and 6th December, 1979, mimeo.

Bhagwati, J. N. (1964) 'The pure theory of international trade: a survey', *Economic Journal*, vol. 74.

Bhagwati, J. N. (1970) 'Comment' in R. Vernon (ed.), *The Technology Factor in International Trade*, New York, NBER/Columbia University Press.

Bhagwati, J. N. (1989) 'Is free trade passé?', *Weltwirtschaftliches Archiv*, vol. 125.

Blecker, R. A. (1985) 'A model of capital accumulation in an open economy', Washington, DC, Dept of Economics, The American University, mimeo.

Blejer, M. I. (1978) 'Income per capita and the structure of industrial experts: an empirical analysis', *Review of Economics and Statistics*, vol. 60.

Bodenhofer, H. J. (1976) 'Technischer Fortschritt, Forschung und Entwicklung und Internationaler Handel, der Fall der Bundesrepublik Deutschland', *Jahrbücher für Nationalökonomie und Statistik*, vol. 190, pp. 151–79.

Bowles, S. (1981) 'Technical change and the profit rate: a simple proof of the Okishio theorem', *Cambridge Journal of Economics*, vol. 5.

Boyer, R. (1988) 'Formalizing growth regimes?' in G. Dosi *et al.* (eds.), *Technical Change and Economic Theory*, London, Pinter Publishers.

Boyer, R. and Mistral, J. (1983) *Accumulation, Inflation, Crises*, Paris, PUF, 2nd edn.

Boyer, R. and Mistral, J. (1984) 'The present crisis – from an historical interpretation to a prospective outlook', Paris, CEPREMAP, mimeo.

Boyer, R. and Petit, P. (1980) 'Employment and productivity in the EEC', *Cambridge Journal of Economics*, vol. 5.

Brander, J. A. (1981) 'Intra-industry trade in identical commodities', *Journal of International Economics*, vol. 11 (February), pp. 1–14.

Brander, J. A. (1987) 'Shaping comparative advantage: trade policy, industrial policy and economic performance', in R. B. Lipsey and W. Dobson (eds.), *Shaping Comparative Advantage*, Toronto, Prentice Hall.

Brander, J. A. and Krugman, P. R. (1983) 'A "Reciprocal Dumping" model of international trade', *Journal of International Economics*, vol. 15 (November), pp. 313–21.

Branson, W. and Monoyios, N. (1977) 'Factor inputs in US trade', *Journal of International Economics*, vol. 7.

Brander, J. A. and Spencer, B. (1983) 'International R & D rivalry and industrial strategy', *Journal of International Economy*, vol. 14 (Spring), pp. 225–35.

Brander, J. A. and Spencer, B. (1985) 'Export subsidies and international market share rivalry', *Journal of International Economics*, vol. 17 (February), pp. 83–100.

Buckley, P. and Casson, M. (1976) *The Future of the Multinational Enterprise*, London, Macmillan.

Buckley, P. and Casson, M. (1981) 'The optimal timing of a foreign direct investment', *The Economic Journal*, vol. 91.

Buer, P. (1982) Investigation of Consistent Make or Buy Patterns of Selected Process Machinery in Selected US Manufacturing Industry, Cambridge (Mass), Sloane School of Management. MIT, Ph.D Dissertation.

Cantwell, J. A. (1989) *Technological Innovation and Multinational Corporations*, Oxford, Basil Blackwell.

Cantwell, J. A. and Dunning, J. H. (1986) 'The changing role of multinational enterprises in the international creation, transfer and diffusion of technology', paper presented at the conference on Innovation and Diffusion, Venice, 17–22 March.

Cape, R. E. (1980) 'The impact of bioengineering', in *Opportunities in Innovation*, A symposium sponsored by the Sperry Rand Corporation, New York, Rye.

Carter, A. P. (1970) *Structural Change in the American Economy*, Cambridge (Mass), Harvard University Press.

Caves, R. (1980) 'International trade and industrial organisation introduction', *Journal of Industrial Economics*, vol. 29.

Caves, R. (1982) *Multinational Enterprise and Economic Analysis*, Cambridge, Cambridge University Press.

Caves, R. (1985) 'Trade exposure and changing structures of US manufacturing industry', Cambridge (Mass), Harvard University, paper presented at the conference on International Competition, 7–9 March 1985.

Caves, R., Porter, M. E. and Spence, A. M. (1980) *Competition in the Open Economy: A Model Applied to Canada*, Cambridge (Mass), Harvard University Press.

CEPII (1983) *Economie Mondiale: La Montée des Tensions*, Paris, Economica.

Chenery, H. B. and Bruno, M. (1962) 'Development alternatives in an open economy: the case of Israel', *Economic Journal*, vol. 72.

Chenery, H. B. and Strout, A. (1966) 'Foreign assistance and economic development', *American Economic Review*, vol. 56.

Chesnais, F. and Michon-Savarit, C. (1980) 'Some observations on alternative approaches to the analyses of international competitiveness and the role of the technology factor', Science and Technology Indicators Conference, OECD, Paris, 15–19 September 1980.

Chipman, J. S. (1965–6) 'A survey of the theory of international trade', *Econometrica*, vol. 34.

Chipman, J. S. (1970) 'Induced technical change and patterns of international trade', in R. Vernon (ed.), *The Technology Factor in International Trade*, New York, NBER/Columbia University Press.

Cimoli, M. (1988) 'Technology gaps and institutional asymmetries in a North-South model with a continuum of goods', *Metroeconomica*, vol. 40.

Cimoli, M. and Soete, L. (1988) 'A generalised technology gap trade model', paper presented at the conference on Technological Innovations and Organization, Trieste, September.

Cimoli, M., Dosi, G. and Soete, L. (1986) 'Innovation diffusion, institutional differences and patterns of trade: a North-South model', Brighton, SPRU, University of Sussex, paper presented at the conference on Innovation Diffusion, Venice, 17–21 March 1986.

Clarke, K. B. and Griliches, Z. (1984) 'Productivity growth and R & D at the business level: results from the PIMS data base', in Z. Griliches (ed.), *R&D, Patents and Productivity*, Chicago, NBER/Chicago University Press.

Cohen, S., Teece, D., Tyson, L. and Zysman, J. (1984) *Competitiveness*, Berkeley, BRIE, University of California, Working Paper.

Cole, S. (1980) 'Product versus process innovation, technology transfer and the world distribution of incomes', Brighton, SPRU, University of Sussex, mimeo.

Cooper, R. (1983) 'A process model for industrial new product development' *IEE Transactions on Engineering Management*, vol. 30.

Corden, W. (1979) 'Intra-industry trade and factor proportions theory' in H. Giersch (ed.), *On the Economics of Intra-Industry Trade*, Tübingen, J. C. B. Mohr.

Coriat, B. (1979) *L'Atelier et le Chronomètre*, Paris, Christian Bourgois.

Coriat, B. (1983) *La Robotique*, Paris, La Découverte/Maspero.

Cornwall, J. (1977) *Modern Capitalism: Its Growth and Transformation*, London, Martin Robertson.

Cox, D. and Harris, R. (1986) 'The economic consequences for Canada of sectoral free trade with the United States', *Canadian Journal of Economics*, vol. 19, August.

David, P. A. (1975) *Technical Choice, Innovation and Economic Growth*, Cambridge, Cambridge University Press.

David, P. A. (1985) 'Clio and the economics of QWERTY', *American Economic Review*, vol. 75(2), May, pp. 332–7.

David, P. A. (1986) 'Technology diffusion, public policy and industrial competitiveness', in R. Landau and N. Rosenberg (eds.), *The Positive Sum Strategy: Harnessing Technology for Economic Growth*, NAS, NAP, Washington.

David, P. and Olsen, T. E. (1984) Anticipated Automation. A Rational Expectation Model of Technological Diffusion, Stanford, Stanford University, CEPR Discussion Paper.

Davidson, W. (1976) 'Patterns of factor-saving innovation in the industrialised world', *European Economic Review*, vol. 8.

Davidson, W. (1979) 'Factor endowment, innovation and international trade theory', *Kyklos*, vol. 32.

Deardorff, A. V. (1984) 'Testing trade theories and predicting trade flows' in R. W. Jones and P. B. Kenen (eds.), *Handbook of International Economics*, Amsterdam, Elsevier–North-Holland.

Deaton, A. and Muellbauer, J. (1980) *Economics and Consumer Behaviour*, Cambridge, Cambridge University Press.

De Marchi, N. (1976) 'Anomaly and the development of economics', in S. J. Latsis (ed.).

Dixit, A. (1981) 'The export of capital theory', *Journal of International Economics*, vol. 11.

Dixit, A. (1986a) 'Trade policy: an agenda for research' in P. Krugman (ed.), *Strategic Trade Policy and the New International Economics*, Cambridge (Mass), MIT Press.

Dixit, A. (1986b) 'Issues of strategic trade policy for small countries', Princeton University, mimeo.

Dixit, A. and Norman, V. (1980) *Theory of International Trade*, Cambridge, Cambridge University Press.

Dixit, A. and Stiglitz, J. (1977) 'Monopolistic competition and optimum product diversity', *American Economic Review*, vol. 67.

Dornbush, R., Fisher, S. and Samuelson, P. A. (1977) 'Comparative advantage, trade and payments in a Ricardian model with a continuum of goods', *American Economic Review*, vol. 67.

Dosi, G. (1982) 'Technological paradigms and technological trajectories. A suggested interpretation of the determinants and directions of technical change', *Research Policy*, vol. 11, pp. 147–62.

Dosi, G. (1982a) 'La Circolarita tra Progresso Tecnico e Crescita. Alcune Osservazioni sulla "Legge di Verdoorn-Kaldor"', *L'Industria*.

Dosi, G. (1984) *Technical Change and Industrial Transformation*, London, Macmillan.

Dosi, G. (1988) 'Sources, procedures and microeconomic effects of innovation', *Journal of Economic Literature*, vol. 26, pp. 1120–71.

Dosi, G. (1988a) 'Institutions and markets in a dynamic world', *The Manchester School*, May.

Dosi, G., Freeman, C., Nelson, R., Silverberg, G. and Soete, L. (1988) *Technical Change and Economic Theory*, London, Pinter Publishers.

Dosi, G. and Orsenigo, L. (1986) 'Order and change. An exploration of markets, institutions and technology in industrial dynamics', in H. Minsky and P. Ferri (eds.), *Innovation, Financial Structures and Growth Stability*, New York, Sharp.

Dosi, G. and Orsenigo, L. (1988) 'Coordination and transformation: an overview of structures, behaviours and change in evolutionary environments', in G. Dosi *et al.* (eds.), *Technical Change and Economic Theory*, London, Pinter Publishers.

Dosi, G. and Soete, L. (1983) 'Technology gaps and cost-based adjustments: some explorations on the determinants of international competitiveness', *Metroeconomica*, September, vol. 12(3), pp. 357–82.

Dosi, G. and Soete, L. (1988) 'Technical change and international trade' in G. Dosi *et al.* (eds.), *Technical Change and Economic Theory*, London, Pinter Publishers.

Drèze, J. (1960) 'Quelques Réflexions Sereines sur l'Adaptation de l'Industrie Belge au Marché Commun', *Comptes Rendus des Travaux de la Societe Royale d'Economie Politique de Belgique*, no. 275, December.

Drèze, J. (1961) 'Les Exportations intra-CEE en 1958 et la Position Belge', *Recherches Economiques de Louvain*, vol. 27, pp. 717–38.

Dunning, J. H. (1977) 'Trade, location of economic activity and multinational enterprises: a search for an eclectic theory', in B. Ohlin *et al.* (eds.), *The International Allocation of Economic Activity*, London, Macmillan.

Dunning, J. H. (1981) *International Production and the Multinational Enterprise*, London, Allen and Unwin.

Dunning, J. H. (1981a) 'Explaining the international direct investment position by countries: towards a dynamic or development approach', *Weltwirtschaftliches Archiv*, vol. 117.

Eaton, J. and Kierzkowski, H. (1984) 'Oligopolistic competition, product variety and international trade', in H. Kierzkowski (ed.), *Monopolistic Competition and International Trade*, Oxford, Clarendon Press.

Eliasson, G. (1984) 'Micro heterogeneity of firms and the stability of industrial growth', *Journal of Economic Behaviour and Organisation*, vol. 5.

Emmanuel, A. (1969) *L'Exchange Inégal*, Paris, Maspero.

Ergas, H. (1984) 'Why do some countries innovate more than others?' Centre for European Policy Studies, Brussels.

Ethier, W. (1979) 'Internationally decreasing costs and world trade', *Journal of International Economics*, vol. 9, pp. 1–24.

Ethier, W. (1981) 'A reply to Professors Metcalfe and Steedman', *Journal of International Economics*, vol. 11.

Ethier, W. (1982a) 'Decreasing costs in international trade and Frank Graham's argument for protection', *Econometrica*, vol. 50.

European Industrial Research Management Association (EIRMA) (1986), *Developing R&D Strategies*, Working Group Report, Paris, no. 33.

Evans, D. H. (1980) 'Emmanuel's theory of unequal exchange: critique, countercritique and theoretical contribution', Discussion Paper no. 149, Brighton, Institute of Development Studies, University of Sussex.

Fagerberg, J. (1987) 'A technology gap approach to why growth rates differ', *Research Policy*, vol. 16, pp. 87–99.

Fagerberg, J. (1988a) 'International competitiveness', *Economic Journal*, vol. 98, pp. 355–74.

Fagerberg, J. (1988b) 'Why growth rates differ', in G. Dosi *et al.* (eds.), *Technical Change and Economic Theory*, London, Pinter Publishers.

Feinman, S. and Fuentevilla, W. (1976) *Indicators of International Trends in Technological Innovation*, Washington, National Science Foundation.

Fellner, W. (1961) 'Two propositions in the theory of induced innovation', *Economic Journal*, vol. 71.

Ferguson (1978) 'International capital mobility and comparative advantage', *Journal of International Economics*, vol. 8.

Ferrier, F. L. A. (1805) *Du Gouvernement Considéré dans ses Rapports avec le Commerce*, Paris.

Fetherson, M., Moore, B. and Rhodes, J. (1977) 'Manufacturing export shares and cost competitiveness of advanced industrial countries', *Economic Policy Review*.

Field, A. J. (1982) 'Land abundance factor returns and nineteenth century American and British technology: a Ricardian linear production model perspective', in N. Rosenberg (ed.), *Inside the Black Box*, Cambridge, Cambridge University Press.

Findlay, R. (1973) *International Trade and Development Theory*, New York, Columbia University Press.

Findlay, R. (1978) 'Relative backwardness, direct foreign investment and the transfer of technology: a simple dynamic model', *Quarterly Journal of Economics*, vol. 92.

Findlay, R. (1984) 'Growth and development in trade models', in R. W. Jones and P. B. Kenen (eds.), *Handbook of International Economics*, Amsterdam, Elsevier-North-Holland.

Franko, L. G. (1976) *The European Multinationals. A Renewed Challenge to American and British Big Business*, London.

Freeman, C. (1963) 'The plastics industry: a comparative study of research and innovation'. *National Institute Economic Review*, no. 26.

Freeman, C. (1965) 'Research and development in electronic capital goods', *National Institute Economic Review*, vol. 34.

Freeman, C. (1974) *The Economics of Industrial Innovation*, in Harmondsworth, Penguin, (2nd edn: London, Pinter Publishers, 1982).

Freeman, C. (1982a) 'Technological infrastructure and international competitiveness', Brighton, SPRU, University of Sussex mimeo.

Freeman, C. and Soete, L. (1987) *Technical Change and Full Employment*, Oxford, Basil Blackwell.

Freeman, C., Clark, J. and Soete, L. (1982) *Unemployment and Technical Innovation*, London, Pinter Publishers.

Freeman, C., Fuller, J. K. and Young, A. (1980) 'Technological forecasting and trends of innovation in the chemical industry', Brighton, SPRU, University of Sussex, mimeo.

Gardiner, P. (1984) 'Design trajectories for aeroplanes and automobiles during the past fifty years', in C. Freeman (ed.), *Design, Innovation and Long Cycles in Economic Development*, London, Pinter Publishers.

Ghymers, C. (1981) 'Taux de Change Tendanciels et Spécialisation', *Revue d'Economie Politique*, vol. 91.

Gibbons, M. and Johnston, R. (1974) 'The role of science in technological innovation', *Research Policy*, vol. 3, no. 3.

Giersch, H. (1979) (ed.), *On the Economics of Intra-industry trade*, Tübingen, J.C.B. Mohr.

Giovannetti, G. (1985) 'The international transmission of price level and output disturbances between raw material producer countries and industrial countries: a theoretical analysis', *Economic Notes*.

Glejser, H., Jacquemin, A. and Petit, J. (1980) 'Experts in an imperfect competition framework: an analysis of 1446 small country exporters', *Quarterly Journal of Economics*, vol. 94.

Gomulka, S. (1971) *Inventive Activity, Diffusion and the Stages of Economic Growth*, Aarhus, Skrifter fra Aarhus Universtets Okonomiske Institut nr. 24, Institute of Economics.

Gort, M. and Klepper, S. (1982) 'Time paths in the diffusion product innovations', *Economic Journal*, September, vol. 92(367), pp. 630–53.

Gort, M. and Konakayama, A. (1982) 'A model of diffusion in the production of an innovation', *American Economic Review*, December, vol. 72(5), pp. 1111–20.

Grabowski, H. G. and Vernon, J. M. (1984) 'Pioneers, imitators and generics – a model of Schumpeterian competition in the pharmaceutical industry', Duke University, mimeo.

Graham, F. D. (1923) 'Some aspects of protection further considered', *Quarterly Journal of Economics*, vol. 37.

Graham, E. (1979) 'Technological innovation and the dynamics of the US comparative advantage', in C. Hill and J. Utterback (eds.), *Technological Innovation for a Dynamic Economy*, New York, Pergamon Press.

Granstrand, O. (1979) *Technology Management and Markets*, Gothenberg, Chalmers University.

Greenaway, D. and Milner, C. (1986) *The Economics of Intra-Industry Trade*, Oxford, Basil Blackwell.

Griliches, Z. (1984) (ed.), *R & D, Patents and Productivity*, Chicago, NBER/Chicago University Press.

Griliches, Z. and Lichtenberg, F. (1984) 'R & D and productivity growth at the industry level: is there still a relationship?', in Z. Griliches (ed.), *R&D, Patents and Productivity*, Chicago, NBER/Chicago University Press.

Griliches, Z. and Mairesse, J. (1984) 'Productivity and R & D at the firm level', in Z. Griliches (ed.), *R&D, Patents and Productivity*, Chicago, NBER/Chicago University Press.

Grossman, G. and Helpman, E. (1989) 'Product development and international trade', *Journal of Political Economy*, 97 (December).

Grossman, G. and Helpman, E. (1990a) 'Comparative advantage and long-run growth', *American Economic Review* (forthcoming).

Grossman, G. and Helpman, E. (1990b) 'Trade, innovation and growth', *American Economic Review, Papers and Proceedings*, May.

Grossman, G. and Helpman, E. (1990c) 'Quality ladders in the theory of growth', Discussion papers in Economics no. 148, Woodrow Wilson School of Public and International Affairs, Princeton University.

Grubel, H. G. and Lloyd, P. J. (1975) *Intra-Industry Trade: The Theory and Measurement of International Trade in Different Products*, London, Macmillan.

Gruber, W. and Vernon, R. (1970) 'The technology factor in a world trade matrix', in R. Vernon (ed.), *The Technology Factor in International Trade*, New York, NBER/Columbia University Press.

Habakkuk, H. J. (1962) *American and British Technology in the Nineteenth Century*, Cambridge, Cambridge University Press.

Hahn, F. (1984) *Equilibrium and Macroeconomics*, Oxford, Basil Blackwell.

Haitani, K. (1970) 'International differences in capital returns and wage rates', *Kyklos*, vol. 23.

Hanel, P. (1976) The Relationship Existing Between the R & D Activity of Canadian Manufacturing Industries and their Performance in the International Market, Ottawa, Technological Innovation Studies Programme, Office of Science and Technology, Department of Industry, Trade and Commerce.

Harkness, J. and Kyle, J. (1975) 'Factors influencing United States comparative advantage', *Journal of International Economics*, vol. 5.

Harris, R. (1984) 'Applied general equilibrium analysis of small open economies with scale economies and imperfect competition', *American Economic Review*, vol. 74, December.

Hayami, Y. and Ruttan, K. (1971) *Agricultural Development*, Baltimore, John Hopkins University Press.

Heiner, R. A. (1983) 'On the origin of predictable behaviour', *American Economic Review*, vol. 73(4).

Helg, R. and Onida, F. (1985) 'Un'analisi "cross-sectors" sull'Italia', in F. Onida (ed.), *Innovazione, Competitivite e Vincolo Energetico*, Bologna, Il Mulino.

Helleiner, G. K. (1981) *Intra-firm Trade and the Developing Countries*, London, Macmillan.

Helleiner, G. K. and Lavergne, R. (1979) 'Intra-firm trade and industrial exports of the United States', *Oxford Bulletin of Economics and Statistics*, vol. 41.

Helpman, E. (1981) 'International trade in the presence of product differentiation, economies of scale and monopolistic competition: a Chamberlain–Heckscher–Ohlin Approach', *Journal of International Economics*, vol. 11.

Helpman, E. (1984) 'Increasing returns, imperfect markets, and trade theory', in R. W. Jones and P. B. Kenen (eds.), *Handbook of International Economics*, Amsterdam, Elsevier–North-Holland.

Helpman, R. and Krugman, P. (1985) *Market Structure and Foreign Trade. Increasing Returns, Imperfect Markets and International Trade*, Hemel Hempstead, Harvester Wheatsheaf.

Helpman, R. and Krugman, P. (1989) *Market Structure and Trade Policy*, Cambridge (Mass), MIT Press.

Helpman, R. and Razin, A. (1980) Monopolistic Competition and Factor Movements, Stockholm, Institute for International Economic Studies, University of Stockholm, Seminar Paper no. 155.

Henner, H-F. (1984) 'An analytical model of technology transfer', Université D'Orleans, Faculté de Droit et des Sciences Economiques, mimeo.

Hicks, J. (1932) *The Theory of Wages*, London, Macmillan.

Hill, T. H. (1979) *Profits and Rates of Return*, Paris, OECD.

Hirsch, S. (1965) 'The US electronics industry in international trade', *National Institute Economic Review*, no. 34, pp. 92–107.

Hirschman, A. D. (1958) *The Strategy of Economic Development*, New Haven, Yale University Press.

Horn, E-J. (1976) *Technologische Neuerungen und Internationale Arbeitsteilung*, Kieler Studien nr. 139, Tübingen, J.C.B. Mohr.

Horn, J. (1982) *Management of Industrial Change in Germany*, Brighton, University of Sussex, Sussex European Papers.

Horstmann, I. and Markusen, J. (1986) 'Up the average cost curve: inefficient entry and the new protectionism', *Journal of International Economics*, vol. 20, pp. 225–48.

Horstmann, I. and Markusen, J. (1987a) 'Licensing versus direct investment: a model of internalization by the multinational enterprise', *Canadian Journal of Economics*, vol. 20, pp. 464–81.

Horstmann, I. and Markusen, J. (1987b) 'Strategic investments and the development of multinationals', *International Economic Review*, vol. 28, pp. 109–21.

Horstmann, I. and Markusen, J. (1989) 'Firm-specific assets and the welfare effects of direct foreign investment', *Economica*, vol. 56, pp. 41–8.

Houthakker, H. S. and Magee, S. P. (1969), 'Income and price elasticities in world trade', *Review of Economics and Statistics*, vol. 51.

Hufbauer, G. C. (1966) *Synthetic Materials and the Theory of International Trade*, London, Duckworth.

Hufbauer, G. (1970) 'The impact of national characteristics and technology on the commodity composition of trade in manufactured goods', in R. Vernon (ed.), *The Technology Factor in International Trade*, New York, NBER/Columbia University Press.

Hulsman-Vejsova, H. and Koekkoek, K. (1980) 'Factor proportions, technology and Dutch industry's international trade patterns', *Weltwirtschaftliches Archiv*, vol. 116, pp. 162–77.

Hymer, S. H. (1976) *The International Operations of National Firms: A Study of Direct Foreign Investment*, Cambridge (Mass), MIT Press.

Ireland, N. J. and Stoneman, P. (1986) 'Technological diffusion, expectations and welfare', *Oxford Economic Papers*, vol. 38(2).

Isard, P. (1977) 'How far can we push the law of one price?', *American Economic Review*, vol. 67.

Iwai, K. (1981) 'Schumpeterian dynamics, part I: an evolutionary model of innovation and imitation, and part II: technological progress, firm growth and economic selection', New Haven, Yale University, Cowles Foundation Discussion Papers.

Jacquemin, A. (1982) 'Imperfect market structure and international trade – some recent research', *Kyklos*, vol. 35.

Jacquemin, A. and Sapir, A. (1988) 'International trade and integration of the European Community', *European Economic Review*, Special issue, September.

Jaffe, A. B. (1989) 'Characterising the technological position of firm with application to quantifying technological opportunity and research spillovers', *Research Policy*, vol. 18, no. 2.

Johnson, H. (1970) 'The state of theory in relation to the empirical analysis', in R. Vernon (ed.), *The Technology Factor in International Trade*, New York, NBER/Columbia University Press.

Johnson, H. (1975) 'Technological change and comparative advantage: an advanced country's viewpoint', *Journal of World Trade Law*, vol. 9.

Jones, D. T. (1976) 'Output, employment and labour productivity in Europe since 1955', *National Institute Economic Review*.

Jones, R. W. (1970) 'The role of technology in the theory of international trade', in R. Vernon (ed.), *The Technology Factor in International Trade*, New York, NBER/Columbia University Press.

Jones, R. W. (1979) *'International Trade: Essays in Theory*, Amsterdam, Elsevier–North-Holland.

Jones, R. W. (1980) 'Comparative and absolute advantage', *Schweizerische Zeitzchrift fur Volkswirtschaft und Statistik*.

Jones, R. W. and Kenen, P. B. (1984) (eds.), *Handbook of International Economics*, Amsterdam, Elsevier–North-Holland.

Jones, R. W. and Neary, J. P. (1984) 'The positive theory of international trade', in R. W. Jones and P. B. Kenen (eds.), *Handbook of International Economics*, Amsterdam, Elsevier–North-Holland.

Kaldor, M. (1966) *Causes of the Slow Rate of Growth of the United Kingdom*, Cambridge, Cambridge University Press.

Kaldor, M. (1970) 'The case for regional policies', *Scottish Journal of Political Economy*, vol. 17, pp. 337–48.

Kaldor, M. (1975) 'What is wrong with economic theory?', *Quarterly Journal of Economics*, vol. 89.

Kaldor, M. (1978) 'The effects of devaluation on trade', in *Further Essays on Applied Economics*, London, Duckworth.

Kaldor, M. (1980) 'The role of increasing returns, technical progress and cumulative causation in the theory of international trade', Paris, ISMEA, mimeo.

Kamin, J. *et al.* (1982) 'Some determinants of cost distributions in the process of technological innovation', *Research Policy*, vol. 11.

Katrak, H. (1973) 'Human skills, R and D and scale economies in the export of the United Kingdom and the United States', *Oxford Economic Papers*, vol. 25.

Katz, B. and Philips, A. (1982) 'Innovation, technological change and the emergence of the computer industry', in H. Giersch (ed.), *Emerging Technology*, Tübingen, J.C.B. Mohr.

Keesing, D. B. (1965) 'Labour skills and international trade: evaluating many trade flows with a single measuring device', *Review of Economics and Statistics*, vol. 47.

Keesing, D. B. (1967) 'The impact of research and development on United States trade', *Journal of Political Economy*, vol. 75.

Kemp, M. C. (1969) *The Pure Theory of International Trade and Investment*, Englewood Cliffs, Prentice Hall.

Kennedy, C. (1964) 'Induced buyers in innovation and the theory of distribution', *Economic Journal*, vol. 74.

Kennedy, C. and Thirlwall, A. P. (1979) 'Import penetration, export performance and Harod's trade multiplier', *Oxford Economic Papers*, vol. 31.

Kierzkowski, H. (1984) (ed.), *Monopolistic Competition and International Trade*, Oxford, Clarendon Press.

Kindleberger, C. P. (1970) 'Comments', in R. Vernon (ed.), *The Technology Factor in International Trade*, New York, NBER/Columbia University Press.

Klein, B. (1977) *Dynamic Competition*, Cambridge (Mass), Harvard University Press.

Kleinman, H. (1975) Indicators of the Output of New Technological Products from Industry, Report to US Science Foundation, National Technical Information Service, US Department of Commerce.

Kodama, F. (1986) 'Japanese innovation in mechatronics technology', *Science and Public Policy*, vol. 13, no. 1.

Koizumi, I. and Kopecky, K. (1980) 'Foreign direct investment, technology transfer and domestic employment effects', *Journal of International Economics*, vol. 10, pp. 1–20.

Kravis, I. B., Kenessy, Z., Heston, A. and Summers, R. (1975) *A System of International Comparisons of Gross Product and Purchasing Power*, Baltimore, John Hopkins University Press.

Kravis, I. B., Heston, A. and Summers, R. (1982) *World Products and Income. International Comparisons of Real Gross Product*, Baltimore, John Hopkins University Press.

Krugman, P. (1979) 'A model of innovation, technology transfer and the world distribution of income', *Journal of Political Economy*, vol. 87.

Krugman, P. (1979a) 'Increasing returns, monopolistic competition and international trade', *Journal of International Economics*, vol. 19.

Krugman, P. (1979b) 'Comment on Corden', in H. Giersch (ed.), *On the Economics of Intra-Industry Trade*, Tübingen, J.C.B. Mohr.

Krugman, P. (1980) 'Scale economies, product differentiation and the pattern of trade', *American Economic Review*, vol. 70.

Krugman, P. (1981) 'Intra-industry specialisation and the gains from trade', *Journal of Political Economy*, vol. 89.

Krugman, P. (1982) A Technology Gap Model of International Trade, International Economic Association Conference on Structural Adjustment in Trade-dependent Advanced Economies, Yxtahohn, Sweden.

Krugman, P. (1984a) Growth, Trade and Income Distribution Under Increasing

Returns, paper presented at the International Economics Study Group Ninth Annual Conference, Brighton, University of Sussex, 7–9 September 1984.

Krugman, P. (1986) (ed.), *Strategic Trade Policy and the New International Economics*, MIT Press.

Krugman, P. (1987) 'Is free trade passé?' *Economic Perspectives*, vol. 1, no. 2, pp. 131–44.

Krugman, P. and Obstfeld, M. (1988) *International Economics: Theory and Policy*, Scott Foresman/Little Brown.

Kuznets, S. (1967) 'Quantitative aspects of the economic growth of a nation: X level and structure of foreign trade: long term trends', *Economic Development and Cultural Change*, vol. 16.

Lacroix, R. and Scheuer, P. (1976) 'L'Effort de R & D, l'Innovation et le Commerce International', *Revue Economique*, no. 6, pp. 1008–29.

Lafay, G. (1979) *Dynamique de la Spécialisation Internationale*, Paris, Economica.

Lafay, G. (1981) 'Analyse rétrospective des spécialisations internationales et leur conséquence macroéconomiques', *Revue d'Economie Politique*.

Lall, S. (1980) 'Developing countries as exporters of industrial technology', *Research Policy*, vol. 9.

Lancaster, K. (1979) *Variety, Equity and Efficiency*, New York, Columbia University Press.

Lancaster, K. (1980) 'Inter-industry trade under perfect monopolistic competition', *Journal of International Economics*, vol. 10.

Landes, D. (1969) *The Unbound Prometheus*, Cambridge, Cambridge University Press.

Langrish, J. *et al.* (1972) *Wealth from Knowledge*, London, Macmillan.

Leamer, E. (1974) 'The commodity composition of international trade in manufactures: an empirical analysis', *Oxford Economic Papers*, vol. 26.

Leamer, E. (1980) 'The Leontief paradox reconsidered', *Journal of Political Economy*, vol. 88.

Leamer, E. (1984) 'Sources of international comparative advantage: theory and evidence', MIT Press, Cambridge, Massachusetts.

Leamer, E. and Bowen, H. (1981) 'Cross-section tests of the Heckscher–Ohlin theorem: comment', *American Economic Review*, vol. 71.

Le Bas, C. (1982) *Economie des Innovations Techniques*, Paris, Economica.

Leijonhufrud, A. (1981) *Information and Coordination*, Oxford, Oxford University Press.

Leontief, W. (1953) 'Domestic production and foreign trade: the American capital position re-examined', *Proceedings of the American Philosophical Society*.

Leontief, W. (1956) 'Factor proportions and the structure of American trade: further theoretical and empirical analysis', *Review of Economics and Statistics*, vol. 38, pp. 386–407.

Leontief, W. *et al.* (1953) *Studies in the Structures of American Economy*, Oxford, Oxford University Press.

Lerner, A. P. (1953) *Essays in Economic Analysis*.

Levin, R. (1977) 'Technical change and optimal scale: some evidence and implications', *Southern Economic Journal*, vol. 44.

Levin, R., Kleverick, A. K., Nelson, R. and Winter, S. (1987) 'Appropriating the returns from industrial research and development', *Brooking Papers on Economic Activity*, vol. 3.

Lindbeck, A. (1981) 'Industrial policy as an issue in the economic environment', *The World Economy*, vol. 4.

Linder, S. B. (1961) *An Essay on Trade and Transformation*, New York, Wiley.

Linnemann, H. (1966) *An Econometric Study of International Trade Flows*, Amsterdam, Elsevier–North-Holland.

Lipsey, R. B. and Dobson, W. (eds.), (1987) *Shaping Comparative Advantage*, Toronto, Prentice Hall.

Lipsey, R. B. and Kravis, I. B. (1985) 'The competitive position of US manufacturing firms', *Banca Nazionale del Lavoro Quarterly Review*.

Lipsey, R. B. and Weiss, N. Y. (1981) 'Foreign production and exports in manufacturing industries', *Review of Economics and Statistics*, vol. 63.

List, F. (1904) *The National System of Political Economy*, London, Longmans, English translation from German original 1844.

Loftus, P. J. (1969) 'Labour's share in manufacturing', *Lloyds Bank Review*.

Lorenzi, M., Pastre, O. and Toledano, J. (1980) *La Crise du XXème Siècle*, Paris, Economica.

Lucas, R. (1988) 'On the mechanics of economic development', *Journal of Monetary Economics*, vol. 22, pp. 3–42.

Lyons, B. (1986) 'The international trade perspectives of technology policy', in P. Dasgupta and P. Stoneman (eds.), *The Economic Theory of Technology Policy*, Cambridge, Cambridge University Press.

MacDonald, B. N. and Markusen, J. R. (1985) 'A rehabilitation of absolute advantage', *Journal of Political Economy*, vol. 93.

MacDougall, G.D.A. (1951–2) 'British and American exports: a study suggested by the theory of comparative costs', *Economic Journal*, vol. 62.

Maddison, A. (1964) *Economic Growth in the West*, George Allen & Unwin.

Maddison, A. (1987) 'Growth and slowdown in advanced capitalist economies, techniques and quantitative assessment', *Journal of Economic Literature*, vol. 25, pp. 649–98.

Maidique, M. (1983) 'The Stanford innovation project: a comparative study of success and failure in high technology product innovation', Worcester Polytechnic Institute, *Management of Technological Innovation: Facing the Challenge of the 1980's*, Conference Proceedings.

Mansfield, E. (1968) *Industrial Research and Technological Innovation*, New York, Norton.

Markusen, J. (1981) 'Trade and the gains from trade with imperfect competition', *Journal of International Economics*, vol. 11, pp. 531–51.

Markusen, J. (1985) 'Canadian gains from trade in the presence of scale economies and imperfect competition', Canada-United States Free Trade, Volume 11 of the Report of the Royal Commission on the Economic Union and Development Prospects for Canada, University of Toronto Press.

Markusen, J. (1986) 'Explaining the volume of trade: an eclectic approach' *American Economic Review*, vol. 76, pp. 1002–11.

Markusen, J. (1989) 'First mover advantages, blockaded entry, and the economics of uneven development', Department of Economics, University of Colorado, Boulder.

Markusen, J. (1990) 'Derationalizing tariffs with specialized intermediate inputs and differentiated final goods', *Journal of International Economics* (forthcoming).

Markusen, J. and MacDonald, G. (1985) 'A rehabilitation of absolute advantage', *Journal of Political Economy*, vol. 93, pp. 277–97.

Markusen, J. and Melvin, J. (1984) 'The gains-from-trade theorem with increasing return to scale', in H. Kierzkowski (ed.), *Monopolistic Competition and International Trade*, Oxford, Clarendon Press.

Markusen, J. and Melvin, J. (1988) *The Theory of International Trade*, Harper & Row, New York.

Markusen, J. and Venables, A. (1988) 'Trade policy with increasing returns and imperfect competition: contradictory results from competing assumptions', *Journal of International Economics*, vol. 24, pp. 299–316.

Markusen, J. and Wigle, R. (1989) 'Nash equilibrium tariffs for the US and Canada: the roles of country size, scale economies and capital mobility', *Journal of Political Economy*, vol. 97, pp. 368–86.

Marquis, D. G. and Myers, S. (1969) *Successful Industrial Innovations*, Washington, National Science Foundation.

Melvin, R. (1969) 'Increasing returns to scale as a determinant of trade', *Canadian Journal of Economics*, vol. 2.

Melvin J. R. and Warne, R. D. (1973) 'Monopoly and the theory of international trade', *Journal of International Economics*, vol. 3.

Metcalfe, J. S. (1985) 'On technological competition', Manchester, Department of Economics, University of Manchester, mimeo.

Metcalfe, J. S. (1988) 'Trade, technology and evolutionary changes', Manchester University, PREST Discussion paper, mimeo.

Metcalfe, J. S. and Soete, L. (1984) 'Notes on the evolution of technology and international competition', in M. Gibbons *et al.* (eds.), *Science and Technology Policy in the 1980's and Beyond*, London, Longman.

Metcalfe, J. S. and Steedman, I. (1981) 'On the transformation of theorems', *Journal of International Economics*, vol. 11.

Mistral, J. (1982) 'La Diffusion Internationale Inégal de l'Accumulation Intensive et Ses Crises', in Reiffers (ed.), *Economie et Finance Internationales*, Paris, Dunod.

Mistral, J. (1983) 'Competitiveness of the productive system and international specialisation', Paris, OECD, DSTI/SPRU/83.31.

Mistral, J. (1985) *Régime Internationale et Croissance Nationales*, Paris, CEPREMAP.

Modiano, P. and Onida, F. (1983) 'Un Analisi Disaggregata delle Funzioni di Domanda e di Esportazione dell'Italia e dei Principali Paesi Industriali', *Giornale degli Economisit*.

Momigliano, F. (1985) 'Determinanti, Tipologia ed Effetti dell'Innovazione come Fattore di Competitivita', in F. Onida (ed.), *Innovazione, Competitivite e Vincolo Energetico*, Bologna, Il Mulino.

Momigliano, F. and Siniscalco (1984) 'The growth of service employment: a reappraisal', *Banca Naxionale del Laboro Quarterly Review*, September, pp. 269–306.

Mowery, D. (1983) 'The relationship between intrafirm and contractual forms of industrial research in American manufacturing, 1900–1940', *Explorations in Economic History*, vol. 20, no. 4.

Mowery, D. and Rosenberg, N.(1979) 'The influence of market demand upon innovation: a critical review of some recent empirical studies', *Research Policy*, vol. 8, pp. 102–53.

Mowery, D. and Rosenberg, N. (1989) *Technology and the Pursuit of Economic Growth*, Cambridge, Cambridge University Press.

Myint, H. (1958) 'The "Classical Theory" of international trade and the underdeveloped countries', *Economic Journal*, vol. 68.

Nalebuff, B. and Stiglitz, J. E. (1983) 'Information, competition and markets', *American Economic Review*, vol. 73.

National Science Board (1976), (1982) and (1984) *Science Indicators*, Washington, US Department Printing Office.

Nelson, R. (1968) 'A "diffusion" model of international productivity differences in manufacturing industry', *American Economic Review*, vol. 58(5).

Nelson, R. (1981) 'Assessing private enterprise', *Bell Journal of Economics*, vol. 12(1).

Nelson, R. (1981a) 'Research in productivity growth and productivity differences: dead ends and new departures', *Journal of Economic Literature*, vol. 19(3).

Nelson, R. (1984) *Policies in Support of High Technology Industries*, New Haven, Yale University, Insititution for Social and Policy Studies, Working Paper no. 1011.

Nelson, R. (1985) 'Industry growth accounts and cost functions techniques are proprietary', New Haven, Yale University, mimeo.

Nelson, R. (1988) 'Institutions supporting technical change in the United States', in G. Dosi *et al.* (ed.), *Technical Change and Economic Theory*, London, Pinter Publishers.

Nelson, R. and Soete, L. (1988) 'Policy conclusions', in G. Dosi *et al.* (ed.), *Technical Change and Economic Theory*, London, Pinter Publishers.

Nelson, R. and Winter, S. (1977) 'In search of a useful theory of innovation', *Research Policy*, vol. 6(1).

Nelson, R. and Winter, S. (1982) *An Evolutionary Theory of Economic Change*, Cambridge (Mass), The Belknap Press of Harvard University Press.

Nelson, R., Winter, S. and Schuette, H. (1976) 'Technical change in an evolutionary model', *Quarterly Journal of Economics*, vol. 90.

Noble, D. (1977) *America by Design*, Oxford, Oxford University Press.

OECD (1979) *The Case for Positive Adjustment Policies*, a Compendium of OECD Documents, Paris, OECD.

OECD (1983) 'Robots: the users and the makers', *OECD Observer*.

OECD (1983a) Investment, Capacity, Utilisation and the Rate of Growth of Productivity, Paris, OECD, DSTI/IND/83.41.

OECD (1984) *Resources Devoted to R & D*, Paris, OECD.

OECD (1985) 'Trade in high technology products. An initial contribution to the statistical analysis of trade patterns in high technology products', mimeo.

Ohlin, B. (1933) *Interregional and International Trade*, Cambridge, Cambridge University Press revised edition 1967.

Okishio, N. (1961) 'Technical change and the rate of profit', *Kobe University Economic Review*.

Olsson, C. A. (1982) 'Relative factor prices and technical change: some historical and theoretical perspectives', in Jörberg, L. and Rosenberg, N. (eds.), *Technical Change, Employment and Investment*, Department of Economic History, University of Lund.

Onida, F. (1984) *Economia degli Scambi Internazionali*, Bologna, Il Mulino.

Onida, F. (1985) (ed.), *Innovazione, Competitivite e Vincolo Energetico*, Bologna, Il Mulino.

Onida, F. (1990) 'Technological competition, structural change and international integration of the European Single Market', March, mimeo.

Opocher, A. (1986) *Trade and Technical Progress in Alternative Theoretical Perspectives*, Manchester, University of Manchester, unpublished thesis.

Ostry, S. (1990) *Government & Corporations in a Shrinking World. Trade & Innovation Policies in The United States, Europe and Japan*, Council on Foreign Relations Press, New York, London.

Owen, N., White, G. and Smith, S. (1978) *Britain's Pattern of Specialisation*, London, Department of Industry, Economics and Statistics.

Paige, D. and Bombach, G. (1959) *A Comparison of National Output and Productivity of the United Kingdom and the United States*, Paris, OEEC.

Pasinetti, L. L. (1974) *Growth and Income Distribution: Essays in Economic Theory*, Cambridge, Cambridge University Press.

Pasinetti, L. L. (1981) *Structural Change and Economic Growth*, Cambridge, Cambridge University Press.

Pastre, O. and Toledano, J. (1975) Filières d'Entreinement et Effets Externes. Le Development de la Filière 'Composants Electroniques' et ses Effects sur l'Emploi, Chantilly, ADEFI.

Patel, P. and Pavitt, K. (1987) 'Is Western Europe losing the technological race?' *Research Policy*, vol. 16, nos. 2–4.

Patel, P. and Pavitt, K. (1988) 'The international distribution of technological activities', *Oxford Review of Economic Policy*, vol. 4, no. 4.

Patel, P. and Soete, L. (1987) 'International comparisons of activity in fast-growing patent fields', Science Policy Research Unit, Sussex University, mimeo.

Pavitt, K. (1979) 'Technical innovation and industrial development: the new causality', *Futures*, vol. 11, no. 6.

Pavitt, K. (1980a) (ed.), *Technical Innovation and British Economic Performance*, London, Macmillan.

Pavitt, K. (1980b) 'Technical innovation and industrial development: the dangers of divergence', *Futures*, vol. 12, no. 1.

Pavitt, K. (1984) 'Sectoral patterns of technical change: towards a taxonomy and a theory', *Research Policy*, vol. 13, no. 6.

Pavitt, K. (1985a) 'Technology transfer amongst the industrially advanced countries: an overview', in N. Rosenberg and C. Frischtak (eds.), *International Technology Transfer: Concepts, Measures and Comparisons*, New York, Praeger.

Pavitt, K. (1985b) 'Patent statistics as indicators of innovative activities: possibilities and problems', *Scientometrics*, vol. 7, no. 1–2.

Pavitt, K. (1986a) 'Chips and trajectories: how does the semiconductor influence the sources and directions of technical change?', in R. Macleod (ed.), *Technology and the Human Prospect*, London, Pinter Publishers.

Pavitt, K. (1986b) 'Technology, innovation and strategic management', in S. McGee and H. Thomas (eds.), *Strategic Management Research: a European Perspective*, New York, Wiley.

Pavitt, K. (1988) 'International patterns and technological accumulation', in N. Hood and J-E. Vahlne (eds.), *Strategies in Global Competition*, Croom Helm.

Pavitt, K. and Soete L. (1980) 'Innovative activities and export shares: some comparisons between industries and countries', in K. Pavitt (ed.), *Technical Innovation and British Economic Performance*, London, Macmillan.

Pavitt, K. and Soete L. (1982) 'International differences in economic growth and the international location of innovation', in H. Giersch (ed.), *On the Economics of Intra-Industry Trade*, Tübingen, J.C.B. Mohr.

Pavitt, K., Robson, M. and Townsend, J. (1987) 'The size distribution of innovating firms in the UK: 1945–1983', *Journal of Industrial Economics*, vol. 35, no. 3.

Pavitt, K., Robson, M. and Townsend, J. (1989) 'Technological accumulation, diversification and organisation in UK companies, 1945–1983' *Management Science*, vol. 35, no. 1, pp. 81–99.

Peck, M. and Wilson, R. (1982) 'Invention, imitation and comparative advantage: the performance of Japanese colour television set producers in the US market', in H. Giersch (ed.), *On the Economics of Intra-Industry Trade*, Tübingen, J.C.B. Mohr.

Perez, C. (1983) 'Structural change and the assimilation of new technologies in the economic and social system', *Futures*, vol. 15, no. 4, October, pp. 357–75.

Perez, C. (1984) 'Structural change and assimilation of new technologies in the economic and social system', *Futures*, vol. 15, pp. 357–75.

Perez, C. (1985) 'Microelectronics, long waves and the world structural change: new perspectives for developing countries', *World Development*, vol. 13, no. 3, pp. 441–63.

Perez, C. and Soete, L. (1988) 'Catching up in technology: entry barriers and windows of opportunity', in G. Dosi *et al.* (eds.), *Technical Change and Economic Theory*, London, Pinter Publishers.

Perroux, F. (1973) 'L'Effet d'Entreinement: de l'Analyse au Repérage Quantitatif', *Economie Appliquée*.

Petri, P. A. (1980) 'A Ricardian model of market sharing', *Journal of International Economics*, vol. 10.

Ploeg, E. J. van der (1989) 'The political economy of overvaluation', *Economic Journal*, vol. 99(397), pp. 850–5.

Plott, C. R. (1982) 'Industrial organisation theory and experimental economics', *Journal of Economic Literature*, vol. 20.

Popper, K. (1968) *The Logic of Scientific Discovery*, New York, Harper (German original: 1934).

Posner, M. (1961) 'International trade and technical change', *Oxford Economic Papers*, vol. 13.

Prais, S. (1987) 'Educating for productivity: comparisons of Japanese and English schooling and vocational preparation', *National Institute Economic Review*, no. 119, February.

Pratten, C. (1976) *A Comparison of the Performance of Swedish and UK Companies*, Cambridge, Cambridge University Press.

Prebisch, R. (1950) *The Economic Development of Latin America and its Principal Problems*, New York, ECLA, United Nations.

Purvis, D. D. (1972) 'Technology, trade and factor mobility', *Economic Journal*, vol. 82.

Ranci, P. (1983) 'Introduzione' to P. Ranci (ed.), *I Transferimenti dello Stato alle Imprese Industriali Negli Anni Settanta*, Bologna.

Ricardo, D. (1951) *On the principles of Political Economy and Taxation.* (ed.), P. Sraffa, Cambridge, Cambridge University Press.

Robinson, J. (1974) *Reflections on the Theory of International Trade*, Manchester, Manchester University Press.

Robson, M., Townsend, J. and Pavitt, K. (1988) 'Sectoral patterns of production and use of innovations in the UK: 1945–1983', *Research Policy*, vol. 17.

Romer, P. (1986) 'Increasing returns and long run growth', *Journal of Political Economy*, vol. 94 (October), pp. 1002–37.

Romer, P. (1987) 'Growth due to increasing returns based on specialization', *American Economic Review*, vol. 77 (May), pp. 56–62.

Romer, P. (1989) 'Capital accumulation in the theory of long run growth', in R. Barro (ed.), *Modern Business Cycle Theory*, Cambridge (Mass), Harvard University Press.

Romer, P. (1990) 'Endogenous technological change', *Journal of Political Economy* (forthcoming).

Rosenberg, N. (1970) 'Comments', in R. Vernon (ed.), *The Technology Factor in International Trade*, New York, NBER/Columbia University Press.

Rosenberg, N. (1976) *Perspectives on Technology*, Cambridge, Cambridge University Press.

Rosenberg, N. (1982) *Inside the Black Box*, Cambridge, Cambridge University Press.

Rosenberg, N. and Frischtak (1985) (ed.), *International Technology Transfer*, New York, Praeger.

Rothschild, K. W. (1985) 'Exports, growth and catching-up: some remarks and crude calculations', *Weltwirtschaftliches Archiv*, vol. 121.

Rothwell, R. (1979) 'Technical change and competitiveness in agricultural engineering. The performance of the UK industry', Brighton, SPRU, University of Sussex, Occasional Paper Series no. 9.

Rothwell, R. *et al.* (1974) 'SAPPHO updated – Project SAPPHO phase II', *Research Policy*, vol. 3, no. 3.

Rothwell, R. and Gardiner, P. (1984) 'The role of design in product and process change', *Design Studies*, vol. 4(3).

Roy, A. D. (1982) 'Labour productivity in 1980: an international comparison', *National Institute Economic Review*.

Rugman, A. M. (1980) 'Internalisation as a general theory of foreign direct investment: a reappraisal of the literature', *Weltwirtschaftliches Archiv*, vol. 116.

Rumelt, R. P. (1974) *Strategy, Structure and Economic Performance*, Boston.

Sahal, D. (1981) *Patterns of Technological Innovation*, New York, Addison Wesley.

Sahal, D. (1982) (ed.), *The Transfer and Utilisation of Technical Knowledge*, Lexington (Mass), D. C. Heath.

Sahal, D. (1985) 'Technology guide-posts and innovation avenues', *Research Policy*, vol. 14(2).

Salter, W. E. G. (1969) *Productivity and Technical Change*, Cambridge, Cambridge University Press, 2nd edn.

Samuelson, P. A. (1965) 'A theory of induced innovation along Kennedy–Weizsäcker Lines', *Review of Economics and Statistics*, vol. 47.

Schefold, B. (1976) 'Different forms of technical progress', *Economic Journal*, vol. 86.

Schefold, B. (1979) 'Capital, growth and definitions of technical progress', *Kyklos*, vol. 32.

Scherer, F. M. (1965) 'Firm size, market structure and the output of patented inventions', *American Economic Review*, vol. 55.

Scherer, F. M. (1982) 'Inter-industry technology flows in the US', *Research Policy*, vol. 11, no. 4.

Schmookler, J. (1966) *Invention and Economic Growth*, Cambridge (Mass), Harvard University Press.

Shaikh, A. (1980) 'The laws of international exchange', in E. J. Nell (ed.), *Growth, Profits and Property*, Cambridge, Cambridge University Press.

Shaked, A. and Sutton, J. (1984) 'National oligopolies and international trade', in H. Kierzkowsi (ed.), *Monopolistic Competition and International Trade*, Oxford, Clarendon Press.

Silverberg, G. (1987) 'Technical progress, capital accumulations and effective demand: a self-organisation model', in D. Batten *et al.* (eds.), *Economic Evolution and Structural Adjustment*, Berlin, Heidelberg, New York, Tokyo, Springer Verlag.

Silverberg, G., Dosi, G. and Orsenigo, L. (1988) 'Innovation, diversity and diffusion: a self-organising model', *The Economic Journal*, vol. 98, no. 393, pp. 1032–55.

Smith, A. (1937) *An Enquiry into the Nature and Causes of the Wealth of Nations*, New York, Modern Library.

Smith, A. and Venables, T. (1988) 'Completing the internal market in the European Community', *European Economic Review*, Special issue, September.

Smith, A. D., Hitchens, D. M. W. W. and Davies, S. W. (1982), 'International industrial productivity: a comparison of Britain, America and Germany', *National Institute Economic Review*.

Soete, L. (1979) 'Firm size and inventive activity: the evidence reconsidered', *European Economic Review*, vol. 12, pp. 319–40.

Soete, L. (1980) 'The impact of technological innovation on international trade patterns: the evidence reconsidered', paper presented to the OECD Science and Technology indicators Conference, Paris.

Soete, L. (1981a) 'A general test of technological gap trade theory', *Weltwirtschaftliches Archiv*, vol. 117.

Soete, L. (1981b) 'Technological dependency: a critical view', in D. Seers (ed.) *Dependency Theory: A Critical Reassessment*, London, Pinter Publishers.

Soete, L. (1985) 'International diffusion of technology: industrial development and technological leapfrogging', *World Development*, vol. 13, no. 3, pp. 409–22.

Soete, L. (1987) 'The impact of technological innovation on international trade patterns. The evidence reconsidered', *Research Policy*, vol. 16.

Soete, L. and Dosi, G. (1983) *Technology and Employment in the Electronics Industry*, London, Pinter Publishers.

Soete, L. and Turner, R. (1984) 'Technological diffusion and the rate of technical change', *Economic Journal*, vol. 94(375).

Soete, L., Verspagen, B., Pavitt, K. and Patel, P. (1989) 'Recent comparative trends in technology indicators in the OECD area', Workshop OECD, International Seminar on Science, Technology and Economic Growth, June 5–8.

Spaventa, L. (1970) 'Rate of profit, rate of growth and capital intensity in a simple production model', *Oxford Economic Papers*, vol. 22.

Sraffa, P. (1960) *Production of Commodities by Means of Commodities*, Cambridge, Cambridge University Press.

Steedman, I. (1979) (ed.) *Fundamental Issues in Trade Theory*, Cambridge, Cambridge University Press.

Steedman, I. (1980) *Trade Amongst Growing Economies*, Cambridge, Cambridge University Press.

Steedman, I. (1985) 'On the impossibility of Hicks-neutral technical progress', *Economic Journal*, vol. 95.

Stern, R. M. (1962) 'British and American productivity and comparative costs in international trade', *Oxford Economic Papers*, vol. 14.

Stern, R. (1975) 'Testing trade theories' in P. Kenen (ed.) *International Trade and Finance*, Frontiers for Research, Cambridge, Cambridge University Press.

Stern, R. (1976) 'Some evidence on the factor content of West Germany's foreign trade', *Journal of Political Economy*, vol. 84.

Stern, R. and Markus, K. (1981) 'Determinants of the structure of US foreign trade, 1958–1976'. *Journal of International Economics*, vol. 11.

Stern, R., Francis, J. and Schumacher, B. (1976) *Price Elasticities in International Trade*, London, Macmillan.

Stern, R., Tresize, P. and Whalley, J. (1987) *Perspectives on a US-Canadian Free Trade Agreement*, Brookings Institution.

Stiglitz, J. E. (1982) 'Information and the capital market', in W. F. Sharpe and C. Costner (1982) (eds.), *Financial Economics: Essays in Honour of Paul Costner*, Englewood Cliffs, N.J., Prentice Hall.

Stiglitz, J. E. (1984) 'Information and economic analysis: a perspective', *Economic Journal*, vol. 95.

Stiglitz, J. E. (1987) 'Learning to learn, localized learning and technological progress', in Dasgupta, P. and Stoneman, P. (eds.), *Economic Policy and Technological Performance*, Cambridge, Cambridge University Press.

Strassmann, W. P. (1959) 'Interrelated industries and the rate of technological change', *Review of Economic Studies*, vol. 26.

Streit, C. K. (1949) *Union Now: A Proposal for an Atlantic Federal Union of the Free*, New York, Atlantic Union. 2nd edn.

Sylos Labini, P. (1982) *Lezioni di Economia, Vol II*, Rome, Edizioni dell'Ateneo.

Sylos Labini, P. (1983–4) 'Factors affecting changes in productivity', *Journal of Post Keynesian Economics*, vol. 6.

Sylos Labini, P. (1984) *Le Forze dello Svilluppo e del Declino*, Bari, Laterza (*The Forces of Development and Decline*, Cambridge, Cambridge University Press).

Taylor, C. and Silberston, A. (1973) *The Economic Impact of the Patent System*, Cambridge, Cambridge University Press.

Teece, D. (1977) 'Technology transfer by multinational firms: the resource cost of transferring technological know-how', *Economic Journal*, vol. 87.

Temin, P. (1966) 'Labour scarcity and the problem of American industrial efficiency in the 1950's', *Journal of Economic History*, vol. 26.

Terleckyj, N. E. (1974) *Effects of R & D on Productivity Growth of Industries. An Exploratory Study*, Washington, National Planning Association.

Terleckyj, N. E. (1980) 'Direct and indirect effects of industrial research and development', in J. Kendrick and B. Vaccara (eds.), *New Developments in Productivity Measurement and Analysis*, Chicago, NBER/Chicago University Press.

Terleckyj, N. E. (1982) 'R & D and the US industrial productivity', in D. Sahal (ed.), *The Transfer and Utilisation of Technical Knowledge*, Lexington (Mass), D. C. Heath.

Teubal, M. (1982) 'The R & D performance through time of high technology firms', *Research Policy*, vol. 11.

Thirlwall, A. P. (1979) 'The balance of payment constraint as an explanation of international growth rate differences', *Banca Nazionale del Lavoro Quarterly Review*.

Thirlwall, A. P. (1980) *Balance-of-Payment Theory and the United Kingdom Experience*, London, Macmillan.

Thirlwall, A. P. and Vines, D. (1983) 'A general model of growth and development on Kaldorian lines', paper presented at the conference on 'The dynamics of employment and technology: theories and policies', Udine, Italy, 1–3 September 1983.

Tilton, J. (1971) *International Diffusion of Technology: The Case of the Semiconductors*, Washington, The Brookings Institution.

Toledano, J. (1978) 'A Propos des Filières Industrielles', *Revue d'Economie Industrielle*.

Townsend, J. (1980) 'Innovation in coal-mining machinery', in K. Pavitt (ed.), *Technical Innovation and British Economic Performance*, London, Macmillan.

Townsend, J. *et al.* (1981) Innovations in Britain Since 1945, Brighton, SPRU, University of Sussex, Occasional Paper no. 16.

Tucker, J. (1774) *Four Tracts, Together with Two Sermons on Political and Commercial Subjects*, Gloucester.

US Department of Labour (1980) *Report of the President on US Competitiveness*, Transmitted to the Congress, September 1980, Office of Foreign Economic Research.

US Tariff Commission (1973) *Implications of Multinational Firms for World Trade and Investment and for US Trade and Labor*, Washington DC, US Government Printing Office.

Vernon, R. (1966) 'International investment and international trade in the Product Cycle', *Quarterly Journal of Economics*, vol. 80.

Vernon, R. (1970) (ed.) *The Technology Factor in International Trade*, New York, NBER/Columbia University Press.

Vernon, R. (1979) 'The product-cycle hypothesis in a new international environment', *Oxford Bulletin of Economics and Statistics*, vol. 41.

Vernon, R. (1982) 'Technology's effects on international trade: a look ahead', in H. Giersch (ed.), *On the Economics of Intra-Industry Trade*, Tübingen, J. C. B. Mohr.

Von Hippel, E. (1978) 'A customer active paradigm for industrial product idea generation', *Research Policy*, vol. 7, no. 3.

Von Hippel, E. (1982) 'Appropriability of innovation benefit as a predictor of the source of innovation', *Research Policy*, vol. 11, no. 3.

Von Weizsäcker, C. C. (1965) 'Tentative notes on a two-sector-model with induced technical progress', *Review of Economic Studies*, pp. 245–51.

Vona, S. (1979) 'Il Commercio Orizzontale e le Teorie degli Scambi Internazionali', *Rassegna Economica*.

Walker, W. (1979) *Industrial Innovation and International Trading Performance*, Greenwich, Connecticut, JAI Press.

Wilson, C. (1980) 'On the general structure of Ricardian models with a continuum of goods: applications to growth, tariff theory and technical change', *Econometrica*, vol. 48.

Winter, S. (1982) 'An essay on the theory of production', in S. H. Hymans (ed.), *Economics and the World Around it*, Ann Arbor, University of Michigan Press.

Winter, S. (1984) 'Schumpeterian competition in alternative technological regimes', *Journal of Economic Behaviour and Organisation*, September/December, vol. 5(3–4), pp. 287–320.

Wolter, F. (1977) 'Factor proportions, technology and West German industry's international trade patterns', *Weltwirtschaftliches Archiv*, vol. 113.

Wyatt, S. and Bertin, G. (1985) *The Role of Patents in Multinational Corporations Strategies for Growth*, Paris, AREPIT.

Yan, C. S. and Ames, E. (1965) 'Economic inter-relatedness', *Review of Economic Studies*, vol. 32.

Index